POWER AND PRINCIPLE IN THE MARKET PLACE

Law, Ethics and Economics

Series Editors:
Christoph Luetge, University of Munich, Germany
Itaru Shimazu, Chiba University, Japan

Law, Ethics and Economics brings together interdisciplinary books which deal with at least two of the three constituents. Among other subjects, this series covers issues in ethics and economics, law and economics, as well as constitutional issues in law, economics, philosophy and social theory. The focus is on theoretical analysis that goes beyond purely normative considerations, thus aiming at a synthesis of the desirable and the feasible.

Also in the Series:

Absolute Poverty and Global Justice
Empirical Data – Moral Theories – Initiatives
Edited by Elke Mack, Michael Schramm, Stephan Klasen and Thomas Pogge
ISBN 978 0 7546 7849 6

Corporate Citizenship, Contractarianism and Ethical Theory
On Philosophical Foundations of Business Ethics
Edited by Jesús Conill, Christoph Luetge and Tatjana Schönwälder-Kuntze
ISBN 978 0 7546 7383 5

Public Reason and Applied Ethics
The Ways of Practical Reason in a Pluralist Society
Edited by Adela Cortina, Domingo García-Marzá and Jesús Conill
ISBN 978 0 7546 7287 6

Globalisation and Business Ethics
Edited by Karl Homann, Peter Koslowski and Christoph Luetge
ISBN 978 0 7546 4817 8

Deliberation and Decision
Economics, Constitutional Theory and Deliberative Democracy
Edited by Anne van Aaken, Christian List and Christoph Luetge
ISBN 978 0 7546 2358 8

Power and Principle in the Market Place
On Ethics and Economics

Edited by

JACOB DAHL RENDTORFF
Roskilde University, Denmark

Routledge
Taylor & Francis Group

LONDON AND NEW YORK

First published 2010 by Ashgate Publishing

2 Park Square, Milton Park, Abingdon, Oxon OX14 4RN
711 Third Avenue, New York, NY 10017, USA

Routledge is an imprint of the Taylor & Francis Group, an informa business

First issued in paperback 2016

British Library Cataloguing in Publication Data
Power and principle in the market place : on ethics and
  economics. -- (Law, ethics and economics)
  1. Economics--Moral and ethical aspects. 2. Business
  ethics. 3. Social responsibility of business.
  I. Series II. Rendtorff, Jacob Dahl, 1965-
  174.4-dc22

Library of Congress Cataloging-in-Publication Data
Power and principle in the market place : on ethics and economics / edited by Jacob Dahl
Rendtorff.
    p. cm. -- (Law, ethics and economics)
  Includes index.
  ISBN 978-1-4094-0717-1 (hardback)
1. Economics--Moral and ethical aspects. 2. Business ethics. 3. Social
responsibility of business. I. Rendtorff, Jacob Dahl, 1965-
  HB72.P66 2010
  174--dc22

                                                                          2010017362

ISBN 978-1-4094-0717-1 (hbk)
ISBN 978-1-138-26083-2 (pbk)

Contents

List of Figures and Tables

Figures

Tables

*This book is dedicated to the staff of the Goethe-Institut,
cultural institute of Germany in Copenhagen, Denmark,
who organized the conference that made this book possible.
Congratulations!*

Notes on Contributors

Güler Aras is Professor of Finance and Director of the Graduate School at Yildiz Technical University, Istanbul, Turkey. She has published 12 books and has contributed over 150 articles to academic, business and professional journals and magazines and to edited book collections. She has also spoken extensively at conferences and seminars and has acted as a consultant to a wide range of government and commercial organizations. Her research is into financial economy and financial markets with particular emphasis on the relationship between corporate social responsibility and a firm's financial performance.

Michael Blowfield is Teaching Fellow at Oxford University, Organizational Behaviour Development. He conducts professional development programmes for senior managers in multinational corporations and financial institutions on how to incorporate sustainability into management practices and strategies. His latest book *Corporate Responsibility: A Critical Introduction* (Oxford University Press, 2008) provides a comprehensive overview of corporate responsibility as theory and practice; *Business in Society*, his Ford Foundation study of how senior executives see the role of business in society in the twenty-first century, was published in 2007 under the title *Step Up: A Call for Courageous Leadership*.

Maria Bonnafous-Boucher is Professor in Strategy and Organizational Studies and Dean of Research at Advancia-Negocia, Graduate Business School of the Paris Chamber of Commerce and Industry, dedicated to entrepreneurship, trade practices and negotiation. She has worked in the fields of political philosophy, institutional theory, stakeholder theory, corporate governance and corporate social responsibility. She has edited two books, *Stakeholder Theory* (Palgrave, 2005) and *Décider avec les parties prenantes* (*Making Decisions with Stakeholders*) (La Découverte, 2006). She has been Associate Professor in Epistemology and Organizational Studies at the Conservatoire National des Arts et Métiers, Paris, and was a Member of the Collège International de Philosophie from 1995 to 2002.

Janet L. Borgerson is Reader (Associate Professor) in Philosophy and Management at the University of Exeter, UK. Being educated at the University of Michigan, Ann Arbor, and the University of Wisconsin, Madison, she has held faculty positions at the University of Rhode Island and Stockholm University, where she is ongoing Associate Professor. Since 2004, she has been a member of the Editorial Review Board of *Consumption Markets and Culture*. Her research has appeared in various journals and book chapters, among recent publications are: "Living Proof: Reflections on Irreplaceability", in the *CLR James Journal* (2008); "On the Harmony of Feminist Ethics and Business Ethics", in *Business and Society Review* (2007), and with J. Schroeder, M. Escudero-Magnusson and F. Magnusson, "Corporate Communication, Ethics, and Operational Identity", in *Business Ethics: A European Review*. She currently is writing a book-length manuscript on Islamic philosophy and models of subject formation.

Kirsten Marie Bovbjerg is Associate Professor in Educational Anthropology at the School of Education, University of Aarhus. She is educated in European ethnology, and obtained her PhD degree in 2001 on the impact of religious thoughts on business life. Her book, *Ethics of Sensibility – Personality Adjustment in New Age and Modern Management* (*Følsomhedens etik. Tilpasning af personligheden i New Age og moderne management*), Forlaget Hovedland, 2001, explores how a new work ethic has evolved from ideas of personal growth and courses in personal development through work.

Karin Buhmann is Associate Professor of Law at Copenhagen University. She specializes in human rights, business responsibilities and legal and normative development of corporate social responsibility (CSR). She currently works on the emerging regulation of CSR and business responsibilities for human rights at national and transnational, EU and UN levels, looking particularly at the interrelationship between international law and new forms of law and regulatory modalities related to corporate social and human rights responsibilities. She also works on CSR in a Chinese context. She has edited a special issue on CSR of the *Nordic Journal of Human Rights* (issue 4, 2007). Her other recent publications include "Corporate Social Responsibility – what Role for Law? Some legal aspects of CSR", in *Corporate Governance – The International Journal of Business in Society*, Vol. 6, 2006.

David Crowther is Professor of Corporate Social Responsibility at De Montfort University, UK. He has published 26 books and has also contributed 250 articles to academic, business and professional journals and to edited book collections. He has also spoken widely at conferences and seminars and acted as a consultant to a wide range of government, professional and commercial organizations. His research is into corporate social responsibility with a particular emphasis on the relationship between social, environmental and financial performance.

Susanne Holmström is Adjunct Professor at the Department of Communication, Business and Information Technology at Roskilde University, Denmark. Her research and publications focus on the interrelation between society's constitution and organizational legitimacy, based mainly on the sociology of Niklas Luhmann. She is on the board of the Nordic Network for Research on Legitimacy, Organization, Communication and Ethics (LOKE).

Hans Joas is Professor of Sociology at the University of Erfurt and the University of Chicago. His research concentrates on sociological theory and social philosophy, the sociology of Northern America, the sociology of war and sociology of religion. Recently, he has been studying and teaching the development, history and adaptation of human rights and values. One of his most recent publications is *Die Entstehung der Werte* (Suhrkamp Verlag, 2006).

Niels Kærgård has since 1993 been Professor of Agricultural Economics at the Royal Danish Veterinary and Agricultural University (since 2007 the Faculty of Life Sciences, University of Copenhagen). During 1992–2001 he was a member of the presidency of the Danish Board of Economic Advisors, and Chairman from 1995 to 2001. He has been on the board for the Carlsberg Foundation since 2002. He is also a member of a number of expert commissions formed by the Danish Government and the Danish Parliament (concerning such topics as the structure of Danish agriculture, the Danish capital area, pesticides in Danish agriculture, strategy for agricultural research, and integration and migration policy). He has published in Danish and international journals on econometrics, economic history, agricultural economics and economic policy.

Peter Kemp is Emeritus Professor of Philosophy at the Danish School of Pedagogy, Aarhus University. He is educated in theology but has written about many topics of ethics and philosophy. Since 1993, he has been Director of the Independent Centre for Ethics and Law in Copenhagen and he was also co-founder of the Danish Philosophical Forum in Copenhagen. He is a member of the Académie Internationale de Philosophie des Sciences, Bruxelles, Institut International de Philosophie and President of FISP (Fédération Internationale des Sociétés de Philosophie), which is responsible for the organization of the World Congresses on Philosophy. Recently, he has written on the concept of world citizenship.

Peter Koslowski is Professor of Philosophy, especially Philosophy of Management and History of Philosophy, VU University Amsterdam, Netherlands; he is also Chair, Forum for Economic Ethics and Economic Culture, German Philosophical Association; and Chair, Working Group on the Compliance and Ethics in Financial Institutions in the German Business Ethics Network. He is a member of the Executive Committee, International Society for Business, Economics and Ethics. He has authored numerous books, translated in various languages, including *The Ethics of Capitalism* (several English editions, first published 1983, sixth German edition 1998) and *Principles of Ethical Economy* (paperback edition 2001; German original published 1988) and has edited a book series, Studies in Economic Ethics and Philosophy.

Christoph Luetge is Peter Loescher Professor of Business Ethics, Technische Universität München. He taught at the Ludwig–Maximilian University in Munich from 1999 to 2007. A former student of Karl Homann, he studies the idea of an economic ethics. He is co-editor of the series *Law, Ethics and Economics* (Ashgate) and has recently published his study entitled *Was hält eine Gesellschaft zusammen? Ethik im Zeitalter der Globalisierung* (Tübingen, 2007).

Mollie Painter-Morland is an Associate Professor at DePaul University, Chicago, and Associate Director of its Institute for Business and Professional Ethics. As previous Director of the Centre for Business and Professional Ethics at the University of Pretoria in South Africa, she acted as ethics management consultant to various business corporations and the South African government, and pursued research into proactive corruption prevention strategies. Her publications include *Business Ethics, Business Ethos* (Cambridge University Press, 2008), and *Cutting-edge Issues in Business Ethics: Continental Challenges to Theory and Practice* (Springer, 2008). She also serves on the Advisory Board of the Society of Corporate Compliance and Ethics, the Ethics Oversight Board of PwC (PricewaterhouseCoopers) South Africa, and the Editorial Board of *AJOBE*, the *African Journal of Business Ethics*.

Ove K. Pedersen is Professor at the Copenhagen Business School and Director of External Affairs at the International Center for Business and Politics. His primary areas of research are comparative political economy, comparative politics, institutional change, economy of negotiation, theory of democracy and political theory. His publications include *National Identity and Varieties of Capitalism: The Danish Experience* (edited, with John L. Campbell and John A. Hall; McGill–Queen's University Press and Jurist- og Økonomforbundets Forlag, 2006).

Jacob Dahl Rendtorff is Professor of Responsibility, Ethics and Legitimacy of Corporations at the Department of Communication, Business and Information Technologies at the Roskilde University, Denmark. He is Head of Research and also Head of Business Studies at Roskilde University. His publications include a recently published book on business ethics and corporate social responsibility with Copenhagen Business School Press (2009).

Ole Thyssen is Professor of Philosophy at Copenhagen Business School. His research interests include philosophy and social theory, ethics, aesthetics, communication, leadership and management. He has written on the sociology and social theory of Niklas Luhmann. He has also worked on values-based management and ethical accounting. Publications include *Værdiledelse. Om organisationer og etik* (*The Philosophy of Organizational Values*) (Copenhagen, 1997, 5th revised edition 2007).

Chapter 1

Introduction

Jacob Dahl Rendtorff

The problem of ethics and economics has been a major topic in recent debates about the development of global markets in relation to issues of social cohesion, justice and political stability. Indeed, this issue has been an important challenge in relation to the discussion of global business ethics and the social responsibility of corporations, which is becoming more and more important in the ongoing discussions of the relation between market institutions and democratic governments. This is an important cultural issue concerning the ethical foundations of economic institutions, which the financial crisis in 2008 put on the agenda as an important topic for the development of the world.

It is the task of this book to clarify this relation between ethics and economics as a contribution to political theory and the philosophy of economics. The chapters deal with central issues of the philosophical foundations of the relation between ethics and economics, but they also deal with concrete and current aspects of international business and human rights. We think that international debates about business ethics and economics, for example bank ethics, can be inspired by this approach.

The chapters of this book address the social and political foundations of economics by asking the question whether there is connection between ethics and economics. A unity or harmony between the two concepts is considered by many sceptical critics an *oxymoron*, i.e. a contradiction in terms, an impossible metaphor and an expression that is an opposition in itself and therefore without any real meaning. That there is an opposition involved in the confrontation between the two terms is expressed in our ordinary definitions of ethics and economics. We understand economics as being based on egoistic actions that aim to obtain as much economic gain for the individual as possible, and we define ethics as composed of generous actions that aim at the good for everyone and the common good for community. It seems as though the two concepts – individual egoism versus altruistic concern for community – cannot really be combined.

Such an understanding of the two terms as being opposed to one another has also been present in the history of theoretical and political economy. The tradition from Karl Marx is that economics is a question of profits, and when there is economic surplus, someone must be being morally exploited. Even though Adam Smith originally considered economics as a moral science, neoclassical economics was based on the idea of an egoistic utility-maximizing subject as the basis for economic action. According to critics, this subject does not act altruistically but only seeks to serve its own interests and therefore the economic subject cannot be said to act ethically but is rather considered as a selfish egoist that never serves the community. The only way we can talk about ethics is to refer to the invisible hand – if everybody follows their own interests then this will in the end benefit the community.

This egoist ethics that thinks that only individual interests and preferences can be the aim of our actions can also be found in modern economic science. In the case of game theory, which deals with the calculation of the most efficient actions, it is based on the "prisoner's dilemma", that is the presupposition that every prisoner has to decide whether it is rational to cooperate with other prisoners in order to be released. If a prisoner calculates that she has more chance of surviving, then she chooses only the solution that promotes individual interests rather than out of concern for the community.

In the prisoner's dilemma there is no possibility for a concern for the common good that precedes the interests of individuals. Moreover, in the so-called "neo-institutional" economics that has become mainstream economic theory in the last 20–30 years, the importance of the institutions of community for economic action is highly valued. However, despite the continuant *embeddedness* in institutions, the individual may still relate in an egoistic and opportunistic manner to those institutions.

The consequence of this economic egoism can be said to be showing itself in today's globalized economy. We are confronted with increasing numbers of always larger multinational corporations, for example Walmart, McDonalds and Coca Cola, that have a power, economic turnover and cash flow that are larger than those of small developed states like Denmark or the economies of many developing countries. However, these companies have little tradition or ability to conceive their role in society as being anything other than the maximization of economic gain. On the international scale the dogma about the individualized free market economy states that it is difficult to control growth in countries like China, where the economic growth may also have unintended social and environmental consequences. Not least the issues of climate change, where the international community and corporations have known the possible consequences of CO_2 release in the atmosphere for at least 30 years without doing something about it, shows the problem of uncritically sticking to a concept of an economy that is based on egoistic preference maximization without concern for the common good.

We therefore need another concept of economics, and we need to think about a closer connection between ethics and economics; this will happen by seeking an altruistic and community-oriented economics. In fact, we do not need to go very far from the existing concepts of economics in order to integrate ethical and altruistic concerns into the economy. If we start to analyse the concepts of economics more deeply, we see the possibility of deconstructing the concepts of the already existing political economy and of the economic subject. Originally economics meant exchange, and exchange must be mutual if the capacity to exchange relates to power. However, the greatest power includes the capacity to give, and a real demonstration of power in exchange therefore includes generosity and gifts; it is only possible to give by transcending the exchange relationship. To show off oneself, to be respected and to receive recognition from the community one must give gifts and become generous. It quickly becomes very clear that the egoistically utility-maximizing individual in the case of the surplus that emerges from the economic success of a society is in fact forced to transcend herself and become generous and willing to give to society.

So in order really to become ourselves we need an economics of generosity where every individual and organization agrees to contribute to the common good in society. This includes the statement that the changed conditions for economic responsibility in modern society propose new conditions for economic action where everybody will contribute to the creation of the common good. Talking about corporate citizenship therefore includes stating that corporations have a social and societal responsibility that transcends individual responsibility and gives corporations duties corresponding to individual duties towards society. Therefore, we can say that corporations and organizations have to function as responsible actors in a society that, as individual citizens, has responsibility for the common good.

In the economy of the common good that is built on the good corporate citizenship of corporations, social responsibility will be a central aspect. Within the theory of social responsibility there has historically been a distinction between four basic kinds of responsibility that can be ascribed to a corporation, an organization or an institution, namely economic, legal, ethical and philanthropic responsibility. Economic responsibility concerns the capacity for making the corporation economically beneficial and profitable. A concrete way to realize economic responsibility is work on the triple bottom line that combines concern for economics, environment and social aspects in the evaluation of the profitability of the corporation. Economic responsibility can in this sense be extended to responsibility for sustainable and environmentally acceptable production that does not have a destructive effect on the environment. Legal responsibility expresses a responsibility to stick to the law and to live up to the legal rules of and regulation of society, not least when dealing with ethical rules that have been proposed as the basic guidelines and codex for the actions of companies. Ethical responsibility is the basic responsibility behind economic and legal responsibility. The ethics of this responsibility is expressed in the unity that defines legal as well as economic responsibility. Sometimes ethical responsibility becomes philanthropic responsibility, that is, responsibility for gift-giving, which is the real responsibility in the economy when it is developed into an economics of generosity that aims at the common good.

Finally these four concepts of responsibility can be included in the concept of political responsibility, which expresses good corporate citizenship as the essence of corporate social responsibility. In the international community good corporate citizenship is realized through the responsibility of human beings and corporations to realize the common good for humanity.

We begin this anthology with a chapter on the philosophy of economics. Peter Koslowski, Professor of Philosophy, Vrije Universiteit, Amsterdam, Netherlands opens the discussions with a chapter on the relation between ethics and economics. In his chapter "Ethical Economy and Business Ethics: On the Relationships between Ethics and Economics" he addresses the presupposition that the synthesis of ethics and economic criteria is the central task in judging individual and collective human action.

Seeing the role of business in the light of *ethics and economics* is, according to this view, central for business and public policy. In modifying Walter Rathenau, Koslowski argues that one could say that the economy is one of the determinants of our fate. In this sense the chapter addresses the close relationship between ethics and economics.

Hans Joas, pragmatic sociologist, Universities of Erfurt and Chicago, goes on to discuss problems of "Value Generalization – Limitations and Possibilities of a Communication about Values".

His contribution is an attempt to demonstrate that the concept of "value generalization" is of considerable importance for moral philosophy and therefore hopefully also for those interested in business and economic ethics. The importance of this concept lies in its relevance for what one could call "the logic of a communication about values". This logic is different from the structure of rational-argumentative discourse in a strict sense, but also far from a mere clash of values or identities or civilizations or any form of irrationalist decisionism, as if ultimate values could only be chosen in an existential way without any reasoning and intersubjective plausibility.

Niels Kærgård, Professor of Economics, Copenhagen University, discusses in his chapter "Corporate Social Responsibility, Economic Optimality and the Interests of the Poor" how the market economy is based on the actions of selfish agents. If the relevant rules are established by government, the price mechanism gives the profit-maximizing firm incentives to do what is optimal for the society. This means that it is far from obvious that altruistic action is more socially responsible than profit maximizing. Therefore Kærgård is rather critical of the social responsibility movement because he argues that social responsibility and other ethical arguments can often be used to legitimate economically and socially suboptimal actions. Profound analysis of the consequences is normally better for everybody than imprecise positive intentions.

Maria Bonnafous-Boucher, Director of Research, National Chamber of Commerce, Paris, has given her chapter the title "Stakeholders, Corporate Social Responsibility and Global Markets". She looks at how power is displaced and how principles are deconstructed. The sudden emergence of Corporate social responsibility (CSR) and social stakeholder theory (STH) 20 or so years ago – and its growing influence since then – has occurred in a very specific context characterized by the displacement of sovereignties and, consequently, of powers. This displacement deconstructs the foundations and principles of political philosophy: from the conception of the public good to perceptions of sovereignty and how it is exercised. It would be hard to imagine CSR without taking these important changes into account.

Christoph Luetge, Peter Loescher Professor of Business Ethics, Technische Universität München, takes the concept of economics ethics as the basis of business ethics in his chapter "Economics and Ethics: How to Combine Ethics and Self-Interest". The starting point is that the economy plays a dominant role in the global society. After the downfall of communism, a globalized market has emerged that extends across nearly all countries and regions. However, in theoretical discussions as well as in public opinion, the role of the economy is often in doubt. This is especially the case in ethics: on the one hand, there are those who see the capitalist market economy as the key to the promotion of ethical ideals like peace and prosperity. On the other hand, there are many others who believe the same market economy to be a major threat to national and international solidarity, to cultural pluralism and to a sense of community. Who is right?

Jacob Dahl Rendtorff, Roskilde University, the editor of this anthology, proposes in his chapter "Business Ethics between Politics, Ethics and Economics" to address the relation between business ethics and market institutions. He investigates how the problem of the relation between ethics, economics and market institutions in business concerns the concept of economic action and the role of ethical responsibility in economics. The debate about market institutions, economic rationality and political philosophy depends on the problem of whether there can be something like a common good or social justice for all members of society. From the standpoint of mainstream economics we can say that this problem is a problem of how to deal efficiently with limited resources. In this sense we may argue that neoclassical economic theory is a system of thought that seeks to deal rationally with the problem of sacrifice, that is, the problem of who, how or what society should sacrifice in order to seek optimal and efficient use of resources. With the separation of economics from political philosophy, economics has become the rational use of resources based on the principles of the rational profit maximizer of "homo economics" in the market institutions of individualist capitalism.

Güler Aras, Professor of Finance and Director of the Graduate School at Yildiz Technical University, Istanbul, and David Crowther, Professor of Corporate Social Responsibility at De Montfort University, propose in "Developing Durability: A Re-examination of Sustainable Corporate Social Responsibility" a new and critical understanding of the concept of sustainability. For more than 20 years the starting point for any discussion of sustainable corporate activity has been the Brundtland Report. Its concern with the effect that action taken in the present has upon the options available in the future has directly led to simplistic assumptions that sustainable development is both desirable and possible and that corporations can demonstrate sustainability merely by continuing to exist into the future. There have been various descendants of Brundtland, including the concept of the triple bottom line. This in turn has led to an assumption that addressing the three aspects of economic, social and environmental is the epitome of corporate social responsibility. It is Aras and Crowther's argument that this notion is not just incorrect but also positively misleading through an obfuscation of the key issues surrounding such responsibility. It is therefore time to re-examine the legacy of Brundtland and to redefine what is meant by sustainable activity. In order to do this they reject the accepted term of "sustainability", preferring instead the term "durability" to emphasize the change in focus. From this Crowther and Aras argue for a rejection of the triple bottom line and a redefinition of corporate social responsibility, using alternatives developed from their own work.

Mollie Painter-Morland, Associate Professor at DePaul University, Chicago, and Associate Director of its Institute for Business and Professional Ethics, explores in "Global Principles (as)(or) Ethical Responsiveness: The Case of Sustainability Rhetoric" the possibility that, in our preference for standardizing good conduct by means of global principles, we may have lost the ethical moment itself. She will argue that ethical responsiveness occurs only in a relationship, and that losing sight of the specific relationships that inform global principles threatens the principles themselves. The questions Painter-Morland would like to pose might even be more troubling: could it be that our current use of global principles undermined and contradicted ethics as such? Or that well-intentioned global principles contain elements that are irredeemably oxymoronic? For the purposes of this chapter, she is focusing on the notion of sustainability and the global principles that have been developed and advocated around it. Painter-Morland analyses prevalent global sustainability rhetoric, and seeks to indicate that, in and of themselves, these principles do little to foster ethical responsiveness. Does this mean that such principles have to be abandoned? Not necessarily. It does, however, mean that terms associated with them constantly need to be re-evaluated, which will include an ongoing reassessment of the relational dynamics informing them. This process may be performative in nature and may include grappling with the relationship between ethics and aesthetics.

Susanne Holmström, Roskilde University investigates in the chapter "Society's Constitution and Corporate Legitimacy, or Why it Might be Unethical for Business Leaders to Think with Their Heart" the new corporate legitimacy in the relation between ethics and economics. Is the perspective of ethics sensitive to the social complexity of the changes within the legitimating notions which determine the role and responsibility of economy and business companies within contemporary society? On the scientific dimension, taking the human being as ultimate reference or endeavouring to provide organizations with human qualities may represent sociological under-complexity. On the practical dimension, catchphrases such as "managers must learn to think with their heart" may risk leaving corporate executives in the lurch, considering the immense and increasing social complexity constituting and surrounding organizations today. Instead, from a sociological perspective, the new legitimating ideals empirically expressed in the thematization of ethics and concepts such as CSR and the triple bottom line are reconstructed as reflection, the specific second-order observation mode of self-referential social systems such as economy and companies. This reconstruction sees the changing interrelation between organization and society in relation to the societal structure and evolutionary processes. It is based mainly on Niklas Luhmann's theories which empty society of human beings as well as any teleology or content apart from the highly improbable ability to reproduce itself.

Ole Thyssen, Professor of Philosophy, Copenhagen Business School, analyses in "Hide and Seek in the Dark – on the Inherent Ambiguity of CSR" whether we can talk about an inherent ambiguity of CSR. He begins with the presupposition that, when civilizations clash, it is all about values. However, the battlefield is not only civilizations, but also organizations. In the last 30 years, values have invaded business life and created new agendas, as not only economic, but also ethical, human, social, environmental and a host of other values fight for a place in the sun.

Kirsten Marie Bovbjerg, Associate Professor, University of Aarhus, discusses in the chapter "'Ethics of Sensitivity' – Towards a New Work Ethic: New Age in Business Life" how courses in personal development and staff recruitment have become the site of a remarkable alliance between modern working life and new religious practice. Many of the methods and philosophy for developing the Self in work-life have their origin in modern religious, New Age thoughts such as Zen Buddhism, Landmark, neurolinguistic programming (NLP) and meditation techniques. How do religious methods give meaning in business life? Approaching this question about religious practice in modern business life, the work of Max Weber seems to be an obvious starting point. In his famous work on the rise of a protestant ethic in the early phase of modern capitalism as we know it in the West, Weber put attention on the fact that, in particular, the new protestant ethic and the protestant idea of salvation had an important influence on the development of a new economic behaviour and attitude towards work. The trend towards personal development shows an increasing interest in other aspects of an employee's competence than his professional qualifications. Courses in personal development often have a therapeutic dimension, deliberately intended to change people's behaviour or self-perception by a particular method. In her research, Kirsten Marie Bovbjerg has focused on the relationship between New Age and modern management and the development of a new work ethic based on sensitivity. From a critical perspective she has examined the use of personal development courses in business in recent decades and the increasing interest in the cultivation of the Self and how this trend has found expression in New Age as well as in modern management.

Karin Buhmann, Associate Professor at the University of Copenhagen, has a legal perspective on corporate social responsibility. In the chapter "Public–Private Development of CSR on the International Stage: Reflexivity and Legitimacy" she maintains that corporate social responsibility should only be understood as being beyond the law. Based on observations of developments on CSR and business responsibilities for human rights, this chapter argues that there is a closer relationship between CSR and law than is often recognized. Drawing in particular on the role of international law as a normative source of CSR as well as on soft, indirect and incentives-based modalities employed by governmental and intergovernmental authorities to regulate business behaviour with regard to social and human rights responsibilities, the chapter discusses the relationship between CSR and law, and argues that the insistence on CSR and law being distinct is misconceived and not beneficial to long-term development of CSR. The chapter discusses law in terms of regulatory methods and normative sources rather than positive requirements.

Michael Blowfield, Teaching Fellow at Oxford University, Organizational Behaviour Development, develops the legal perspective in the chapter "Business and Poverty – Bridges and Divides" into a political discussion of poverty. Globalization is variously portrayed as alleviating, exacerbating or ignoring poverty. For those who see liberalism as essential to economic growth, democracy and peace, corporate responsibility is potentially damaging to the globalization project. For those concerned about disparities in global equality, corporate responsibility is sometimes depicted as a way of securing more beneficial social and environmental outcomes than free markets alone could achieve. Yet is either of these positions justified? Is corporate responsibility in theory or in practice able to affect the way business relates to issues such as poverty, inequality and marginalization? This chapter examines poverty as it is experienced by business, and explores how business is responding. It examines the intent, possibilities, extent and limitations of corporate responsibility as a contribution to global development, and whether it ultimately constitutes a systematic or arbitrary, innovative or exploitative, effective or random way to tackle the challenges of the globalization project.

Ove K. Pedersen, Professor at the Copenhagen Business School and Director of External Affairs at the International Center for Business and Politics, addresses in "The Ethical Moment: Ethics and Economy in Public Administration" the problem of ethics in relation to public affairs. It has become common over the last 25 years to formulate general ethical standards for the management of public administration, not only in developing countries, but also in most Western democratic societies. Standards of ethical conduct currently exist for public managers in the USA, the UK, New Zealand, Canada, Australia and a number of other countries. They apply to members of the civil service on the basis of professional merits (meritocracy) as well as to public officials on the basis of their political appointment (politocracy). Ove K. Pedersen argues that public managers are compelled to make decisions to an increasing extent in situations of a "legal void". In addition, he uses the introduction of new public management to explain why situations of ethical moments have become an important topic of contemporary public administration. Much of this discussion focuses on the Nordic countries (Denmark and Norway) but it also includes examples from the USA and other Anglo-Saxon countries.

Janet L. Borgerson, Reader (Associate Professor) in Philosophy and Management at the University of Exeter, discusses in "On Witnessing Global Ethics: A Case of International Health Research Involving Human Subjects" a case of exploitation of human subjects in the process of globalization. She begins with a discussion of a point of view of Derrida. Derrida argues that the Witness attempts to make present a singular and irreplaceable experience, not as proof, but as testimony. Perhaps, then, the Witness is a worthy figure to evoke in attempts to observe, articulate, manifest and even manage global ethics. The context of international health research involving human subjects, and this should appear obvious, is the global human community. Yet, the geography, both planetary and human, in international health research is so vast, and the boundaries of countries and the boundaries of acceptability so porous and moveable, that the concern for human beings, apparently so foundational, may lose centrality. Borgerson traces a narrative inspired by a university programme on the ethics of international health research involving human subjects. She focuses, in particular, upon the pedagogic rhetoric, then moves to issues around a standard of care. She draws upon philosophers John Rawls, Claudia Card and Allen Buchanan to discuss concerns regarding the "least advantaged members of society", "the unnatural lottery" and "global basic structure" in the context of global inequality. Beyond exploring fundamental issues, the chapter emphasizes that, in processes of writing codes and guidelines for international health research involving human subjects, the authors are as much subjects of inquiry as the guidelines themselves.

Peter Kemp, Professor Emeritus of Philosophy, Danish School of Education, Aarhus University, presents in "The Cosmopolitan Story" a view of ethics and economics in the process of globalization. The current crisis of the world economy follows nearly eight years of crisis of international law. The political reaction, in particular by the Bush administration (2001–2009), to the terrorist attack on 11 September 2001 shook for many people the conviction they had that international law was respected, at least to some degree, by the major powers in the world. The idea that all nations must respect a certain world order, including the right to basic goods for all people, was developed from Francisco Vitoria (1483–1546), Francisco Suarez (1548–1617), Hugo Grotius (1583–1645) and Samuel Pufendorf (1632–1694) up to the international agreement on the Charter of the United Nations in 1945 and the Geneva Conventions from 1949, adopted by all major powers. However, this idea went into deep crisis after 11 September. People became demoralized. Not only was a military intervention made against Iraq without the required permission from the Security Council of the United Nations, but prisoners from the wars in Afghanistan and Iraq were also treated inhumanely in prison camps at Guantánamo and elsewhere. These prisoners have not been given the right to a fair trial according to the Geneva Conventions and later supplements.

Finally, Jacob Dahl Rendtorff concludes with "Conclusion: Outline of an Epistemological Methodology for Integrating Ethics and Economics". This conclusion deals with the relation between ethics and economics as a problem of integrative business ethics. Business ethics is not a field of pure philosophy but a kind of social theory and applied philosophy that addresses normative issues of values and norms in economic systems. Business ethics should be conceived as an interdisciplinary field of study, which proposes a broad and open concept of economics. Business ethics is, according to Jacob Dahl Rendtorff, conceived as a normative argument about good business values. However the field of study does not only depend on philosophical methods of arguments of meaning and interpretations of relevant textual material. Although it is a field of theoretical clarification of arguments as the basis of concrete action, business ethics also relies heavily on the type of knowledge generated by the social sciences. Therefore, research in business ethics cannot be separated from social sciences because it is enriched by the knowledge and methodology of the social sciences. However, this implies reflection about the kind of research to be undertaken in this intersection between the social sciences, business, ethics and economics.

All the chapters of this anthology were originally presented in preliminary form at a conference in Copenhagen, Denmark, 12–14 September 2008, "Power and Principle in the Market Place", organized together with the German Cultural Institute – the Goethe Institute of Copenhagen, Copenhagen Business School and Roskilde University. The conference was very fruitful and the authors benefited from the discussions in order to prepare their chapters for publication. We are thankful for the support of the Goethe Institute, Copenhagen Business School and Roskilde University for the conference and for publication of this anthology.

Indeed, we would like to congratulate Professor, Dr. Per Øhrgaard of the Copenhagen Business School and in particular, Director, Dr. Matthias Müller-Wieferig and his staff from the Goethe Institute of Copenhagen who did so much of the work of organizing the conference.

Chapter 2

Ethical Economy and Business Ethics: On the Relationships between Ethics and Economics

Peter Koslowski

Business ethics deals with the ethical duties, values and virtues of the commercial, profit-oriented and not-for-profit organization. It is ethical economy as the synthesis of economic and ethical theory applied to management and business. Ethical economy is the foundational theory of business ethics. Most deep choices have an ethical and an economic dimension. The optimization of a decision requires doing justice to both of these dimensions. Ethical economy is the theory of this synthesis. It is more than applied ethics. It is a foundational theory of its own kind, not the application of ethical principles to concrete cases. A number of general and rather abstract principles are derived from this theoretical synthesis and serve in turn to make the combination of ethical and economic criteria operational. If the theory of ethical economy is applied to business and economic organizations, it is the ethical economy of business or business ethics.[1]

Ethical Economy as the Economy of Ethics

The Principle of the Aspired Compatibility of Morality and Advantage

The first question of the economics of ethics concerns the conditions under which efficient rule adherence can be expected. Under which conditions do individuals have incentives to follow the ethical norm? Ethical economy as the economy of ethics gives an answer to the question of what economic reasons motivate individuals to follow ethical norms.

How can ethics be formulated in such a way that it is incentive-compatible or congruent with self-interest? The motivational part of the economy of ethics is concerned with the question of how ethics can be made effective by harmonizing it with economic incentives. Economic ethics demands that situations are avoided

---

1   Cf. Koslowski (2002c). J. M. Buchanan subsumes parts of what is called here "ethical economy" under the concept of "the constitutional economics of ethics" (cf. Buchanan 1992).

in which ethical demands are incentive-adverse and contradict the incentives individuals have. In contrast to situations in which ethical motivation and rule are contrary to self-interest and economic incentive, ethical economy as the economy of ethics proposes that the social and ethical order are constituted in such a way that, by following the ethical rule, persons acting in the economy face no net loss of wealth and do not violate their self-interest.

Breaking through the Infinity of Opportunity Cost and Negation

Since any course of action excludes another opportunity for action, every action has a cost which can, in one way or another, be expressed by its opportunity costs. The cost of an opportunity forsaken is not the same as a cost actually incurred, since we never know exactly how much another opportunity would have cost in real terms since it will never occur. Nevertheless, opportunities forsaken imply a forsaken utility and therefore an opportunity cost for economic theory and an opportunity forsaken for ethical theory. This is particularly true for irreversible decisions in which the opportunity cost of the decision cannot be revised at any cost. Irreversible decisions are particularly ethical decisions since they encounter prohibitive costs of revision.

The concept of opportunity cost resembles but is not identical to the principle of negation. Spinoza introduced the principle of negation of which Hegel made ample use: every determination is negation. If determination or decision-making is the negation of all other attributes, possibilities or decision outcomes, it will never reach the point of determinedness or decision since there are infinite possibilities to be negated. The logic of determination and the logic of decision are similar in logics, ethics and economics. In the logics of logics and in the logics of choice, negation is a central principle, but it is not the only and metaphysical principle of reality or decision-making.

By making an ethical or economic decision we do not negate infinite other possibilities but negate only a finite number of alternatives or opportunities. We negate the opportunities that we are able to imagine and that are actually open to us. It requires all our imagination and analysis as well as all our ethical honesty to recognize what our opportunities really are and which of these opportunities we will forsake. Decision-making in ethics and economics demands identification of the relevant and real opportunities we actually have; it does not demand negation of all possible opportunities in all possible worlds.

Ethical Economy as the Theory of the Ethical Presuppositions of the Market Economy

Perfect competition has no need for ethics since it is assumed that the market price and the quality of the goods are perfectly transparent. Furthermore, perfect competition tends to squeeze out non-remunerative incentives in the labour market since all suppliers have to provide the same working conditions to attract labour. It drives out non-remunerative incentives in the market for goods since consumers have no other incentive but the market price if the goods offered by suppliers are the same. Consumers can only differentiate in the quality of goods being sold on the market by moving to substitutes of the goods in question. David Gauthier describes the ideal market of perfect competition as a "morals-free zone" (Gauthier 1985).

The Principle of the Need for an Internalized or External Third in Contracts

There is, however, a difficulty in the model of the market of perfect competition which concerns the workings of the invisible hand in the coordination of self-interested action. The business contracts might not be self-enforcing even under perfect competition – they seem to require a third party to enforce them.

In his *Leviathan*, Hobbes writes about the nature of humankind's desires: "So that in the nature of man, we find three principall causes of quarrell. First, Competition; Secondly, Diffidence; Thirdly, Glory. The first, maketh men invade for Gain; the second, for Safety; and the third, for Reputation. ... Hereby it is manifest, that during the time men live without a common Power to keep them all in awe, they are in that condition which is called Warre; and such a warre, as is of every man, against every man" (Hobbes, 1909, p. 43).

Human beings need a third party to control their desire to invade each other for gain, greater safety or more glory. Human beings understand that they can improve their lot by entering into agreements not to invade for greater gain, safety or reputation, but their rational self-interest to come to mutual agreements might be not as strong as their reluctance to keep these agreements. This is why a social contract of association, a contract between two parties, Ego and Alter, is not sufficient for a civil state of contract compliance. Without a third party who enforces compliance, human beings are always tempted to breach their contracts.

All agreements, be they civil or public, need the third party to guarantee their fulfilment and to ensure certainty of expectation, which is the core of legal safety. Without the third party, Ego and Alter have no certainty that their agreements will be observed and that their expectations about the future will be fulfilled. They cannot plan for the future without an external or internalized third party guaranteeing observance of the contracts.

The Principle of the Ethical Assurance of Loyalty to Contracts

As soon as there is a time-lag between contracting and observing the contract, uncertainty enters as to whether the contract will be observed as agreed upon. This uncertainty is reduced by the third party, the legal guarantor of contracts; by long-term business relationships, repeat business; or by an effective business ethics code. The legal monitoring and enforcement of contracts is costly. Legal costs occur, and the contract enforcement is only realized later when the damage caused by the delay in honouring the contract and by the non-realization of the contract-based expectations about the future have already occurred. Even if the law enforces a contract, the plans of the contracting partner for the future made on the basis of the contract have already been disrupted.

Long-term business relationships and repeat business do not rely on ethical considerations, but on the formation of habits and the expectation of lower transaction costs by replicating the same business. The same process that creates economic advantages and the formation of trust, however, is also subject to the possibility of being exploited by both sides. The more often a business transaction is repeated and the more a habit of doing business is established, the more both sides are locked into the business relationship. Repeat business is economically and ethically ambivalent. Not only does it create cost-saving opportunities but it also increases the possibility of losses from being locked into a relationship and being exploited in it.

Contractual relationships in the market can be monitored by more than fear of legal punishment or the establishment of long-term business relationships. Ethical codes and ethical convictions serve as a substitute for legal enforcement and monitoring, and as a way to reduce the exploitation potential in long-term business relationships. An ethos of observing contracts leads to a market environment that is superior to an environment where only lawyers or mere habits ensure that contracts are served.

Pacta sunt servanda is a central norm of the economy that is not secured by self-interest alone. Even in a market with well-functioning legal enforcement of contracts, there are many contracts that are incomplete, ill-defined or indeterminate with regard to the contractual obligations. Ethics and religion are a means of giving substance to the expectation that the contracting partner will observe the contract and keep the promises made in the contract.

Reliability and mutual trust on the part of business partners result in reduced costs of economic exchange. Trust reduces transaction costs, since the contracting partners can come to an agreement more rapidly. They face fewer monitoring costs.

Individuals may react in three ways to this relationship between trust and freedom of contract. First, individuals can behave unconditionally morally. They understand the common economic need in ethical behaviour as the *motive* for their *own* behaviour. This person turns common interest into his own interest, i.e. the person behaves morally irrespectively of the behaviour of the others (*case 1*). For example, a firm employee tries to do his best irrespective of what others achieve, or a business person tries to remain fair even if widespread forms of unfair behaviour are to be found in the industry.

Second, a person can behave conditionally morally. This person is ready to follow ethical rules if the others or the majority also follow them, but violates the rules if she feels that she alone "will be the fool" (*case 2*). This contracting partner fulfils the contractual obligations only if everybody else does so as well.

Third, persons may appreciate that a better situation for everybody is achieved if everybody follows the rules, but consider the best situation to be one in which everybody but them follows the rules (*case 3*). This is the pattern of behaviour assumed by the famous prisoner's dilemma in game theory. A firm knows that it is best for the industry if every firm sticks to the rules and no bribing of business partners or other form of corruption takes place, but it prefers to make an exception for itself and to support contracting by doing favours for business associates.

Case 3 of the behavioural options presents a typical dilemma situation in which one cannot remain. The dilemma describes a situation in which everybody benefits if *everybody* follows the rules and in which each person is interested in being the only one who can violate the rules. As a consequence, the rule will be violated if it is not enforced by external control and sanctions, or if it is not affirmed by the individuals on ethical grounds. Case 3 will then be transformed either into the ethical options of case 1 or 2 or into a system of external monitoring and enforcement.

Case 2, in which one acts morally if everyone else does too, is a typical intermediate situation that seems to be acceptable to most people. One behaves morally if others do the same; one stops behaving morally if one feels oneself to be the only person behaving morally. Ethics is a means of transforming the situation of a prisoner's dilemma into a situation of trust or assurance. The general acceptance of and compliance with ethical rules would transform the isolation paradox, named after Amartya Sen (1967, p. 112), of case 2 into a situation of relative certainty. The isolation paradox implies that individuals will not follow the rules under conditions of isolation and uncertainty about others' behaviour since they are afraid of being deceived, although they are actually ready to follow the general rule in other circumstances.

However, case 2 is not stable, as the certainty that at least most of the others will follow the rules is always vague and limited. Sen, though, assumes that generally acknowledged moral values transform case 3, the situation of the prisoner's dilemma, into case 2, the situation of certainty or assurance, into an "assurance game". When moral values are generally acknowledged, the individual is no longer uncertain about the moral preferences of the others. However, Sen's position is begging the question – a *petitio principii* remains. If one says that individuals have further motivation to behave morally if ethical behaviour is general, i.e. that "values" are recognized, this begs the question of whether the values are indeed generally acknowledged. How is it possible to make sure that moral "values" are generally acknowledged, that the others also behave morally and that the individuals make the rule their motive? The element of uncertainty remains here; assurance is only relative. Case 2 is more stable than case 3, as in case 2 the individuals are at least partially moral and cooperating, but case 2 cannot ensure absolute certainty about the moral behaviour of the others and provide secure grounds for trust.

In case 2, in the situation of the isolation paradox, two questions arise: "How long will the individuals be ready to follow the moral rules if most of the others violate them or if they are not certain about the others' actual behaviour?" and "How may the uncertainty about the behaviour of the others be reduced?" Both questions cannot be solved by ethics alone. Answering the questions by pointing to the need for a general ethics leads again and again to the *petitio principii* that the ethics will be accepted by the individuals and find general recognition if this already enjoys general recognition, and that the isolation paradox of the acceptance of ethics may be overcome if the ethics is already generally effective.

Case 2 shows that the prisoner's dilemma and isolation paradox may be solved by ethics only if individuals recognize the moral rule naturally and irrespectively of the behaviour of the others – if they make the moral rule their individual motive also. As uncertainty about the others' behaviour cannot be eliminated, the moral rule can win recognition only if it is recognized despite the others' behaviour.

The failure of ethics requires a corrective. Kant, in his *Critique of Practical Reason*, sheds light on this problem of ethics failure. If a moral individual follows the categorical imperative while all the others follow the rule of personal happiness, the harmony between one's own morality and pursuit of happiness is destroyed. Kant thought that this problem could be solved by the "postulates of practical reason". The postulates of practical reason – God, liberty and the immortality of the soul – restore trust in the meaningfulness of moral behaviour, and in the harmony between morality and advantage. Religion here is a postulate guaranteeing the exigency of being moral. It helps build up a social capital on which trust can be founded.

There is a sequence of compensations for failure. When self-interest fails, there is ethics; when ethics fails, there is religion. This structure of failure compensation has been analysed in greater detail in the author's *Principles of Ethical Economy* (Koslowski, 2002c).

The Principle of Double Effect: Handling Externalities of Economic Action

The assumption of market theory is that the market price includes or internalizes all benefits and costs caused by the exchange to both sides. Both sides confirm that all benefits and costs are internalized by their consent to the exchange. Third parties that are not part of the exchange are not concerned. There are, however, exchanges that have side-effects or externalities on others that are not internalized in the exchange, like environmental pollution. When pollution on third parties originates from a contract between two parties, the principle of internalization is violated.

Side-effects are a classical problem of moral philosophy and of economics. Moral philosophy developed the theory of the principle of double effect, which can be considered to be a transcendental principle of handling side-effects and is a central principle of ethical economy and of business ethics.

Most ethically relevant decisions in business do in fact have side-effects and, therefore, are ill-structured decision problems under uncertainty. They cannot be converted into well-structured decision situations by calculi unless with unrealistic, scientistic premises, such as premises that the results of actions can be known with certainty or that the probability distribution of the possible effects of actions and outcomes is known. The principle of double effect is, in contrast to the principle of the categorical imperative, concrete and makes it possible to perform comparisons of goods. It is, therefore, an important complement to the universalization principle, which is weak in judging the concrete case.

The principle reads: an action with negative side-effects is sensible and permitted, if the following four conditions are met:

1. The goal of the action must be good and sincere (i.e. the acting person may not intend a bad and impermissible effect). The side-effects must be *praeter intentionem*.
2. The type or form of the action must be intrinsically good.
3. The negative side-effects must be true *side*-effects. They must objectively have the character of accidental effects arising in the pursuit of other goals, and may not serve as means to the good effect.
4. There must be a proportionately grave reason to perform the action. The acting person may not be obligated by other duties to refrain from it completely.

The Principle of Hyper-Motivation: Incentives of Self-Justification as Economic Incentives

The idea of the right structure of incentives and contributions is a central concept of economic and management theory. There exist, however, not only incentives but also right and wrong incentives in business, science and technology. The remuneration of managers according to the rise or fall of the share price of the firms they manage creates incentives to arrange their performance primarily on this goal and to neglect other duties.

Motivation structures and contributions can be intensified in their effect through motivation boosters, as the history of entrepreneurship, technological invention and scholarship demonstrates. Max Weber's Calvinist entrepreneur becomes creative and is motivated for high performance through religious incentives. Because he understands his economical success as a proof of being in the state of grace, he experiences additional religious incentives to be successful in business.

Cultural and economic incentives and motives overlap. Culturally defined incentives enhance economic creativity and business performance. Re-grandizement of meaning are central phenomena of cultural and economic enforcement of motivation. One can call this meaning enforcement a "hyper-motivation" by cultural incentives.

Business Ethics as Applied Ethical Economy

An essential starting point of business ethics is the management of firms. Because the management task is not restricted to the commercial enterprise, business ethics affects all organizations.

The firm or organization is a possible subject of business ethics because organization failure exists as failure of the institutional norms and control mechanisms. Organization failure furthers individual failure, which therefore cannot be blamed on the individual organization member who acts unethically. The institutionalization of ethical codes and compliance officers who are in charge of controlling and enforcing the compliance of the legal and ethical rules is used for the prevention of ethical organization failure. Both measures were made obligatory in the USA after the Enron scandal through the Sarbanes–Oxley Act and influenced business ethics rules in all international large-scale corporations.

The compliance and development of rules in complex organizations is a task which must be fulfilled by the firms themselves, since the legislator and the courts can develop and enforce the appropriate rules for the rapidly changing world of business and technology only together with the corporations and industries. Business ethics plays an important role in the legislative process of civil and corporate law.

Business ethics and business compliance are instruments of risk management. The risks which arise from unethical or even criminal behaviour of members of an organization consist of the damage to the reputation and the brand of the firm as well as possible payments for penalties and compensations. The enterprise must minimize the risk arising from the non-observance of the rules of business ethics and law through the implementation and sanctioning of business guidelines which illustrate the basic ethical principles of the organization to all organization members. Business ethics is part of the risk management of the enterprise against risks of reputation loss and penalties.

The duties of the manager are determined by her position as the director of the enterprise, employed by the owners of the firm as the director of the firm and as their agent. The manager is, however, not only the agent of the owners (principals), but also the manager or director of the entire enterprise. She is obliged to the enterprise as a whole and to its common good. The manager of a large-scale corporation is not only the agent of the owners or shareholders, but also their fiduciary and the trustee of those that work under her management. It is part of her fiduciary duty towards the owners to act at the same time as the trustee of the entire enterprise.

As a concept of business ethics, the fiduciary duty contains the following particular duties: the duty of good faith (*bona fide*), the duty of loyalty, the duty of care and prudence, the duty of disclosure and the duty to avoid and disclose possible conflicts of interest. In fulfilling these duties, managers are not free to follow their own interest at the expense of the enterprise. The fiduciary relationship implies a kind of self-binding of the owners and the managers which goes beyond the mere self-interest of shareholders and managers and beyond the idea that management is only the owners' agent.

The duty of loyalty in the fiduciary duties commits the manager to undivided and unselfish loyalty towards the corporation, not only towards the shareholders. It is more than a mere contract. It is an obligation towards the corporation as a whole. The duty of care and prudence obliges the manager to act in the interests of the corporation, and not only in her own interest, with due care and diligence. The duty of disclosure obliges the managers not to take any advantage from facts gained confidentially in the pursuit of their tasks or from being informed by the firm's owners. The fiduciary duty of disclosure excludes the possibility of making use of or taking advantage of this knowledge as insider knowledge in the course of the fulfilment of the management task or as a private person. The prohibition of the use of insider knowledge and the duty of disclosure follow from the manager's trustee position towards the enterprise as whole, not only from her position as an agent of the owners. This is confirmed by the fact that the prohibition of insider trading also holds in cases where a major shareholder authorizes the manager to make use of insider knowledge for private interest. The common interest of the corporation and the right of all shareholders to the insider knowledge forbid the use of insider knowledge through the managers even in cases where the main shareholder exempts them from their duty to avoid insider deals.

The duties that follow from a fiduciary relationship are valid for all fiduciary relationships, for the relationship of the bank employees and financial consultants with their customers, for the doctor with the patient, for the architect with the house owner, and so forth.

The definition of the relationship between the enterprise and the manager as a principal–agent relationship only and the compensation of the managers according to the development of the share price alone leads to the disregard of criteria of success other than the development of market capitalization. It furthers a hit-and-run-mentality. Business ethics has the task of examining whether incentives are set correctly since there also exist perverse incentives that do not lead to a realization of business objectives. It is necessary not only to set incentives, but also to set economically and ethically right incentives to achieve the right contributions to the firm's success.

State compulsion is replaced by voluntary self-obligation of corporations in movements such as the Global Compact Initiative and the Global Reporting Initiative. These movements attempt to reduce environmental damage and to pay attention to the rights of future generations by corporate self-binding. Respecting the natural capital in environmental protection creates a reputation for the firm which is also acknowledged by investors and considered as additional value in the evaluation of the market capitalization of firms. Investors are increasingly and more frequently ready to pay an additional price for companies which have a higher reputation for observing ethical principles such as the protection of the environment or the rights of future generations – be it that this evaluation is done within the framework of institutionalized ethical investing or in the general stock market.

The consideration of the effects of the corporation's action on the natural and social environment of the firm in the triple bottom line according to economic performance indicators, environmental performance indicators and social performance indicators is another means of achieving higher ethical performance of corporations. The triple bottom line causes a greater inclusion of ethical criteria and of corporate social responsibility – such as services of the enterprise to its social and natural environment or observation of intergenerational justice – within the evaluation of the total corporate performance than accounting according to a single bottom line. The new weight of the ethical, environmental and social indicators forces in turn the management and the shareholders to pay more attention to these indicators of corporate success in their management decisions if they want to be able to compete successfully for investors, consumers and employees.

Four Elements of Corporate Social Responsibility, their Legitimacy and Limits

At present, firms seem to be more interested in corporate social responsibility (CSR) than business ethics. Business schools seem to be more eager to have CSR than business ethics courses in their curriculum. Is CSR a substitute for business ethics?

Corporate social responsibility[2] includes several elements: (1) voluntary social action for the employees of the firm in the tradition of social policy or corporate social welfare; (2) environmental action as an expression of the ecological responsibility of the firm; (3) corporate citizenship rendering the firm as a legal person into a corporate citizen, promoting human rights and political change through civic political action; (4) philanthropy as support of philanthropic purposes in culture, the arts, sport, science, etc.

It should be noted that there are semantic differences between the different Western countries. In English, social responsibility comprises all societal actions of the firm, "social" meaning societal in the most general sense and social in the sense of social welfare, social policy and social support. In German and, as I have learned from Jacob Dahl Rendtorff from Roskilde University, Denmark, also in Danish, *sozial* or "social" means primarily social policy-oriented action whereas the wider orientation on all kinds of activites aimed at society in general is usually called "societal" or in German *gesellschaftlich* (from *Gesellschaft* = society).

The four classes of corporate social responsibility listed above are often introduced as ethical activities and duties following from business ethics consideration. The CSR activities of a firm are, however, not strict duties but virtuous acts. They represent supererogatory acts of virtue. As such they are to be applauded. The emphasis on CSR is problematic when these acts are demanded as voluntary acts that are at the same time substitutes for formerly legally organized

---

2   See Crane et al. (2008).

activities. Take activity (1), voluntary social action for employees. If the firm claims that formerly legal social rights are now transferred to weak claims of virtue on the firm, the danger of down-sizing of these activities and their transformation into mere voluntary acts of benevolence is present. With this transformation comes the danger of under-institutionalization, lack of public debate and control. If social policy were transferred to management discretion, it would further aggrandize the "manager-leader" and the personality of the CEO and reduce the public responsibility for social policy. It would also lead to a de-professionalization of social policy. It is also likely that the voluntary social policy of firms would be down-sized and would underperform as compared with the strict legal rules of social policy.

In addition, environmental action should not be considered to be a voluntary act of discretion and virtue, but should be either the consequence of the principle of no harm to third parties in the production process and, therefore, a strict consequence of civil law or a norm set by the government for all firms of an industry if some pollution is allowed. Environmental protection is neither a supererogatory act of social thinking, philanthropy or corporate citizenship but an obligation derived from the no-harm principle.

Corporate citizenship as a need that the firm becomes also a political actor applies mainly to those countries in which the natural citizen or the natural, in contrast to legal, persons cannot influence politics in such a way that their rights as humans and as citizens are affirmed. Under these circumstances, firms can become proxies for their employees in the political process and further enforce their employees' rights by using political influence. If powerful firms do the same in countries where the human and political rights of their employees are secure, the effect is totally different and adverse. Corporate citizenship as the corporate citizen's right to influence politics in countries where personal political rights are secured would give a mandate to exert political influence to already powerful corporate actors. It would combine economic and political power and influence in corporate actors and cause a development that is detrimental to the democratic process.

Corporate social responsibility as a duty to perform philanthropic acts is not an obligation that can be ethically justified. Philanthropy is a supererogatory act. The funds for philanthropy can only be taken from corporate resources if they add to the value creation of the firm by public relations and advertising activities that further the economic purpose of the firm. If they do not further the economic goal of the firm, philanthropy as pure donation must be left to the owners of the firm, who can use their dividends or capital gains obtained from the firm after taxes or after being freed from taxes for these contributions to philanthropic purposes by the government.

If the management used the firm's funds for philanthropy that did not further the purpose of the firm and was a mere cost for it, the firm's management would be using funds that are due to the shareholders or the claimants of wages or income for purposes that are external and alien to the purpose of the firm. The idea that philanthropy can correct the distribution of income arising from the market is mostly mistaken if the philanthropic funds are partly financed by the tax advantage given by them, since the tax advantage is financed, in turn, by the loss of government income and, therefore, by the tax payer.

To summarize the problem of CSR: to affirm the duty of the management to engage in CSR measures and the right of the public to CSR activities contradicts the purpose of the firm and violates the shareholders' property rights and the employees' rights to their share of the firm's value creation. It allocates further discretionary power to the management without institutionalizing additional checks and balances within corporate governance for this power. The de-institutionalization caused by this extension of the management's power of discretion is not helpful.

A plain affirmation of CSR contradicts the principle of the division of labour between the firm and other institutions like the state and non-governmental organizations. CSR can have the effect of a de-legitimization since CSR-decisions are not checked by consumer sovereignty in the market or voter sovereignty in politics. CSR is in danger of creating a third zone between the state and the market where managers have great discretionary power unchecked by the firm's shareholders or employees and are not accountable to the market, the government, or the voter.

References

Bowie, N. E. (2002), A Kantian Approach to Business Ethics, in *A Companion to Business Ethics*, R. E. Frederick (ed.). Oxford: Blackwell, pp. 3–16.

Brady, F. N. (1990), *Ethical Managing: Rules and Results*. New York: Macmillan.

Buchanan, J. M. (1992), Die konstitutionelle Ökonomik der Ethik, in *Neuere Entwicklungen in der Wirtschaftsethik und Wirtschaftsphilosophie*, P. Koslowski (ed.). Berlin: Springer, pp. 21–46.

Coleman, J. S. (1993), Social Organization of the Corporation, in *Ethical Issues in Business. A Philosophical Approach*, 4th edn, T. Donaldson and P. H. Werhane (eds). Englewood Cliffs, NJ: Prentice Hall, pp. 172–190.

Crane, A., McWilliams, A. and Matten, D. (2008), *The Oxford Handbook of Corporate Social Responsibility* (Oxford Handbooks). Oxford: Oxford University Press.

Donaldson, T. and Dunfee, T. W. (1994), Toward a Unified Conception of Business Ethics: Integrative Social Contracts Theory. *Academy of Management Review*, 19, 252–279.

Evan, W. M. and Freeman, R. E. (1993), A Stakeholder Theory of the Modern Corporation: Kantian Capitalism, in *Ethical Issues in Business. A Philosophical Approach*, 4th edn, T. Donaldson and P. H. Werhane (eds). Englewood Cliffs, NJ: Prentice Hall, pp. 166–171.

Gauthier, D. (1985), *Morals by Agreement*. Oxford: Oxford University Press.

Hartman, L. (2004), *Perspectives in Business Ethics*. New York: McGraw-Hill/ Irwin.

Hobbes, T. (1909), *Leviathan*, W.G. Pogson Smith (ed.). Oxford: Clarendon Press. Reprint of the edition of 1651, Chap. XIII. *Of the Natural Condition of Mankind, as Concerning their Felicity, and Misery*, reprinted as online edition in The Online Library of Liberty, Liberty Fund, 2005; http://oll.libertyfund. org/.

Homann, K. (2002), *Vorteile und Anreize*. Tübingen: Mohr Siebeck.

Johnston, J. F. (2005), Natural Law and the Fiduciary Duties of Business Managers, in *Business and Religion: A Clash of Civilizations*, N. Capaldi (ed.). Salem, MA: M&M Scrivener Press, pp. 279–300.

Koslowski, P. (1991), *Gesellschaftliche Koordination: Eine ontologische und kulturwissenschaftliche Theorie der Marktwirtschaft*. Tübingen: Mohr Siebeck.

Koslowski, P. (1992), Ethical Economy as Synthesis of Economic and Ethical Theory, in P. Koslowski (ed.), *Ethics in Economics, Business, and Economic Policy*. Berlin: Springer, pp. 15–56.

Koslowski, P. (1995), The Ethics of Banking. On the Ethical Economy of the Credit and Capital Market, of Speculation and Insider Trading in the German Experience, in *The Ethical Dimension of Financial Institutions and Markets*, A. Argandoña (ed.). Berlin: Springer, pp. 180–232.

Koslowski, P. (1996), Ethics of Capitalism, in *Ethics of Capitalism and Critique of Sociobiology*, P. Koslowski (ed.), Two Essays with a Comment by James M. Buchanan. Berlin: Springer.

Koslowski, P. (2002a), The Shareholder Value Principle and the Purpose of the Firm: Limits to Shareholder Value, in *Rethinking the Purpose of Business: Interdisciplinary Essays from the Catholic Social Tradition*, S. A. Cortright and M. J. Naughton (eds). Notre Dame, IN: University of Notre Dame Press, pp. 102–130.

Koslowski, P. (2002b), Economics as Ethical Economy and Cultural Economics in the Historical School, in *The Historicity of Economics: Continuities and Discontinuities of Historical Thought in 19th and 20th Century Economics*, H. H. Nau and B. Schefold (eds). Berlin: Springer, pp. 139–173.

Koslowski, P. (2002c), *Principles of Ethical Economy*. Dordrecht: Kluwer, paperback edition. German original (1988), *Prinzipien der Ethischen Ökonomie. Grundlegung der Wirtschaftsethik*. Tübingen: Mohr Siebeck.

Koslowski, P. (2006), The Common Good of the Firm as the Fiduciary Duty of the Manager, in *Global Perspectives on Ethics of Corporate Governance*, G. J. Rossouw and A. J. G. Sison (eds). New York: Palgrave Macmillan, pp. 67–76.

Sen, A. (1967), Isolation, Assurance, and the Social Rate of Discount. *Quarterly Journal of Economics*, 81, 112–124.

Solomon, R. C. (1993), *Ethics and Excellence: Cooperation and Integrity in Business*. Oxford: Oxford University Press.

Velasquez, M. G. (2005), *Business Ethics: Concepts and Cases*, 5th edn, Englewood Cliffs: Prentice Hall.

Weber, M. (2005), *The Protestant Ethic and the Spirit of Capitalism* (1904/1905), translated by Talcott Parsons with an introduction by Anthony Giddens. London: Routledge Classics.

Chapter 3

Value Generalization[1] – Limitations and Possibilities of a Communication about Values

Hans Joas

This chapter is an attempt to demonstrate that the concept of "value generalization" – a concept that has been developed in one of the most ambitious sociological theories of social change – is of considerable importance for moral philosophy and therefore hopefully also for those interested in business and economic ethics. The importance of this concept lies in its relevance for what one could call "the logic of a communication about values". My claim is that this logic is different from the structure of rational-argumentative discourse in a strict sense, but also far from a mere clash of values or identities or civilizations or any form of irrationalist decisionism, as if ultimate values could only be chosen in an existential way without any reasoning and intersubjective plausibility. I will proceed in four steps: after a reflection on the limitations of rational discourse and a typology of the alternatives to the idea of an inevitable clash of values and identities, I will present the concept of "value generalization" in some detail and then illustrate it by mentioning certain empirical processes in the field of value change and value innovation to which it can be applied.

Why do we need a specific theory of the communication about values? Why can we not be satisfied given the elaboration of an extremely sophisticated version of discourse ethics in the works of the German philosophers Jürgen Habermas and Karl-Otto Apel? Inspired by the path-breaking work of Charles Sanders Peirce, the founder of American pragmatism, but also taking up suggestions from analytical philosophers and linguists and above all from Stephen Toulmin's (1958) work *The Uses of Argument*, these two thinkers have elaborated a comprehensive model of rational-argumentative discourse about cognitive, normative and other validity claims. This model can certainly be considered the most consistent such theory that is currently available. The basic idea here is that all rational discourse has its point of departure in speech acts in which a speaker pursues the illocutionary goal to convince the listener that his or her implicit or explicit validity claims are justified. The listener is then expected not simply to listen, but also to accept

---

1 Originally published in *Zeitschrift für Wirtschafts- und Unternehmensethik*, 9 (2008), 88–96.

the validity claim – or otherwise to give better reasons why he or she cannot or can only partially agree. In this case the speaker is confronted with an alternative validity claim which implies that he is now expected to accept the views of his partner on this matter or again to give reasons why he cannot do so. The ensuing process is considered a process of mutual modification of the original validity claims so that, if there are no time constraints or other external restrictions on the forces of argumentation, this discourse will reach an "organic" end-state in which the participants will have reached an unenforced consensus. Habermas and Apel are both well aware that this model is an idealization of empirical processes of argumentation, but they consider the idealization not a worthless abstraction, but a regulatory idea (l) that guides us in our empirical world. All objections directed against the alleged naïvetè of this model are therefore misplaced. However, this does not mean that it is the last word about discourse or about ethics. In my writings I have brought up a long list of critical reservations with regard to this model, mostly concerning the motivation to enter into such a discourse or to act in accordance with the results of such argumentation, the relationship between discursive "justification" and practical "application" and the problems that are related to the distinction between different types of validity claims (see above all Joas, 2000, Chap. 10). All this has to be left aside here. The exclusive focus of the following remarks is on the question of whether we can imagine having such a purely rational discourse about values and, if not, whether the only alternative is the nihilism of pure confrontation or decision.

I assume that many of us share the intuition that there is a third way between rational discourse and the conflict of competing values or value systems; just think of inter-religious dialogues, for example between Christians and Jews in postwar Germany or between Christians and Buddhists in contemporary East Asia. Jürgen Habermas (1992, p. 202) himself readily admits that, in the case of values, no clear separation of questions of validity from questions of genesis is possible and that values therefore cannot be submitted to the same argumentative procedure as cognitive and normative validity claims. Yet this does not lead him to specify what the logic of a communication about values would look like; for him the main consequence from this insight is that values are inherently particular and do not allow for universalization in the same sense that cognitive and normative propositions do. What is more, for Habermas to be "particular" means for him to be "particularist"; i.e. for him there can be no such thing as a universalist value orientation, which means that all hope for universalization lies in the spheres of law and morality in a normative sense. This is inappropriate not only with regard to post-axial religious worldviews and ethics,[2] but also with regard to the specific structures of our communication about values.

---

2   Following Karl Jaspers, sociologists and historians of religion speak of an axial age (800–200 before Christ) as the time in which the idea of "transcendence emerged" (for a good summary see Bellah, 2005).

I see at least three differences between a rational-argumentative discourse and our communication about values. The first is that, when we talk about values, a strongly affectual dimension comes in. Although all values can be reformulated in propositional form as statements like "It is good to do X" or "It is evil to do Y", and although all religious and secular encompassing worldviews contain factual statements like "Jesus has risen from the dead" or "Muhammad is the prophet", our commitment to these is different from our commitment to purely cognitive validity claims. We have to take seriously the fact that we cannot simply "have" values as we may have opinions, but that we have to feel strongly committed to them if the word "value commitment" is to make any sense. William James (1902/1982), on whose thinking I rely in this respect (Joas, 2000, Chap. 3), emphasized that there are parallels between our commitment to values and our commitment to persons, for example between religious faith and love – and this not so much in the sense of a religion and an ethics of love, but mostly in the sense that our commitment to particular values is similar to our commitment to particular persons in our life. When we are asked why we love a certain person, let us say why I love my wife, my son, my closest friends, we realize that it may be inappropriate to derive our feelings of love from a list of specific attributes, talents or achievements of the beloved person. Even personal relations do have a cognitive side; they are based on certain assumptions about the character and behaviour of the beloved person in the past, present and the future. In that sense we can certainly make plausible where our commitment to that person comes from, but our expectations with regard to the listener are very different from rational discourse. It is neither our expectation nor our intention that those to whom we speak share our feelings and instantly fall in love with the same person. As compared with a discourse about norms, the goal of plausibility may look more modest than the goal of consensus. On the other hand, the fact that we cannot talk about values without referring to feelings and experiences makes a communication about values also much richer than purely rational discourse.

The second difference to be mentioned here is a difference with regard to the negation of validity claims. It has often been recognized that the falsification of a cognitive proposition in a religious worldview in most cases does not weaken the commitment of believers to this faith. In their perspective the factual statements of their faith can be rather flexible. Their basic feeling of certainty is neither grounded in quasi-empirical statements nor shattered by their falsification. From a strictly empiricist standpoint, this, of course, makes believers look like narrow-minded dogmatists who are not willing to adjust their convictions to scientific progress and enlightened insight. However, since the publication of Ludwig Wittgenstein's reflections *On Certainty* in 1969 at the latest, it has become clear in the Anglo-Saxon philosophical tradition that all cognitive frameworks are based on "certainties" that are constitutive even for the procedures of falsification. These certainties themselves are not fallible in the same sense in which all individual propositions in the constituted framework are. When our basic values are affected, our reaction with regard to doubt or the person articulating this doubt will often not be the modification of our conviction, but a devaluation or derogation of that person. Let me quote from Bernard Williams's magisterial book *Ethics and the Limits of Philosophy* a short passage that seems particularly pertinent:

> One does not feel easy with the man who in the course of a discussion of how to deal with political or business rivals says, "of course, we could have them killed, but we should lay that aside right from the beginning." It is characteristic of morality that it tends to overlook the possibility that some concerns are best embodied in this way, in deliberative silence. (Williams, 1985, p. 185)

Some of you might say that this second difference between a communication about values and the rational-argumentative discourse is an implication of the first insofar as our unwillingness to submit to falsification is a consequence of our affectual commitment to values. However, I think this second difference has more to do with the constitutive role of evaluations for the basic structures of our cognitive frameworks.

The third difference I would call the necessary narrativity of a communication about values. Hilary Putnam (1981) in his book *Reason, Truth, and History* claims in the context of a thought experiment about the question of whether we submit mere preferences to acts of moral judgment that value judgments are not isolated judgments, but form groups or clusters, and that we find only those preferences morally indifferent which are not in a closer connection with other preferences that are for us morally relevant. I fully agree, but I would go a step further and extend this idea of groups of value judgments so that it includes the temporal dimension. We cannot make plausible and defend our value commitments without telling stories – stories about the experiences from which our commitments arose, stories about other people's experiences or about the consequences a violation of our values had in the past. Biographical, historical and mythological narration in this sense are not just a matter of illustration for didactic purposes, but a necessary part of our self-understanding and of our communication about values. The insight that in the case of the communication about values a strict separation of genesis and validity is impossible should not lead to an exaggerated understanding of their separability in the case of cognitive and normative validity claims, but instead inspire us to take seriously the connection between narration and argumentation in all attempts to justify values. What we need is a structure of argumentation that is "genealogical" because of the contingency of the genesis of values, but not "destructive" in the way Nietzsche and Foucault thought it to be.

If my ideas about the specificities of our value commitments are convincing, one might now assume that they will intensify the fear of those who think that power struggle is the only alternative to rational discourse here. If strong emotions, an unwillingness to draw conclusions from empirical falsification and an entanglement with history and mythology are unavoidable in the case of values, does that not entail that values should be excluded from the public sphere so that the public sphere can remain an arena of rational discourse? Does my whole line of argumentation not support a strictly liberal view according to which all citizens with strong convictions have to leave their particular worldviews about which no rational consensus is possible behind them when they enter the public sphere? I obviously cannot discuss all aspects of this fundamental question here, but I would like to mention that this fear is an overgeneralization of important negative experiences and based on a reification of the concept of values. Values and value systems are treated as entities that exclude one another and can even get into conflict with one another. However, from a strictly action-oriented perspective, be it pragmatist or Weberian, it is only human beings, their organizations and institutions that can act, not values or value systems. There can be logical inconsistencies between cognitive propositions and between values, but the human beings who believe in them, feel committed to them or act on their basis have to detect these inconsistencies and cope with them. The strictly liberal position is one possibility for human beings to act together, a possibility that is based on a bracketing of value commitments. Whether liberal or not, we all constantly interact and cooperate with others without paying attention to our value-related differences. Yet there are several other possibilities for dealing with such differences. We can, for example, take elements from other cultural traditions and fit them into our original framework in creative ways. Traditions are not hermetically closed, self-referential frameworks. They have to be actively perpetuated, and this happens under specific circumstances and in risky ways. Since values, value systems and traditions are not entities, but articulations of experience, it can also happen that we share experiences without sharing values. Experiences are articulated in different, maybe opposite ways, and we can feel committed to people without sharing their values and committed to shared values without really feeling committed to certain people with whom we share these values. In the public discussion about German and European values we can often find a conflation of all these dimensions so that it looks as if states have one unitary and homogeneous culture. And in addition to the "bracketing" of value commitments, creative incorporation of other components, and differentiation between experiences and values, we can also enter into a process of value generalization.

As I said in the introduction, this concept stems from the theory of social change as it has been developed by the most influential American sociologist of the 1950s and 1960s, Talcott Parsons. In reaction to the many criticisms of his work that blamed his so-called structural-functionalism for being unable to deal with social change, he applied his theory of the four basic functions each system has to fulfil to the area of social dynamics. The four functions were called adaptation to the environment, goal-attainment, integration and maintenance of the value patterns characteristic for a social pattern. In a dynamic perspective this means that all social change has to have four dimensions as well, namely adaptive upgrading, social differentiation, inclusion of more and more members of society in the status of full citizenship and, lastly, value generalization. The fullest exposition of Parsons's ideas on value generalization can be found in his essay "Comparative Studies and Evolutionary Change", published in a volume on comparative methods in sociology in 1971.[3] Parsons, in whose theory the concept of "value" was absolutely crucial, had for a long time "treated institutionalized value-patterns as a primary, indeed in one special respect the most important single structural component of social systems" (Parsons, 1971, p. 307). For him such value systems have "considerable stability transcending the shorter-run change in the structure of particular societies – meaning time periods up to several centuries" (Parsons, 1971, p. 307). However, it now became more and more clear to him that social differentiation cannot progress without affecting the dimension of institutionalized values in very important ways. This led him to the following basic proposition:

> The more differentiated the system, the higher the level of generality at which the value-pattern must be 'couched' if it is to legitimate the more specified values of all of the differentiated parts of the social system. (Parsons, 1971, p. 307)

It is evident that the concrete example Parsons has in mind here is the differentiation of church and state and the institutionalization of a "moral community" within a society "which both cuts across 'denominational' lines – in the more narrowly religious sense – and those of ethnic culture" (Parsons, 1971, p. 308). "Cutting across" here means – and this can be taken as a definition of value generalization – "the inclusion, under a single legitimizing value-pattern, of components which are not only diverse and differentiated from each other, but many of which have, historically, claimed some sort of an 'absolutistic' monopoly of moral legitimacy" (Parsons, 1971, p. 308).

Parsons is fully aware that value generalization can only be conceived of as a process, and he has interesting things to say about the stages and the character of this process. He follows Karl Mannheim and sees "utopias" – such as the liberal-democratic and the socialist-communist utopias – as helpful for a process of value generalization. Pluralism for him is an early stage in this process, and growing moral autonomy of the individual a later stage. Values have to be specified to be relevant in concrete action-situations; the more differentiated a society is, the more different these specifications will be. To bring them together, a redefinition of what holds them together has to happen. This process of value generalization "is very often fraught with conflict in concrete situations" (Parsons, 1971, p. 311). Some groups will protest against "any alteration of their concrete commitments" and see this as "a surrender of integrity to illegitimate interests" (Parsons, 1971, p. 312). Parsons calls this the "fundamentalist" reaction. Others will be motivated to discredit the fundamentalists and to hinder or reverse differentiation in their plea for radical innovation.

Parsons himself certainly considered his ideas about value generalization a contribution to an empirical theory of social change, but if you listen carefully

---

3   Parsons (1971, pp. 97–139); reprinted in Parsons (1977, pp. 279–320), cf. above all p. 307ff.

to the way he phrased his claim, you realize that there is a certain ambiguity in his thinking at this point. In an autobiographical statement ('On Building Social System Theory') he qualifies his understanding of value generalization "as the mode of change required to complete such a phase for the system, *if it is to have the prospect of future viability*" (Parsons, 1977, pp. 22–76, here 51; emphasis added). Value generalization for him has been "necessitated" by the industrial, the democratic, and the educational revolutions, but what exactly does it mean to call a process "required" or "necessary"? It is one of the crucial weaknesses of a functionalist approach to deducing a process from a functional requirement. Why should it be that what is necessary does indeed happen? One of the points where contemporary neo-Parsonians like Jeffrey Alexander differ from Parsons is exactly here. They realize that Parsons fell prey to a kind of evolutionary optimism that is not really supported by the historical realities of the twentieth century. If we want to make the concept of value generalization fruitful, we certainly have to liberate it from Parsons's functionalist assumptions.

In his interpretation of Parsons in the *Theory of Communicative Action*, Jürgen Habermas (1981) realized this and radicalized it beyond a mere antifunctionalist statement to a critique of an understanding of modernization in which tensions between the different dimensions of social change have been excluded from the outset. Not only does value generalization not simply follow from functional differentiation, it could even be that there are systematic tensions between ongoing differentiation and a specific process of value generalization. However, Habermas's intention at this point is almost the opposite of what I am pursuing here. For Habermas (1981, Vol. 2, p. 268) value generalization leads to an uncoupling of communicative action from all concrete normatively binding behavioural patterns. Social integration for him is achieved more and more through rational discourse and no longer based on any religiously anchored agreement. This is what he called the "linguistification of the sacred" – one of the most radical versions of the secularization thesis we have! What Parsons had in mind when he developed the idea of "value generalization" ran completely counter to such an idea. For him the crux of the matter was that different value traditions can indeed produce a more general, mostly also more abstract, understanding of their common features without losing their roots in the specific traditions and experiences to which actors feel affectually committed. In its current articulation a value may be the result of a particular cultural tradition – human rights, for example, are claimed to be a result of the Judaeo-Christian tradition or of the Enlightenment – but this does not mean that other cultural and religious traditions cannot be reinterpreted, or rather, cannot reinterpret themselves in view of this articulation of a value so that their own potential to articulate this same value comes to light. Such a reinterpretation must not be an intellectualization. Disconnected from the affectual side of a tradition, it would remain ineffective. Value generalization as one possible result of a communication about values would then be neither a consensus about a universalistic principle which everybody has to accept as valid nor a mere decision to live in peaceful coexistence despite value disagreement. Again the result of the communication about values can at once be more and less than the result of rational discourse: not a full consensus, but a dynamic mutual modification and stimulation toward renewal of one's own tradition.

While the concept of value generalization obviously has its pitfalls in the study of social change, it seems to me a highly valuable concept for the study of communication about values. It certainly has its predecessors and companions in the philosophical, theological and juridical literature. I have the impression that Ernst Troeltsch, for example, argued in a similar way against a strong tendency in religious studies in the nineteenth century (Troeltsch, 1895/1896); John Rawls after his *Theory of Justice* revised his position and allowed for a plurality of so-called comprehensive doctrines and what he called an "overlapping consensus" (Rawls, 1996, p. 133ff). This idea is similar in some aspects to Parsons's "value generalization", but Parsons's concept is superior because it does not describe a static constellation of the coexistence of doctrines, but a dynamic process of their mutual modification, and it is not restricted to a communication about constitutional or political principles that leaves the deeper layers of these value systems or traditions unaffected. In legal theory – for example in the work of German theorist Winfried Brugger – we can find a distinction between different levels of generality in the articulation of values that is also intended to describe processes of value generalization that are not disconnected from the experiential level (Brugger, 1999). Perhaps one could say all theoretical attempts that deny both indisputable ethical foundations in the sense of natural law doctrines and the impossibility of any reasonable foundation in a Rortyan sense have to have some equivalent to Parsons's idea of value generalization. However, in my eyes none of these "equivalents" is as inspiring as the concept of value generalization.

At this point one would have to demonstrate the fruitfulness of this concept in specific applications to concrete cases of a communication about values and mutual modification. One can mention the studies on the drafting of the UN Declaration of Human Rights in 1948 published by Mary Ann Glendon (2001) and Johannes Morsink (2000) as cases in point. They do not use this concept, but what they describe is one of the most consequential processes of value generalization in modern history. Proponents of the most diverse value traditions came together, united in their rejection of Nazism and Fascism, and formulated a declaration that does not have one rationalist justification but presents itself as the shared articulation of all the value traditions that had been part of the process. As I mentioned before, interreligious dialogues, but also religious-secular dialogues, if successful, are illuminating examples of value generalization (Joas, 2007, pp. 19–32). In her dissertation, Hella Dietz (2007) studied the process in which anti-Stalinist Marxists and progressive "personalist" Catholics gradually learned to redefine their self-images and the images of the other and began to define human rights as the common denominator of their originally extremely different value systems – and she found out that there is no better term for an analysis of this process than the term "value generalization". Obviously, the debate about European values is such a process of value generalization as well. There is no better way to exemplify how my views on this process could be translated into a concrete statement about European values, the plurality of traditions, the positive and negative experiences connected with them than to quote the proposed preamble for a European constitution written by the Polish journalist Stefan Wilkanowicz (2003):

> We, Europeans:
>
> aware of the richness of our heritage, drawing from the wealth of Judaism, Christianity, Islam, Greek philosophy, Roman law, and humanism with both religious and non-religious roots;
>
> aware of the values of Christian civilization, which is the basic source of our identity;
>
> aware of the frequent betrayals of these values by both Christians and non-Christians;
>
> aware of the good and the evil that we have spread to the inhabitants of other continents;
>
> bemoaning the social catastrophe caused by the totalitarian systems that have originated within our civilization,
>
> would like to build our common future on the basis of profound respect for every man and recognition of his or her inalienable dignity (…).

References

Bellah, R. N. (2005), What is Axial about the Axial Age? *European Journal of Sociology*, 46, 69–90.

Brugger, W. (1999), *Liberalismus, Pluralismus, Kommunitarismus*. Baden-Baden: Nomos.

Dietz, H. (2007), *Von der Opposition der Werte zu den Werten der Opposition – Eine pragmatistische Rekonstruktion der zivilgesellschaftlichen Opposition in Polen*. Dissertation at the Max Weber Center for Advanced Cultural and Social Studies – University of Erfurt.

Glendon, M. A. (2001), *A World Made New. Eleanor Roosevelt and the Universal Declaration of Human Rights*. New York: Random House.

Habermas, J. (1981), *Theorie des kommunikativen Handelns*, 2 Vols. Frankfurt am Main: Suhrkamp.

Habermas, J. (1992), *Faktizität und Geltung*. Frankfurt am Main: Suhrkamp.

James, W. (1902/1982), *The Varieties of Religious Experience*. New York: Penguin Books.

Joas, H. (2000), *The Genesis of Values*. Chicago, IL: University of Chicago Press.

Joas, H. (2007), Werte und Religion, in *Werte. Was die Gesellschaft zusammenhält*, L. Mohn, B. Mohn, W. Weidenfeld and J. Meier (eds). Gütersloh: Bertelsmann, pp. 19–32.

Morsink, J. (2000), *The Universal Declaration of Human Rights. Origins, Drafting, and Intent*. Philadelphia, PA: University of Pennsylvania Press.

Parsons, T. (1971), Comparative Studies and Evolutionary Change, in *Comparative Methods in Sociology*, I. Vallier (ed.). Berkeley, CA: University of Chicago Press, pp. 97–139; reprinted in Parsons, T. (1977), *Social Systems and the Evolution of Action Theory*. New York: Free Press, pp. 279–320.

Parsons, T. (1977), On Building Social System Theory, in *Social Systems and the Evolution of Action Theory*, Parsons, T. (ed.). New York: Free Press, pp. 22–76.

Putnam, H. (1981), *Reason, Truth, and History*. Cambridge: Cambridge University Press.

Rawls, J. (1996), *Political Liberalism*. New York: Columbia University Press.

Toulmin, S. (1958), *The Uses of Argument*. Cambridge: Cambridge University Press.

Troeltsch, E. (1895/96), Die Selbständigkeit der Religion. *Zeitschrift für Theologie und Kirche*, 5, 361–436; 6, 71–110 and 167–218.

Wilkanowicz, S. (2003), *Tygodnik Powszechny*, 29 June 2003; English translation (2003), *World Press Review*, 50, 9.

Williams, B. (1985), *Ethics and the Limits of Philosophy*. London: Fontana Press.

Wittgenstein, L. (1969), *On Certainty*. New York: Harper Torchbooks.

Chapter 4

Corporate Social Responsibility, Economic Optimality and the Interests of the Poor

Niels Kærgård

The Market Economy

This article makes some comments about altruism, ethics and economic optimality from the point of view of hard-core economics. This point of view is of course not the whole story; modifications, more precision and the specification of exceptions are needed, but there is no room for these in a short article. Therefore, the article takes just one clear line: describing the problematic aspects of ethics and corporate social responsibility in relation to economic and social optimality.

The main point to underline is that a market economy – given certain assumptions – generates some sort of optimal allocation of resources and commodities even if no one worries about this optimum. An "invisible hand" guides selfish individuals to act in a socially optimal way. This hand is the price mechanism. If there is scarcity of a commodity in a society, the price will be high; this means high profits from producing the commodity, and selfish capitalists will accelerate its production. The production of the scarce commodity will increase.

From Adam Smith's *Wealth of Nations* to modern mathematical economists, this has been the viewpoint in mainstream economics. A couple of famous quotations from Adam Smith are particularly relevant in this context:

> It is not from the benevolence of the butcher, the brewer, or the baker that we expect our dinner, but from their regard to their own interest. We address ourselves, not to their humanity but to their self-love, and never talk to them of our own necessities but of their advantages. (Smith, 1776; see for example Sæther and Sæther, 1997, p. 13)

and

> He intends only his own gain, and he is in this, as in many other cases, led by an invisible hand to promote an end which was no part of his intention. Nor is it always the worse for the society that it was no part of it. By pursuing his own interest he frequently promotes that of the society more effectually than when he really intends to promote it. I have never known much good done by those who affected to trade for the public good. It is an affectation, indeed, not

very common among merchants, and very few words need to be employed in
dissuading them from it. (Smith, 1776; see Boserup, 1976, pp. 69–70)

Modern economists like Kenneth J. Arrow (Nobel Prize winner 1972) and Frank
H. Hahn support this point of view.

> The immediate 'common sense' answer to the question 'What will an economy
> motivated by individual greed and controlled by a very large number of different
> agents look like?' is probably: There will be chaos – Our answer is somewhat
> different. There is by now a long and fairly imposing line of economists from
> Adam Smith to the present who have sought to show that a decentralized economy
> motivated by self-interest and guided by price signals would be compatible with
> a coherent disposition of economic resources that could be regarded, in a well-
> defined sense, as superior to a large class of possible alternative dispositions.
> (Arrow and Hahn, 1971; see Eriksson, 1997, p. 58)

It is the main point of this argument that the agents do not have to be altruistic; on
the contrary, as another Nobel Prize winner Friedrich A. von Hayek (Prize winner
1974) said:

> The deliberate striving for the common good would distract you from doing
> what you are most suited for – using your particular knowledge of time and
> space – and so decrease the overall effectiveness of the system. Furthermore,
> with the complex division of labour we have today you cannot have an overview
> of what the common good is. (Hayek, 1988; see Eriksson, 1997, p. 116)

The attitude of mainstream economics was summarized clearly by Laurence S.
Moss (researcher in the history of economics and former president of History of
Economics Society):

> The economics that I know and love had its origins in the work of that accused
> seventeenth century atheist Thomas Hobbes, who asked how a community
> of selfish and cheating individuals could ever get organized. Bernard de
> Mandeville, the Dutch cynic of the early eighteenth century, suggested it is
> the private vices of the masses that supply the social glue. Adam Smith argues
> that in a well-governed society, self-interest could promote the public interest,
> and in the twentieth century economists such as Ludwig von Mises defined a
> 'well governed' society as one in which property rights were clearly defined
> and private contracts about the exchange of those rights enforced. The great
> insight of our discipline – most recently sensationalized in Coase theorem – is
> that competition can serve to secure efficiency and meaningful organization.
> (Moss, 1996, p. 493)

In relation to corporate social responsibility, the Nobel Prize winner (1976) Milton Friedman makes the provocative statement that:

> There is one and only one social responsibility of business – to use its resources and engage in activities designed to increase its profits so long as it stays within the rules of the game, which is to say, engages in open and free competition without deception or fraud. (Friedman, 1970)

All these economists knew that the market mechanism takes care of neither justice in the income distribution nor social security for the poor. People get high incomes in a market economy not because they are hard-working, very skilful or have great needs, but because they are scarce. If there is only one, perhaps lazy, baker in the city he will get a higher income than the many hard-working butchers. This is unjust but gives the right incentives. Neither does the market automatically take care of the environment or of an optimal use of common natural resources. All this is known to all mainstream economists, and because of these things many of them do not support an unregulated market. However, regulations are matters for the government and legislative power. Some economists – like Milton Friedman – are generally sceptical towards public regulation, but most are pragmatically searching for an appropriate balance between market and regulation. Very few think it possible to create something like a social optimum by appealing to firms' voluntary altruistic or semi-altruistic actions.

We have seen a lot of unacceptable short-run profit maximizing where unrestrained gamblers have made considerable gains. We have seen directors becoming rich because of share options, and sometimes making profits due to appreciation which was not sustainable in the long run. All this has formed a central topic in the recent discussion about the current financial crisis. However, short-run behaviour is not a result of a conflict between ethics and economics; the relevant conflict here is between good and bad economics. An unsustainable exploitation of suppliers, workers or customers can be very costly for the firm in the long run – it is simply bad economics.

The growing interest in ethics, social responsibility and the environment may very well be caused by markets that are too unregulated: the national authorities are not able to control the big multinational firms, and the international authorities (the WTO, EU and UN) have not yet sufficient power to do so. If citizens observe this, they may realize that their only means of gaining influence is to act as "political consumers". Such reactions are highly significant, especially for multinational firms; the international regulations and the legislation in many of the countries where these firms operate are so weak that actions which are completely legal there will be considered to be amoral and shameful by many of the consumers in other countries, and this may consequently result in consumer boycotts. Political consumers are powerful, and none of the multinational firms can ignore them.

If consumers are willing to pay for specific characteristics of the production process, e.g. organic production or high labour welfare, it is of course up to them, and no one will blame them. However, influence via political consumers' boycotts has, compared with public regulation, a number of drawbacks. The behaviour of political consumers is often based on feelings rather than serious analysis to a higher degree, compared with political and administrative decisions. Pictures on television of the killing of baby seals in Canada caused serious damage to sustainable hunting by the Inuit in Greenland, for example. The influence of political consumers is furthermore unequal; there are equal voting rights in the normal political system, but when people act as political consumers they vote with a number of "votes" determined by the size of their consumption. When the market is to "decide" whether farmers should produce *foie gras* or organic vegetables, the various consumers "vote" with their purchasing power. Democratically decided regulations have many advantages compared with regulation via ethically motivated political consumers.

The Hidden Motives

However, could it not be helpful for governments if firms were socially responsible? Perhaps sometimes, but many traditional economists are suspicious, and how helpful depends greatly on the definition of "social responsibility". What is called "ethics" and "corporate social responsibility" is often used just as an instrument for recruiting a highly-skilled labour force (see e.g. Bhattacharya et al., 2008) or in marketing (see e.g. Maignan and Ferrell, 2001). However, if ethics and social responsibility are to mean anything specific, it must be something other than long-run profit maximization. It must include some further restrictions on the actors. All the talk about ethics, corporate social responsibility, the triple bottom line, ethical accounting, etc. can be a veil behind which the economic realities are hidden. Are the firms really altruistic and socially responsible, or do they have hidden selfish motives? A number of possible explanations are available for consideration when the management of a firm declares itself socially and environmentally responsible.

Ethics and corporate social responsibility may, as already mentioned, be part of a firm's PR and advertising strategies. This does not mean that the firm is being altruistic, but rather that they reckon that a good reputation leads to higher profits and attracts well-qualified employees. This is of course completely acceptable. If the consumers want organic food and are willing to pay for it, it is of course optimal both for the firm and for society if firms produce organic food and use money to tell the consumers that they are doing so, but there is clearly a possibility that some of the ethical declarations made may be the result of double standards.

It can sometimes seem as if a manager of a firm is buying himself a reputation for being a humanitarian and benevolent person with the money of the stockholders or the customers. An altruistic image may be an indication of a manager who follows his own interests and not those of the stockholders, and consequently an indication of a weak representation of the stockholders on the board of the firm. It is worth quoting Milton Friedman once again:

> What does it mean to say that the corporate executive has a 'social responsibility' in his capacity as businessman? If the statement is not pure rhetoric, it must mean that he is to act in some way that is not in the interest of his employers. For example, that he is to refrain from increasing the price of the product in the best interests of the corporation. Or that he is to make expenditures on reducing pollution beyond the amount that is in the best interest of the corporation or that is required by law in order to contribute to the social objective of improving the environment. Or that, at the expense of corporate profit, he is to hire 'hardcore' unemployed instead of better qualified available workmen to contribute to the social object of reducing poverty. In each of these cases, the corporate executive would be spending someone else's money for a general social interest. Insofar as his actions in accord with his 'social responsibility' reduce returns to stockholders, he is spending their money. Insofar as his actions raise the price to customers, he is spending the customer's money. Insofar as his actions lower the wages of some employees, he is spending their money. (Friedman, 1970)

Yet "environmental and social responsibility" may also act as hidden obstacles to trade for poor countries, and protection of the production in rich countries. We will not buy products if the producers use workers who are too young, if they do not pay reasonable wages, and if they do not take sufficient care of the environment, but the consequences can be that the poor country with low productivity does not have a chance to compete at all.

The low-productivity countries have to pay lower wages, skip some of the environmental considerations or take less care of safety issues in production; if they do not act in this way, the competitiveness of their industry will not be sufficient. If we restrict our imports to commodities which are produced by organized workers with reasonable wages in factories which take care of the internal and external environment, this is often not good news for the poor countries. It is only protection of the production of the rich countries. To forbid "social dumping" may in the real world often be in the interest of the firms and the workers in the rich countries, and against the interests of the producers and the workers in the poor countries. As formulated by the Nobel prize winner 2008, Paul Krugman:

> Unlike the starving subsistence farmer, the women and children in the sneaker factory are working at slave wages for our benefit – and this makes us feel unclean. And so there are self-righteous demands for international labor standards – This sounds only fair – but is it? Let's think through the Consequences. – The advantages of established First World industries are still formidable. The only reason developing countries have been able to compete with those industries is their ability to offer employers cheap labor. Deny them that ability, and you might well deny them the prospect of continuing industrial growth, even reverse

the growth that has been achieved. – A policy of good jobs in principle, but no job in practice, might assuage our consciences, but it is no favour to its alleged beneficiaries. (Krugman, 1999, pp. 84–85).

Unintended Consequences

The low-productivity countries can only compete on international markets if they accept low wages, less safety, and lower quality of the internal and external environment. If we in the rich countries do not accept commodities produced with less safety and lower quality of the internal or external environment, we force the poor countries to take the whole effects of their low productivity as low wages and low material consumption. It is far from sure that this is in accordance with the preferences of poor countries. When we were poor (low productivity), we accepted a number of problematic effects for the working environment, industrial accidents and damage to biodiversity because we wanted a higher level of material consumption and economic growth (see Table 4.1).

The first two columns of the table show the year and the per capita income in Denmark in that year. The per capita income is given in 2005 dollars. The per capita income for 1825–1975 is taken from the series of incomes in 1929 prices in Hansen (1977) and supplemented with modern national accounts figures from Statistics Denmark. These figures in 1929-kroner have been transformed into 2005 dollars by multiplying each of them by the ratio for the year 2005 between the figure for Denmark in dollars given in World Bank (2007) and the figure in kroner from the Danish sources. The third column indicates the point of time for some of the major reforms in Denmark related to labour and environmental protection. In the last column the per capita income in 2005 for different countries is shown; the figures are placed at around the point of time when Denmark had the same level of income per capita.

When the population in Denmark before 1870 had an income less than 3000 dollars per capita per year, it was felt necessary for the survival of families for children to contribute to the income of those families – Cambodia, Pakistan, Bangladesh, Nepal and some African states today have levels of income that are lower than that. We in Denmark began public control of factory machinery and industrial safety in the inter-war period when we had a per capita income similar to those of Panama and China today. When we in Denmark in the 1970s began to make public institutions for environmental protection and appointed a cabinet minister for this area, we had a per capita income higher than that of Eastern Europe today. Perhaps the poor countries have the same preferences as we had when we were poor.

Table 4.1 Income per capita in Denmark 1825–2005 and in different countries in 2005, and environmental and labour protection in Denmark

Year	Income per capita in Denmark, 2005 ($)	Labour and environmental protection in Denmark	Corresponding 2005 income in different countries; 2005 ($), PPP values
2005	33,973		
1995	29,409		Germany 29,461
1985	25,407		New Zealand 23,381
1975	20,310	1973: Government department of environmental protection	Portugal 20,410
1965	15,392		Poland 13,847
1955	10,404		Mexico 10,751
1945	7,183		Thailand 8,677
1935	7,772	1933: General public control of factory machinery	Panama 7,605
1925	6,210	1916: Compulsory labour accident insurance	China 6,757
1915	5,403	1915: Voting rights for women	The Philippines 5,137
1905	4,783	1901: Ban on employment of children under the age of 12.	Morocco 4,555
1895	3,958		Indonesia 3,843
1885	3,247	1873: Ban on employment of children under the age of 10; maximum of 6 daily working hours for children of age 10–14.	India 3,452
1875	3,020		Vietnam 3,071
1865	2,684	1866: Supervision of phosphor in the match industry	Cambodia 2,727
1855	2,636		Pakistan 2,370
1845	2,217		Bangladesh 2,053
1835	1,973		Nepal 1,550
1825	1,881		Tanzania 744
			Kenya 1,240

Source: Hansen (1977), Statistics Denmark and World Bank (2007).

This does of course not mean that we have to accept the exploitation of poor countries with weak institutions by big international firms. However, it is far from always being true that "altruistic" acting multinational firms, following the preferences of the customers in the rich countries, are an optimal solution to a situation with imperfect markets and exploitation. We know that an ideal situation with perfect markets is unrealistic, but it is very difficult to say how we can reach some sort of a second best solution. The right thing to do can often be to support the local authorities, and if the domestic authorities and the local citizens in the poor countries prefer higher consumption and economic growth instead of a good working environment and biodiversity, we have no right to dispute their choice.

We can prefer that they give priority to, for example, a high degree of biodiversity and low pollution, but if this is not their preference we have to support them in doing so by paying the cost ourselves. The choice is theirs. The rich countries have to be careful not to use a double standard according to which they demand, for example, a cap on pollution at current levels, when the richest countries pollute considerably more than the developing countries will come to do in any foreseeable future.

Ethical and social responsibility can also be problematic in domestic policy both in the developed and the developing countries. Many firms argue that, because of their ethical attitude and social responsibility, they have good working conditions and high wages. This means that they can demand high productivity and can attract the most highly skilled workforce. However, the main problem in almost all societies is getting the least skilled elements of the workforce into employment. Very few societies have problems with employment for highly skilled workers. This means that it is probably more important for countries to have firms with poor working conditions and low wages if as a consequence they are able to employ low-skilled people. Firms with good working conditions, high wages and low-skilled workers are an unrealistic dream.

This does not mean that we never see firms taking care of suppressed minorities, but if a minority is discriminated against it also means that it may be possible to hire very skilful people from such a group (immigrants, ethnic minorities, women, etc.) at a lower wage than people from the majority. To hire a talented immigrant who is without a job or has a wage below average because he is discriminated against is not only social responsibility and altruism, but also rational economics.

Kicking Away the Ladder

It is relevant to supplement the arguments in the previous section with a short summary of some of the arguments from development economists such as Ha-Joon Chang of the University of Cambridge. He compares what we demand of the developing countries in relation to "good policies" and "good institutions" with what the rich countries actually do when they become rich. The title of Ha-Joon Chang's book is inspired by a quotation from the German economist Friedrich List (1789–1846):

> It is very common clever device that when anyone has attained the summit of greatness, he kicks away the ladder by which he has climbed up, in order to deprive others of the means of climbing up after him. (Chang, 2003, p. 4)

Chang studies the history of the now-developed countries and especially the start of what we now call "good institutions". His results are summarized in

Table 4.2. Chang's conclusion is that the "good institutions" came historically remarkably late:

> I conclude that contemporary developing countries actually have much higher levels of institutional development than the now-developed countries did at comparable stages of development. (Chang, 2003, p. 111)

Or

> From these examples we can conclude that, in the early days of their economic development, the now-developed countries were operating with much less developed institutional structures than those which exist in today's developing countries at comparable level of development. Needless to say the level of institutional development in the now-developed countries fell well short of the even higher 'global standards' to which today's developing countries are being told to conform. (Chang, 2003, p. 121)

Table 4.2 Time of introducing institutions in the now-developed countries

Country	Universal male suffrage	Universal suffrage	Industrial accident institutions	First regulation of child labour
Austria	1907	1918	1887	1787
Belgium	1919	1948	1903	1878
Denmark	1849	1915	1898	1873
France	1848	1946	1898	1841
Germany	1849	1946	1871	1839
Italy	1919	1946	1998	1902
Norway	1898	1913	1894	1892
Portugal	n.a.	1970	1962	1913
Spain	n.a.	1931/1977	1900	1873
Sweden	1918	1919	1901	1846
Switzerland	1879	1971	1881	1877
UK	1918	1928	1897	1802
USA	1870/1965	1965	1930	1842

Source: Chang (2003, pp. 73, 104 and 108).

Chang is far from convinced that this high level of demand is optimal for the developing countries:

> What seems clear from our analysis here is that institutions have typically taken decades, if not generations, to develop. In this context, the currently popular demand that developing countries should adopt 'world standard' institutions right away, or at least within the next 5 or 10 years, or face punishments for not doing so, seems to be at odds with the historical experiences of the now-developed countries that are making these very demands. (Chang, 2003, p. 117)

Ha-Joon Chang is afraid that we are kicking away the ladder for the developing countries.

> I would agree that, if done in a realistic way and if combined with the right policies, international pressures for institutional improvements can play a positive role in the developmental process. However, the current push for institutional improvements in developing countries is not done in this way and is likely to end up as another 'ladder-kicking' exercise. By demanding from developing countries institutional standards that they themselves had never attained at comparable levels of development, the now-developed countries are effectively adopting double standards, and hurting the developing countries by imposing on them many institutions that they neither need nor can afford. (Chang, 2003, pp. 134–135)

Ha-Joon Chang is very sceptical with regard to pressure on developing countries from the now-developed countries and international institutions. These countries are not ready for the institutions we want them to introduce, and it is not in their interests to introduce them. Corporate social responsibility is in many cases part of this pressure, and the firms and organizations supporting corporate social responsibility should be very careful not to be part of a "ladder-kicking exercise".

Conclusion

Something must be done for the environment, for the poor people in our own countries and for the less developed countries, but it is important that our possible goodwill and willingness to pay for these things have the right consequences. Ethics, social responsibility and environmental responsibility are rather imprecise terms which can be used as arguments for a lot of behaviour which is not optimal for society, for weaker citizens, for poor countries or for the environment. Rational analysis of the consequences and a sceptical investigation of the different groups' real, perhaps hidden, interests often provide much better protection of the interests of the weaker members of society and of the world community than goodwill and vague references to ethics and responsibility. Or as Paul Krugman formulated the message:

> And when the hopes of hundreds of millions are at stake, thinking things through is not just good intellectual practice. It is a moral duty. (Krugman, 1999, p. 85)

References

Arrow, K. J. and Hahn, F. H. (1971), *General Competitive Analyses*. Holden Day, San Francisco, CA.

Bhattacharya, C. B., Sen, A. and Korschun, D. (2008), Using Corporate Social Responsibility to Win the War for Talent. *MIT Sloan Management Review*, 49(2), 37–44.

Boserup, M. (1976), *Deres egne Ord (Their Own Words)*. Akademisk Forlag, Copenhagen.

Chang, H. -J. (2003), *Kicking away the Ladder: Development Strategy in Historical Perspective*. Anthem Press: London.

Eriksson, R. (1997), *Essays on the Methodology and Ethics of Economics*. Åbo Akademi University Press: Åbo.

Friedman, M. (1970), The Social Responsibility of Business is to Increase its Profit. *The New York Times Magazine*, 13 September.

Hansen, S. A. (1977), *Økonomisk vækst i Danmark (Economic Growth in Denmark)*, Vols I–II, 2nd edn. G. E. C. Gads Forlag, Copenhagen.

Hayek, F. A. von (1988), The Fatal Conceit, in *The Collected Works of F.A. Hayek* W.W. Bartley (ed.). London: Routledge.

Krugman, P. (1999), *The Accidental Theorist and other Dispatches from the Dismal Science*. London: Penguin Books,

Maignan, I. and Ferrell, O. (2001), Corporate Citizenship as Marketing Instrument. *European Journal of Marketing*, 35(3–4), 457–484.

Moss, L. S. (1996), Review of H.G. Brennan and A.M.C. Waterman (red.): Economics and Religion: Are they Distinct?, *European Journal of History of Economic Thought*, 3, 490–494.

Sæther, A. and Sæther, B. (1997), Self-interest as an Acceptable Mode of Human Behaviour. Paper presented at European Conference on the History of Economics, Athens.

Smith, A. (1776), *An Inquiry into the Nature and Causes of the Wealth of Nations*. Edinburgh. (Considerable number of editions, e.g. Random House, 1937, and University of Chicago Press, 1976.)

World Bank (2007), *World Development Indicators*. World Bank: Washington, DC.

Chapter 5

Stakeholders, Corporate Social Responsibility and Global Markets

Maria Bonnafous-Boucher

Introduction

Business ethics, the major source of stakeholder theory, stipulates a kind of implicit contract between the firm and society in which the former has obligations towards the latter. In 1975, there were approximately 7000 multinational companies in the world. In 1994, there were some 37,000 (Schwartz and Gibb, 1999). In 2003, the number of parent companies was estimated at 65,000, and those companies were thought to have 850,000 associated foreign subsidiaries (Bauchet, 2003). From the mid-1980s, the implicit contract between business and society has become increasingly more explicit: a certain number of actors openly admonish multinationals about their responsibilities and the impact of their activities both on the market and on society as a whole. Following hard on the heels of the financial crisis of 2007–2008, the economic crisis of 2008 and 2009 has fuelled desires to see that contract become even more explicit.[1]

In view of the above observations, this chapter adopts a heuristic approach by seeking to move beyond both a description of the expectations expressed by stakeholders in terms of the actions of multinationals, and a prescriptive and normative formulation of recommendations to multinationals stipulating what they should do in order to meet stakeholder expectations. In so doing, the legitimacy of those who would judge business morality, and the interests that underlie such judgments, is called into question.

The term "multinational" will be used in reference to the definitions elaborated by the International Labour Organization in 1997 and the UN in 2003. In the light of these definitions of "multinational" and "transnational" companies, stakeholder theory will be considered as an analytical tool which provides a broad perspective on business (stakeholders) and, more particularly, on the multinational, as opposed to a narrow perspective on the firm focusing on its shareholders. The term "globalization" will be used in reference to a trend in which barriers established

---

1   In France in 2008, for example, corporate social responsibility investment funds expanded although they account for only 1–1.4 per cent of French funds as a whole. The creation of around 50 new funds of this type suggests that the crisis has not put a stop to this trend. Sources: Novethic & Morningstar, *Le Monde*, 9 February 2009.

by individual countries to protect their capital, goods and services, as well as to control patterns of migration, were replaced by a distinctly less protected market in which capital, goods and services and people circulated more freely.

The aim of this chapter is to address power and principles in the market place. More specifically, the chapter looks at how power is displaced and how principles are deconstructed with regard to globalization and multinationals.

Stakeholder Theory and Multinationals: Three Critiques

The sudden emergence of corporate social responsibility and stakeholder theory in the 1980s – as well as their growing influence since then – occurred in a very specific context characterized by the displacement of sovereignties and, consequently, of powers. These displacements deconstructed the foundations and principles of political philosophy, from the conception of the public good to perceptions of sovereignty and how it is exercised. It would be hard to imagine corporate social responsibility without taking these important evolutions into account. Such changes are linked to the emergence of demands from stakeholders.

A number of definitions should be provided with a view to situating the point of departure. Stakeholder theory is at the heart of corporate social responsibility. It might even be said that stakeholder theory and corporate social responsibility are indissociably linked. Corporate social responsibility derives from expectations that are external to decision-makers (directors and shareholders); it is a response to demands from consumers, investors, salaried employees and, more generally, citizens, who would like to see business more effectively integrated into public life. The number and intensity of such demands has increased because business policies, particularly those of multinationals operating simultaneously in various regions throughout the world, have considerable social, cultural and environmental consequences. Multinational companies are an expression of contemporary economic globalization and of the predominant role of financial capitalism. In its *Tripartite Declaration of Principles Concerning Multinational Enterprises and Social Policy*, the International Labour Organization states that: "Multinational enterprises include enterprises, whether they are of public, mixed or private ownership, which own or control production, distribution, services or other facilities outside the country in which they are based […]. The term 'multinational enterprise' designates the various entities (parent companies or local entities or both or the company as a whole) according to the distribution of responsibilities among them." In 2003, the UN published *Norms on the Responsibilities of Transnational Corporations and Other Business Enterprises with Regard to Human Rights*. The UN's definition focuses on the term "transnational" rather than "multinational". According to the document, "a 'transnational corporation' refers to an economic entity operating in more than one country or a cluster of economic entities operating in two or more countries – whatever their legal form, whether in their home country or country of activity, and whether taken individually or collectively".

Such companies have replaced national firms which, thanks to their efficiency, have succeeded in significantly augmenting investment abroad.[2] However, multinationals have been criticized on a number of grounds, namely: (1) for causing negative effects; (2) for orchestrating globalization; and (3) for manipulating reformist theses. Multinationals are, therefore, the object of a great deal of criticism. However, it would be useful to distinguish between criticism concerning the direct activities of multinationals and their negative impact, the globalized economic system as it is perceived in terms of its inherent injustice and threat, and the debate about the ways in which a more equitable world can be created (Renouard, 2007, p. 11). However, it should be borne in mind that multinationals have been the object of criticism for many decades. Criticism was first levelled in the late nineteenth century at a time when trade within colonial empires was developing apace. The phenomenon intensified after the Second World War as decolonization took hold and attempts were made to define approaches to fostering increased growth in the countries of the South using, amongst other approaches, import-substitution strategies. During this period, although multinational companies were suspected of violating national integrity, they were welcomed in that they represented factors of industrial growth for host countries. In the 1970s, criticism, particularly of US firms operating in Africa and those suspected of helping to bring down democratically elected regimes, became harsher. Reaction to the fall of President Allende in Chile and the setting up of a UN centre for monitoring the activities of transnational corporations and providing legal aid to host countries are just two examples of the mood of the time. However, let us return to the three types of criticism encompassing the negative effects occasioned by the activities of multinational companies mentioned above.

The *first critique* concerns the negative effects of the *direct activities of transnational corporations abroad*. In 2003, a major European oil company generating between 80 and 90 per cent of its profits from non-European countries, redistributed a mere 10 per cent of its profits despite the fact that 55 per cent of its staff came from those countries. Many commentators were quick to conclude that certain multinationals used the profits generated in operations in the countries of the South to pay wage bills in Europe. Consequently, in the decade from 1990 to 2000, critics of the negative effects of the activities of multinationals shifted their emphasis from the problem of the exploitation of natural resources to the issue of human resources and the exploitation of the labour force in host countries. This change in emphasis mirrored the change in foreign direct investment strategies since the 1960s. Originally based on using and transforming natural resources abroad, these strategies had shifted to a focus on the commercial aspects of local markets. In spite of such new strategies, which appeared to be favourable to consumers in host countries, the earnings of local employees were still considered a mere adjustment variable dwarfed by the overriding needs of capital. The assets of the

---

2   Renouard (2007). I have used the arguments developed by the author in research that she carried out between 2005 and 2007, research which gave rise to the book referred to.

100 top multinationals increased by 697 per cent between 1980 and 1995 while, during the same period, direct employment provided by those companies declined by 6.7 per cent.[3] In fact, in the 1990s, annual profit estimates from shareholder equity rose by 15 per cent, a far higher rate than the average rate of share return over the course of the century (around 10 per cent).

It is thought that outsourcing and a greater recourse to service companies in the period from 1980 to 1990 had the effect of bringing down salaries, although the average salary paid by Western multinationals in host countries was higher than that paid by local companies (Bhagwati, 2004, p. 173). However, while multinationals often paid better than other companies, they also employed increasingly fewer people.

The *second critique* levelled at multinationals casts them as *the lynchpins of globalization*. Multinationals are currently generating a great deal more profit from the global market than they did from the first phase of globalization which occurred at the start of the twentieth century. Suzanne Berger (2002) observes that the years preceding the First World War differed from the timeframe spanning 1980–2000 in that, in the earlier period, state governments controlled the movement of capital and goods even if foreign direct investment and migration were both increasing. Consequently, the second critique concerns the global scope of the activities of multinationals, which undermines the creation of an equitable world. It remains, however, that the link between globalization and increased inequality is by no means clear; several studies demonstrate that "open" countries have a faster growth rate than "closed", protectionist ones. In effect, "from 1975–1995, the group of open economies grew at an average annual rate of 4.5%, while the GDP of closed economies grew at a rate of only 0.7% per year" (Cohen, 2004). It should also be observed that, in terms of management, open economies are better integrated into the global network of ideas, markets, technologies and innovations (Sachs, 1999). Nevertheless, wealth is still unequally distributed (Renouard, 2007; Peyrelevade, 2005): the United States possesses half the world's market capitalization, Europe 25 per cent, and Japan, whose 300 million people account for 5 per cent of the world's population, 15 per cent. Thus, the second critique levelled at multinationals as lynchpins of globalization, implies that economic growth favours the rich and that wealth redistribution is an issue that has not yet been properly addressed.

Multinationals are also open to a third form of criticism, expressed by Cécile Renouard in the following terms: "they have appropriated the notion of sustainable development and emptied it of its transformative potential" (Renouard, 2007, p. 28). In effect, multinationals sensitive to the times and to the unresolved problems that characterize them, attempt to weather the storm by taking criticism on board and offering to modify their practices.

In a relatively old article entitled "Corporate Social Responsibility Revisited, Redefined", Jones (1980) defined corporate social responsibility as "the notion

---

3   Sources: *Transnational Corporations in World Development: Trends and Prospects*, UN 298, World Investments Reports, UN, 1997.

that the corporations have an obligation to constituent groups in society other than stockholders and beyond that prescribed by law or union contract, indicating that a stake may go beyond mere ownership". Who are these groups? How many of these groups must be catered for? Which of their interests are the most important? How can their interests be balanced? According to Mitchell et al. (1997), "these questions are still being explored in stakeholder literature". After posing a succinct and surprisingly complex question – who are these stakeholders? – the authors isolate around 20 different definitions within the literature itself. In general, researchers working on stakeholder theory follow Freeman, who provides two definitions, the first "broad", the second "narrow". The "broad" definition casts the stakeholder as a person or entity which "can affect or who is affected by the achievement of an organization's objectives". In the "narrow" definition, the stakeholder is a person or entity "on which the organization is dependent for its continued survival". It is generally considered that Freeman's narrow definition is more easily applied in practical situations. In 1997, Ronald P. Mitchell used it as the basis for a classification of stakeholders encompassing three criteria: power, legitimacy and urgency. These criteria are piloting tools for business leaders.

While both interesting and rewarding, it is, nevertheless, a curious reversal of perspective to see that stakeholder theory is most useful to business leaders disoriented by the emergence of new actors, and original, sometimes urgent demands. It is for this reason that the philosophical foundations of stakeholder theory should be re-examined. Corporate social responsibility and stakeholder theory (since such a theory does exist) is, above all, heuristic. In Greek, "heuriskein" means "to find". In other words, it is a theory used to discover things, a theory that constitutes a direction-giving idea. Otherwise expressed, stakeholder theory, like corporate social responsibility, is not just (or even) a warning, sent out by alarmist parties or victims, to the business world, but a genuine paradigm change in the history of ideas, in attitudes and in the concrete world of systems of production and nation-states.

The Heuristic Function of Stakeholder Theory and Corporate Social Responsibility

An examination of the theory reveals a number of heuristic aspects. Firstly, stakeholder theory asks questions about the displacement of sovereignties, for example the transition from national public institutions to international organizations and global private firms. Secondly, taking into account this displacement of sovereignties, stakeholder theory demands that global firms contribute to both the common good and the public good. This poses a major problem in terms of arbitrage and legitimacy, particularly if, as some authors maintain, corporate social responsibility can be used as a foundation for a new social contract. Thirdly, however, the elaboration of the common good as based on stakeholders theory founders on the rock on which the theory is built: the origin of inequality and the possibility of redistributing wealth (distributive justice) between proprietors and non-proprietors.

Stakeholder Theory and the Displacement of Sovereignties

Stakeholder theory asks questions about the displacement of sovereignties, or, in other words, about the transition from national public institutions to international organizations and private global firms. First and foremost, stakeholder theory overturns the financial view of the firm. The firm is often represented as a technical–economic unit or a local social organization, but stakeholder theory casts it as "a public arena entity" (Martinet, 1984; Martinet and Reynaud, 2004). It therefore asks the firm to play a new role as a prescriptor of the common good and of the public good, a task formerly carried out by the government and its agencies in the public sphere. Why is this? Is it a question of principle? Is it merely a normative guideline? Or does the emergence of stakeholders represent a total reconfiguration of sovereignties and the creation of an entirely new strategic and political horizon? If so, what is this strategic and political horizon?

By constructing a new centre of gravity, private international organizations create an economic sovereignty that, in effect, sets itself up as a rival to public sovereignty. Consequently, the equilibrium inherited from the liberal philosophies of the eighteenth and nineteenth centuries is disintegrating. This equilibrium was founded on an alliance between a public space, the state and public organizations (which usually depend on nation-states), and a private space (national civil societies). Such an observation could be seen as highly questionable, or even as a stereotype, but it is no more and no less than a convincing observation made by the most critical sociologists. Thinking of Ulrich Beck (2002, 2003, 2005), we can say that the gradual displacement of sovereignty's centre of gravity raises the question of its legitimacy. Can multinational companies present themselves as third parties? Can they act as arbiters on behalf of stakeholders? Do stakeholders replace national civil society by constituting themselves as a global civil society because they engage in an unmediated dialogue with multinational companies? Before the advent of this phenomenon, the dual relationship between liberal democracies and capitalist systems of production was based on an external regulating authority, that of the state of law which guaranteed the autonomy of civil society.

These questions demonstrate that stakeholder theory is positioned within the context of a latent conflict of interest between spheres of sovereignty not shared by a number of institutions and organizations. More concretely, sovereignty used to be based on the exclusive right to exercise political authority (legislative, judicial and executive) in a particular geographical territory or over a group of peoples. Yet while, for example, the sovereignty of the United Nations survives, it has nevertheless diminished in the post-Second World War period, notably due to economic globalization.

The erosion of sovereignty is exemplified by several phenomena. The first is the development of international organizations, principally those whose aim is to coordinate activities involving different states. The European Union[4] is a prime example, but others should also be mentioned: the United Nations, the World Trade Organization, the International Criminal Court, the International Fund for Agricultural Development, the International Monetary Fund and the International Labour Organization. Yet other international bodies whose objective is to defend the interests of entire regions can be added to the list: the Association of South-East Asian Nations, the European Bank for Reconstruction and Development, the International Bank for Reconstruction and Development and the Inter-American Development Bank.

The second phenomenon is non-governmental organizations,[5] whose field of action is at once local and global and who deal primarily with global actors such as multinationals and intergovernmental organizations. Another is the economic clout of multinational companies, whose turnovers are sometimes bigger than the GDPs of developed countries. For example, in 2005 Exxon Mobil's turnover was US$358.9 billion, more than the GDP of Sweden (ranked twentieth in the world), which amounted to US$354.1 billion. BP's turnover of 249.4 billion dollars was just behind Denmark's GDP of 254.4 billion dollars (ranked twenty-sixth). As well as this financial clout and the power to act that it provides, multinationals also exert considerable influence on the economic and trade policies of nation-states. Furthermore, they often lead the way in terms of defining geographical spheres of competition. Finally, they often employ more people than the government administrations running nation-states. All these factors mean that global firms are, to all intents and purposes, sovereign actors on the international scene.

To sum up, international companies are powerful actors which stand almost alone since other organizations are either in decline (the nation-state) or in the processes of being constructed (regional organizations like the EU, inter-governmental organizations like the WHO and organizations whose ultimate aim is to provide a global regulation mechanism).

In *Power in the Global Age*, Ulrich Beck posits that the abolition of economic, political and societal borders marks the beginning of a new struggle between power and counter-power. Institutions no longer provide the space or framework in which organizations can carry out their policies. Thus, the organizational sphere has overtaken its institutional counterpart, a phenomenon particularly noticeable

---

4   The EU retains a certain degree of sovereignty due to its legislative impact in key fields, including energy, the environment, chemicals and agriculture. Between 60 and 70 per cent of new legislation in these areas is produced by the EU. It should also be noted that a single currency – the euro – is used in a high proportion of the economic exchanges carried out within the Union.

5   The phrase "intergovernmental organization" often evokes the idea of international associations working for increased recognition in such fields as sustainable development, human rights and consumer rights (some "altermondialists" actively lobby for alimentary sovereignty: the right to eat). Other bodies, including the International Chamber of Commerce, fall into the same category.

in organizations "which exist outside the institutional framework and dispense with the national *a priori* of political action" (Beck, 2002).

This transformation, initiated by, amongst others, the counter-powers of civil society, appears to be irreversible, since the distinction between the terms "national" and "international" has become meaningless: we now act within the context of a global interior policy; the abolition of economic, political and societal borders marks the beginning of a new struggle between power and counter-power. There is no doubt that stakeholder theory questions the traditional borders between the public space and the private space. It deconstructs the categories of political philosophy, ethics, the economics of organizations and corporate strategy, and provides a fresh approach.

The Traditional Borders between Public and Private Spheres and the Common Good

Until recently, the common good was the fruit of the democratic development of what is good for people living in a polis in which the public good and the personal good do not conflict with each other. The idea of the common good is different from the following two conceptions of society: firstly, the idea that society is an agglomeration of individuals who are forced to cooperate with each other, or who can only cooperate under the pressure of an individual-to-individual contract; and, secondly, the idea according to which individual interests are subordinated to the economic objectives of society as a whole. Stakeholder theory underlines the fact that the state justifies its existence by means of the defence and promotion of the public good, or in other words, the common good of civil society, citizens and intermediary institutions. Corporate social responsibility and stakeholder theory demand that the business world – through the mechanisms of corporate governance – contribute to defining the common good by putting their private and particular interests to one side. Stakeholder theorists who foreground the common good postulate a kind of harmony between business and society. After all, business and society are both members of the same civil society. Consequently, their individual interests will tend to converge towards common ends. In fact, for stakeholder theorists focusing on the common good, firms, which are organizations within society, contribute to the common good by providing capital and work. For a business, the common good consists of creating the necessary conditions for people involved in it to achieve their personal goals.

Nevertheless, the common good formulated by the firm is not the sum of individual goals since such goals imply more than what a firm can make possible and the firm only indirectly facilitates the processes of realization of personal goals. After all, the objectives of the firm are paramount. The common good provided by the firm also includes its long-term capacity to develop, amongst the personnel, a desire to work there, as well as the mutual goodwill of the parties involved, and the confidence of financial institutions. A list of particular kinds of common good could be drawn up based on the industries in which firms operate, but that is not the issue. What is important is that a solid foundation is provided for stakeholder theory by means of a common good that can be shared by both firms and stakeholders.

The Common Good and the Social Contract

If the common good is that which is good for everybody and which does not conflict with individual interests, and if this good is none other than the public good considered as the possibility of living together, then it is conditioned by a social contract that derives from contractualist political philosophy. The social contract is supported by a sociality which pre-exists it, a sociality which is itself a tacit contract rather than an explicit one. In fact, stakeholder theory uses the idea of the common good to reinvigorate the social contract.

The social contract has a variety of applications in management and business ethics. Many of these applications were developed in the 1980s. In 1982, Donaldson elaborated the terms of an agreement between business and society and followed this hypothesis in 1990 in an article addressing social contract and later with a book, *Ties That Bind: a Social Contracts Approach to Business Ethics* (Donaldson and Dunfee, 1999). In the same vein, Bowie published a special issue in the *Journal of Business Ethics* entitled "Business Ethics" (Bowie, 2004), in which he outlined a Kantian hypothesis based on the possibility of creating a social contract. In *Morale et contrat* (Morals and Contract), Gauthier (2000) developed the idea of "contract by agreement" and used the concept of economic rationality to advance the idea of a hypothetical accord accommodating individual economic interests and providing a collective moral foundation. In 1988, Keeley developed a social contract governing organizations. Although deviating from the letter of the social contract, he saw the firm as "a series of contract-like agreements about social rules". However, the authors most convinced by the possibility of applying a social contract to both the political and economic spheres are Dunfee and Donaldson (Donaldson, 1982; Dunfee, 1991; Donaldson and Dunfee, 1995, 2008). Donaldson and Dunfee (1999) interpret the social contract as an implicit agreement between society and an artificial entity, as a sort of gentleman's agreement, a handshake that brings to mind Adam Smith's invisible hand. They accept the idea that it is not a real contract, no more than were the social contracts of Hobbes, Locke and Rousseau. For Donaldson and Dunfee, it is a matter of accepting the fiction of an implicit agreement between parties, a fiction which serves as the cornerstone of liberal societies. "Social contract has been a powerful image for the support of democratic forms of governance. In effect, a mythical agreement is used to give legitimacy to a very real set of laws and institutions" (Axelrod, 1986). The fiction is, in effect, contained within the contract. According to Donaldson and Preston: "If the contract were something other than a *fiction* it would be inadequate for the purpose at hand, namely revealing the moral foundations of productive organizations."

Stakeholder theory "models" the theory of social contract and transposes the pre-conditions of an agreement. Just as contractualists posit ideal conditions of government in view of the transition from a monarchical system to the rational foundation of a system of representative government, in the business world, some conditions are more equitable than others in terms of setting up productive organizations and getting involved in trade. Thus, implicitly, "we should let business people get on with their business and let them either use or own natural resources in exchange for which they will assume ethical obligations vis-à-vis each individual member of society". The minimum demanded in return by society is that profits do not incur disadvantages to society's members. It should be noted that this contract is entered into (by free consent) by rational, autonomous individuals, each of whom has their own economic and political preferences (the contrary of Rawls's "Veil of Ignorance"), and who are all guided by hyper-norms which are, in effect, the norms by which other members of society judge them. Quoting Taylor (1989), Walzer (1992) claims that the greatest good is justice, which is constituted by "standards to which all societies can be held – negative injunctions, rules against murder, deceit, torture, oppression and tyranny". This initial level of contract based on sociability could not be put into effect were it not for the existence of a second, more concrete level.

Moving away from the abstract versions posited by political philosophers such as Hobbes, Locke and Rousseau and indeed more recently by Rawls, Donaldson and Dunfee offer an integrative approach to the social contract: integrative contract social theory, ICST. ICST affects a convergence between the macro level and the micro level. The macro level reflects a hypothetical agreement between rational members of the community, while the micro (or broad) level reflects a real agreement within the community. These ethical principles are accepted by the professions – lawyers, accountants, etc. – but they can also be applied to communities categorized by political and economic entity (European Community, United States, New Jersey), by industry (chemicals, software companies), by company (Canon, Microsoft, United Way of America), by organizational unit (Department of Human Resources, etc.), by informal communities within organizations (women managers, Afro-American managers) or as partners, professional associations, transaction communities, unions or trade organizations (International Chambers of Commerce).

As we can see, the institutional context of this form of social contract is markedly different from the one posited by contractualist political philosophers like Hobbes, Locke and Rousseau, and much more recently by Rawls. This version is informed by a crisis of the nation-state. Who is to be the arbiter of a contract drawn up between society and a multinational? For such a contract to be effective, the firm will have to make a pact with non-owners by creating an arena of dialogue and deliberation which accommodates them. The expectations of non-shareholders, who nevertheless have rights (and who are impacted by the activities of the firm) will have to be taken into account. This seems somewhat problematic. Business ethics, one of stakeholder theory's major sources, stipulates a kind of implicit contract between the firm and society in which the firm has obligations towards society, which, in turn, has the right to monitor the firm. However, the theorists of business ethics do not raise the question of arbitrage. Donaldson and Dunfee's notion of a new social contract seems plausible, but it is nevertheless built on moral foundations rather than on political philosophy.

The Limits of the Stakeholder Theory-Based Social Contract

A social contract that comes from classical political philosophical is based on (1) a tacit, pre-existing sociality rather than a real contract; (2) the fact that the social contract is different from a contract between two individuals; and (3) an arbitration body governing the parties to the contract, or an entity that does not have the same status as the parties (individuals, members, etc.). However, the new kind of social contract emerging from the demands of stakeholders contains a major flaw: there is no regulatory instance other than a pact between stakeholders and firms (Argandona's (1989) theory of the common good). The question of legitimacy and of arbitration between the parties is immediately raised. Who is the regulatory instance going to be? Clearly, if we allow every individual to be the judge, we will end up with a situation in which only individual interests exist. Such a situation would make a social contract impossible. For a social contract to be able to function, certain actions must be exempt from all questioning. They must have the status of law. Contractualist philosophy eventually provides two solutions. The first involves the two parties waiving their rights in favour of a third party beneficiary (Hobbes). The second consists in the people striking a contract with themselves (Rousseau),[6] thus guaranteeing the viability of the social contract through the equal reciprocity of the parties involved. However, this equal reciprocity is based on a pact considered as a social body. It is a pact in which the collectivity considered as a single person strikes a reciprocal contract with each member taken individually.[7] This hypothesis pre-supposes that the sovereign is not an individual but a "collective moral body" whose subjects are its members. Consequently, "the social contract needs no other

---

6 Contrary to most thinkers, who regard the social contract as the basis of political authority and as a pact of submission (*pactum subjectionis*) by means of which a people agrees, either because they are constrained by necessity (a form of submission produced by conquest or the right of war) or because they voluntarily acquiesce, to accept the authority of a sovereign. For Pufendorf, in either case, the pact is based on the model of the pact of slavery. Just as the slave gives himself a master, a people gives itself a king. For Rousseau, however, the terms of the pact compromise any form of social contract (see the chapter on slavery in *Du contrat social*, which constitutes a thoroughgoing critique of the pact of submission).

7 Rousseau (1762a): "according to the social pact, the sovereign power is only able to act through the common, general, will; so its decrees can only have a common, general aim; hence it follows that a private individual cannot be directly injured by the sovereign, unless all are injured, which is impossible, for that would be to want to harm oneself."

guarantor than public force, because individuals can never break or harm it".[8] In the absence of any shared superior, the only guarantor of the commitment made by individuals to the collectivity is public force: "thus the fundamental pact tacitly encompasses this commitment, which alone can give strength to all the others; anyone who refuses to obey the general will, will be constrained by the whole body".[9] The result is exactly the same as in Hobbes: the sovereign instance is the only judge of the execution of the contract and wields absolute power over all the other members of the community.

There is a second problem with the new social contract: the fact that stakeholders are fragmented, leading to the risk that the social contract may degenerate into a contract between individuals and private interests. Stakeholder theory has no answer to this question, which was already raised by Rousseau in the *Social Contract*.[10] In fact, the issue is not even raised, as if the existence of civil law and business law is enough. Strangely, the problem is not addressed by business ethics, even though, as mentioned above, it is one of the major sources of stakeholder theory. Business ethics entirely ignores the neo-institutionalist conception of the contract and the force of orthodoxy of the theory of the firm. Thus, the business ethics view of the contract is situated within the framework of a "soft law" which does not constitute an alternative to the neo-institutionalist current. In effect, the business ethics current known as "corporate social responsibility", which was first developed in the 1960s and 1970s,[11] stipulates a kind of implicit contract between the firm and society (according to which the firm has obligations to society, which, in turn, has the right to monitor the firm). In fact, "CSR demands it be recognized that attention should be paid to social demands" while bearing in mind that such recognition is entirely dependent on the goodwill of the firm.[12] Robert Frank (1993) suggests a contractualist perspective in view of a market regulation policy.

---

8   Rousseau (1762b): "The sovereign, being formed wholly of the individuals who compose it, neither has nor can have any interest contrary to theirs; and consequently the sovereign power need give no guarantee to its subjects, because it is impossible for the body to wish to harm all its members."

9   Rousseau (1761).

10   "In order to discover the rules of society best suited to nations, a superior intelligence beholding all passions of men without experiencing any of them would be needed. This intelligence would have to be wholly unrelated to our nature, while knowing it through and through; its happiness would have to be independent of us, and yet ready to occupy itself with ours."

11   Pesqueux and Biefnot (2002): "It is likely that the issue was first mooted by H. R. Bowen in his book *The Social Responsibilties of the Business Man* and developed by Eels and Walton 1961, McGuire 1963, and Davis and Blostrom 1975."

12   In effect, if we distinguish *corporate social responsibility* from *corporate social responsiveness* we can say that the former concerns "all the obligations of society, encompassing all the categories of economic, legal, ethical and discretionary performance" (Caroll, 1979, 1998). *Corporate social responsiveness*, on the other hand, consists of "taking into consideration the fact that society issues certain demands to which organisations

On the Origin of Equality

Stakeholder theory addresses the distinction between shareholders and non-shareholders. This distinction reveals disparities that can only be resolved by redistributing profits from shareholders to non-shareholders who have contributed, either directly or indirectly, to the firm. The aim of the contractual approach is to go back to the source of inequality. The objective of the social contract is to break free of the effects of this source of inequality.

Two hypotheses are available. The first is a return to an equilibrium between the parties (non-shareholders and shareholders). In this case, stakeholder theory posits the extension of shareholders' rights to everyone. The second hypothesis encompasses a tolerance of the inequality inherent in society characterized by a given system of production – capitalism – if, and only if, it does not negatively influence its stakeholders' fundamental freedoms. Such inequality must be in accord with the idea of freedom as a primary value that is inalienable vis-à-vis all other social values. The first hypothesis focuses on creating a balance between stakeholders and shareholders by extending stakeholders' property rights (Bonnafous-Boucher, 2004, 2006). The second hypothesis – "tolerable inequality"[13] – posits that stakeholder theory highlights a disparity between shareholders – who receive profits from their shares – and non-shareholders (who receive no share of the profits, but who are nevertheless impacted by the activities of the firm and who often contribute to it). In reality, Rawls rarely addresses economic and financial disparities, and even when he does so, he never develops his analyses very far. Instead, he prefers to apply the principle of equity to social justice rather than to economic circumstances. In other words, he addresses social and economic inequalities and the way in which they can be remedied in two contexts: (1) in situations characterized by equal opportunities; and (2) in situations in which the greatest benefit is sought for the society's least advantaged members.

Theory of Justice and Distributive Justice[14]

In attempting to re-establish an equality of treatment between shareholders and non-shareholders, stakeholder theory effectively demands that shareholders meet the expectations of people subject to the actions of capitalists, expectations which, according to part of the theory, are intrinsically legitimate. One approach

---

must respond" (Wartick and Cochran, 1985). In the first case, the firm produces values corresponding to those of its stakeholders; in the second, the firm is a receptacle of society's expectations. Evidently, the concept of a social contract requires that expectations concerning change linked to corporate responsibility be identified and analysed with a view to determining an approach able to react to demands for change and implementing appropriate responses to social problems.

13   Since it refers directly to Rawls's second fundamental principle.
14   Matland (2001); Philipps and Reichart (2000); Rendtorff (2005).

is to redistribute profits and reduce the gap between rich and poor (distributive justice). However, who creates share value? Is not reducing the gap, redistributing dividends or becoming a shareholder when you are not one tantamount to creating an inverse situation of inequality – a situation which is unequal for the richest and egalitarian for the poorest. What about redistribution at source (equality, equality of opportunity) and the concepts of "equal freedom" and "equity" in stakeholder theory? All these questions are raised by stakeholder theory and by corporate social responsibility within the context of a global market.

Conclusion

The aim of this chapter was to address power and principles in the market place. More specifically, I have looked at how power is displaced and how principles are deconstructed by the displacement of sovereignties and, consequently, of powers. I have analysed the foundations and principles of public and private spaces: from the conception of the public good to perceptions of sovereignty and how it is exercised. It would be hard to imagine corporate social responsibility without taking these important changes into account.

I have therefore concentrated on the heuristic function of stakeholder theory and corporate social responsibility, examining three aspects:

1. Stakeholder theory asks questions about the displacement of sovereignties, for example the transition from national public institutions to international organizations and global private firms.
2. Taking into account this displacement of sovereignties, stakeholder theory demands that global firms contribute to both the common good and the public good. This poses a major problem in terms of arbitrage and legitimacy, particularly if, as some authors maintain (such as Donaldson and Dunfee), corporate social responsibility can be used as a foundation for a new social contract. Who is to be the arbiter of a contract drawn up between society and a multinational? There is no regulatory instance other than a pact between stakeholders and firms, but the social contract cannot be founded on a contract between two entities. The fragmentation of stakeholders leads to the risk that the social contract may degenerate into a contract between individuals or private interests. On the other hand, the arbitration body governing the parties to the contract cannot be an entity that has the same status as the parties (individuals, members, etc.). The question of legitimacy and of arbitration between the parties is raised. Who is the regulatory instance going to be?
3. However, the elaboration of the common good as based on stakeholder theory founders on the rock on which the theory is built: the origin of inequality and the possibility of redistributing wealth (distributive justice) between proprietors and non-proprietors.

References

Argandona, A. (1989), The Stakeholder Theory and the Common Good. *Journal of Business Ethics*, 17, 9–10.

Axelrod, R. (1986), An Evolutionary Approach to Norms. *American Political Science Review*, 80(4), 1095–1111.

Bauchet, P. (2003), *Concentration des multinationales et mutation des pouvoirs de l'état*. Paris: CNRS Editions, p. 66.

Beck, U. (2002), *Macht und Gegenmacht im globalen Zeitaler*. Suhrkamp: Frankfurt am Main.

Beck, U. (2003), *Pouvoir et contre-pouvoir à l'ère de la mondialisation*. Paris: Aubier, p. 27.

Beck, U. (2005), *Power in the Global Age: A New Global Political Economy*. London: Polity Press.

Berger, S. (2002), *Notre Première mondialisation*. Paris: Le Seuil.

Bhagwati, J. (2004), *In Defense of Globalization*. Oxford: Oxford University Press, p. 173.

Bonnafous-Boucher, M. (2004), Some Philosophical Issues in Corporate Governance: The Role of Property in Stakeholder Theory. *The International Journal of Business in Society*, 5(2), 34–48.

Bonnafous-Boucher, M. (2005), From Government to Governance, in *Stakeholder Theory, a European Perspective*. New York : Palgrave Macmillan.

Bonnafous-Boucher, M. (2006), Décision stratégique et vitalité de la philosophie politique de la théorie des parties prenantes, in *Décider avec les parties prenantes*. Paris: Editions La Découverte, pp. 239–268.

Bowen, H. R. (1953), *Social Responsibility of the Business Man*. New York: Harper.

Bowie, N. E. (2004), Business Ethics, a Kantian Perspective. *Journal of Business Ethics*, 50(4).

Caroll, A. B. (1979), A Three Dimensional Conceptual Model of Corporate Performance. *Academy of Management Review*, 4(4), 500.

Carroll, A. (1998), The Four Faces of Corporate Citizenship. *Business and Society Review*, 100(1), 1–17.

Cohen, D. (2004), *La mondialisation et ses ennemis*. Paris: Grasset.

Davis, K. and Blostrom, R. C. (1975), *Business and Society*. New York: McGraw-Hill.

Donaldson, T. (1982), *Corporations and Morality*. Englewood Cliffs, NJ: Prentice-Hall.

Donaldson T. (1990), Can There be a Social Contract with Business? *Journal of Business Ethics*, 9(2).

Donaldson, T. and Dunfee, T. W. (1995), Contractarian Business Ethics, Current Status and Next Steps. *Business Ethics Quarterly*, 5, 173–186.

Donaldson, T. and Dunfee, T. W. (1999), *Ties that Bind. A Social Contracts Approach to Business Ethics*. Boston, MA: Harvard Business School Press.

Donaldson, T. and Dunfee, T. W. (2008), Four Design Criteria for any Future Contractarian Theory of Business Ethics. *Journal of Business Ethics*, 81(3).

Dunfee, T. W. (1991), Business Ethics and Extant Social Contracts. *Business Ethics Quarterly*, 1(1), 23–51.

Eels, R. and Walton, C. (1961), *Conceptual Foundations of Business*. Homeward: Richard D. Irwin.

Gauthier, D. (2000), *Morale et contrat*. Paris: Editions Mardaga.

Frank, R. (1993), A New Contractarian View of Tax and Regulatory Policy in the Emerging Market Economies. *Social Philosophy and Policy*, 258–281.

Jones, T. M. (1980), Corporate Social Responsibility Revisited, Redefined. *California Management Review*, 22(2).

Keely, M. (1988), *A Social-Contract Theory of Organizations*. Notre Dame: Notre Dame University Press.

Martinet, A. C. (1984), *Management stratégique: Organisation et Politique*. Paris: McGraw-Hill.

Martinet, A. C. and Reynaud, E. (2004), Entreprise durable, finance et stratégie. *Revue Française de Gestion*, 152(5), 121–136.

Matland, I. (2001), Distributive Justice in Firms: Do the Rules of Corporate Governance Matter? *Business Ethics Quarterly*, 2(1).

Mitchell, R. K., Agle, B. R. and Wood, D. J. (1997), Toward a Theory of Stakeholder Identification and Salience: Defining the Principle of Who and What Really Counts. *Academy of Management Review*, 22(4), 853–886.

Pesqueux, Y. and Biefnot, Y. (2002), *L'éthique des affaires, Management par les valeurs et responsabilité sociale*. Paris: Editions d'Organisation.

Peyrelevade, J. (2005), *Le capitalisme total*. Paris: Le Seuil, p. 41.

Philipps, A. and Reichart, J. (2000), The Environment as a Stakeholder? A Fairness-based Approach. *Journal of Business Ethics*, 23, 185–197.

Rendtorff, J. D. (2005), Des principes de justice pour les parties prenantes, in *Décider avec les parties prenantes*. Paris: Editions La Découverte.

Renouard, C. (2007), *La responsabilité éthique des multinationales*. Paris: Presses Universitaires de France, collection ethique et philosophie morale.

Rousseau, J. J. (1761), *Manuscrit de Genève,* Du pacte fondamental. Paris: La Pléiade, Editions Gallimard, I, 3, pp. 289–294.

Rousseau, J. J. (1762a), *Emile ou de l'éducation*. Paris: Editions Garnier Flammarion, V, pp. 465–629.

Rousseau, J. J. (1762b), *Du Contrat social, Du souverain*. Paris: La Pléiade, Editions Gallimard, I, 7, pp. 362–364.

Sachs, J. (1999), *The Lexus and the Olive Tree*. New York: Anchor Books, p. 227.

Schwartz, P. and Gibb, B. (1999), *When Good Companies Do Bad Things*. New York: Wiley.

Taylor, M. C. (1989), *Source of the Self: The Making of the Modern Identity*. Boston, MA: Harvard University Press.

Walzer, M. (1992), *Civil Society and American Democracy*. Hamburg: Rotbuch Verlag.

Wartick, S. L. and Cochran, P. L. (1985), The Evolution of the Corporate Social Performance Model. *Academy of Management Review*, 10, 758–769.

Chapter 6

Economics and Ethics: How to Combine Ethics and Self-Interest

Christoph Luetge

Introduction: A Survey on Profits and Morals

The current banking crisis has led to a decline in the reputation of banks and of managers in general. In the view of many public voices, managers are reckless and greedy and should exercise temperance. Banks in particular, but corporations in general too, are looked at with quite sceptical eyes.

This is not a new view, however. According to a 2005 survey of the Association of German Banks (Bundesverband Deutscher Banken 2005), the German public already then had a rather critical image of the engagement of corporations in matters of corporate social responsibility (CSR): Although this engagement had increased significantly in recent years, this was not being recognized by the public. Rather, 60 per cent of German people believed that only a few corporations were doing more than promoting their own interests and engaging in social affairs – 7 per cent even believed that there were *no* corporations doing more than this. In total, in the eyes of more than two-thirds of the people, corporations were not doing enough in this regard.

Moreover, more than half of the people (51 per cent) thought that the engagement of corporations had decreased during recent years. Only 11 per cent believed it had increased. Clearly, the public image was not in line with what was actually the case: according to a survey by the Forsa Institute conducted in the same year (2005), only 12 per cent of the entrepreneurs interviewed had decreased their CSR activities during recent years.[1]

Thirdly, apart from public opinion on CSR activities, there was a more general tendency visible: while most activities of corporations were not viewed as morally problematic *per se*, they were however not viewed as morally *desirable* either. In particular, while 58 per cent regarded large profits of corporations as morally acceptable in principle (37 per cent said that large profits were morally unacceptable), 75 per cent equally said that these large profits did not benefit the society as a whole.

---

1   Some 24 per cent had increased their activities, while 64 per cent had not made any changes. This study has been one of the largest studies on CSR in Germany; cf. http://www. insm.de/campaigns/cooperations/forsa/csr/.

This is a view that is not limited to Germany, but widely held in many parts of the world. While people do not subscribe to blatant anti-capitalist positions any more, the activities of corporations, in particular large company profits, are still widely regarded as morally *neutral*. Profits are believed to benefit only the corporations, but not larger parts of society.

More generally speaking, self-interest and ethics are not seldom still seen as strictly distinct and separate fields. I would like to sketch a conception of ethics, however, that combines economics and ethics. It is called *order ethics* (Ordnungsethik).[2]

A Justification of Order Ethics: Combining Economics and Ethics

The conception of order ethics relies heavily on contractarianism, especially on James Buchanan's work.[3] Unlike many other conceptions of ethics, it does not start with an aim to be achieved, but rather with an account of what the social world – in which ethical norms have to be implemented – is like. Our social world is different from the pre-modern one. Pre-modern societies played zero-sum games in which people could only gain significantly at the expense of others. The types of ethics that we are still used to today have been developed within these pre-modern societies.

Modern societies, by contrast, can be characterized – by economists and other social theorists alike – as societies with continuous growth. This growth has only been made possible by the modern competitive market economy which enables everyone to pursue their own interests *within a carefully devised institutional system*. In this system, positive-sum games are played, which makes it in principle possible to improve the position of every individual at the same time. Most kinds of ethics, however, resulting from the conditions of pre-modern societies, ignore the possibility of win–win situations and instead require us to be moderate, to share and to sacrifice, as this would have been functional in zero-sum games. These conceptions distinguish – in more or less strict ways – between self-interest and altruistic motivation. Self-interest, more often than not, is ultimately seen as something evil.

Such an ethics cannot be functional in modern societies, but this becomes clear, for example, in business ethics, only when regarding norms from a theoretical viewpoint. Intuitive, or everyday, or pragmatic deliberation cannot lead us to recognize this systematic "disfunctionality". Ethical concepts lag behind. Within zero-sum games, it was necessary to call for temperance, for *moderate* profits or for a condemnation of lending money at interest. Within positive-sum games, however, the morally desired result of a social process cannot be brought about by changes

---

2   Cf. Homann and Luetge (2005) and Luetge (2005, 2006b).

3   See Luetge (2005, 2006a). For contrasting views on contractarianism and other approaches, see Conill et al. (2008).

in motivation, by switching from "egoistic" to "altruistic" motivation. Instead, in the modern world, the individual pursuit of self-interest can promote traditional moral ideals in a much more efficient way: these ideals are implemented in the institutional framework of a society. They govern the market, and via competition on the market, the position of each individual can be improved: the positive-sum results. This positive sum is visible in the form of innovative products at good value for money, jobs, income, taxes and so on. So within the positive-sum games of modern societies, the individual pursuit of advantages is in principle compatible with traditional ethical ideas like solidarity.

After focusing on the conditions of modern societies, the second theoretical element introduced by order ethics is the distinction between actions and rules, which has already been mentioned. Traditional ethics concerns actions: it calls directly for changes in behaviour. This is a consequence of pre-modern conditions: people in the pre-modern world were only able to control their actions, and rather less the *conditions* of their actions. In particular, rules like laws, constitutions, social structures, the market order and also ethical norms have remained stable for centuries.

In modern societies, this situation has changed entirely. The rules governing our actions have increasingly come under our control. (Not only can we change rules like laws and constitutions, we are even beginning to change our genetic makeup.)

In this situation, ethics has to focus on rules. These rules themselves cannot, however, be recognized by pragmatic or common sense approaches to business ethics. Morality has to be incorporated in incentive-compatible rules. Direct calls for changes in behaviour without changes in the rules lead only to an erosion of compliance with moral norms. Individuals who continue to behave "morally" will be singled out, because the incentives have not been changed. There are three problems here. The first is that only changes in rules can change the situation for all participants involved *at the same time*. The second is that only rules can be enforced by sanctions – which alone can change the *incentives* in a *lasting* way. Third, only by incorporating morality in the rules can competition be made productive, making individuals' moves moral-free *in principle*. With the aid of rules and adequate conditions of action, competition can realize advantages for everyone involved. In this way, Adam Smith's classic idea of the market promoting the interests of all can be (re-)captured: if the rules are set adequately, self-interest as the dominant motive in actions can bring about the ethically desired results.

Thus, rules open up new opportunities in actions, but there is an even more important lesson to be learned from this theoretical perspective: rules and actions must be prevented from getting into opposition with one another. Ethical behaviour on the level of actions can only be expected if there are no counteracting incentives on the level of rules. In the classic model of the prisoner's dilemma, the prisoners cannot be expected to cooperate, because the conditions of the situation (the "rules of the game") are such that cooperation is punished by defection on the part of the other player: morality gets crowded out. This lesson is certainly incorporated in some pragmatic approaches to business ethics as well, at least in principle, but within order ethics, this lesson can be derived systematically, and thus made much more convincing.

Actions are governed by rules, but what about rules themselves? In this picture, rules are governed by other rules of higher order. Higher order means that there is a greater degree of consent needed to put these rules in effect or to change them – as is the case with laws and constitutional rules, for example.[4] Ultimately, the only normative criterion that is needed here is consent.[5] This criterion has been the core of social contract theory from Hobbes and Spinoza to Rawls. Other normative criteria, such as justifying norms by reference to the will of God, to the law of nature, to reason or to intuition cannot count on acceptance in the modern pluralistic world any more.

Most ethical theories, whether consequentialist or deontological, proceed by first giving a justification for their norms and then looking for ways of putting these norms into effect. The problem here is that the social conditions for implementation, especially in modern societies, are taken into consideration only *after* a justification has already been established. In this way, there is no room for the idea that a norm may not be justifiable *because* there is no way to implement it: ought implies can. Consequently, order ethics changes the theoretical precedence: discuss problems of implementation already in the process of justification.

It must therefore be clear that moral norms which are to be justified cannot require people to *abstain* from pursuing their own advantage. People abstain from taking "immoral" advantages only if adherence to ethical norms yields greater benefits over the planned *sequence* of actions than defection in the single case. Thus "abstaining" is not abstaining in the long run; it is rather an investment in expectations of long-term benefits. By adhering to ethical norms, I become a reliable partner for interactions. The norms do indeed constrain my actions, but they simultaneously expand my options in *inter*actions. People consent to rules only if these rules hold greater advantages for them, at least in the long run.

In general, ethics cannot require people to abandon their individual calculation of advantages. However, it may suggest *improving* one's calculation, by calculating in the long run rather than in the short run, and by taking into account the interests of our fellows, as we depend on their acceptance for reaching an optimal level of well-being, especially in a globalized world full of interdependence. (This global interdependence has become especially visible since the events following 11 September 2001.)

---

    4   Cf. Buchanan (1975). For the ethical dimension of Buchanan's work, see Luetge (2006a).

    5   Herein lies an important difference between a contractarian and a rule-utilitarian approach: the contractarian rejects the idea of adopting a rule *because* it maximizes some collective utility. Instead, in a contractarian setting, there has to be some level in the hierarchy of rules where every single individual must agree to a rule for it to be adopted. Thus, suppressing minorities becomes less probable than in a rule-utilitarian setting.

The problem of implementation can now be placed at the beginning of a conception of order ethics, justified with reference to the conditions of modern societies I have sketched. Under the conditions of pre-modern societies, an ethics of temperance had evolved that posed simultaneously the problems of implementation and justification. The implementation of well-justified norms or standards could then be regarded as unproblematic, because the social structures allowed for a direct face-to-face enforcement of norms. Pre-modern societies not only favoured an ethics of temperance, they also had the instrument of face-to-face sanctions within their smaller and non-anonymous communities. This instrument is no longer functional in modern anonymous societies (cf. Luhmann, 1989), and so we have to face up to the problem of implementation right at the start of our ethical conception. Simultaneously, an order ethics relies on the implementation of sanctions for enforcing *incentive-compatible rules*. In modern societies, rules and institutions, to a large extent, must fulfil the tasks that were, in pre-modern times, fulfilled by moral norms, which in turn were sanctioned by face-to-face sanctions. Norm implementation in modern societies thus works by setting adequate incentives in order to prevent the erosion of moral norms, which would happen if "moral" actors were systematically threatened with exploitation by other, less "moral" actors.

Combining Economics and Ethics:
Self-interest and Morals in the Ethical Tradition

As I have remarked, the conception laid out here makes changes in ethical categories necessary. Instead of calling for temperance and sacrifice, ethics should promote investing. Instead of demanding redistribution, it should favour exchange. Self-interest should not be "domesticated", but unleashed. What does this have to do with ethics?

Looking back at the (Western) ethical tradition, neither the Golden Rule, which has sometimes been regarded as the common core of all conceptions of ethics across cultures, nor Kant's categorical imperative deny the legitimacy of the individual pursuit of advantages. They indeed take it for granted, and then aim at constraining it. The new element within the conception of institutional ethics advocated here is just that these constraints are themselves justified by the expectation of greater benefits across a sequence of actions.

Many ethical conceptions do not recognize this, but rather derive the constraints from some form of "higher" morality, from "reason" or from the "human condition". The most prominent one of these, Kantian ethics, is commonly seen as being directly opposed to an ethics based on the pursuit of individual advantages, but some elements of Kant's original conception are commonly overlooked. In his *Groundwork of the Metaphysics of Morals*, Kant states: "denn dieses Sollen ist eigentlich ein Wollen" ("for this properly an 'I ought' is properly an 'I would'", Kant, 1785/1974, p. BA 102). Even for Kant, the core of normativity is made

of "wants", of interests, namely the interests of perfectly rational beings. We –
as beings that are not perfectly rational, but that are also affected by "springs"
("Triebfedern") of a different kind – we may sometimes get astray, but this
"getting astray" can in my view only be interpreted as the impossibility for people
of escape from social dilemma situations. In these situations, individual rationality
indeed leads us to act against our own interests. Therefore, we have to establish
rules for overcoming these situations, but these rules are themselves legitimated
by our (long-term) interests.

Getting back to Kant, I maintain that, for Kant, interests are the legitimate basis
of norms, but these interests must pass two filters – according to the categorical
imperative: (a) They have to be pursued within a *long-run* perspective (based on a
"maxim" (Maxime), not on a single opinion); and (b) we have to take into account
the vital interests of others, as we need their (at least implicit) agreement or toleration
(maxim as a basis for a general law; "Maxime des Willes zugleich als Prinzip einer
allgemeinen Gesetzgebung"). So even for Kant, ethics does not require us to abstain
from seeking advantages, but rather to improve our calculation of advantages by
taking a long-run rather than a short-run perspective and by taking a social or
cooperative rather than individual view. Again, abstaining is not really "abstaining",
but investment in the stability and further development of the social order.

Responsibilities of Corporations

At this point, it could be objected that order ethics neglects situations where
no viable framework exists, and it could be argued further that these situations
increase greatly in number under conditions of globalization. According to M.
Friedman's famous dictum, "the social responsibility of business is to increase its
profits" (Friedman, 1970), corporations would have – at most – responsibilities for
the order framework of the market. However, we observe corporations doing much
more, like providing social welfare and engaging in environmental protection or in
cultural and scientific affairs. Order ethics proceeds by extending the concept of
"order" to other, less formal orders.

In a world where incomplete contracts play a vital role, corporations have
responsibilities that can be differentiated into three dimensions:[6]

The first is that corporations are responsible for their actions and the immediate
consequences resulting from them. This can be defined as their *action responsibility*.
Corporations must comply with laws, and they are responsible for entities like
their products, their marketing methods, their employment policy, their corporate
culture, and so on. Also, philanthropic activities fall into this category.

In an extended sense, action responsibility also encompasses activities that
go beyond the traditional, rather passive meaning. Here, investing in educational

---

6   I am following an idea by K. Homann here.

programmes, fighting directly against corruption and discrimination or founding trusts can be located. These are important activities in the globalized world. However, they have mostly (a) local or regional character, and they are (b) mostly uncoordinated, because corporations hesitate to cooperate in this field with others who are normally their competitors. Thus, the structural problems of the world like hunger, poverty, terrorism and destruction of the environment are not dealt with systematically.

In the second step, corporations are responsible for the social and political order framework. In the national setting, this framework is easily identified, but in the global setting, it does not (yet) exist, and there is not much reason to suggest that it will come into existence in the near future. Thus, there is room for the *order responsibility* of corporations, which can have much greater impact than their action responsibility. The main task is to help in establishing basic human rights, a trustworthy judicial system, property rights and so on. This in turn improves the conditions for future, long-term company benefits. However, the main criticism here is that corporations that take their order responsibility seriously are simply engaging in lobbyism.

This leads directly to the third and most important, yet often overlooked element – which may also create a bridge to the discourse approach: the mental models people have greatly influence their actions. They can block necessary reforms and create vehement opposition to globalization. Many people even regard it as their *moral duty* to oppose "neoliberalism" and the market.

These people can however not be convinced by "economic" benefits, narrowly understood, by improving factors like GNP, but only by engaging in a discourse about the social and economic structures and factors that shape the world. From the perspective of order ethics, for example, it can be shown that many traditional moral ideals are better served by *intensifying*, not by slowing down, competition within an adequate institutional framework, but this must be convincingly shown, by way of argumentation. What is called for is the *discourse responsibility* of corporations. Corporations must engage in (public) discourse about the social and political order of the global society. People who cannot reconcile this social and political order with their own normative self-image, with their moral or ethical views, will stand in the way of many mutually fruitful and productive cooperations.

In several cases, these people are indeed reinforced in their opinions by bad arguments in favour of the market: for example, if the market is justified by calling it an expression of human freedom – the classic Friedman (1962) view – this creates immediate opposition in many people who daily experience otherwise. Many people in Germany (taking just one example) see a growing danger in globalization and in the activities of corporations. Five million people who are out of work, and many more who are afraid of losing their jobs, experience mainly *pressure* from competition, not freedom. It is therefore vital to stress that freedom and pressure always go hand in hand in the market economy: pressure on suppliers creates freedom of choice for consumers.

Another popular argument, used for example, in virtue ethics, is that the market is not as bad as some think – because we also find virtues like reliability or loyalty in the market. This in turn reinforces the view that, as a *general* rule, the market is bad and immoral. Virtues are only there to remedy the general immorality of the market. Moreover, reliability and loyalty can also be found in organized crime.[7]

Finally, my last example is again a German one. The German system of the "social market economy" is quite often justified – or equally criticized by others – by saying that the role of the "social" is to *correct* the "anti-social" consequences of the market. In this picture, the market in itself is regarded as morally dubious, to say the least. A better view, and one that the discourse responsibility of corporations should find it worthwhile to take into consideration, would be that the word "social" can only mean to create a better, more productive and thus ethically more desirable market. This argument would proceed by showing that people can take more risks as market competitors if they know that the social system will support them. If the concept of a social market economy is to make sense at all in the globalized world, then this strategy of argumentation should be followed.

However, two major criticisms are raised regularly against the political activities of corporations:

1. The first one is that corporations are "only" maximizing their profits and are therefore "only" following their own interests. In the political sphere, this is supposed to amount "only" to lobbyism. What about this charge? Certainly, no corporation can control the global social order on its own. It has to justify its actions in public, and that is not the only means of *controlling* companies. This leads us to the second criticism.

2. It is often alleged that corporations lack democratic legitimation, as CEOs and managers are not elected "democratically". This argument presupposes that democracy can be reduced to elections and to the vote of the majority – in a Lockean sense. However, following authors like Popper,[8] the main function of democracy is not majority vote, but *control*. In a democracy, control is exercised through many mechanisms, of which voting is only one. Others include competition in markets and public discourse, but also control of politics through corporations: bad politics must reckon with the possibility of being "punished" on capital markets. These control mechanisms exist likewise in a global setting, with the addition of non-governmental organizations – who are of course no more "democratically" elected (in the traditional sense) than corporations. The democratic legitimation of corporations depends on these control mechanisms being in place. By making their activities more transparent, corporations can

---

7   Cf. Gambetta (1993).

8   Popper famously wrote that the main advantage of democracy is to be able to get rid of governments "without bloodshed – *for example*, by way of general elections" (Popper, 1945/1966, Vol. 1, p. 124, my italics). Note the wording "for example".

enhance their acceptance and equally their democratic legitimation. This is in their own interest – and not simply a *moral duty* for a "good corporate citizen".

Conclusion

I have presented order ethics as a view on ethics which draws some of its main theoretical resources from economics. This conception points especially to the distinction between actions and rules and to the role of implementation in ethics.

Besides action responsibility and order responsibility, corporations can be assigned a discourse responsibility, which calls for caring about the ethical arguments used in public discourse. I have given an example of how a bad argument can be detrimental to an adequate understanding of business and ethics in the globalized world – and also to companies themselves. Of course, corporations cannot fulfil their discourse responsibility on their own. Here, business ethics can be of help in developing, shaping and promoting ethical ideas about – business. In the current financial crisis, it is especially important to be aware of the lessons ethics holds for a more efficient *and* more ethical way of doing business.

References

Buchanan, J. M. (1975), *The Limits of Liberty. Between Anarchy and Leviathan.* Chicago, IL: University of Chicago Press.

Bundesverband Deutscher Banken (2005), *Die Zukunft der Sozialen Marktwirtschaft.* Umfrage im Auftrag des Bundesverbandes deutscher Banken, November.

Conill, J., Luetge, C. and Schönwälder-Kuntze, T. (2008), *Corporate Citizenship, Contractarianism and Ethical Theory. On Philosophical Foundations of Business Ethics.* Aldershot: Ashgate.

Friedman, M. (1962), *Capitalism and Freedom.* Chicago, IL: Chicago University Press.

Friedman, M. (1970), The Social Responsibility of Business is to Increase its Profits. *The New York Times Magazine*, 13 September 1970, 32f and 122–126.

Gambetta, D. (1993), *The Sicilian Mafia. The Business of Private Protection.* Cambridge, MA: Harvard University Press.

Hobbes, T. (1651/1991), *Leviathan* (ed.), R. Tuck. Cambridge: Cambridge University Press.

Homann, K. and Luetge, C. (2005), *Einführung in die Wirtschaftsethik*, 2nd edn. Münster: LIT.

Homann, K., Koslowski, P. and Luetge, C. (eds) (2007), *Globalisation and Business Ethics.* Aldershot: Ashgate.

Kant, I. (1785/1974), *Grundlegung zur Metaphysik der Sitten*. Frankfurt am Main: Suhrkamp (in English: *Groundwork of the Metaphysics of Morals*).

Luetge, C. (2005), Economic Ethics, Business Ethics, and the Idea of Mutual Advantages. *Business Ethics: A European Review*, 14(2), 108–118.

Luetge, C. (2006a), An Economic Rationale for a Work and Savings Ethic? J. Buchanan's Late Works and Business Ethics. *Journal of Business Ethics*, 66(1), 43–51.

Luetge, C. (2006b), Against Dualisms: What I Try to Achieve by Teaching Business Ethics. *Journal of Business Ethics Education*, 3, 75–82.

Luetge, C. (2007), *Was hält eine Gesellschaft zusammen? Ethik im Zeitalter der Globalisierung*. Tübingen: Mohr Siebeck.

Luhmann, N. (1989), Ethik als Reflexionstheorie der Moral, in *Gesellschaftsstruktur und Semantik*, Vol. 3. Frankfurt am Main: Suhrkamp, pp. 358–447.

Popper, K. R. (1945/1966), *The Open Society and its Enemies*, 2 Vols, 5th edn. London: Routledge and Kegan Paul.

Spinoza, B. (1670–1677/1965), *The Political Works* (ed.), A. G. Wernham. Oxford: Clarendon.

Chapter 7

Business Ethics between Politics, Ethics and Economics

Jacob Dahl Rendtorff

The aim of this chapter is to discuss the relation between economics and ethics as justification for the rationality of values-driven management in business institutions. In the context of values-driven management we often meet debates about the relation between economic values and ethical values. Concepts like "ethics pays", "corporate social responsibility 'simply works better'" and "good business is good ethics" indicate such a connection between ethics and economics.[1] However, the mixture of arguments also indicates some confusion of ethics and economics.[2] In the following I want to argue that there is a mutual connection between ethics and economics. Together with legal regulation (for example property and contract law) and as a rational justification of such regulation of free markets, business ethics will primarily be conceived as an external constraint on economic markets. Accordingly, ethics is considered as the foundation of economic action.[3] However, I do not think that it is valid to argue that the relation between ethics and economics should be conceived exclusively in terms of considering ethics as a kind of "king of economics", where economics is always submitted under the sovereign leadership of ethics. We should rather admit that there is an economic aspect of ethics and that economics also helps to shape ethics. So even though ethical values are external constraints on economic action and market behaviour, we cannot exclude that economics may help to define ethics and to clarify ethical arguments.

We may argue that there is a "dialectical relation" between ethics and economics and that the two disciplines mutually shape one another.[4] We will look into the concept of economic anthropology, which is the discipline in which

---

1   These "sayings" are for example promoted by the European Academy of Business in Society and the lobby organization for corporate involvement in business ethics in Europe, CSR Europe. The economic arguments for corporate social responsibility have also become very important for the efforts of the European Commission to "mainstream corporate social responsibility" as an integrated part of Good Corporate Governance.

2   Amartya Sen (1987), *On Ethics and Economics*, Cambridge, MA: Blackwell.

3   François-Régis Mahieu (2001), *Éthique économique, fondements anthropologiques*, Paris: Bibliothèque du développement, L'Harmattan, p. 67.

4   This reflects the method of critical hermeneutics, which often argues from dialectical tensions between different disciplines in order to find the right mean between the different viewpoints. See Jacob Dahl Rendtorff, Critical Hermeneutics in Law and Politics, in Lars

one can find implicit or explicit ethical views.[5] Traditional economic theory is based on the idea of "Homo economicus", indicating that economic action is based on "rational utility maximizing" individuals.[6] However, this view of the economic actor has been exposed to strong criticism stating that it implies a too simple concept of anthropology. Human beings are not isolated individuals but they are parts of complicated networks of reciprocity and social interaction. We can propose an ethical correction of the traditional concept of economic anthropology (Aristotle). Ethical theory primarily is based on a vision of the good life in community for and with the other person. This vision is limited by a universal ethics of rules and categorical imperatives (Kant). After this analysis in the perspective of "Communitarian Kantianism"[7] or rather *ethical liberalism* we may introduce utility- and welfare-based analysis based on the idea of the "greatest happiness to the greatest number". Indeed, even this restricted rule utilitarianism may be viewed as a correction of economic action, which is based on personal rather than common utility maximization. However, the utilitarian approach also gives possibilities of seeing economic calculation as a critical reply to ethical argument.[8]

We will discuss this relation between business, economics and ethics in the following sections: (1) Values, Ethics and Economic Reason; (2) Economic Anthropology between Ethics and Politics; (3) Ethico-legal and Political Constraints on Economics; (4) Ethics out of Economics; and (5) Business Ethics between Ethics and Economics.

Values, Ethics and Economic Reason

The problem of the relation between ethics and economics in business concerns the concept of economic action and the role of ethical responsibility in economics. The idea of economic rationality depends on the concept of economic action.[9] This concept is marked by a tension between individualism and altruism and personal responsibility for economic actions. The idea of an ethical correction of economic action implies a critical attitude to the concept of self-interest as the basis for economic action. It is argued that economic calculation should exclusively be based on individual utility maximization but include an altruistic concern for the

---

Henrik Schmidt (1995), *Paul Ricoeur in the Conflict of Interpretations*, Aarhus: Aarhus University Press.

5   Mahieu, *Éthique économique, fondements anthropologiques*, ibid., pp. 183–229.

6   Sen, *On Ethics and Economics*, ibid.

7   You can find an explicit elaboration of the concept of Communitarian Kantianism or "ethical liberalism" in my discussion of Paul Ricoeur's political philosophy. See Rendtorff, Critical Hermeneutics in Law and Politics, ibid.

8   John Broome (1999), *Ethics out of Economics*, Cambridge: Cambridge University Press.

9   Sen, *On Ethics and Economics*, ibid.

common good and for other human individuals. In the perspective of such an ethical correction of economics, we think of the economic actor as an individual, who makes an economic calculation which is extended to include the responsibility for other human beings and society, integrating economic calculation in well-founded moral norms and ethical customs of society.

Looking at the relation between business and ethics in the perspective of economic history we can see that the idea of the rational profit-maximizing individual based on self-interest is a newcomer for understanding economics.[10] Although we find preliminaries of the concept in the classical materialist philosophy of Epicure, it is only with the modern economic thinkers in the sixteenth and seventeenth centuries in combination with the emergence of an autonomous capitalist economy based on efficiency and utility that this view of economic actors becomes predominant. The concept of the political and social neutrality of the market has emerged in this context of independent economic markets. In classical political economy, market action was conceived in the perspective of political community. Aristotle argued, for example, that wealth and money are not goods that man seeks for their own value but rather as a means to obtain the good life in community. Thomas Aquinas developed the doctrine of the "just price" in which economic exchange relations were based on respect for the natural law and political justice in society.[11]

Even though he was the founder of the modern economic doctrines of self-interests and the invisible hand, a similar conception of economy as science of the good for community can be found in the works of Adam Smith.[12] In the *Theory of Moral Sentiments* (1759) Smith seems to argue that the relation between persons and other mutual moral sentiments are the basis for economic action. Self-interest is only one among the human virtues and of the natural inclinations of human nature. Therefore, even Smith argued that utility maximization has to be seen in the perspective of other virtues like generosity and justice.[13] Therefore rational economic calculation is founded on a broader view of human nature than of the idea of "economic man" that has become predominant in neoclassical economics.

In the perspective of the history of political economy we find that economics originally was viewed as a moral science, not as a mechanical natural science, but as a part of the art of "good government". According to Amartya Sen, among others, this view of economics has been forgotten in modern economics, which is more interested in the engineering problems of economic efficiency than in ethical and political problems of rights and social achievement.[14] This tradition includes classical authors like Ricardo and Malthus and was continued by the neoclassical

---

10   Henri Dennis (1966), *Historie de la pensée économique*, Paris: Thémis, PUF, pp. 7–91.

11   Ibid., pp. 74–75.

12   Patricia Werhane (1991), *Adam Smith and his Legacy for Modern Capitalism*, Oxford: Oxford University Press.

13   Sen, *On Ethics and Economics*, ibid., pp. 22–23.

14   Ibid., p. 6.

tradition of Leon Walras and Jevons and developed by authors like Alfred Marshall in his *Principles of Economics*,[15] which focuses exclusively on individual utility and seems to forget the importance of concerns for the common good in economic theory. This concentration on self-interest economic theory and the idea of economic rationality is exposed to a strong tension with deontological constraints on economic markets based on the protection of rights, interest and freedoms of other human beings.[16] According to this view the concepts of well-being and rationality in neoclassical economic thought must be rethought in accordance with ethical principles. We should look more closely on the ethical aspect of human motivation and integrate questions of the good life into economics. Therefore, without dropping all the important insights of descriptive positive economy, we may argue for a normative view of economic theory in saying that business ethics is providing us with the "missing link" between traditional "political economy" and micro-economic rationality.

In order to provide such a link between ethics and economic rationality, we have to look closer to the neoclassical view of economic rationality and its possible ethical implications. The neoclassical concept of rationality implies an unlimited conception of rationality according to which economic agents have unlimited competencies of decision-making in order to maximize personal self-interest within an exogenous space of possibilities.[17]

The ideal of perfect competition in neoclassical economics is based on the presuppositions of perfect competition, rational independent decision-making, a perfect market, a homogenous product, many competing sellers and free possibilities of entry/exit into economic markets. It is presupposed that the firm consists of one rational individual rather than a group or coalition of individuals. The firm is a category of the individual and a production unit in order to provide goods to be exchanged on economic markets.[18]

In the view of neoclassical economy, ethics is regarded as external limitations of the market. A presupposition is that the conditions of fair competition and perfect markets should be accepted by all participants in economic competition, which is restricted by the rules of the game, for example property rights and contract law. I would argue that the only ethics present in this doctrine is the ethics of competition, which is to maximize self-interest and personal utility. A promise of total opportunistic and selfish action is a handshake, as some have characterized this ethics of competition. In this way ethics seems to be an exogenous element of social action at the limits of economic rationality.

Even though they heavily disagree with neoclassical economic theory, some other paradigms of economics – for example game theory and agency theory

---

15   Alfred Marshall (1920), *Principles of Economics*, 8th edn, New York: Macmillan.

16   Sen, *On Ethics and Economics*, ibid., p. 15.

17   Christian Knudsen (1995), *Økonomisk metodologi II*, Copenhagen: Jurist og Økonomforbundets forlag.

18   Ibid., p. 66.

– seem to share the same view of the separation between ethics and economics and of the idea of egoistic rational utility-maximizing individuals as the ideal of economic action.

Game theory contributes to solving an important problem in neoclassical economic theory – the problem about harmonious equilibrium leading to monopoly, which is contradictory to the ideal of perfect competition.[19] In order to avoid static harmony, game theory operates with "non-cooperative games as the ideal of economic interaction". According to the economic mathematician Nash, a situation of equilibrium is the case where every participant in the game chooses a strategy that is the best response to compete with the strategies of the other. Perfect equilibrium in non-cooperative game theory is a combination of strategies in which no player has reason to choose another strategy to improve pay-off.[20] Indeed, this theory of competition presupposes external limitations on markets and firm behaviour. The players have to play within certain rules and they have to share the same concept of rationality considering economic actors as self-interested utility maximizers.

A similar view of economic man may be said to be present in agency-theory building on rational individual agents acting in firms in order to maximize their own interests. In agency theory corporations are primarily viewed as instruments and devices to maximize profits.[21] We may even mention some views of economic man in transaction cost economics, arguing that, if we look at men "as they really are", we are likely to meet not only self-interested utility maximizers, but also potential opportunistic individuals who, even though they are not rational in any ideal sense, in their daily actions, with limited knowledge are likely to follow a non-ideal strategy of personal utility maximization.[22] Even though transaction cost theories argue for the importance of governance structures and agree that cooperation, personal honour and integrity matter,[23] this institutional economics regards self-interest as the primary motive for action.

We can say that we are confronted with an instrumental concept of economic reason, which is presupposed rather than explicitly argued for. Yet why consider self-interest as the only motive for economic action when we know that real people also are motivated by a plurality of values and ethical choices.[24] Economics is viewed, not as a science applied to a specific realm of being, but rather as a general method that can be applied as a fundamental method in all aspects of human life.

---

19 Ibid.

20 Ibid., p. 96.

21 Michael Jensen (2000), *A Theory of the Firm, Governance, Residual Claims and Organizational Forms*, Cambridge, MA: Harvard University Press; Michael C. Jensen and William H. Meckling, Theory of the Firm: Managerial Behavior, Agency Costs and Ownership Structure, *Journal of Financial Economics* (1976) 3, 305–360.

22 Oliver Williamson (1989), *The Economic Institutions of Capitalism*, New York: The Free Press.

23 Ibid., p. 63.

24 Sen, *On Ethics and Economics*, ibid., pp. 19–20.

The foundation of this concept of economics is anthropology of the individual as maximizing self-interest and personal utility – even under conditions of bounded rationality and finitude of voluntary reflexivity.

Economic Anthropology between Ethics and Politics

The debate about the relation of economics to ethics and politics centres on the view of economic anthropology and on the motives for action of human individuals. As mentioned, common criticisms of the idea of the self-interest of economic actors argue that human beings are not egoist utility maximizers but belong to human communities and social cultures where concerns for the common good cannot be excluded from understanding motives for economic action.[25] Moreover, neoclassical presuppositions of ideal situations of economic action are conceived to be very far from the conditions of action in concrete social contexts of economic life.

Arguments for a broader ethical foundation of economic action state that economic anthropology is characterized by a tension between egoism and altruism.[26] Communitarian authors argue that wise economic action implies reciprocity and concern for other human beings.[27] Therefore, self-interest is never the only motive for economics. In opposition to such a social view on economic action, economists like Gary Becker have defended altruism as an advanced form of individual utility maximization. Becker advances the so-called "Rotten Kid Theorem", stating that people acting altruistically do so in order to improve their self-interest – like the child who behaves nicely in order to get a great reward from her parents.[28] In this perspective strategies of cooperation and sympathy are only forms of advanced self-interest recognizing the importance of truth-telling, promise and contract keeping for future collaboration and exchange. This argument has been fully developed by Axelrod who, in his book *The Evolution of Cooperation* (1984), argues that cooperative behaviour can be founded on individual maximization of utility because cooperative strategies in the long run will benefit individuals more than opportunistic strategies.[29]

When John Rawls takes the starting point from self-interest and situates the rational theory within a Kantian construction of universal norms in his discussion of the "veil of ignorance" in his famous *A Theory of Justice* (1971), he can be said to formulate a rational foundation of economics between ethics and politics.[30] The

---

25   Mahieu, *Éthique économique, fondements anthropologiques*, ibid., p. 299.

26   Ibid, p. 152.

27   Amartya Etizioni (1988), *The Moral Dimension. Towards a New Economics*, New York: Collier Macmillan.

28   Mahieu, *Éthique économique, fondements anthropologiques*, ibid., p. 164.

29   Axelrod, R. (1984), *The Evolution of Cooperation*, New York: Basic Books.

30   John Rawls (1971), *A Theory of Justice*, Cambridge, MA: Oxford University Press.

veil of ignorance means that individuals do not know their personal position in a future society and therefore it is most rational to choose the same basic conditions and principles of justice, which are valid for everyone in a future society. In this construction Rawls does not ignore individual rational choice, nor does he make it the only basis for rational action. It is important to emphasize that this Kantian constructivism cannot exclude a concern for justice in political community and the common good, when Rawls argues that individuals under the "veil of ignorance" ought to choose principles of justice for future communities which are valid for everyone.[31] Moreover, this concept of society presupposes a broader conception of the human self than the one which is proposed by neoclassical economics. We can therefore state that political rationality implies social reciprocity and commitment to a common political community. In this context the concepts of altruism of Becker and Axelrod do not take account of what altruism really is.[32] They are begging the question of altruism because they only want to count altruism in terms of enlightened egoism.

Lévinas helps to enlarge the ethical foundation for Rawls's theory of justice in political community. Lévinas proposes a phenomenology of the intimate encounter of the other human being as the basis for our view of human motivation.[33] The encounter of the other human being is an infinite demand of responsibility and self-sacrifice. This concern for the other is the basis for social relations and the reciprocity with the other should not be defined as a relation of "alter ego", but rather the other is someone fundamentally different from me. In the perspective of Lévinas, the fundamental respect for the other as other is the foundation of ethical relations, and this concern for "the other as other" precedes the relation of economic egoistic exchange. The ethical relation is more fundamental than economic relations and this ethical ideal of respect for the other as other is the foundation and condition of possibility for economic exchange.[34] Therefore, Lévinas says that ethics precedes reciprocity as mutual recognition and altruism as enlarged self-interest.

In order to situate economics between ethics and politics we summarize our view of economic anthropology by stating that the traditional view of "economic man" is transcended by the Kantian constructivism of John Rawls, which is submitted to the communitarian criticism of the self-interested, rational and isolated liberal individual as situated in a community with fellow human beings searching for the common good. The political perspective is supported by Lévinas's ethical anthropology, which situates economic action as secondary to the fundamental

31　Michael Sandel (1982), *Liberalism and the Limits of Justice*, Cambridge, MA: Oxford University Press.

32　Mahieu, *Éthique économique, fondements anthropologiques*, ibid., p. 164.

33　Emmanuel Lévinas (1961), *Totalité et infini, Essai sur l'extériorité*, The Hague: Martinus Nijhoff; Mahieu, *Éthique économique, fondements anthropologiques*, ibid, p. 159.

34　Lévinas, *Totalité et infini*, ibid.

human responsibility for "the otherness of the other" as revelation of the innermost purpose of human action. This implies that economic action is embedded in larger social structures and economic rationality cannot be separated from ethical and political rationality.

These perspectives of political justice in community and ethical care for the human being as the most fundamental condition for human existence must lead to the idea that economics is seen as being dependent on politics and ethics. The ontology of economics and the reach of economic method cannot be conceived as all-encompassing and absolute, but economic rationality is secondary to political and ethical reciprocity. From such a point of view, economic decision-making should have external restrictions in the laws of political justice and the ethical principles based on fundamental principles of human existence. Economic reason is submitted to the ethical ideas of universal moral rules, to the search for justice in political communities and to considerations of community welfare.

In the perspective of the philosophy of Lévinas we may say that responsibility for the human being conditions the legitimacy of economic action.[35] Moreover, viewed from the ideals of political community, responsibility is not only an intimate relation with the other but also should be extended in time and space to society as a whole. This is the argument of the German philosopher Hans Jonas, who argued that responsibility does not only concern present human activities but should be extended globally in time and space and include the future of humanity.[36]

However, such an integration of ethics and politics in economic rationality is not without a price, because basic economic considerations are considered as relative to ethical principles.[37] Concepts of efficiency, utility, production, demand, consumption and accumulations of goods and property are not considered as intrinsic values, but as only valid insofar as they do not violate basic ethical principles and as dependent on their ability to contribute to the common good of political community. Ethical and political limitations of economic action propose a system of laws and rights as the basis for social regulation of economic action.

We can even find support for such a critical limitation of economic action within the institutionalist conception of organization theory, questioning some of the central principles of neoclassical economic thought.[38] In particular, the behaviouralistic paradigm of organization and management theory questions the purity of the neoclassical concept of economic rationality. These approaches to organization theory both argue that the ideal of economic man as a rational self-interest maximizing actor does not correspond to the reality of corporate action or to the idea of the firm as a "loosely coupled system".[39] Simon and March stated in

---

35   Ibid.

36   Hans Jonas (1979), *Das Prinzip Verantwortung*, Frankfurt am Main: Insel Verlag.

37   Mahieu, *Éthique économique, fondements anthropologiques*, ibid., p. 168.

38   Walter W. Powell and Paul J. DiMaggio (1991), *The New Institutionalism in Organizational Analysis*, Chicago, IL: The University of Chicago Press.

39   Knudsen, *Økonomisk metodologi II*, ibid., p. 114.

1958 that the concept of maximization of profits does not explain how individuals operate in daily economic life. Economic actors are not rational in any ideal sense, but depend on many different personal interests, preferences and property rights. The firm does not represent a rational hierarchical engine of production, but may be viewed as an open political system of interacting individuals in a complex environment.[40]

This view of economic action does not necessarily introduce a normative theory of foundation of economics in ethics and politics, but it implies that economic systems cannot be viewed as closed systems of efficiency rationality. Organizations are much more complex, because they are social systems with mutually dependent actors who act according to organizational goals and particular structures of reward and incentives. Moreover, individuals take part in organizations according to personal judgments of possible benefits and organizations only function if there are good reasons for individuals to work in them.

By considering organizations as "political coalitions" March and Cyert developed in 1962 a criticism of the neoclassical conception of economic markets and firms as "black boxes" determined by ideal economic rationality.[41] Emphasizing imperfect knowledge and open complexity in firms, organizations are in opposition to fully rational systems viewed as adaptive rational systems characterized by the "garbage can model", where ideal economic rationality is viewed as dependent on particular decisions and horizons of decision-making.

This view of organizational rationality has further been described by Herbert Simon by the concept of "procedural rationality", which considers factual decision-making as dependent on "bounded rationality", meaning that alternatives are limited, absolute knowledge is impossible and full knowledge about personal future preferences is impossible.[42] James March argues that neoclassical "logic of consequences" must be replaced by a "logic of appropriateness" as a condition for economic action. Bounded rationality means that it is impossible to work with a strict separation between exogenous and indigenous aspects of economics. Internal economic rationality is influenced by external social values and conditions.

Accordingly we may say that the evolution of organization theory supports the idea of external ethical and political limitations of economic rationality. When Simon argues that the substance of neoclassical economic rationality is replaced by "procedural rationality in organizations as 'adaptive, political coalitions'", we may say that this shows how ethics and other values than economic values cannot avoid influencing organizational decision-making. Thus, organizational theory and the institutionalist paradigm in economics help to give descriptive arguments for a close relation between ethics and economics.[43] In this sense economic stability

---

40 Ibid., p. 118.
41 Ibid., p. 124.
42 Ibid., p. 159.
43 See Powell and DiMaggio, *The New Institutionalism in Organizational Analysis*, ibid.

and competitive equilibrium are dependent on institutions and institutional arrangements. These arrangements cannot exclude ethical values and political considerations, which become a part of bounded and procedural rationality in firms as political coalitions.

Ethico-Legal and Political Constraints on Economics

What we can learn from this analysis of economic reason as based on bounded rationality and the "garbage can" conditions of decision is not that business decisions are exclusively ethical or economic in any ideal sense, but rather that decision-making is based on a kind of "mixed rationality" including elements from both economic and ethical rationality but certainly also other fields like politics and law. Yet in a deeper sense, we can also conceive business ethics as the foundation of decision-making, because business ethics is not only about economic means and rationality but also about social and political goals of economic behaviour. However, now the problem is how to define this political and ethical rationality as a basis for economic action.

In this context my starting point is the "vision of ethics as the good life for and with others in just institutions".[44] This approach was initiated by Aristotle in his ethics and politics. If we follow Aristotle's economics, the market system is nothing but a means to facilitate exchange in order to create a good political community.[45] Such a virtue ethics would consider every firm and organization as a part of a broader social context. The firm may be viewed as "a form of life", a community of excellence based on virtuous and good behaviour, building moral character through experience. The aim of work is not primarily to earn money but to cultivate an ability contributing to the good life of community.[46] Individuals are required to act according to the virtues and fulfil required standards of excellence as participants of the firm as a culture of excellence. This is done by continuous formation, elevation and education of the faculty of judgment.[47] Judgment is the capacity to act according to the virtues. This communitarian approach to ethics is based on the view of the firm as belonging to a culture and a society with particular traditions and standards of excellence which always should be respected in corporate economic action.

According to communitarian theory such limits on corporate action are based on the view of corporations as institutions which should contribute to the good life in society. However, ethics face the problem of the relation between community and universal norms of society. Therefore from our concept of ethical liberalism

---

44   Paul Ricoeur (1990), *Soi-même comme un Autre* (One-Self as Another), Paris, p. 202. See also Rendtorff, Critical Hermeneutics in Law and Politics, ibid.

45   Dennis, *Historie de la pensée économique*, ibid., pp. 36–54.

46   Ibid., pp. 36–54.

47   Ibid., pp. 36–54.

we have to argue for a universal dimension of business ethics. This approach is based on the deontological ethics of Immanuel Kant. Kant's philosophy can be used to propose a "contractual theory of business ethics".[48] The basis for Kant's philosophy is the categorical imperative which in this deontological view is based on universal protection of fundamental rights. It states that: (1) an action to be morally acceptable must be possible as a universal law; and (2) human beings should never be treated only as means but also always as ends in themselves.[49] According to Kant a just society should be conceived as the kingdom of ends in themselves where people live together in just institutions. In this perspective it is not only the good life or economic utility, but firstly the protection of universal rights and of human dignity, which is the most important goal of ethics.

In the Kantian perspective limits of economic rationality are based on protection of personal rights, human rights and property rights. Today the foundation for this kind of ethics may be found in the Universal Declaration of Human Rights from 1948. Rights are founded in reason, they are natural and rational and human beings cannot lose their basic rights. From the point of view of rights theory respect for basic rights and dignity of workers and employees are fundamental external limitations on economic action.[50] To the moral rights of employees corresponds duties of the firm to respect these rights. Some argue that it is difficult to cope with conflicts of rights and to deal with possible exceptions from strict moral rules. In order to cope with this difficulty we must be precise with regard to definitions of rights. Rights can be divided into negative and positive rights. Negative rights like the right to employee privacy are rights not to have others intervene in your private affairs. Positive rights are like the right to work and the right to property positive requirements to be respected.

Rights are in the perspective of deontological ethics founded in a social contract institutionalizing freedom in social institutions.[51] Justice in the firm may also be considered in terms of rights and contract, but there is a close link between the concept of right and the legal notion of contract, which is essential to business interactions. The ethical principles of business contracts are that (1) contracts and agreements should be based on informed consent among partners; (2) moreover, facts that are the basis for the agreement should be reliable; (3) no one can be forced to make a contract; and (4) the agreement must never bind partners to immoral action.[52]

In the Kantian framework the ethical theory of rights is combined with a conception of justice. In the perspective of business ethics, justice on economic

48 Manuel Velasquez (2002), *Business Ethics. Concepts and Cases*, 5th edn, Englewood Cliffs, NJ: Prentice Hall.

49 Immanuel Kant (1999), *Grundlegung zur Metaphysik der Sitten* (1785), Hamburg: Felix Meiner.

50 Velasquez, *Business Ethics. Concepts and Cases*, ibid., pp. 94–96.

51 Ibid., p. 90.

52 Ibid., pp. 94–95.

markets and in relations between firms may be conceived in terms of "fairness", implying a fair distribution of benefits and burdens. Thus, we may refer to three forms of justice: (1) distributive justice, (2) retributive justice and (3) compensatory justice.[53] These forms of justice may be taken into account when we determine the right principles of property and contract law in relations between firms.

As we have argued, John Rawls's theory of justice can be considered as a modern version of the Kantian deontological approach to justice. According to this view two substantial principles of justice that individuals would choose impartially in the initial situation of selection behind the "Veil of ignorance" would be (1) the principle of equal liberty and (2) the principle of difference (that inequality can only be justified if it may be advantageous for the worst off), implying that everyone should have the same opportunities from the beginning of their lives.[54]

This view of justice as fairness based on the principle of difference can be considered as justification of a liberal market economy.[55] Even though it eventually implies great difference in economic wealth, economic freedom on competitive markets will in the long run be for the benefit of the worst off in society. Retributive and compensatory forms of justice may also be taken into account when we deal with contracts and other interactions based on agreements on a voluntary basis. However, we ask the question whether distributive justice can be included in justice as fairness in economic markets. What is the Kantian and Rawlsian response to radical libertarian belief in the virtues of the free market?

Against Kant and Rawls, Milton Friedman would argue that individual economic freedom should not be restricted by retributive compensation. The Libertarian would follow Locke in emphasizing that individual property rights are essential for personal freedom in a liberal society.[56] Everyone should be free to choose with minimal intervention of the state. According to the Libertarian, such freedom in the market within ethical custom is the best argument for human happiness and luck.[57] It may be argued that economic equality cannot be viewed as important in competitive markets based on economic freedom. Neoclassical economic thought based on the pursuit of self-interest implies the view of human beings as competitive by nature. Property rights liberalism does not imply any principles of equality as the basis for economic markets because economic freedom is essential to property rights. It is argued to be paternalistic to limit human freedom by rules of justice in economic markets. Radical libertarians and some liberals are indeed somewhat critical of the deontological perspective, because it implies moral restrictions on personal liberty.

---

53   Ibid., pp. 107–111.
54   Rawls, *A Theory of Justice*, ibid.
55   Ibid., p. 105–106.
56   Ibid., pp. 175–176.
57   Milton Friedman (1962), *Capitalism and Freedom*, Chicago, IL: Chicago University Press.

However, from the perspective of consequentialist welfare economics the libertarian attitude is not considered sufficient to ensure efficient allocation of resources and justice in society. In opposition to radical libertarianism's emphasis on self-interest, consequentialism argues for a rational distribution based on "the greatest good to the greatest number". However, utilitarians are not less satisfied with the deontological approach, which is in danger of creating a strong divide between the right and the good. Kant was very strict and he stated that there could be no exceptions from moral law, even in cases where we think that such exceptions may lead to greater utility for all. Against this approach an economic ethics would always emphasize the need for efficiency rather than rules in order to achieve the highest and greatest good.[58]

Indeed, we may argue that utilitarianism and consequentalism already function as the foundation of modern economics. Utilitarianism is a philosophy which is based on cost–benefit calculation and on the rational balancing of different kinds of goods. However, as welfare economics searching to maximize "the greatest good for the greatest number", utilitarianism implies a concept of the common good and this philosophy is not solely a definition of utility as individual profit maximization.[59] However, utility is generally defined in terms of "personal and subjective preferences" of each individual. Jeremy Bentham argued for pain and pleasure as the indicators of the utility of different goods. Against Bentham's somewhat simple view of pleasure and pain, John Stuart Mill argued for a less materialistic and hedonistic conception of personal preferences, stating that it is better to be an "unsatisfied Socrates rather than a happy pig".

As a consequence of this individualist definition of pleasure and pain, modern consequentialists operate with the idea of preferences being subjective and personally dependent on whatever preferences individuals may have. In this sense the foundation of ethics is the subjective perception of utility, pleasure and pain, which can be conceived as personal welfare. Indeed, the concept of welfare has been influential in modern economics, considering economics as the science of maximization of welfare, which is for example proposed by Samuelson. Thus, according to the theory of business organizations, we may argue that the ethics of business is to make the corporation contribute to maximization of welfare for the greatest number in society.[60]

The result is that the organization before doing an action always should weigh the implied benefits and harms for different stakeholders of the corporation. In this sense utilitarian philosophy implies a rather critical view of neoclassical economics if economic action is considered solely in terms of egoistic procurement of goods. Self-interested economic action can only be said to be justified if it will have better consequences for the greatest number in society. The ethical limitations of utilitarian ethics on business may indeed be rather strict. An example is the

---

58 Broome, *Ethics out of Economics*, ibid., 1999.
59 Velasquez, *Business Ethics. Concepts and Cases*, ibid., p. 77.
60 Ibid., p. 78.

discussion of affluence and famine by modern consequentialists, arguing that the marginal utility of material goods of citizens in a welfare society is so low that there is no justification for increase in their wealth.[61]

The ethical foundation of my discussion of business ethics can on this basis be defined as an ethical liberalism or republican business ethics combining the teleological approach to the good life with others in community with the deontological restrictions on actions that cannot be universalized. With John Rawls we can say that the "the good shows the point, justice draws the limit". This idea of an ethical liberalism is viewed as the limit of utilitarian and pragmatic actions and decision-making. This connection between teleology, deontology and utilitarianism is proposed as the normative framework for business and economic markets. Thus, we can argue that ethics functions as the basis for a normative use of economics. When we analyse decision-making and organizational actions of firms in the framework of ethical theories, we are integrating the perspective of ethical responsibility for the good life and universal norms as a basic limitation for the economic calculation of efficiency in the perspective of rational choice individualism, welfare-utilitarianism or liberalism of unlimited personal freedom.

To resume our view of republican business ethics we can say that the concern for the good life materialized in the idea of "good corporate citizenship" where the corporation not only wants to earn money on the economic market, but also seeks to contribute to the common good of the community. The idea from Ricoeur of "the good life for and with the other in just institutions" can be considered as the fundamental ethical basis for economic action. Within the teleological concern for the good life, rights and duties conditioned by the Kantian categorical imperative propose restrictions and limitations of economic action based on respect for human dignity, property rights and other relevant legal principles. Only on such a universal foundation may we take into account the utilitarian welfare calculations of John Stuart Mill and Jeremy Bentham about the greatest good for the greatest number.

We can find support for such subordination of economic action of the ethical perspectives of republican business ethics as the basis for good corporate citizenship in James Buchanan's theories of constitutional economics and of public choice as social choice.[62] In the perspective of political economy, the market action of the firm is not independent of general political consideration. According to the theory of constitutional economics, we can say that managers on the boards of corporate governance are very much like governmental leaders or writers of constitutions who are deliberating not only about strategic rules but also about which ethical principles and values the firm should follow. Moreover, the firm is to be viewed as much more than a nexus of contracts. It is rather a constitutional arrangement where management and the board as a kind of constitutional governance mechanism are

---

61   See for example Peter Singer (1993), *Practical Ethics*, Cambridge: Cambridge University Press.
62   Knudsen, *Økonomisk metodologi II*, ibid., p. 245.

formulating basic principles and values for the corporations. As a constitution the basic ethical values and principles are not limited to the realm of the organization – in the words of Douglass North, "the institutional arrangements of the organizations" – but may also be said to refer to the "institutional environment of the firm".[63]

To use the idea of the constitution as a metaphor for what the board or the general assembly does when it formulates basic norms and values for the organization is to focus on corporate governance and decision-making processes as based on business ethics judgments. In these processes the ethical theories of Aristotle, Kant and Mill function as external limits of self-interested action. Therefore we can define business ethics as kind of "economics of self-control", making an institutional and constitutional arrangement fundamental for management and relations with stakeholders.[64] Thus, we will argue for a "tensional integration" of the different views of the firm in business ethics. The rational choice view and stakeholder theory should be considered in the perspective of ethical liberalism, which again can be considered as a kind of "integrated social contract theory" emerging as a republican view of the firm as a "good corporate citizen". The basis for this convergence of ethics and economics in constitutional economics is a combination between Herbert Simon's idea of "procedural rationality" combined with John Rawls's idea of the "veil of ignorance" and Jürgen Habermas's concept of communicative rationality as the basis for organizational decision-making.[65]

Ethics Out of Economics

In the previous section we focused on ethics as a limitation of economics. However, we may also argue that there is an internal ethical dimension of economics and even that it is possible to define what can be considered as valid ethical behaviour out of economic reason.[66] The issue is what economics can help to say about the good life and how economics as a moral science contributes to a better society. According to the Austrian economists like Karl Menger, Von Miss and to some degree Alexander Hayek, economics may be considered as a kind of "praxeology", a normative science of practical reason, based on universal categories of human

---

63 Ibid., p. 254.

64 Ibid., pp. 263–264.

65 Jürgen Habermas (1981), *Theorie des kommunikativen Handelns I–II*, Frankfurt: Suhrkamp Verlag.

66 See for example Broome, *Ethics out of Economics*, ibid., 1999. Broome even thinks that ethics and politics should learn a lot from economics. However, Broome seems to work within the utilitarian tradition of welfare economics and it is not clear whether he would opt for the neoclassical view of the necessity of a market without legal and political restrictions. Broome's views seem to impose rather strict limitations on economic markets in comparison to the radical libertarianism of Robert Nozick and also Milton Friedman, who both argue for an ethics implicit in economic markets.

action and helping to realize the human good.[67] They proposed a rationalistic and interpretative paradigm of economics in which it was argued that economics could be based on synthetic *a priori* principles. There is also much convergence between utilitarian ethics and traditional views of normative economics. Economics is viewed as the science of calculation of efficiency, profit and maximization of personal and common human preferences.

In-so-far as institutional organization theory is founded on ideas of self-interest and efficiency in the maximization of profits, it seems to presuppose some kind of utilitarian ethics. However, this is utilitarianism with a strong emphasis on personal and egoistic interests. Indeed this is the case with neoclassical economics and we have seen how the concept of human beings as self-interested and potentially opportunistic actors has been taken over by theories of economic organization like transaction costs economics and agency theory. Transaction cost economics considers firms as contractual relationships among individuals who seek to maximize self-interest, and the fight against opportunism on the basis of lawful behaviour within contracts can be considered as a defence of an ethics of good governance and high performance in efficient economizing market institutions.[68] Agency theory focuses on economic property rights as the basis for economic behaviour.[69] When we propose an ethics of constitutional economics, we are not only looking at the firm in the light of micro-economics, but we also consider the organization as integrated in larger social and political systems.[70] We want to state that individual instrumental economic reason only has significance in the framework of ethics subordinating individual goals to the common interest of community.

In opposition to this view we have to admit that there may be many important aspects of economic principles of self-interest and rational action that can help to shape ethics. Orthodox economists argue that efficient allocation of scarce resources is based on minimal governmental and legal intervention and that free actors are the best placed to know how to respect the norms of the market and ethical customs of society.[71] Major economists like Adam Smith and Milton Friedman, but also John Stuart Mill, believed that the economic rationality of seeking self-interest and profit maximization in economic markets on its own contain an important form of rationality where everyone, by seeking to fulfil their own interests, will contribute to the common good. Business ethics cannot ignore this ethics of the market, which can contribute to an economic shape of ethics

---

67   Mahieu, *Éthique économique, fondements anthropologiques*, ibid., p. 120.
68   Williamson, *The Economic Institutions of Capitalism*, ibid., p. 129.
69   Jensen, "A Theory of the Firm, Governance, Residual Claims and Organizational Forms", ibid.
70   Knudsen, *Økonomisk metodologi II*, ibid., p. 262.
71   Diane L. Swanson (2002), Business Ethics and Economics, in *A Companion to Business Ethics*, Blackwell Companions to Philosophy, Oxford: Blackwell, pp. 207–217, at p. 210.

within the rules of market economy. Within such a view of the ethical rationality of economic thinking we describe below the norms of economics that are important for the common good of society.

According to what may be called the cost–benefit efficiency view of economic ethics, free economic action in economic markets is the best way to deal with scarce resources.[72] This view may have two formulations. The first stresses the role of the state in establishing a dynamic market economy and the second stresses that the autonomy of the private sector is the most efficient way to allocate scarce resources. Economic actors are characterized by responsible, conscious use of scare resources. Economics is about efficiency and prudent use of resources. Moreover, organizational action should be profitable. According to economic rationality, we cannot ignore the bottom line of income and expenditures for the success of corporate action. Economics is about creating value and maximizing profits in terms of individual or social wealth and utility. Economics is the science of efficiency and utility for society and economic action is about ensuring the most efficient way to deal with scarce resources.

Economics can also be considered from the perspective of social development. Utility theory is based on Pareto optimality (that is a situation of economic arrangements where a change of the situation cannot make the situation better for some without making it worse for others).[73] Welfare economists stress the role of the state in such situations while libertarians consider that the free market gives the best optimality. Thus economics is the science of how to compare and weigh the different goods of society and allocate scarce resources most efficiently. Economic action is about how to contribute to creating wealth in markets and thereby create wealth in society. It is advisable to contribute to economic goods within the basic rules and ethical principles of society, and it would not be just to not respect the laws and principles of economics when acting in economic markets. Economic action based on utility contributes to maximization of efficiency within limits of respect for basic rights.

An important aspect of such a concept of economic ethics is the idea of the "invisible hand" from Adam Smith, stating that, if everyone acts according to his own interests respecting the rules of fair competition in economic markets, society will flourish and individual self-interested action will be a contribution to the common good. We also find this idea of the ethical consequences of individual self-interested action in Alexander Hayek's philosophy of the "spontaneous order" of economic and social development. During evolution based on interaction among self-interested individuals, those practices which are based on individual freedom and rational choice of the most efficient alternative will in the long run contribute to social betterment. Indeed, better legal and moral systems will be a result of this spontaneous order. Fair competition and healthy economic institutions will in an economic system based on fair competition contribute to a better society. In this

---

72   Ibid., p. 211.
73   Ibid., p. 210.

perspective the idea of competition includes an ethical dimension of fairness and transparency contributing to the spontaneous order of society.

If we conceive economics as implying a particular ethical rationality, we may consider how economic institutions contribute to ethics. The ethics of economics in institutional arrangements is the promotion of rational self-interest and fair competition as an instrument for economic progress. As John Dienhart acknowledges, according to the institutional view of economics, markets are considered as "ethical engines".[74] The aspect of economizing that we have discussed may very well be considered as a part of economic institutions as ethical engines. However, the concept of economic rationality is broader and more pluralistic than the view of fair economic markets as exclusively based on the pursuit of self-interest.

Thus we can distinguish between an internal and an external approach to ethics and economics. According to the external approach economic rationality is based on self-interest and there is complete separation between ethics and economics.[75] Economic engines can help us to attain ethical values, but economics as such is neutral. However, as we have seen, there seems to be an ethics implied in economic rationality. Therefore, we can argue for an internal approach according to which ethics is not only considered as an external limitation to economics but also as part of economics. The internal approach does not necessarily have to rely on a utilitarian and neoclassical concept of economic ethics, though. Rather we can have a pluralistic approach to the ethical values that have an impact on economic action. Thus, ethics is to be considered as an internal aspect of economic institutions and there is an ethical dimension to economic concepts like property, risk-reward structures, information and competition.

This implies that we should have an institutional approach to economics emphasizing that institutions determine economic action.[76] The constitutive rules and principles of economic markets based on property, risk-reward structures, information and competition include certain ethical ideas which are the conditions for development of economic systems. Douglass North has, for example, shown how the act of promising is a condition for good contracts that in turn conditions predictions of future economic action.[77]

When we deal with the institutional aspects of property rights, risk–reward structures, information and competitive relationships, we may say that the internal ethics of the economics of fair markets is about how to organize scarce resources in economic systems in a fair way. To respect property rights is viewed as the

---

74   John W. Dienhart (2000), *Business, Institutions and Ethics. A Text with Cases and Readings*, Oxford: Oxford University Press, p. 145.

75   Ibid., p. 146.

76   See Powell and DiMaggio, *The New Institutionalism in Organizational Analysis*, ibid., p. 293ff.

77   Dienhart, *Business, Institutions and Ethics. A Text with Cases and Readings*, ibid., p. 149.

foundation of the economic system and part of fair competition is not to question basic property rights. Adam Smith and after him most libertarian economists have, for example, always been saying that property rights should be considered as the foundation of the economic order.[78] We may say that our use and definitions of property rights in the centre of a corporation is based not only on considerations about self-interest, but rather on a combination between teleological, deontological and utilitarian considerations. External intervention is necessary when basic rights are not respected in economic transactions on economic markets. This is the case when we encounter widespread corruption with regard to property rights in economic systems.

Concerning contracts, we can also emphasize some implicit ethical values that are required to be fulfilled in economic interactions. This is evident when some transaction cost theorists have stated that governance structures to avoid opportunism as well as to maintain confidence and promise-keeping matter for economic interaction.[79] With regard to information, we may also encounter certain ethical principles within economic interactions. Correct and reliable information is a condition for trustful relations of economic action on different economic markets. It is a requirement for good contracts that they are based on reliable information.

The principles of fair and healthy competition may indeed also be an important aspect of the ethical principles of competitive markets.[80] Norms about monopolistic practices constitute internal limitations on economic interactions. It is a widespread belief that monopolistic action is at the limits of economic systems and possible economic behaviour in liberal economic markets.

If we analyse the ethics of transaction costs economics it may be argued that a contract view of the firm is not sufficient to conceptualize the ethical dimensions of organizations. Organizations are not only universes of micro-contracts but are based on values that function as organizational goals for corporate behaviour. Transaction costs economics addresses ethical problems in organizations when it discusses problems of opportunistic behaviour with regard to information, agency and liability of individuals, but it cannot explain loyal and altruistic behaviour in organizations. It may be true that organizations try to control organizational behaviour and ensure efficiency in competition by setting up institutional infrastructures based on contracts.[81] However, the question is if this really is sufficient to understand cases of lack of opportunistic behaviour in organizations?

With Herbert Simon we can argue that transaction cost economics cannot explain why people identify with organizations and feel much more committed than is

---

78   Ibid.

79   Williamson, *The Economic Institutions of Capitalism*, ibid., p. 63.

80   See for example Milton Friedman's discussions of healthy markets in *Capitalism and Freedom*, ibid.

81   Dienhart, *Business, Institutions and Ethics. A Text with Cases and Readings*, ibid., p. 177.

required from the perspective of self-interest.[82] Authority–employee relationships and motivation cannot be understood as incomplete contracts, but rather as being based on the goals and values of the organization as implicit premises for decisions. Employee motivation is therefore not only based on economic incentives but also on loyalty with the goals of the organization. Moreover, organizations should not only be understood as micro-markets of competitive contracts but rather as also instruments for coordination of human action, which facilitate action on economic markets.[83] In such a goal-based view, the rationality of utility based on "economic man" cannot be the only explanation of the function of organizations on economic markets, but goal-oriented and community-based behaviour is a much more important aspect of organizational action. However, within new institutional theory we can perceive an orientation towards integration of different aspects of rationality when dealing with economic institutions.[84] Therefore it may be possible to find a sort of convergence between a goal-based and a contract-based view of organizations.

From this initiative to deduce ethics out of economics we may conclude that ethics is not always external but also sometimes implicit in economic rationality. We can say that ethical aspects of economics are based on the values of the basic concepts of economic systems. We can point to organization of market structures and the most important concepts of economic markets: "property, risk–reward relationships, information and competition".[85] The system of these concepts is not neutral but cannot but imply ethical values. These values are not only based on economic efficiency but include a plurality of ethical rationality reflecting individual goals, organizational values and community values. Moreover, economic organizations are not only determined by self-interested individuals acting according to utility values, but the ethical values of economic organizations are more complex and they also include personal values of individual members of organizations.[86] However, the plurality of values also implies great tension between traditional economic values of utility and self-interest with community values based on ethical liberalism.

---

82   Herbert Simon (1995), Organizations and Markets, *Journal of Public Administration Research and Theory*, 5(3), pp. 273–293.

83   Dienhart, *Business, Institutions and Ethics. A Text with Cases and Readings*, ibid., p. 180.

84   Powell and DiMaggio, *The New Institutionalism in Organizational Analysis*, ibid., 1991, p. 294.

85   Dienhart, *Business, Institutions and Ethics. A Text with Cases and Readings*, ibid., p. 182.

86   Ibid., p. 182.

Business Ethics between Ethics and Economics

We can now conceive this tension between economics and ethics as the methodological framework for business ethics. The starting point is the pluralism of ethical values within the economic systems, which, however, includes utility and efficiency as predominant values. After this we can conceive the ethical foundation of economics with the principles of republican business ethics as external limitations of economic action. Ethics may be conceived as a kind of political theory of market economies and we cannot ignore the perspective of the state.[87] Business ethics is not only about the relation between ethics and economics, but it is also about finding the right balance between political governance of market economies with legislation and legal incentives for economic behaviour.

In this way we can say that the centre for business ethics is the problems of ethical behaviour of the firm in relation with its surroundings at the market and in society at large. Business ethics is about the right values at the micro-level of organizations, but also about individual behaviour in organizations and at the macro-level. In this sense business ethics is about defining acceptable ethical positions of the firm within society and in relation to the state. Business in the ethical perspective is not only a descriptive and positivist discipline about the factual values of organizations, individuals and market systems, but also concerns the normative question of which values should be promoted for the relation between organizations, individuals, and market economies in a broader social and political context.

Thus business ethics can be conceived as being based on an interdisciplinary approach to the social sciences integrating views from economics, sociology, political science, law, organization theory and ethics in order to discuss the right values and ethical principles to be promoted in business life. From our discussion of the dialectical relation between ethics and economics, we have learned that ethical liberalism proposes a broader concept of "social man" as the foundation for economic anthropology than the strong idea of "economic man" only following self-interest as the foundation of business ethics. Utility-maximizing individuals are not guided by absolute principles of utility, but personal preferences only acquire meaning within the context of a "vision of the good life for and with the others in just institutions".[88]

Even though we have proposed the ideas of the vision of the good life and the universalistic restrictions on acceptable moral action, which should be based on the Kantian categorical imperative, we have also admitted that there is a tension between the economic principles of maximizing self-interest and the ethical principles of community and respect for the moral law. Business ethics has always to deal with this tension between narrow economic perspectives of efficiency and utility and broader concepts of social justice in the perspective of the interests

---

87 See Rendtorff, Critical Hermeneutics in Law and Politics, ibid.
88 Ricoeur, *Soi-même comme un Autre*, ibid., p. 202.

of community and society. We cannot dissolve this tension between ethics and economics, but we can try to search for decision-making and action, which can promote a convergence between ethics and economics.

When we analyse the notion of rational choice and decision-making of the firm, we can perceive how organizational behaviour and decision-making are characterized by what we may call impure "economic reason". Decision-making does not only follow the ideals of economic man, but it is based on "bounded and procedural rationality", which does not exclude ethical and political dimensions of decision-making. These aspects of organizational decision-making represent a documentation of the fact that firms are not isolated economic entities, but they should be conceived as social units, implying pluralistic concepts of rationality.

Within this view of economic action, rationality in economic theory is not based on "Homo economicus of individual preference maximization", but on individuals who are integrated in social relations of reciprocity and exchange. This social notion of rationality places the economic actor within an ethical community of values and therefore the firm must be conceived in the perspective of broader institutional and social dimensions.[89] It is reciprocity and exchange of social man in community which constitutes the basis for understanding economic action.

From this starting point our considerations on business ethics and values-driven management view the vision of the good life with others in community as the outer determination of economic action. This vision of the good life can be explained as the "licence to operate of the firm". However, we cannot have the vision of the good life without testing this vision on the perspectives of universal principles of the categorical imperative, so that a licence to operate should require universalistic foundations. On these foundations we can then look at economic action in the perspectives of utility and self-interest and this economic action may contribute to shaping our perception of ethical dilemmas and opportunities for economic action. On this basis we may take into account the practical reality of economic action as conditioned by pressures of time, competition and resources, which we would have to shape and evaluate in terms of the values of business ethics.

An important faculty to promote mediation and decision-making in the application of ethical principles in relation to concrete situations of economic decision-making and action is the idea of moral and ethical judgment.[90] The concept of judgment as Immanuel Kant develops as a universal faculty is his *Critique of Judgment*.[91] The Kantian concept of judgment extends the Aristotelian idea of practical reason, *phronesis*, which is the capacity of deliberation and reasoning for the good life in community according to the moral sense and habitus of the experienced moral actor. In this context judgment finds the right place of action,

89　Mahieu, *Éthique économique, fondements anthropologiques*, ibid., p. 314.

90　Lynn Sharp-Paine (1994), Law, Ethics and Managerial Judgment, *The Journal of Legal Studies Education*, 12(2), 153–159.

91　Immanuel Kant (2004), *Kritik der Urteilskraft* (1794), Frankfurt: Suhrkamp Werkausgabe.

the mean of virtue and consistency between extremes. Kant not only considers the importance of the mean for finding the good life, but he also points to the moral sentiments and common morality of human beings, *sensus communis*. Moral judgments find universal validity in the appeal to common sense and shared values of human beings.

Determinate judgment is the capacity to apply already established general rules to concrete cases. Reflective judgment is the ability to find new rules for new cases where there are no pre-established rules or principles that are intuitively given or self-evident. Judgment in business ethics is only the application of ethical principles to factual cases. Rather it should also be responsible for mediating between ethics and economics in relation to other disciplines of social sciences which are important for decision-making and research. What is required in reflective judgment is moral imagination and the ability to integrate and weigh up judgments in different disciplines and from different viewpoints with regard to concrete decision-making. The faculty of judgment – applied to decisions-makers in the good citizen corporation – can be said to have two major results: economic efficiency and contribution to the integration and development of society towards the ideal of a community of ends in themselves.

In this case reflective judgment also constitutes the mediating bridge between micro-economic rationality of free market economics, based on individual economic actors on the one hand and macro-economic rationality of welfare and rights in political community on the other. Ethical liberalism uses the faculty of judgment in order to celebrate the internal ethical dynamics of micro-economics, but also to set external ethical limits on economic actions in order to contribute to social justice in community. This means that business ethics does not only operate on the micro-level of ethical behaviour of individual rights and ethics in firms. It also operates at the level of organizational behaviour and more broadly at the level of market institutions. However, business ethics goes further and takes the point of view of state regulation and macro-economic ethics concerning the significance of the organization of market economies for the general development of society.

It is the task of reflective judgment to mediate between these different ethical fields. It is very important to have an integrated perspective on the relations between micro- and macro-levels of ethical reflections. Therefore, we neither opt exclusively for an ethics of the lonely "moral manager", nor solely for an ethics of the economic market or of the business system as a structural totality, nor for an ethics of political welfare economics, based on allocation of goods and services by democratic political authorities. To focus exclusively on one of these fields of ethics may lead to negligence of important knowledge. However, even though reflections on basic ethical principles and values of business should integrate these fields, the main focus of the present discussion is situated at the level of the firm. From this viewpoint we will discuss problems of tensions between economic efficiency and ethics at the other levels of application of reflective judgment.

Indeed, the concern for justice as the ultimate horizon for analysis of ethics and values should be mentioned. The concern for human realization and freedom may be based on such a concern for ethical aspects of justice. John Rawls's concept of justice as fairness is an important basis for evaluation of values-driven management, which focuses on efficiency and utility in neoclassical economics. This ethical horizon for economics based on social justice as optimum equality of the market place is not only based on economic concerns for just distribution of marginal utility, but we may also consider the satisfaction of the basic social needs of citizens, provision of an institutional framework for enabling human freedom and the rights of citizens to satisfy their need for self-respect and dignity as a part of this normative approach to business and economics.[92]

This normativity implies that we conceive the concepts of wants, utility (pleasure), competition and freedom to consume in neoclassical economics to be in tension with social values like needs, self-actualization, cooperation, freedom to grow and self-realization through work as potential goods.[93] These ideas may be considered necessary in order to promote justice as fairness as the basic structure of society. It is, in the perspective of business ethics, the aim of business institutions to contribute realization of the vision of the good life within just institutions and to help to improve fair coexistence in the framework of the Kingdom of Ends in themselves.

---

92   Mark A. Lütz and Kenneth Lux (1979), *The Challenge of Humanistic Economics*, Menlo Park, CA: Benjamin Cummings, p. 171.

93   Ibid. p. 160.

Chapter 8

Developing Durability: A Re-Examination of Sustainable Corporate Social Responsibility[1]

Güler Aras and David Crowther

Introduction

One of the most used words relating to corporate activity at present is the word "sustainability" (Aras and Crowther, 2008a), which seems to appear in every corporate report and is ubiquitous in the business press. Indeed it can be argued that it has been so heavily overused, and with so many different meanings applied to it, that it is effectively meaningless. For example, according to Marrewijk and Werre (2003), there is no specific definition of corporate sustainability and each organization needs to devise its own definition to suit its purpose and objectives, although they seem to assume that corporate sustainability and corporate social responsibility (CSR) are synonymous and based upon voluntary activity which includes environmental and social concern, implicitly thereby adopting the EU approach. There are a number of problems with the popular understanding of the term sustainability – not least that it is about environmental issues – which we intend to discuss in this chapter. It is our argument that the misunderstandings have prevented serious discussion of the most important features of sustainability, which we redefine and use the term durability to signify a stronger form of sustainability.

There has been considerable change in the emphasis of a corporation's reporting of its activity which has taken place in recent years, not least of which are the extension of disclosure and the re-designation of CSR activity as sustainability action. This change is not just in terms of the extent of such reporting, which has become more or less ubiquitous throughout the world, but also in terms of style and content. When researching into corporate activity and the reporting of that activity in the 1990s, it was necessary to acknowledge (Crowther, 2002) that no measures of social or environmental performance existed which had gained universal

---

1 The ideas in this chapter are a development of the ideas in our recent book, *The Durable Corporation: Strategies for Sustainable Development* (Aras and Crowther, 2009). Inevitably there is some repetition of some of those ideas in order to situate the development of the ideas in this chapter, and some of the ideas form the basis of various papers published elsewhere. Anyone interested can pursue these through the book and the papers referred to in this chapter.

acceptability. Good social or environmental performance was subjectively based upon the perspective of the evaluator and the mores of the temporal horizon of reporting. Consequently no report concerning such performance could easily be made which would allow a comparative evaluation between corporations to be undertaken. Sustainability has always been one of the key principles of CSR, but recently it has become the most ubiquitous one, with all corporations claiming to address it and many replacing their CSR reports with Sustainability reports.

Sustainability is of course merely the latest concept to be adopted by corporate managers in their reporting/publicity – the two are often indistinguishable (see Aras and Crowther, 2008b). Prior to this the term "corporate responsibility" – or "corporate social responsibility" – had been in vogue and before this terms such as the "triple bottom line" and "business process re-engineering" can be used to trace the concepts back through the idea of the balanced scorecard to the early days of TQM.[2] One question that arises, therefore, concerns whether these are truly new techniques or refinements of existing management techniques. We argue that this does not matter but the concepts do force a re-evaluation of what is meant by competitive advantage and how it can be sustained. In this paper we examine its philosophical and practical foundations, reject them and develop our own concepts with practical applications. This commences with a brief review of utilitarianism and its problems.

The Development of Utilitarianism

Classical liberal theory started to be developed in the seventeenth century by such writers as John Locke as a means of explaining how society operated, and should operate, in an era in which the divine right of kings to rule and to run society for their own benefit had been challenged and was generally considered to be inappropriate for the society which then existed. Classical liberalism is founded upon the two principles of reason and rationality: reason in that everything has a logic which can be understood and agreed with by all, and rationality in that every decision made is made by a person in the light of what their evaluation has shown to be their greatest benefit. Classical liberalism therefore is centred upon the individual, who is assumed to be rational and make rational decisions, and is based upon the need to give freedom to every individual to pursue his or her own ends. It is therefore a philosophy of the pursuance of self-interest. Society, insofar as it exists and is considered to be needed, is therefore merely an aggregation of these individual self-interests. This aggregation is considered to be a sufficient explanation for the need for society. Indeed Locke argued that the whole purpose of society was to protect the rights of each individual and to safeguard these private rights.

---

2   Total quality management – one of the earliest of the programmed change initiatives stemming from the work of Peters and Waterman (1982).

There is, however, a problem with allowing every individual the complete freedom to follow his or her own ends and maximize his or her own welfare. This problem is that in some circumstances this welfare can only be created at the expense of other individuals. It is through this conflict between the rights and freedoms of individuals that problems occur in society. It is for this reason, therefore, that de Tocqueville argued that there was a necessary function for government within society. He argued that the function of government therefore was the regulation of individual transactions so as to safeguard the rights of all individuals as far as possible.

Although this philosophy of individual freedom was developed as the philosophy of liberalism, it can be seen that this philosophy has been adopted by the Conservative governments throughout the world, led by the Thatcherite[3] UK government in the 1980s. This philosophy has led increasingly to the reduction of state involvement in society and the giving of freedom to individuals to pursue their own ends, with regulation providing a mediating mechanism where deemed necessary. It will be apparent, however, that there is a further problem with liberalism, and this is that the mediation of rights between different individuals only works satisfactorily when the power of individuals is roughly equal. Plainly this situation never arises between all individuals and this is the cause of one of the problems with society. This disequilibrium in power relationships means that the markets based upon individual freedom and predicated on the perfect competition assumptions of elementary economics can never exist. This can also be seen to be one of the root causes of the governance failures of the 2008 financial crisis.

While this philosophy of liberalism was developed to explain the position of individuals in society and the need for government and regulation of that society, the philosophy applies equally to organizations. Indeed liberalism considers that organizations arise within society as a mechanism whereby individuals can pursue their individual self-interests more effectively than they can alone. Thus firms exist because they are a more efficient means of individuals maximizing their self-interests through collaboration than is possible through each individual acting alone – primarily through enabling the raising of capital and the supposed lowering of transaction costs. This argument provides the basis for the Theory of the Firm, which argues that, through this combination between individuals, the costs of individual transactions are reduced.

The concept of utilitarianism was developed as an extension of liberalism in order to account for the need to regulate society in terms of each individual pursuing, independently, his or her own ends. It was developed by people such as Bentham and John Stuart Mill, who defined the optimal position for society as being the maximizing of good (utility) and is commonly – but mistakenly – interpreted as the greatest good of the greatest number; they argued that it was the government's

---

3 Margaret Thatcher is well known for having pronounced that there is no such thing as society. Many would say that the actions of her government were designed to make this statement true.

role to mediate between individuals to ensure this societal end. In utilitarianism it is not actions which are deemed to be good or bad, merely outcomes. Thus any means of securing a desired outcome is deemed to be acceptable and, if the same outcomes ensue, then there is no difference, in value terms, between different means of securing those outcomes. Thus actions are considered to be value neutral and only outcomes matter. This is of course problematical when the actions of firms are concerned because firms only consider outcomes from the point of view of the firm itself. Indeed accounting, as we know, only captures the actions of a firm insofar as they affect the firm itself and ignores other consequences of the actions of a firm. Under utilitarianism, however, if the outcomes for the firm are considered to be desirable, then any means of achieving these outcomes is considered acceptable. In the nineteenth and early twentieth centuries this was the way in which firms were managed and accounting information was used purely to evaluate actions and potential actions from the point of view of the firm itself. It is only in more recent times that it has become accepted that all the outcomes from the actions of the firm are important and need to be taken into account.

The development of utilitarianism led to the development of economic theory as means of explaining the actions of firms. Indeed the concept of perfect competition is predicated in the assumptions of classical liberal theory. This is a problem because it encourages selfish and exploitative behaviour. Therefore, we can either believe that the market will mediate in an optimal way – which is complete nonsense – or we can suggest that ethical understanding will compensate – also nonsense. Or we must look for an alternative.

In 1762 Jean-Jacques Rousseau produced his book on the social contract, which was designed to explain – and therefore legitimate – the relationship between an individual and society and its government. In it he argued that individuals voluntarily gave up certain rights in order for the government of the state to be able to manage for the greater good of all citizens. This is of course in sharp contrast to the angry rhetoric of Tom Paine.[4] Nevertheless the idea of the social contract has been generally accepted. More recently the social contract has gained a new prominence as it has been used to explain the relationship between a company and society and legitimate the existence of corporate social responsibility. In this view the company (or other organization) has obligations towards other parts of society in return for its place in society. Most people would argue that the extension of the social contract to corporations provides an answer, through a voluntary giving up of some autonomy for the greater good and subjection to regulation. We do not believe that this is the answer.

---

4   "It is impossible that such governments as have hitherto existed in the world could have commenced by any other means than a total violation of every principle sacred and moral" (Paine, 1792).

Brundtland and Sustainability

Sustainability is a controversial topic because it means different things to different people. Nevertheless, there is a serious debate about what sustainability means and the extent to which it can be delivered by multinational corporations in the easy manner they promise (United Nations Commission on Environment and Development; Schmidheiny, 1992). The starting point must be taken as the Brundtland Report (WCED, 1987) because there is explicit agreement with that Report and because the definition of sustainability in it is pertinent and widely accepted. Equally, the Brundtland Report is part of a policy landscape being explicitly debated by the United Nations, nation-states and big business through the vehicles of the World Business Council for Sustainable Development and ICC (see for example, Beder, 1997; Gray and Bebbington, 2001). Its concern with the effect which action taken in the present has upon the options available in the future has directly led to glib assumptions that sustainable development is both desirable and possible and that corporations can demonstrate sustainability merely by continuing to exist into the future (Aras and Crowther, 2008b). It is important therefore to remember the Brundtland Commission's definition (WCED, 1987, p. 1) of sustainable development, which is one of the most accepted definitions and provides the foundation to all approaches to sustainability. It is that sustainable development is "development that meets the needs of the present without compromising the ability of future generations to meet their own needs".

This definition is, of course, problematic and a moment's reflection will show it to be meaningless and impossible to enact. Mankind has been affecting the choices available to future generations for at least 10,000 years, since the giant fauna were hunted out of existence and trees subsequently chopped down to make farmland. Nevertheless this report makes institutional and legal recommendations for change in order to confront what are described, and generally acknowledged, as common global problems. Increasingly, therefore, there is a growing consensus that firms and governments in partnership should accept moral responsibility for social welfare and for promoting individuals' interests in economic transactions (Amba-Rao, 1993).

Significantly, however, the Bruntland Report made an assumption, which has been accepted ever since – that sustainable development is possible – and the debate since has centred on how to achieve this. Thus ever since the Bruntland Report was produced by the World Commission on Environment and Development in 1987 there has been a continual debate concerning sustainable development (Chambers, 1994; Pretty, 1995). Similarly emphasis has been placed on such things as collaboration, partnerships and stakeholder involvement (Brown et al., 2002). It has, however, been generally accepted that development is desirable and that sustainable development is possible – with a concomitant focus on how to achieve this. Quite what is meant by such sustainable development has, however, been much less clear and a starting point for any evaluation must be to consider quite what is meant by these terms.

There is a considerable degree of confusion surrounding the concept of sustainability: for the purist sustainability implies nothing more than stasis – the ability to continue in an unchanged manner – but often it is taken to imply development in a sustainable manner (Marsden, 2000; Hart and Milstein, 2003) and the terms "sustainability" and "sustainable development" are for many viewed as synonymous. For us, we take the definition as being concerned with stasis (Aras and Crowther, 2008a); at the corporate level, if development is possible without jeopardizing that stasis, then this is a bonus rather than a constituent part of that sustainability. Moreover, sustainable development is often misinterpreted as focusing solely on environmental issues. In reality, it is a much broader concept as sustainable development policies encompass three general policy areas: *economic*, *environmental* and *social*. In support of this, several United Nations texts, most recently the 2005 World Summit Outcome Document, refer to the "interdependent and mutually reinforcing pillars" of sustainable development as economic development, social development and environmental protection.

Although it is over 20 years old, the starting point for any review of sustainability must be the Brundtland Report (WCED, 1987), because its definitions have been universally accepted. According to this report sustainability is concerned with the effect which action taken in the present has upon the options available in the future, and of course if resources are utilized in the present then they are no longer available for use in the future.

The problem with Brundtland is that its concern with the effect which action taken in the present has upon the options available in the future has directly led to glib assumptions that sustainable development is both desirable and possible and that corporations can demonstrate sustainability merely by continuing to exist into the future (Aras and Crowther, 2008c). It has also led to an acceptance of what must be described as the myths of sustainability:

- sustainability is synonymous with sustainable development;
- a sustainable company will exist merely by recognizing environmental and social issues and incorporating them into its strategic planning.

Both are based upon an unquestioning acceptance of market economics predicated in the need for growth and are based upon the false premise of Brundtland, to which we will return later. An almost unquestioned assumption is that growth remains possible (Elliott 2005) and therefore sustainability and sustainable development are synonymous. Indeed the economic perspective of post-cartesian ontologies predominates and growth is considered to be not just possible but also desirable (see for example Spangenberg, 2004). Therefore, it is possible for Daly (1992) to argue that the economics of development is all that needs to be addressed and that this can be dealt with through the market by the clear separation of the three basic economic goals of efficient allocation, equitable distribution and sustainable scale. Hart (1997) goes further and regards the concept of sustainable development merely as a business opportunity, arguing that once a company identifies its environmental strategy then opportunities for new products and services become apparent.

Sustainable development is a notoriously ambiguous concept, as wide arrays of views have fallen under its umbrella. The concept has included various notions of weak sustainability, strong sustainability and deep ecology with different meanings attached to them. The meanings attached to these different conceptions also reveal that there is a strong tension between ecocentrism and anthropocentrism, with corporations tending to assume the anthropocentrism position. Thus, the concept remains weakly defined and contains a large amount of debate as to its precise definition. Nevertheless it is generally accepted that environmental degradation[5] is occurring and that in the short-term, environmental degradation leads to declining standards of living, the extinction of large numbers of species, health problems in the human population, conflicts, sometimes violent, between groups fighting for dwindling resources, water scarcity and many other major problems.

As far as corporations and sustainability are concerned, however, it is essential to recognize the realities of the global environment (see Aras and Crowther, 2007a, b) insofar as the company is firmly embedded into a global environment which necessarily takes into account the past and the future as well as the present. This effectively makes a stakeholder out of everything and everybody both in the present and in the future. Sustainability therefore requires a distribution of effects – positive and negative – in a way which eliminates conflict between all of these and pays attention to the future as well as the present. Thus a short-term approach is no longer acceptable for sustainability

Developing a Full Discourse of Sustainability

One of the roles of accounting is of course to exercise control through the measurement of performance. The inadequacy of accounting has been recognized by many, such as Johnson and Kaplan (1987), who argue that the role of accounting has changed so that it is no longer relevant to managerial needs. It has also been argued (Crowther, 2002) that, although one aspect of managerial need is that of internal control of organizational activity and resource allocation, this is not in fact the prime need for accounting information which is used for the semiotic purpose of creating the desired impression of an organization.

We argue that the accounting discourse of operational performance is predicated in cost reduction as a means of achieving efficiency, while the sustainability discourse is predicated in other factors. For example, one factor it is predicated in is the environmental sustainability discourse, which is epitomized by such work as Jacobs (1991), Welford (1997) and Gray and Bebbington (2001). Equally, a second is predicated in the going concern principle of accounting as epitomized

---

5   At present one of the topical issues is, of course, climate change, which is almost universally accepted as occurring.

by the corporate reporting described earlier. Thus the two discourses tend to run in parallel without actually communicating – and corporate sustainability requires this communication. Although seemingly incompatible, all of these discourses are actually based on an acceptance of a conventional view of the transformational process, as shown in Figure 8.1.

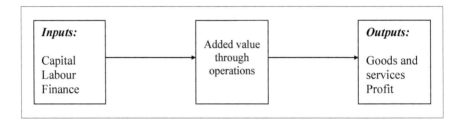

Figure 8.1 The traditional transformational process

This model assumes that inputs (of capital, labour and finance) are used to make goods and services through the employment of the operational factors of production (e.g. employees, suppliers) in order to make goods and services with a resultant profit. The implications of this conventional view of the transformational process are that the inputs can be freely acquired in the desired quantities and that the operational factors of production are commodified. This view of the process enables mediation through the market and is legitimated by the views of such as Spangenberg (2004), referred to earlier.

There are, however, two fundamental flaws with this form of analysis, from a sustainability perspective:

1. The input referred to as capital actually represents environmental resources and these are quite definitely finite in quantity (Daly, 1996). Thus the market cannot mediate adequately as the ensuing competitive bidding will raise the price but will not bring more of the resource into the market because there is no more in existence. Substitution can compensate for shortages only to a limited extent: it is difficult, for example, to see the extent to which more finance or labour can compensate for the absence of oil or any other fuel.
2. The factors of production are not actually commodities: rather they are stakeholders of the organization. It may aid analysis to commodify them but they require benefits from the organizational activity. In particular, when resources are recognized to be finite, market mediation in this way does not satisfactorily accommodate the requirements of all stakeholders to the organization. Thus these stakeholders need to become a part of the output section of the transformational process.

The transformational process therefore needs to be redefined (see Aras and Crowther, 2009) and the revised transformational process is therefore depicted as shown in Figure 8.2.

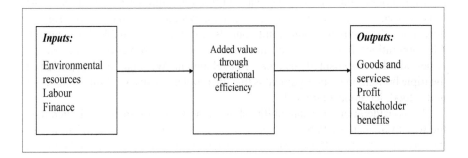

Figure 8.2 The revised transformational process

As far as inputs to the transformational process are concerned, it is apparent that environmental resources are finite and effectively fixed. Currently all the environmental resources of the planet are in use (some would say overuse) and, with no more available, then the resources for one corporation can only be increased by taking them from another through the process of competition in the market place. From a global perspective, rather than that of an individual firm, then this highlights two alternative routes to development. The first is through the substitution of environmental resources with other inputs – labour or finance. The second is through making better use of the available environmental resources – effectively doing more with less. Both require technological development in order to bring them into effect and so sustainable development essentially requires technological development – also known as research and development – in order to be tenable. This is the first point of intersection whereby sustainability comes into conflict with organizational accounting. Technological development for sustainability requires the more efficient use of environmental resources whereas accounting efficiency requires the more effective use of financial resources, with a focus on cost reduction. Sustainable development, therefore, requires greater use of human resources, particularly highly skilled people, in order to develop that technology, and this of course will incur additional cost. Accounting efficiency requires the replacement of people – particularly skilled and therefore expensive people – with relatively low-cost techniques such as programmed change initiatives, business process re-engineering, etc., and computer based management systems. We therefore argue that the use of conventional accounting to a large extent is in direct opposition to the concept of sustainability.

As we have seen, the universally accepted definition of sustainability is that it is concerned with the effect which action taken in the present has upon the options available in the future. The problem is that this concern has led people to simply accept that sustainable development is both desirable and possible. More importantly, it has effectively prevented discussion about the real issues concerning sustainability.

There have been various descendants of Brundtland, including the concept of the triple bottom line. This in turn has led to an assumption that addressing the three aspects of economic, social and environmental is all that is necessary in order not only ensure to sustainability but also to enable sustainable development. All corporations imply that they have recognized the problems, addressed the issues and thereby ensured sustainable development. We argue for a rejection of the triple bottom line; our argument is that the problem of sustainability is not even understood, let alone addressed.

A reconsideration of sustainability shows that when resources are limited then the way to manage sustainable development is through the more efficient use of those resources. Thus all corporations are practising cost management and efficient operational management as a matter of course but also as a means of achieving sustainability.

Conventionally corporations grow by consuming more resources but redefining the problem shows us that natural resources are finite and fully committed, so growth through the use of more natural resources is not possible. These are the scarce resources – not finance. Consequently efficiency must be redefined away from financial efficiency and applied to the use of natural resources. Growth requires us to do more with less, so innovation, technology and R&D become more important. Therefore, we must redefine the transformational process to provide a more realistic description of the input resources used and the potential for substitution, and to highlight that growth must come through technological improvement rather than through the use of more resources.

This gives a different model of sustainability and in this model it is also important to note that none of the stakeholders are merely factors of production but are also affected by, and hence concerned with, the results of corporate activity, as described through the transformational process. At this point therefore we deliberately use the term *distributable sustainability* in order to reflect one of the key components of this argument. This is that true sustainability depends not just upon how actions affect choices in the future but also upon how the effects of those actions – both positive and negative – are distributed among the stakeholders involved. A central tenet of our argument is that corporate activity, to be sustainable, must not simply utilize resources to give benefit to owners, but must recognize all the effects upon all stakeholders and distribute these in a manner which is acceptable to all of these – both in the present and in the future. This is in effect a radical reinterpretation of corporate activity.

It is necessary to consider the operationalization of this view of sustainability. Our argument is that sustainability must involve greater efficiency in the use of resources and greater equity in the distribution of the effects of corporate activity. To be operationalized then, of course, the effects must be measurable and the combination must of course be manageable. This can be depicted as a model of sustainability (Figure 8.3). This acts as a form of balanced scorecard to provide a form of evaluation for the operation of sustainability within an organization. It concentrates upon the four key aspects, namely:

- strategy;
- finance;
- distribution;
- technological development.

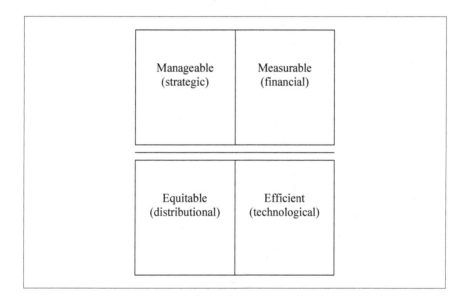

Figure 8.3 The facets of sustainability

Moreover it recognizes that it is the balance between these factors which is the most significant aspect of sustainability. From this plan of action it is possible for an organization to recognize priorities and provide a basis for performance evaluation.

Creating and Sustaining Excellence

It is our argument that each of these four components is a necessary component of sustainable competitive advantage but none is sufficient by itself. It is the combination which is essential for that competitive advantage and it is only when the four coincide that this is achieved. This can be expressed differently in terms of profitability, sustainability, good governance and corporate reputation as a means of achieving business excellence (Aras and Crowther, 2009). This excellence is represented by the segment of overlap in Figure 8.4. Moreover, each component addresses both short-term and long-term performance in order to create competitive advantage, although each component addresses the two in a different balance.

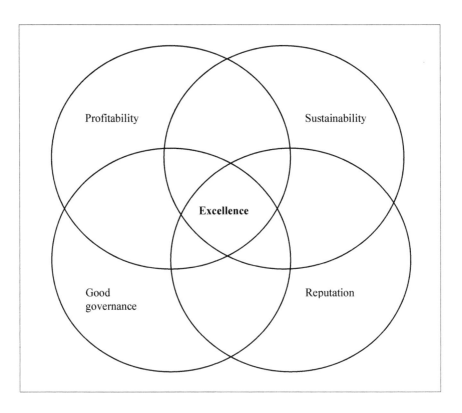

Figure 8.4 Business excellence for competitive advantage

Over 25 years ago Peters and Waterman (1982) considered business excellence in terms of managerial behaviour. Our re-evaluation is more holistic, being concerned with the company as a whole: indeed each of our components is focused upon this. Moreover we have not sought to suggest that any single factor is more important than the others, although we recognize that their relative importance may well vary from one company to another or from one time period to another, depending upon the economic and market factors that might be faced. Essentially, however, our argument consists of not superordinating any one of these factors. It does not matter which of them is the most important as it is the balance between them which is the key to excellent performance. This balance therefore is also the key to creating and sustaining competitive advantage. Effectively therefore this combination can be considered to be a form of balanced scorecard as a guide to managing a business. Like any generic balanced scorecard, of course, it needs to be adapted to individual circumstances and merely acts as a point of focus.

Developing Durability

To summarize, sustainability requires a radical rethink and a move aware from the cosy security of the Brundtland definition, which we consider to have prevented any serious debate about the issues concerned.[6] We therefore reject the accepted terms of sustainability and sustainable development, preferring instead to use the term "durability" to emphasize the change in focus. We describe durability as a stronger and more robust form of sustainability, the essential features of which can be described as follows:

- Efficiency is concerned with the best use of scarce resources. This requires a redefinition of inputs to the transformational process and a focus upon environmental resources as the scarce resource.
- Efficiency is concerned with optimizing the use of the scarce resources (i.e. environmental resources) rather than with cost reduction
- Value is added through technology and innovation rather than through expropriation.
- Outputs are redefined to include distributional effects to all stakeholders.

Durability is more than a focus upon the triple bottom line. It requires a rethink of organizational processes. It is also more than success – which is achieving organizational objectives such as growth as well as profit – and of course it is more than profit. However, all of these are aspects of durability. It is necessary of course to consider the operationalization of our view of durability. Our argument is that durability must involve greater efficiency in the use of resources and greater equity in the distribution of the effects of corporate activity. To be operationalized then, of course the effects must be measurable and the combination must be manageable. This acts as a form of balanced scorecard, as described earlier. Moreover it recognizes that it is the balance between these factors which is the most significant aspect of durability. We can depict durability as illustrated in Figure 8.5.

The two key components of durability therefore are efficiency and equity, but efficiency needs to be redefined to prioritize the efficient use of environmental

---

6   We do not suggest of course that this prevention of serious debate was deliberate. It was an unintended consequence brought about by the universal and unquestioning acceptance of the Brundtland definition. Similarly it is an unfortunate consequence of the sustainability debate being hijacked by the environmental lobby and therefore the debate being restricted primarily to environmental issues when in reality it is much more complex than that.

resources rather than the efficient use of financial resources, and equity requires as a minimum the satisficing[7] of all stakeholders, and not merely the provision of returns to owners and investors. These are the prerequisites for any kind of sustainable development.

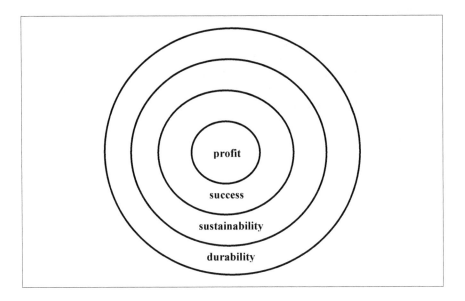

Figure 8.5 The durable company

These can be considered as a hierarchy of organizational behaviour – from profitability to success to sustainability to durability, with durability at the pinnacle as the ideal (Figure 8.6). All are necessary for the survival of the organization – and also to the survival of the planet as we know it.

We can also look at it the opposite way – in terms of corporate potential. A durable company practises sustainability through its concern for the social and environmental as well as the economic, and a sustainable company is of course successful, and a successful company is of course profitable. However, all of this is potential for any company but realized for a durable company – both in the present and in the long term (Figure 8.7). Our argument is that, once the problem is redefined, then equity becomes inevitable – it is in everyone's interests, and moral behaviour becomes enacted through the market.

_____

7   Satisficing is a term coined by Simon (1957) to mean the making of decisions which are good enough – rather than optimal – when there are multiple and competing objectives. In this case we mean that all stakeholders must consider the distribution of effects to be acceptable.

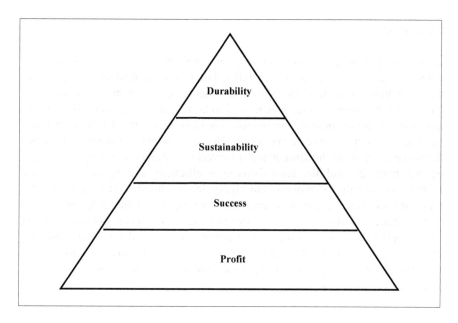

Figure 8.6 Developing a durable company

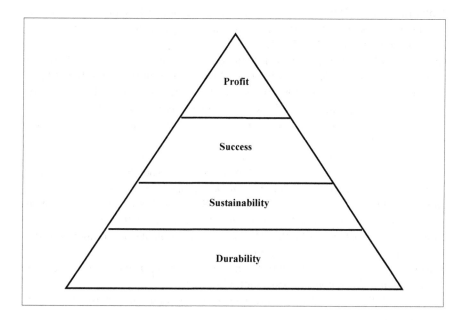

Figure 8.7 The potential of a durable company

Conclusions

As we have shown, the focus of corporate activity has shifted recently to a greater concentration upon sustainability, but in this context our argument is that Brundtland, with its definition of sustainable development, has misdirected concern to the wrong issues, which need to be re-examined. Rather than trying not to affect future choices – an obvious impracticality – the debate must focus upon the efficient use of scarce resources. Hence we refer to "durability" to signal the move away from the Brundtland misdirection. Moreover we argue that any debate about sustainability must focus upon efficiency and equity – efficiency in the transformational process and equity in the distribution of effects. The focus of such concern cannot be upon the three aspects of the triple bottom line – another misdirection. Instead we have introduced our concept of durability as an appropriate vehicle for corporate strategic planning and for sustainable and long-lasting development. In doing so our aim is to move the discourse to the next level and enable some progress to be made in addressing the real issues regarding sustainable corporate activity.

References

Amba-Rao, S. C. (1993), Multinational Corporate Social Responsibility, Ethics, Interactions and Third World Governments: an Agenda for the 1990s. *Journal of Business Ethics*, 12, 553–572.

Aras, G. and Crowther, D. (2007a), Is the Global Economy Sustainable?, in *The Geopolitics of the City*, S. Barber (ed.). London: Forum Press, pp. 165–194.

Aras, G. and Crowther, D. (2007b), Sustainable Corporate Social Responsibility and the Value Chain, in *New Perspectives on Corporate Social Responsibility*, D. Crowther and M. M. Zain (eds). Shah Alam, Malaysia: MARA University Press, pp. 119–140.

Aras, G. and Crowther, D. (2008a), Governance and Sustainability: An Investigation into the Relationship between Corporate Governance and Corporate Sustainability. *Management Decision*, 46(3), 433–448.

Aras, G. and Crowther, D. (2008b), Corporate Sustainability Reporting: a Study in Disingenuity? *Journal of Business Ethics* 98(suppl. 1), 279–288.

Aras, G. and Crowther, D. (2008c), The Social Obligation of Corporations. *Journal of Knowledge Globalisation*, 1(1), 43–59.

Aras, G. and Crowther, D. (2009), *The Durable Corporation: Strategies for Sustainable Development*. Aldershot: Gower.

Beder S. (1997), *Global Spin: the Corporate Assault on Environmentalism*. London: Green Books.

Brown, K., Tompkins, E. L. and Adger, W. N. (2002), *Making Waves: Integrating Coastal Conservation and Development*. London: Earthscan.

Chambers, R. (1994), The Origins and Practice of Participatory Rural Appraisal. *World Development*, 22(7), 953–969.

Crowther, D. (2002), *A Social Critique of Corporate Reporting*. Aldershot: Ashgate.

Daly, H. E. (1992), Allocation, Distribution, and Scale: Towards an Economics that is Efficient, Just, and Sustainable. *Ecological Economics*, 6(3), 185–193.

Daly, H. E. (1996), *Beyond Growth*. Boston, MA: Beacon Press.

Elliott, S. R. (2005), Sustainability: an Economic Perspective. *Resources, Conservation and Recycling*, 44, 263–277.

Gray, R. and Bebbington, J. (2001), *Accounting for the Environment*. London: Sage.

Hart, S. L. (1997), Beyond Greening: Strategies for a Sustainable World. *Harvard Business Review*, 75(1), 66–76.

Hart, S. L. and Milstein, M. B. (2003), Creating Sustainable Value. *Academy of Management Executive*, 17(2), 56–67.

Jacobs, M. (1991), *The Green Economy – Environment, Sustainable Development and the Politics of the Future*. London: Pluto Press.

Johnson, H. T. and Kaplan, R. S. (1987), *Relevance Lost: The Rise and Fall of Management Accounting*. Boston, MA: Harvard Business School Press.

Marrewijk, M. van and Werre, M. (2003), Multiple Levels of Corporate Sustainability. *Journal of Business Ethics*, 44(2/3), 107–119.

Marsden, C. (2000), The New Corporate Citizenship of Big Business: Part of the Solution to Sustainability. *Business and Society Review*, 105(1), 9–25.

Paine, T. (1792), *The Rights of Man*, many editions.

Peters, T. J. and Waterman, R. H. (1982), *In Search of Excellence*. New York: Harper and Row.

Pretty, J. N. (1995), Participatory Learning for Sustainable Agriculture. *World Development*, 23(8), 1247–1263.

Rousseau, J.-J. (1762), *The Social Contract, Or Principles of Political Right*, many editions.

Schmidheiny, S. (1992), *Changing Course*. New York: MIT Press.

Simon, H. A. (1957). *Models of Man: Social and Rational*. New York: Wiley.

Spangenberg, J. H. (2004), Reconciling Sustainability and Growth: Criteria, Indicators, Policies. *Sustainable Development*, 12, 74–86.

WCED (World Commission on Environment and Development) (1987), *Our Common Future* (The Brundtland Report). Oxford: Oxford University Press.

Welford, R. (1997), *Hijacking Environmentalism – Corporate Responses to Sustainable Development*. London: Earthscan.

Chapter 9

Global Principles (as)(or) Ethical Responsiveness: The Case of Sustainability Rhetoric

Mollie Painter-Morland

Introduction

When a small child shares his favourite sweets without being asked to do so, or when a person behind you on the train picks up the $100 dollar bill you dropped and returns it, or a stranger sees that you are lost in a new city and offers advice, when you gaze in a loved one's eyes, something happens. Something that makes life seem worthwhile and makes the world a better place. What we tend to do when thinking about these events is to find something "general" to celebrate, or to infer from it general "rules of good practice". We are quick to name it "justice", "kindness", "altruism" (or even "true love"). We may even claim: "Well, everyone knows what the right thing to do is". Much has been written about the fallacy of this kind of sophistry, and I will not dwell too much on these arguments. What I want to consider is whether we do not employ the same kind of slippage when we formulate global principles in business ethics and corporate social responsibility (CSR). Could it be that in our fervour to standardize good conduct, we have lost the ethical moment itself – the moment of ethical responsiveness that happens only in a relationship, that is lost when that specific relationship is forfeited and that has to be reinvented constantly as the relationship changes.

The question that I would like to address is whether it is still possible to view the existence of global principles *as* ethical responsiveness? Could it be that global principles undermine and contradict ethics as such? That they contain elements that are inextricably oxymoronic? For the purposes of this chapter, I will be focusing on the notion of sustainability and the global principles that have been developed and advocated around it. I will be analysing prevalent global sustainability rhetoric, and seeking to indicate that, in and of itself, these principles do little to foster the ethical responsiveness required to procure "sustainability". Does this mean that it has to be abandoned? Not necessarily. It does mean that the terms associated with it constantly need to be re-evaluated, which includes an ongoing reassessment of the relational dynamics informing it. This process may be performative in nature and may include grappling with the relationship between ethics and aesthetics.

Global Principles (and) Ethical Responsiveness

There are a few ways in which global principles may undermine ethical responsiveness. Global principles operate on a level of generality that allows them to be relevant regardless of context. These principles purport to shed light on certain fundamental beliefs and seek to set standards that should be applied consistently. Now this may seem like a good thing in a world within which we would like to encourage certain behaviours and hold corporations accountable. However, paradoxically, we may be undermining our most important ethical "talent", i.e. the capacity for ethical responsiveness. In my mind, ethical responsiveness entails at least the following: (1) the capacity for re-evaluation; (2) the possibility of a unique response, also called discretion; and (3) the capacity for questioning. I will argue that, as it stands, global sustainability principles, left to their own devices, do little to contribute to any one of these facets of ethical responsiveness.

Ethical Responsiveness as the Capacity for Re-evaluation

> What then is truth? A mobile army of metaphors, metonyms, and anthropo-
> morphisms – in short, a sum of human relations, which have been enhanced,
> transposed, and embellished poetically and rhetorically, and which after long use
> seem firm, canonical and obligatory to people: truth are fictions about which has
> been forgotten that this is what they are: metaphors which are worn and without
> sensuous power; coins which have lost their pictures and now only matter as
> metal, no longer as coins. (Nietzsche, 1954, p. 42)

Global principles are truth statements – statements about what we believe the right thing to do *is*. Typically, they do not contain "ifs" or "buts", but make rather categorical claims about the nature and characteristics of good conduct. As such, they seek to represent a "picture" of ethical responsiveness. The question becomes, however, whether ethical responsiveness can be "pictured" in the way that global principles hope to do and what happens when these pictures become "standard practice".

What seems to be at stake here has to do with language, and with what it can and cannot do. Nietzsche came to the conclusion that every language is a dictionary of faded metaphors. He believed that figures of speech and rhetoric preceded all conceptualization. In this respect, his definition of tropes, or "figures of speech" is unique. He did not believe that tropes stood in contrast to literal uses of language, because all language relies on indirect designations.[1] In his view tropes should therefore be considered the fundamental linguistic paradigm and not

---

1 See in this regard Christian Emden's research in his book *Nietzsche on Language, Consciousness and the Body* (2005) for a discussion of how Nietzsche drew on the work of Jean Paul and a host of other scholars of his time to develop his metaphoric account of truth.

a deviation. Nietzsche argues that all language displays certain anthropologically necessary constructions that help us to organize our environment and make sense of experience (Emden, 2005, p. 79).

Since his account of language and his view of the body are closely related, Nietzsche's trope-ical account of language is grounded in both rhetoric and physiology. Our awareness of our bodies and our desire to interact with others prompt us to use words as "uncertain allusion to things". In the process, we relate our awareness of objects and experiences to other objects and experiences. Because each designation draws on a broad network of references, it is capable of drawing together a variety of symbols, images and allusions in a dense network of meaning.

Nietzsche argues that truth is essentially an estimation of value linked to very practical concerns. "Truth" is the result of human attempts to create a stable point of reference from which to deal with particular relational dynamics. Although "truth" is a useful construction, it becomes a lie when people begin to see it as something permanent and unchangeable. Truth can therefore never be fixed, because to do so would be to deny life's vitality (Heidegger, 1987, p. 66). In Heidegger's reading of Nietzsche, values are part of the process by which we schematize chaos just as much as is required to move us in the direction of self-transcending enhancement (ibid., p. 80). For Nietzsche, the ongoing reconstruction of values is part of the creative process that keeps us alive, both physically and mentally. Heidegger (1987, p. 76) points out that the Greek word "khaos" literally means, "the gaping". For him chaos denotes a peculiar preliminary projection of the world and the forces that govern its dynamics. This schematizing takes place in and through our embodied existence. As such, life for Nietzsche is "bodying writ large". Nietzsche became convinced that our experience as embodied beings determines not only *what* and *how* we see, but also what we imagine. He believed that it is from the particularity of our embodied experience that we begin to discover the relative value of that which we encounter in the world.

There is an opportunity and a threat hidden in an acceptance of the fact that we navigate our environments and relationships by accepting language as this trope-like encounter with the world. The danger lies in believing that all moral truth has become completely relative, that a person literally makes it up as she or he goes along. This threat only exists if we believe that individuals live in a solipsistic cave of isolation and self-sufficiency. We do not live in isolation though … and it is precisely our relationships that make the trope-like nature of values an opportunity rather than a threat. It can mean that, as relationships change, we can re-evaluate the term based on the changing relational dynamics we have to people and places. This is the ethical opportunity.

Regarding our topic here today, the question that Nietzsche would have us ask is: what have we come to accept as "truth" when it comes to global sustainability principles? When reading sustainability principles, they seem again, relatively self-evident. What I would like to argue is that it is precisely the fact that these principles seem "self-evident" that allows the hidden relational constructs that underpin them to go unchallenged.

The typical definition of sustainability is: "Meeting our current needs without compromising the ability of *others*, or *future generations* to meet their needs". What is often not considered is the relational content assumed in the notion of "need". We typically treat the needs of others as instances or slightly different iterations of our own needs. We seldom allow our interactions with others to challenge the legitimacy of our own needs. Instead, we unproblematically assume that it is the right thing to do to give the whole world what the First World has. Man's needs have become defined as consumer needs, and if these consumers do not exist, they are quickly created. We never stop to consider whether the needs of others can in fact be represented in this way. We have no insight into the fact that need itself is a completely relational construct that hardly makes sense outside of relationships. What needs to be considered is the relational dynamic within the various contexts within which "sustainability projects" are launched. One sees, for instance, that small and medium-sized enterprises will not employ the term CSR, although they do respond to community need in their own ways, and use different concepts to talk about these "needs".

What seems to be happening is that certain relational constructs, normally designed by those of power and influence, have become entrenched as the fixed foundation from which "need" is defined and operationalized. The "need" that no one questions is the need to maintain the profit interest of those who claim to bring democracy to the world. Paradoxically, it slips very specific ideological contents into the notions of "freedom", "democracy" and "rights", and ultimately, "sustainability".

Banerjee (2006) argues that American foreign policy that claims to be aimed at "spreading democratic values" is in fact aimed at promoting a brand of American liberal democracy to "create a global system based on the needs of private capital including the protection of private capital and open access to markets". What is even more problematic, Banerjee points out, is that not all aspects of democracy are considered equal in this process: property rights and rule of law are a must, but fair elections, active civil society, etc., are not considered indispensable. In the process, freedom becomes the freedom to consume, which of course creates markets for First World products. Free trade becomes the process of creating conditions for the exploitation of developing countries' resources, both natural resources and cheap labour. Democracy becomes the process by which oil interests and the First World lifestyles that depend on it are protected. Sustainability is too often defined as the ability to thrive into perpetuity, but should any business be perpetuated? What is not questioned is growth for growth's sake, the "profit-motive", and the power disparities that often remain unchallenged in much of CSR and sustainability rhetoric.

Also, the real context of limited global resources is conveniently left out of the equation. China has 1.3 billion people, and India nearly as many, who want to live like Americans. This is just not possible in terms of limited energy resources.

The whole concept of need will have to be re-evaluated from the perspective of multiple relational dynamics that have changed and continue to change globally. The question is whether it is possible for it to be redefined? We cannot know the "need" of future generations, yet this renders us *more*, not less responsible. It is a responsibility to second-guess ourselves, to acknowledge the fact that we cannot know, and that we therefore have to be very, very careful in what we assume. We also have to prepare ourselves to be surprised, as the world is changing very quickly and we may just be confronted with the need to respond to a set of unique dynamics. Rehearsing the same strategies and repeating old mantras may fail us.

The Possibility of a Unique Response

Acknowledging the fact that the values underpinning sustainability rhetoric may be questionable is only part of the process. What may be even more pressing is the need to rediscover the kind of responsiveness that makes specific moral acts possible. In very simple terms, the question that we have to confront is whether various singular acts of kindness, justice, love, etc., are instances of the same global principles that we keep reiterating. If it is, then the formulation of global principles is indeed a helpful and consistent application of these essential, but if there is something unique to an ethical response, something that requires a specific relationship to make any sense, the general formulation may fall short. In fact, it may serve as a mere reminder of the impossibility of repeating or applying the ethical notion of which it speaks in any real sense. The work of Derrida made us aware of the impossibility of applying, or arriving at, "justice", or "forgiveness" in any final sense. This impossibility should, however, not render us helpless to seek out causes worth mobilizing around. Our dilemma lies precisely in the fact that we want to resist the totalizing effect of universal constructs and remain critical of their political, ideological assumptions, without losing the ability to use those very terms to instil hope and lobby around social causes. This dilemma is the one we have to confront in being ethically responsive.

The problem of the relationship between the general and the specific has plagued philosophy for centuries, but thought about it was given new impetus in twentieth-century poststructuralist philosophy. Our very capability of referring to objects and making sense of our world and our relationships with and within it depends on the ability to formulate concepts that can make sense beyond the various specific instances out of which it originated. The downside, however, is that, in order to speak generally, we have to gloss over some of the characteristic specific events or objects. We lose sight of the fact that the specific does to some extent conform to the name it is given, but never completely. This is of course the central idea behind Derrida's notion of *différance*. Meaning is always different from that which a word is trying to represent, and it is always deferred, i.e. never final, always postponed. However, instead of always having some awareness of how it always remains different, and how it changes over time, it is of course easier to work with how it does conform.

Simon Critchley (1992, p. 37) points out that, for Derrida, all language and codes are constituted as and by a weaving of differences. It is precisely these differences that render mute the distinction between text and context, or what has become known in applied ethics as the application of text to context. Text is context, context is text. The relational dynamics within which the ethical demand presents itself is principled, unconditionally so, but the principles have no existence outside of this relational dynamic. The question then becomes how to remind ourselves of these differences, these postponements. How can we keep the context alive in the text? How do we remind ourselves that the text is in fact (con)text? How do we protect the singular ethical demand that only happens in relationship when making a statement in a context in which the relational dynamics are not immediately clear, or at least have been watered down. This question becomes especially poignant in the context of international business where relationships have become fluid, faceless and merely functional.

What seems to be needed is an awareness of the fact that meaning is always a result of how a word, concept or experience relates to other words, concepts or experiences, which may of course change over time. A concept like "justice" therefore does not represent a "thing", but is rather a reflection of relationships between people over time, and as such, *in* and *through* time. Foucault's analysis of this problem in his work on the famous Magritte's painting, in his book by the same name, *This is not a Pipe* (1973), sheds light on the way in which Magritte manages to combine words and images to put at risk precisely those representational references that both the words and images rely upon in order to make sense. In his interpretation of Foucault's distinction between similitude and resemblance, Mark Taylor (2001) reminds us that resemblance gives way to similitude when meaning is relational rather than referential. In my mind, we have come to mistake the principles that we have so cleverly formulated as ethics itself. The picture of the pipe is seen as the pipe itself, and we have lost the self-reflexive feedback loop that reminds us of the relational play of similitude that makes the concept meaningful in the first place.

How do we rediscover the self-reflexive moment in our formulation and use of global principles? Exploring the diachronic process of ethical responsiveness in and through the synchronic ontological frames of reference that formulations of global principles inevitably confront us with may be our most serious challenge. Many authors have tried to explain why this is such a problem. Levinas brings us to the paradoxical discovery that, in making ethical statements, we are covering over and losing sight of precisely that which we are trying to elucidate. In other words, the basic problem with the employment of ethical statements and directives, as with all philosophical language, is precisely the fact that it aims to enlighten, to shed light, to provide clarity.

Phenomenology has been offered as a response to this problem, but Derrida makes it clear that, despite its best intentions, phenomenology also perpetrates this "violence of light" (Derrida, 1978, p. 104). As Michael Naas (2003, p. 98) explains, it is precisely this light that blinds the (non)relation to the other. In a sense, this leads to a conundrum for those of us wanting to question the way in which we use global principles. The language of ethics cannot critique ethical violence without employing precisely such violence, or as Derrida (1978, p. 114) puts it, all languages do combat within the light. It is, however, in acknowledging and accepting this inevitable violence that the self-questioning that resists ethical violence is precipitated.[2]

What does this tell us about the relationship between global principles and the specificity that is required for them to have any real force? Derrida made a distinction between the law in general (*la loi*) and the law in the strict sense or legal justice (*le droit*). It is therefore possible to allow for the existence of the law (*la loi*) without necessarily referring to legal matters. Yet one cannot make a specific legal judgment, for instance, without invoking the other, more general form of law, i.e. *la loi*. Similarly, *la loi* only comes into operation within institutions that give it its force. Any form of law (*le droit*) therefore inevitably evokes various aporias. The judge must refer to the notion of law in her judgment, but in order to appeal to the law (*le loi*) she is expected to judge anew at the same time, as if constantly reinventing the law anew. Derrida's discussion of the judge's obligation to follow the rule and not to follow the rule helps us develop a sense of the kind of task that is at hand in using global principles. Ethical responsiveness is at once regulated and unregulated. Johan Van der Walt (2005) argues that Derrida's Force of Law describes the kind of judgment that involves a phenomenological suspension of the rule. This also entails a suspension of the natural consciousness operative in the "reductions" that typically constitute the phenomenological method. When confronted with any specific decision, we are charged with the responsibility to follow its gist and yet redefine what it means. As Critchley (2004, p. 180) explains, the rule itself takes shape within that decision, it is not formulated beforehand. Yet the criterion by which the rule emerges is universal. Within ethics, it is also the point where we confront the question of what to do or how to proceed. It is not so much the "application" of some generalized truth to a specific problem, but rather "the invention of" an ethical response that displays some congruence to the normative framework that exists, yet can and should never be consumed by or conflated with it.

We draw on what we have come to associate with a term such as "justice", but justice is always somehow new when seen in a new con-text and if we want to speak of ethical responsiveness it is our responsibility to facilitate this process. Something in the specificity of the moment or historical juncture that we are confronted with must unearth the sedimented understandings of the concepts we

---

2   Much has been written on the relationship between the law and the violence that founds it. See in this regard the discussion of the work of Agamben and Derrida in Johan van der Walt's book *Law and Sacrifice* (2005). For Agamben, the law lives off what it excludes, what can be constituted as the exception – what it sacrifices. For Derrida, the law relies on the mystical foundation of authority that entails a judgment that speaks to what exceeds the law, and yet grounds/founds the law.

mindlessly employ and problematize the violence it entails, yet we must always return to the concept again in order to give the principle its force. This is a tall order that does not just miraculously occur when we read global principles, sign on to them or develop strategies around them. It requires something more.

Authors such as Levinas have argued that the possibility of employing philosophical language only ever opens up as a result of the language of the Face that constitutes the ethical relation. That is, the encounter with the Other and the question of justice towards all the other others disrupts the ontological closure of the self as *said*. Since global principles tend to generalize and hence efface instead of facilitate face-to-face relations, one may ask whether this does not foreclose the possibility of ethics in the first place. It does not get us out of the entrapment of language either – the ethics of the face-to-face encounter is equally reliant on the existence of a language within which any response would take place. Since it is clear that many business interactions are "faceless", how is it possible for global business principles to help us re-imagine or relive the face-to-face encounters through which these principles come into existence in the first place?

Derrida makes it clear that every law or commandment confirms and encloses the possibility of the question. Yet there is very little of this questioning left in the functioning of global principles. From a Levinasian perspective, global principles translate the Other in terms of the self, making them palatable, safe. They incorporate and thereby obliterate the challenges made to the self.[3] Note for instance, the following excerpt from a multinational corporation's (Anglo-American's) set of "business principles":

> Though providing strong returns for our shareholders remains our prime objective, we do not believe that these can or should be achieved at the expense of social, environmental and moral considerations. Indeed, a long-term business such as ours will only thrive if it also takes into account the needs of other stakeholders such as governments, employees, suppliers, communities and customers.

Shareholders come first – by definition, they "share" the self-interest that defines corporate reality. In current corporate rhetoric, the "stakes" of the other others are defined in terms of the long-term interests of the self. As such, we lose the various interrelationships that should allow us the self-reflexivity we need. How do we get out of this bind? Derrida (1997) explores Levinas's concept of the third to discuss the relationship between ethics and politics, and as such, between impossible ethical demands and institutional realities. The third, and the question of justice, emerges from the first instance in the face-to-face encounter, as any response to this encounter presupposes language. When the face-to-face relationship between me and the other precipitates a consideration of all the other others who have

---

3   It has to be noted that many Levinas scholars have argued that "corporations" cannot be seen as moral agents in the way that individuals are.

to be included in the ethical demand, I am in fact considering the question of justice. Naas (2003, p. 105) refers to this as a possibility of "contra-diction", a contra-saying that happens when the existence of multiple Others (thirds) crash into our neat understanding of "principle".[4] The third as the very possibility of "counting" or "reckoning" may present us with a way to rethink the accountability of corporations and its agents in the specificity of corporate interactions.

Something of the critical interaction between philosophy as the "power and adventure of the question itself" and philosophical texts that function as events or turning points within this adventure has to be recaptured (Derrida, 1997, p. 99). What we have to rediscover is the relational and con-textual aspect of language alluded to above. It is the fact that language is supposed to be about relationship that seems to be missing – within global principles, the possibility of multiple face-to-face encounters may lie hidden from view, and this may allow us to view ourselves differently. Ethics relies on the kind of relationship that puts the self at risk – that puts everything back in play. Naas explains that the other interrupts ontology, but the third interrupts this very interruption in order to return to ontology with all its terms, and to allow for the possibility of phenomenological experience and analysis. It allows the welcoming of the Other, and the other others, whose existence may put me and my actions in question (Naas 2003, p. 108). Naas argues that, with the question that arises in and through the third, intentional consciousness, thematization, objectification, understanding and even calculation become possible. Without it, a consciousness of the ethical question, conscience itself, does not present itself. The question, according to Naas, is located at the threshold between ethics and politics. The third, and the question, allow for an intelligibility that presents the possibility of political and, as I will argue, institutional challenges. The questioning precipitated by the third allows justice to be thought. It allows us to navigate the ethical space between the immediate ethical demand occurring between me and the Other and the question of justice for, and accountability towards, all the other others. The fact that this broader political, juridical and institutional question is raised puts the one (the person or institution) asking the question in question. It precipitates the question: "Who am I?" or, "Who are we as a corporation?" As Levinas puts it, "To welcome the other is to question my freedom".

Ethical Responsiveness as the Capacity for Questioning

What I have proposed so far is that we may have to use the "(con)textual infrastructure" of global principles to draw out the kind of relational dynamic that could lead to rethinking ethical possibility in various contexts. With careful scrutiny, we may find that the global principle itself is a play of differences, and set

---

4   I argue this more fully in my paper, "Codes of Ethics: Ethical Questioning (and)(or) Questionable Ethics", presented at the Derrida and Business Ethics Conference on 15 May 2008.

of questions that could unsettle even the most self-contained egos. The question is – what would allow this kind of problematization, or contestation of the self, of the understanding of the self, to take place? As such, the language of self-interest may be precisely the point where we have to start the self-questioning, so as to provide us with ways in which the moral conscience may be stimulated. Even this language reflects a certain understanding of relationship – and we may have to start our questioning right here.

What is the "need" that sustainability rhetoric speaks of? *Whose* need does it speak of? Re-evaluating sustainability will mean rethinking our needs, and in order to do this, we will have to rethink who we are as individuals, and what corporations are.

The typical way of thinking about the corporation is as the epitome of private interest, as a means of production of goods and profit. However, in a global environment, the corporation is an investment vehicle "owned" by multiple, variable entities, and also by pension funds, by people like you and I. As such, our views on "need" and "justice" matter.

Yet even "social investment" still implies the demand for growth and profit maximization. Some authors, like James Gustave Speth (2008) would go even further to suggest a form of post-growth capitalism, which challenges the idea that "growth" is how corporate success has to be defined. He argues convincingly that consumer capitalism is incompatible with quality of life for most on the planet. Speth argues that growth is how Western societies attempt to reconcile liberty and equality – the only problem is that it does not work. His basic argument seems to be that progress has to be defined in terms of our relationships with other people.

The key to rethinking sustainability may lie in rethinking business as such. Why do corporations exist? What is their role in society? Within the recent CSR literature, corporations are defined as "citizens" of multiple societies, and even as political actors more influential than national governments.[5] Should we not stop to consider what this means? Multinational corporations (MNCs) increasingly seem to be cast in a political role, yet they do not share the other characteristics required to qualify them as political "agents". This is a scary notion if we take into consideration that corporations do not get elected and have very little capacity to represent the interests of the majority of people.

Corporations are also typically depicted as the centre of the stakeholder map. We may want to consider whether this reflects our current relational reality. In the face of current complex dynamics, the corporation finds itself in various positions on the stakeholder map, and has to redefine its response to stakeholders in more contingent terms. This would entail a process by which a corporation may rethink its growth targets in the light of the relationships it wants to foster and sustain, instead of the profit margins it wants to sustain. Some companies have already started doing this. Some decide against growth because they feel that sustaining

---

5   See Andrew Crane and Dirk Matten's research: *Corporate Citizenship: Towards an Extended Theoretical Conceptualization*, no. 04-2003 ICCSR Research Paper Series.

their current product line, employee base and interactions with communities makes more sense as a sustainable relational reality. Maintaining relational ties to customers and suppliers, fostering good relationships with their employees and strong teams and staying in touch with their local community are some of the most pressing concerns for these companies (Burlingham, 2005).

Unfortunately, this relational dynamic seems to be abandoned within large multinational corporations. Instead of viewing relationships as ends in themselves, they are defined in much more instrumental terms. Relationships typically have to serve the corporation's profit or reputational interest. In their triple bottom line reports, corporations tend to claim credit for social and environmental performance in their supply chain when this has reputational value. At the very same time, MNCs are quick to pass the buck down the supply chain when it comes to accountability for the violation of social and environmental standards – both in terms of attributability and costs.

The rhetoric of seeking the "moral high ground" in terms of social and environmental standards may in some cases be a convenient ruse that MNCs employ to yield benefit without reconsidering their own business model. In many cases, it allows them to pass on the costs of monitoring and auditing CSR standards to their supply chain, who can often not afford this additional burden (we found this in our research on small and medium-sized enterprises). The paradoxical result is that some of these international "CSR" initiatives in fact increase poverty instead of advancing sustainable development. The problem with these standards also includes the fact that they typically reflect the prevailing technologies and best practices of the countries in which they were developed and are not suited to the context in developing countries (UNIDO, 2002, p. 49).

In the current use of sustainability rhetoric, it is therefore not difficult to see that the motivation for sustainability is cast in terms of the longevity of the corporation itself. There is seldom any evidence of a self-reflexive moment, because current sustainability rhetoric relies on a one-directional representation of the other in terms of the self. The instrumental nature of the formulations we employ when making arguments for why certain global standards have to be upheld points to an inability of corporations to truly question their current business model. Instead, the legitimacy of sustainability projects, or any CSR action of the corporation for that matter, is typically defined in terms of efficiency *within* the current business model. We tend to think that, if the one cannot be translated into the other, it constitutes a dichotomy, a crisis of confidence, an impasse. Banerjee (2006, p. 62) argues that the problem with this dichotomy lies in the fact that, in public policy, legitimacy is subordinate to efficiency. What in effect happens is that "notions of legitimacy are discursively produced and defined by economic efficiency criteria".

The multiple attempts to indicate the relationship between social and financial performance is a case in point. One of the most comprehensive arguments on the merits of a broader sustainability approach to business is provided by Freeman et al. (2000), who argue that the business model that most corporations work with can and should be rethought considerably if businesses want to maintain long-term viability and profitability. Scholars who argue for a positive relationship between financial results and social and environmental concerns include Waddock and Graves (1997), Verschoor (1999, 2004, 2005) and Tsoutsoura (2004). Unfortunately, there seem to be as many dissidents who claim no positive correlation between social and environmental agendas and business result, and who dispute the methodology of scholars who argue otherwise (McWilliams and Siegel, 2000). Lynn Sharp Paine (2000, p. 319) points out that the relationship between ethics and economics has been highly variable, to say the least.

Despite the limited success in making this argument, boards still require proof that triple bottom line success is translatable to financial success. The "non-financial" must be translated to financial terms in order to have value, i.e. it has instrumental value only. This of course requires incommensurable goods to be compared on a single scale in order to make the "equation" work. If anything, the preoccupation with this rather meaningless exercise offers a distraction from the more pressing questions that will provide a more meaningful (con)text for the notion of sustainability. Questions about what is valued, why it is valued and by whom it is valued, never arise. Could it be that certain things that are valued are by nature "unsustainable"? Could it be that there is something in this logic of exchange that makes ethical responsiveness impossible? If we fail to engage with these questions, "sustainability" loses any real meaning.

What we may want to consider here is the implications of the fact that sustainability is always measured in monetary terms. Monetary interaction and calculation is the supreme vehicle of neutralization and generalization and as such it renders conversations about sustainability incapable of fostering the kind of ethical responsiveness that we seek. Bauman, in his analysis of Simmel's work, describes money as "that *Eigenschaftlos* abstraction of pure and neutral quantity devoid of substance and qualitative differentiation" (Bauman, 1992, p. 152). Transactions that involve money can be performed properly only under conditions of emotional neutrality, and as such, it depends on our ability to be completely without affect.

It is this affectless, bodiless nature of the world we have come to live in that makes it very difficult to reweave the relational fabric in and through which we come to understand notions such as "need", "care" and "justice" that underpin sustainability. Without the singularity of bodies, emotions, events, general global principles have lost the con-texts that make it a viable text. Seyla Benhabib (1992) makes this point well when she argues that the "generalized other" of moral philosophy is supposed to represent everyone, but in reality it represents the powerful. What she proposes instead is an "interactive universalism" that regards difference as starting point. In her view, when we arrive at a moral standpoint we should perceive it as a contingent achievement instead of as a timeless standpoint of legislative reason. It is maintaining this contingency within our commitment to global principles that remains a challenge within a global business environment. This insight has been acknowledged by more recent iterations of stakeholder theory that make reference to the "names-and-faces" approach to dealing with stakeholder interests (McVea, Freeman and Edward, 2005).

Rediscovering Global Principles (as) Ethical Responsiveness:
Ethics and Aesthetics

We have seen that if we want to rediscover the social, political and economic dynamics that underpin global principles, we have to go beyond the reassurances of the seemingly "self-evident" formulations of global principles. Much lies *between* the lines and *within* the very concepts employed by these formulations. We need to rediscover the possibility of being disturbed, disrupted and interrupted by the specificity of moral demands that originate from the relational dynamics in which we are immersed (Painter-Morland, 2008). The question is how to sustain this responsiveness without giving up all consistency in our commitment to general principles. This entails stimulating the kind of self-reflexivity capable of taking the moral appeal of a global principle seriously, whilst maintaining the acceptance of the differences that such a principle itself contains. This is, however, unlikely to take place deliberately, rationally, as any such a conscious process entangles us even further in the universalizing traps of language and instrumental argumentation. Many authors have turned to the aesthetic dimension is seeking a way out of the mastery of the rational subject and the inevitable solipsism and arrogance it entails.

Aesthetics has long been credited with the capacity to mediate between the general and the specific, and between rational autonomy and relational affect. In the work of Immanuel Kant, we see the belief that it is the aesthetic that contains the capacity to mediate between cognition (reason) and volition (will). Kant's third critique helps us to understand how it is possible that something like moral law can coexist with the belief in autonomous moral agency. This seems like quite a feat, and it is one that may contain some clues as to how restore global principles *as* ethical responsiveness. Mark Taylor (2004) argues that, for Kant, the beautiful work of art is a "self-organized being", operating according to an inner teleology which emerges out of a complex interplay of its parts.[6] This complex interplay constitutes the activity of the whole. Means and ends are internally related and co-constitute each other, making possible a self-reflexivity that is non-utilitarian. Herein lies the clue towards thinking about sustainability principles in non-utilitarian, non-instrumental terms. There is dynamics operative in the notion of sustainability itself that should allow for self-reflexivity, but in order to explore this, we may need aesthetics, rather than cognition.

It is the capacity of the aesthetic to bypass the iron grasp of reason and to draw on the tacit, subconscious and affective aspects of our subjectivity that makes the avenue many poststructuralist, postmodernist and critical theorists have pursued. For Nietzsche, the rich variety and sheer dynamism of the world that we encounter as embodied beings can never be adequately reified as truth or knowledge. He

---

6 Kant's distinction between mechanisms and organisms rests on the fact that mechanisms are driven by external purposes, i.e. utility, whereas organisms display an inner teleology or "intrinsic finality".

therefore suggests that we turn to art to make sense of our experience. For him, art allows us to reveal the order of the world as a body writ large in symbols, images and approximations. There is something in the aesthetic that allows us to tap into the wisdom that the body developed in and through the relational dynamics of many generations. This helps us to find out what we really care about and to discover aspects of ourselves that exist as a sheer possibility. One of Nietzsche's most succinct articulations of the relationship between emotions and moral convictions is his claim that morality is the "sign-language of the emotions" (Nietzsche, 1973, p. 92). Nietzsche challenges his readers to acknowledge the nature of values and to choose values that give creative form to the lives they desire.

There is, however, the risk that the aesthetic becomes just another form of solipsism, where each agent becomes the creative author of his own story. The postmodern *flâneur* with his fluid, non-committal stance and fleeting interactions is certainly not the ethically responsive agent that we are seeking. His self-written text is not the relational con-text that we have in mind in drawing out the interrelationships that could breathe life into global principles.

What seems to be needed instead is the kind of aesthetic engagement that taps into the relational fabric that is created over and *in* time. This relational fabric constitutes our subjectivity and that operationalizes differences in and through its engagements with various experiences, institutions, discourses, media and artistic genres. It is this kind of aesthetic that Brenda Carr Vellino (2004) writes about in her analysis of Bronwyn Wallace's talking lyric. She believes that the "network of relations" that informs this form of poetry leads to an ethical interdependence in which the subject is always speaking *from* and spoken *by* fragile, contingent and interdependent webbed communities. In her hybrid lyric form, Wallace weaves literary, visual, musical and documentary media together. This does not just break down the hierarchies between elite and popular culture, it also allows for discourses that are not typically part of academic ethics discourses to surface. Many of these discourses are those of abused women and other marginalized groups who typically do not have voice within principled ethical conversations precisely because of the fact that much of their suffering goes un*said*. It is the capacity of certain aesthetic forms to go beyond what can be said, precisely articulated and categorized within a principle, which may offer us the mediation between the specific and the general. It is often the silences that require our attention if we want to claim to be ethically responsive. In this silence there is an awareness of contingency that makes the principle real.

Part of what would be important here is the act of witnessing over time, telling stories, in various ways and in various voices. This creates an awareness of the fact that every generalized moral statement is only possible because of many experiences, relational dynamics and real events that occurred over time. Contrary to the way we normally phrase the relationship between general and specific, it is not the general global principle that gets applied to the context. Various con-texts over time create the principle, and could make it meaningless too. The storytelling weaves the fabric that gives the principle substance. There is something in interacting with the stories people tell over time that breaks through the neutral generality that effaces relationships. The story will most likely not be a neat grand narrative, with a single storyline and clear protagonist. In fact, if the story reads like this we should be worried. Many subjugated voices lie in the margins of such stories, and it is here that "sustainability" ends or begins. We may therefore have to read for the gaps. It may be precisely the breakdown of the story at certain points that makes a different kind of engagement possible.

In her poetry, Wallace employs "intervals", i.e. moments of silence, or pause, to evoke the impossibility of speaking in the face of specific traumas. It allows her to mediate between the specific experience that cannot be conveyed in words, and the use of words that allows us to engage with this experience. The silence (evoked through a "gap" in the writing) and words that follow put each other in perspective. They create, in Mark Taylor's phrasing, a "self-reflexive loop" that allows us to face up to the responsibility of speaking without saying too much and in the process reifying and undermining the ethical moment.

What does this mean for our re-evaluation of sustainability principles? Well, in the first place, it will ask us to explore the relational dynamics that underpin our understanding of sustainability rhetoric and to see the (con)textual richness that is to be found there. This process entails much more than a conscious content analysis. It will entail listening to the stories that have been told around sustainability over many decades, even before the term started gaining currency. The (con)text of these principles was not only woven in the academic discourses around this term, but in newspapers, the popular media, NGO activity, etc. Most importantly, the contours of "sustainability" principles are woven around campfires where elders were telling stories about how life used to be and where community leaders were discussing how to meet their fishing needs in changing times.

We will also have to develop a keen eye for the histories that inform our current agency – both on a personal and a corporate level. We can only understand who we are when we know where we come from. We also have to develop a sense that we will never know all we need to know about where we come from. Sustainability rhetoric tends to focus on current needs and those of the future, but surely the notion current "need" can only be understood if the various (con)texts that were woven into this understanding are explored. Could we therefore be so bold as to suggest that Anglo-America unpacks its sustainability principles in terms of its past, as well as its future? What are the histories that informed and continue to inform who it is becoming today. Does its understanding of itself, and of "sustainability" include the histories of mining in South Africa and Zimbabwe? Can this corporation truly commit to sustainability without taking into consideration this past? Rediscovering this past may require more than reading records of shareholder returns or even history books. Some of the history survives in the miners' gumboot dancing and songs that are still sung in some mines. And sometimes, we may want to look at photographs, or paintings, of lives lived over time. Photography can be a gesture that does not aim to represent. Photographs allude to final judgments that may be made, that are always already made by the mere fact that the person in this photograph existed.[7]

In the process of discovering the counter-images, the contra-dictions inherent in sustainability principles, accepting our limitations is crucial. It may be precisely our incapacity to articulate what Derrida calls "the mystical foundation of authority" that underpins our judgment that allows it to function in the first place. To find, or to found, this "foundation" in any final way, would be to annihilate it. This entails a delicate suspension that avoids both a too strong grasp *and* a complete disempowerment that forecloses any action. It allows us to have principled concerns, commitments that continue to challenge us and draw us beyond ourselves in our everyday interactions with others. Yet it is equally important not to try and "own" the truth it speaks by describing its draw in final terms. Georgio Agamben (2007, p. 22) alludes to what this may mean by pointing out that justice, like magic, is nameless. Photographs may help us get a sense of what this means:

> The photograph is always more than an image, it is the site of a gap, a sublime breach between the sensible and intelligible, between copy and reality, between a memory and a hope. (Agamben, 2007, p. 26)

Where does this leave us as "moral agents"? Again, Agamben also helps us get a sense of who we may be as moral agents by describing passion as the tightrope between Ego and Genius – between that which is thoroughly individual and specific and the Genius that transcends it. In my mind, ethical responsiveness requires this kind of passion. Ethical responsiveness happens where the individual comes into interaction with the non-individualizable, with that which transcends her. This is the specific moment in which we experience what we want to call "beauty", "justice", "happiness", "love", but manage to refrain from doing so. As Agamben points out, what we love in another is not what that person is, but the rapid back and forth between genius and character, between that person's identity and capacity to be more than that.

A poem called "Bones", in Bronwyn Wallace's (1987) collection *Stubborn Particulars*, provides us with clues of how this may happen:

> A story of yours got this one going,
> so I'm sending it back now, changed of course,
> Just as each person I love
> is a relocation, where I take up
> a different place in the world.

If we understand anything of "sustainability", it is because of stories that many people told over time. These stories change, and so they should if the concept is

---

7   See in this regard Agamben's thoughts on the relationship between photography and judgment in his book *Profanations* (2007).

to remain meaningful. It is up to us to continue rewriting them, with great care, based on our singular interactions and experiences. Sometimes we may even have to accept that a story no longer makes sense, and abandon it. In doing so, each context we may encounter challenges us to be more, to do more, than we previously thought possible. And this may be what ethical responsiveness is all about.

References

Agamben, G. (2007), *Profanations*. Cambridge, MA: Zone Books.

Banerjee, S. B. (2006), The Ethics of Corporate Responsibility, in *Management Ethics. Contemporary Contexts*, S. R. Clegg and C. Rhodes (eds). Abingdon: Routledge.

Bauman, Z. (1992), *Postmodern Ethics*. Oxford: Blackwell.

Benhabib, S. (1992), *Situating the Self, Gender, Community and Postmodernism in Contemporary Ethics*. Abingdon: Routledge.

Burlingham, B. (2005), *Small Giants: Companies that Choose to be Great Instead of Big*. Portfolio Press.

Critchley, S. (1992), *The Ethics of Deconstruction: Derrida and Levinas*. Edinburgh: Edinburgh University Press.

Critchley, S. (2004), Five Problems in Levinas's View of Politics and the Sketch of a Solution to Them. *Political Theory*, 32(2), 172–185.

Derrida, J. (1978), Violence and Metaphysics. In *Writing and Difference*. London: Routledge.

Derrida, J. (1997), *Adieu to Emmanuel Levinas*. Stanford, CA: Stanford University Press.

Emden, C. J. (2005), *Nietzsche on Language, Consciousness and the Body*. Chicago, IL: University of Illinois Press.

Foucault, M. (1973), *This is Not a Pipe*. Stanford, CA: University of California Press.

Freeman, R. E., Pierce, J. and Dodd, R. H. (2000), *Environmentalism and the New Logic of Business*. Oxford: Oxford University Press.

Heidegger, M. (1987), *Nietzsche Vol III & IV The Will to Power as Knowledge and as Metaphysics and Nihilism*, D. F. Krell (ed.). London: HarperCollins.

McVea, J., Freeman, F. and Edward, R. (2005), A Names-and-Faces Approach to Stakeholder Management: How Focusing on Stakeholders as Individuals Can Bring Ethics and Entrepreneurial Strategy Together. *Journal of Management Inquiry*, 14(1), 57–69.

McWilliams, A. and Siegel, D. (2000), Corporate Social Responsibility and Financial Performance: Correlation or misspecification? *Strategic Management Journal*, 21(5), 603–609.

Naas, M. (2003), *Taking on the Tradition. Jacques Derrida and the Legacies of Deconstruction*. Stanford, CA: Stanford University Press.

Nietzsche, F. (1954), On truth and lie in an extra-moral sense, in *The Portable Nietzsche*, W. Kaufman (ed. and trans.). London: Penguin Books.

Nietzsche, F. (1973), *Beyond Good and Evil*, Section 187. London: Penguin Books.

Paine, L. S. (2000), Does Ethics Pay? *Business Ethics Quarterly*, 10, 319–330.

Painter-Morland, M. (2008), Codes of Conduct: Ethical Questioning or Questionable Ethics. Conference Paper, "Derrida and Business Ethics", University of Leicester.

Speth, J. G. (2008), *The Bridge at the End of the World: Capitalism, the Environment, and Crossing from Crisis to Sustainability*. New Haven, CT: Yale University Press.

Taylor, M. (2001), *The Moment of Complexity: Emerging Network Culture*. Chicago, IL: University of Chicago Press.

Taylor, M. (2004), *Confidence Games, Money and Markets in a World without Religion*. Chicago, IL: University of Chicago Press.

Tsoutsoura, M. (2004), *Corporate Social Responsibility and Financial Performance*. Berkeley, CA: University of California, Berkeley, Center for Responsible Business.

UNIDO (2002), *Corporate Responsibility: Implications for Small and Medium Enterprises in Developing Countries*. Vienna.

Van der Walt, J. (2005), *Law as Sacrifice: Towards a Post-Apartheid Theory of Law*. Johannesburg: Witwatersrand University Press.

Vellino, B. C. (2004), A Network of Relations: Ethical Interdependence in Bronwyn Wallace's Talking Lyric, in B. Gabriel and S. Ilcan (eds), *Postmodernism and the Ethical Subject*. Canada: McGill–Queen's University Press.

Verschoor, C. (1999), Corporate Performance is Closely Linked to a Strong Ethical Commitment. *Business and Society Review*, 104, 407–415.

Verschoor, C. (2004), Does Superior Governance still Lead to Better Financial Performance? *Strategic Finance*, 86, 13–14.

Verschoor, C. (2005), Is there Financial Value in Corporate Values? *Strategic Finance*, 87, 17–18.

Waddock, S. A. and Graves, S. B. (1997), The Corporate Social Performance – Financial Performance Link. *Strategic Management Journal*, 18(4), 303–319.

Wallace, B. (1987), *The Stubborn Particulars of Grace*. McClelland & Stewart.

Chapter 10

Society's Constitution and Corporate Legitimacy, or Why it Might be Unethical for Business Leaders to Think with Their Heart

Susanne Holmström

Die Frage ist vielmehr, ob und unter welschen Umständen es sinnvoll oder gar geboten sein könnte, sich an der *Unterscheidung* von gut und schlecht bzw. gut und böse zu orientieren. [...] Für die Ethik im üblichen Sinn ist das keine Frage, für sie versteht es sich von selbst, dass es gut ist, zwischen gut und schlecht zu unterscheiden. [Rather, the question is if and under which circumstances it could be meaningful or even required to orientate oneself according to the *distinction* between good and bad and between good and evil respectively [...] To ethics in the usual sense it is no question, since ethics automatically understands it as good to distinguish between good and bad.] (Luhmann, 2008, pp. 198–199)

Introduction

When the sociologist behind one of Germany's most important contributions to the understanding of the challenges facing contemporary society, Niklas Luhmann, in 1993 was asked to speak on the theme of business ethics, he commented that,

Es ist mir nicht gelungen, herauszubekommen, worüber ich eigentlich reden soll. Die Sache hat einen Namen: Wirtschaftsethik. Und ein Geheimnis, nämlich ihre Regeln. Aber meine Vermutung ist, dass sie zu der Sorte von Erscheinungen gehört wie auch die Staatsräson oder die englische Küche, die in der Form eines Geheimnisses auftreten, weil sie geheim halten müssen, dass sie gar nicht existieren. (Luhmann, 2008, p. 196)[1]

---

1 "I have not succeeded in working out what I am really supposed to talk about. The matter has a name: business ethics. And a secret, namely its rules. My assumption is, however, that it belongs to the sort of phenomena as the state reason or the English kitchen, which appear in the form of a secret, while they have to keep it secret that they do not exist at all."

I admit to having related reservations, and shall suggest that the rhetoric and rationale of ethics is an inadequate reduction of complexity when the problems of economy's negligence and the interrelation between business and society are addressed. Applying the human being as ultimate reference, using catchwords such as "business leaders must learn to think with their heart" (Pruzan 1998), and endowing organizations with human qualities such as conscience on the one hand represents a sociological under-complexity, and on the other hand leaves business leaders in the lurch. As also Luhmann suggests, then,

> Die Frage bleibt, ob Ethik diejenige Theorieform ist, mit der man angemessen auf die Lage der Gesellschaft am Ende dieses Jahrhunderts [twentieth century, S.H.] reagieren kann. In den guten Absichten der Ethik-Fans könnten sich schlimme Folgen verbergen, nämlich eine Ablenkung von allen ernsthaften Versuchen, die moderne Gesellschaft und in ihr das Funktionssystem Wirtschaft zu begreifen. (Luhmann, 2008, p. 203)[2]

Instead, from a sociological perspective, the new legitimating ideals empirically expressed in the thematization of ethics and concepts such as corporate social responsibility (CSR) and triple bottom line are reconstructed in relation to societal structures and evolutionary processes. I shall suggest that five interrelated structural problems have activated *reflection*, the specific second-order observation mode of self-referential social systems, as a reaction to the strains of the reflexivity of solid modernity's full functional differentiation.

Empirically, the analyses are based on observations of the changing expectations to corporate legitimacy since the 1960s, with the main focus on Denmark (Holmström, 2003, 2005b, 2007, 2008). However, since a key point is that ideals of organizational legitimacy interrelate with societal coordination, generic structures are identified in order for the findings to have global perspectives. Theoretically, the analyses draw mainly upon Niklas Luhmann's theories, which empty society and organizations of human beings as well as any teleology or content apart from the highly improbable ability to reproduce itself.

Following Luhmann, the fundamental premise is to give up the idea that social systems are living systems, and to see them instead as systems whose basic elements consist of subject-less communications, vanishing events in time that, in producing the networks that produce them, constitute emergent orders of temporalized complexity in continuously changing self-referential social systems. Communication comprises the social processes which constitute anything social – society, organization, interactions – and the concept is not confined to

---

2 "The question remains whether ethics is the form of theory with which you can react properly to the situation of society at the end of this century [twentieth century, S.H.]. The good intentions of the fans of ethics may conceal grim consequences, namely a diversion from all serious attempts to understand the modern society and, within it, the functional system of economy."

linguistic processes. For instance, payment processes are seen as communication. Communication takes on its own life in closed, self-referential communication circuits – social systems – which continuously produce meaning. However, they are guided solely by their own horizon of meaning, not the intentions and hermeneutic capacities of a communicating subject. Although meaning is "the universal medium of all psychic and social, all consciously and communicatively operating systems" (Luhmann, 1997a, p. 51), then both types of systems are self-referentially closed and operate simultaneously without interfering with each other at the level of their respective autopoiesis, yet they are structurally coupled. No social system could exist without the environment of psychic systems, and correspondingly, as Knodt observes, "a consciousness deprived of society would be incapable of developing beyond the more rudimentary level of perception" (Knodt 1995, p. xxvii). The interrelation between thoughts and communications activates a complex co-evolution, which however is not linear. The communicative resonance provoked by a psychic system is always self-referentially conditioned by the social system, and vice versa. Baecker (2006) comments that

> Das bedeutet nicht, dass man [...] nicht mehr psychisch, sondern sozial zurechnet, sondern das bedeutet, dass man beides tun kann, in jedem Fall jedoch eine Entscheidung treffen muss. Das alleine reichert die analytischen Möglichkeiten enorm an und macht, da die Entscheidung in jeden Fall alles andere als selbstverständlich ist, mit der Ambivalenz als Grundtatbestand individuellen und sozialen Lebens bekannt.[3]

For Luhmann, the intransparency of consciousness from the viewpoint of the social is not an obstacle to be removed but the very condition that activates communication. Systems rationality is about establishing and stabilizing structures of expectation in an otherwise infinite, immense world by reducing complexity and thus rendering probable communication: "Every social contact is understood as a system, up to and including society as the inclusion of all possible contacts" (Luhmann, 1995a, p. 15). The limits of society are established by the limits of communication. Contemporary society is seen as a complex system of communication that has differentiated itself into a network of interconnected social subsystems through which the world is recognized. Society lacks any "super-system" to ensure coordination, let alone direct it teleologically to a better future. We cannot identify a privileged perspective: as a "recursive universe", society is characterized by disorder, non-linear complexity and unpredictability.

---

3 "This does not mean that you [...] refer nothing to the psychic, but only to the social: but it means that you can do both, and in any case have to make a decision. That alone enriches the analytical potential enormously and, as the decision in any case is all but obvious, makes you aware of ambivalence as the basic state of affairs of individual and social life."

As opposed to ethical approaches, this approach *first* can be characterized as anormative "Sozialtechnologie" – once (Habermas and Luhmann, 1971) a condescending description, today increasingly acknowledged as a sensitive scientific approach required to understand contemporary social complexity, as Knodt observes, "because an acceptance without any nostalgia of the structural limitations of modernity – is a precondition, and possibly the only way, of finding creative solutions to its problems" (1995, p. xxxvi). *Second*, the approach dissociates the analytical optics from anthropocentric understandings of society which see the individual as the ultimate reference. Instead, this approach sees only self-referential social systems constituted by communication – and nothing else. *Third*, social problems and dynamics are localized within the self-referential, self-organizing circular communications driven neither by instrumental systems rationality nor oriented towards understanding – but driven by a circular rationality. Evolutionary dynamics are driven only by the compulsion of communicative processes to continue themselves. This apparently simple – but counter-intuitive – dynamics is the basic frame for empirical analyses based on Luhmann. A consequence of this theoretical approach is that problems will always be identified with the communicative processes, more precisely with the continuation of communicative processes which compulsively activates learning processes when they are endangered. Consequently, this approach identifies the evolution of corporate semantics and practices such as ethics and CSR as part of society's learning processes in the endeavours to clear the way for the continuation of the communication processes constituting society.

Reconstructing Legitimating Ideals as Reflection

A basic challenge for the continuation of the communicative processes is the balance between the social systems' open- and closedness. As I shall demonstrate, with full modernity this balance grows a problem on five structural dimensions. *First* is the conflict between society and environment – the problem being society's increasing strains on human beings and nature, finding solutions such as the triple bottom line. *Second* is the increasing gap between organizations as society's predominant decisions-makers and those affected by the decisions, also known as the risk–danger dichotomy, promoting calls for social responsibility, accountability, transparency and sustainability measures. *Third* is the increasing independence with and consequent interdependence between society's differentiated functional systems – which activate solutions such as increasingly complex stakeholder models and polygenous partnerships. *Fourth* are the challenges to politics in coordinating an increasingly complex and diverse (world) society, which activate reflexive law and political initiatives such as polygenous policy networks and CSR in order to encourage corporate self-constraints. *Fifth* are the conflicts between different forms of society as globalization increases the sensitivity and interdependence between societal and cultural forms that were previously separated.

I shall return to these conflicts, however, to confront them; their premises and their potential requires insight into the social dynamics and the premise that the open- and closedness of social systems, including society, are not opposites, but mutual preconditions – in order for the analysis not to jump to easy conclusions and simplified solutions such as more openness, borderless sensitivity or de-differentiation.

With Luhmann, social systems are closed in order to be open, open in order to be closed. *First*, a social system can observe and realize only a segment of the world, depending on the complexity not of the world, but of the system. Observation refers neither to human beings nor to sight, but to social operations. For instance, economy does not have the tools required to see deforestation or human stress until it catches on to the criteria of payments, prices and profits. *Second*, when information is brought into the system's communicative processes, it is recoded and changes its meaning as a systems-internal construction of a systems-external world. The sufferings of millions of Africans afflicted by AIDS cannot be observed directly by society, since they are not social, but organic and psychic processes. However, communication can thematize pain, disease and poverty insofar as society has developed distinctions for observing such matters. Correspondingly, within society, social systems observe and reconstruct each other from each of their specific perspectives. For instance, the political system sees steering objects, news media reconstruct their environment as information and economics sees markets.

If the open observation is not founded in a specific social filter, which is established exactly by means of the closed meaning boundary, then there is nothing to guide the observation; the system drowns in indeterminate complexity. It cannot separate itself from the environment. This goes for any social system – from society to organizations. If the organization cannot determine any premises for its decisions processes – whether it is a business company or a humanitarian organization – then it comes to a halt. The organization dissolves. So, the closed meaning boundaries have a fundamental function, and "When put under a pressure of selection, the system principally synchronizes itself with itself, however [it] can do this in forms that are more or less sensitive to the environment" (Luhmann, 2000a, p. 162). Consequently, in systems theory we can never talk of a linear causality and direct adjustment to the environment, only of a social system's adjustment to itself.

Hence, the conditionality of an observation and the difference between the first-order observation characterized as *reflexivity* and the second-order observation of *reflection* become decisive to the analysis of contemporary ideals of organizational legitimization (Holmström, 1997, 1998, 2002, 2004, 2005b). This apparently small mechanism has crucial implications to the sensitivity and to the sense of responsibility of an organization. *Reflexivity* implies a monocontextual, narcissistic perspective from within which the organization applies distinctions blindly, and from where the organization takes its own worldview for given, takes what it sees to be the one reality, the only truth – and consequently conflicts blindly with different worldviews. In *reflection*, the organizational system sees itself as if from outside and re-enters the distinction between system and environment within the system. "This higher layer of control is attained by social systems' orienting themselves to themselves – to themselves as different from their environments" (Luhmann, 1995a, p. 455). Consequently, reflection is the production of self-understanding in relation to the environment. Therefore, where the reflexive organization is inattentive to the broader context and consequently to the unintended, however often far-reaching, side-effects involved in its decisions, reflection enables the organization to understand itself in a larger interdependent societal context and to develop self-restrictions out of consideration for its environment in order to secure its own independence and self-referential development (autopoiesis) in the long term (Table 10.1).

Table 10.1 Differences between reflexivity and reflection on categories relevant to corporate legitimization

	Reflexivity	Reflection
Level of observation	Monocontextual, narcissistic first-order perspective from within	Perspective rises to a second-order level; facilitates polycontextual worldview
Society's form	Solid modernity; full functional differentiation	Fluid modernity; flexible functional differentiation
Necessary/contingent	Takes own worldview for given; social norms and institutions seen as necessary, natural, inevitable, self-evident	Own worldview as contingent, i.e. product of social choice, could be different
Sensitivity to conflict	Does not see conflicts, tries to silence them, or to dissolve by information	Sees the inevitability of and the potential for conflicts; exposes their background and facilitates exchange of views
Location of responsibility	Responsibility based on society's well-established norms; no responsibility as decision-taker; feels a victim	Sees own decisions as based on choice; assumes responsibility as decision-taker
Law/legitimacy	Relates to law and fixed rules mainly for legitimacy	Continuous reflective and discursive processes of legitimization
Confidence/trust	Relies on passive confidence	Active trust to be continuously generated
Ethics/morals	Business morals	Business ethics

This rise from first-order narrow, unambiguous, monocontextual perspectives to second-order broad, open, polycontextual perspectives has huge implications for the relationship between organization and environment. From interrelations being characterized by prejudice and locked positions, reflection opens up attempts at mutual respect and consequently leads to practices such as stakeholder engagement and partnerships.

This does not mean that relations between reflective systems are free from conflicts. On the contrary, the basic condition of late modernity is conflict. Reflection implies a larger mutual toleration of differences and the diversity, and consequently the possibility to transform conflicts into productive dynamics. Reflective learning processes are empirically expressed in a movement towards polycontextual perspectives and towards mutual considerations – not to dissolve and integrate the differentiated societal rationalities, but to maintain their specialization. Interdependence is acknowledged as a precondition of independence and autonomy, and vice versa.

Society's Problems Strike in Organizations

In order to understand the legitimating ideals reconstructed as reflection – business ethics, CSR, etc. – I suggest that they must be seen in relation to societal evolution, and the co-evolution of society and organization.

In Europe, from the 1600s a new form of primary societal differentiation gradually replaced stratification, which differentiates society into hierarchical layers. In the *functionally differentiated society*, the communicative processes of diverse functional systems are conditioned by specific symbolic media and binary codes and each structure's specific expectations (Luhmann, 1997a). Luhmann describes a principle which he demonstrates in several analyses of some of the more prominent functional systems, e.g. politics (2000b), law (1993b), science (1990), economics (1999), art (2002a), mass media (1996b), education (2002c) and religion (2002b).[4] The function of economy is identified as reduction of scarcity, the medium as money, the binary code as "±pay, own" and the communicative processes as payments. In line with the theory's fundamental idea, profit is not an end but a means to the continuation of communicative processes. Functional systems each produce their specific realities which are incompatible and indifferent to each other, "but this indifference is used as a protective shield to build up the system's own complexity, which can be extremely sensitive to irritations from the environment as long as they can be internally perceived in the form of information"

---

4 The luhmannian theory focuses on process more than on structure and does not claim a once-and-for-all differentiation of certain functional systems. Function does not – as for instance with Parsons (1951) – imply any legitimation but an analytical focus: a system's function is seen as an offer of meaning which is achieved by its specific reduction of the complexity of the world.

(Luhmann, 1998, pp. 35–36). The integrity of functional spheres is a basic ideal of modernity – so that for instance neither religion nor politics strain science, education, economy or news media. The important point is that legitimization processes will work against de-differentiation – since that would ultimately lead to the dissolution of society.

By accelerating a pronounced growth of complexity, functional differentiation has facilitated industrialization and today's knowledge society. This complexity also implies that what in previous societies just happened over the course of time now "demands explicit couplings in the form of decisions in order to secure a connection between past and future" (Luhmann, 2003, p. 53). Therefore, as functional differentiation evolved, it required a supplementing principle of system formation: organization. Organizations establish a social identity (i.e. stable expectations over time), which bridges the gap between past and future. It is by means of its organizations "(and only there!) that a society enables itself to act collectively and to make programmed decisions" (Baecker, 2003, p. 20). Functional systems cannot decide, and consequently, functional systems are referred to organizational systems.

In a luhmannian optic, organizations are constituted not by employees, factory buildings, products or services, but "'consist' of nothing but communication of decisions" (Luhmann, 1997a, p. 833). This means that, just as society would deteriorate if the communicative processes slowed down, organizations depend on strong and dynamic decision processes: "The maintenance and improvement of the competence of deciding (instead of rationality) become the actual criteria of effective organisations" (Luhmann, 2000a, p. 181). Again, the driving dynamics with Luhmann is the continuation of communication – not rationality, nor specific objectives (although this is what is thematized by organizations).

Even if all organizations refer to several functional systems (and almost all in some way to economy), they predominantly identify themselves by means of a primary reference to one of society's functional systems – a business company to economy, a research institution to science, a court of justice to law, and so forth. Each functional reference constitutes specific expectations: it facilitates decision-making processes and strengthens expectations when you know whether you deal with a hospital (health system as functional primacy), a business company (economic system), a humanitarian organization (care system), a law court (law system), a newspaper (mass media system) or a political party (political system). The important point in the context of new legitimating notions is that, although these notions favour an increasing number of functional references, legitimization processes will work against total polygenity of an organization since that would lead to uncertain patterns of expectations – and ultimately to the dissolution of an organization.

Reflection at Two Interrelated Levels

During the twentieth century, functional differentiation has fully developed in some Western societies, with firmly stabilized boundaries and high specialization – and high ignorance towards society's environment as well as the functional systems in between. Old legitimating notions of growth and progress no longer support the continuation of the processes constituting society. They gradually change towards ideals of sensitivity, responsibility, self-constraint and sustainability. I suggest that these legitimating ideals can be paralleled with the social mechanism of reflection – as opposed to reflexivity, which was legitimate during the construction and stabilization of the principle of functional differentiation. With full functional differentiation reflection seems to be provoked by two structural dimensions: the functional and the organizational dimensions. This is a general trait for any functional and for most organizational systems, not only for the economic system and for business companies, defined as organizations with economy as the primary reference of their decision-making. As for the economic system, it is part of the fundamental societal structure, and society's self-continuing dynamics will endeavour to strengthen the functional differentiation constituting modern society since "a society can only imagine a change of its principle of stability and that is to say its form of differentiation [...] as disaster" (Luhmann, 1996a, p. 104).

On this structural dimension, I suggest that we understand the learning processes towards reflection as a means of strengthening the societal skeleton by making it flexible and by reinforcing boundaries at the same time, thus facilitating communicative processes. Applying the luhmannian optics, centuries of turbulence, protests and legitimacy crises seem to help society – including the business community – adjust and preserve itself rather than to threaten it:

> The system [...] does not protect itself *against changes* but *with the help of changes* against rigidifying into repeated, but no longer environmentally adequate patterns of behavior. The immune system protects not structure but autopoiesis, the system's closed self-reproduction. (Luhmann, 1995a, p. 372)

In the second-order perspective of reflection, social systems on the one hand retain and develop their independent complexity, and on the other hand they develop self-restrictions with regard to their interdependence. Medium and code are invariant, whereas evolutionary variations in functional systems are located in their *programmes*: "The economic system will never doubt that there is a distinction between payment and non-payment. Programmes, on the other hand, can be varied" (Luhmann, 1997b, pp. 52–53). Accordingly, as reflective traits are integrated in the programmes of economy, formerly extra-economic considerations such as concerns for nature and human rights as well as respect for other functional systems appear today to be included in economy's programmes without the imperative of profit being afflicted.

Since functional systems have no address, the turbulent environment and the frequent legitimacy crises challenging society's functional differentiation, in particular since the 1960s, strike in organizations. Even if we may ultimately trace back problems to the functional differentiation of society, then society's conflicts surface in organizations. Organizations "equip society with ultra-stability and with sufficient local ability of absorbing irritation" (Luhmann, 2000a, p. 396). The adjustments of society mainly take place in organizations and provoke new coordinating structures such as ethical programmes and stakeholder engagement. Where legitimating notions no longer support the continuation of the communicative processes constituting society (including organizations), they gradually change. Legitimacy is understood as "a generalized preparedness to accept decisions within certain boundaries of tolerance; decisions which are still undecided as regards contents" (Luhmann, 1993b, p. 28). However, as I shall demonstrate, organizations are under double fire. Not only do their functional primates constitute a challenge; so does the character of their principle operations, decisions. And the fundamental premise for understanding this challenge is that an organization exists only as long as it makes decisions – the specific communicative processes constituting organizations. This means that organizations are threatened when their capability to make decisions is threatened.

Five Structural Contexts

Although they are interrelated and together advance new legitimating ideals and legitimizing processes as expressed in the call for corporate social responsibility, ethics or sustainability, the structural conflicts activating learning processes towards reflection can be identified in five different dimensions on the specific stage of full functional differentiation.

On all of these five dimensions, new legitimating notions and practices to some extent solve the structural problems of full functional differentiation; however, they are not miracle cures, and although often presented as simple and self-evident solutions, they are embedded in complex contexts and often provoke new problems.

Society versus Environment: The Triple Bottom Line

As for the first structural dimension, the theoretical premise is that society has to reconstruct its environment into social processes according to society's functional filters – economy, politics, family, science, education, etc. – in order to observe, interpret and communicate organic, chemical, biological, psychic and physiological processes, such as for instance "obesity", "life quality", "climate change" or "animal welfare":

It is not a matter of blatantly objective facts, for example, that oil-supplies are decreasing, that the temperature of rivers is increasing, that forests are being defoliated or that the skies and the seas are being polluted. All this may or may not be the case. But as physical, chemical or biological facts they create no social resonance as long as they are not the subject of communication. [...] Society is an environmentally sensitive (open) but operatively closed system. Its sole mode of observation is communication. It is limited to communicating meaningfully and regulating this communication through communication. [...] The environment can make itself noticed only by means of communicative irritations or disturbances. (Luhmann, 1989, p. 28)

This implies a highly selective resonance to the well-being of nature and human beings. The economic filter will automatically activate questions such as: does it pay? Does it improve our competitiveness? The economic rationale cannot see its strains on nature and human beings until economic criteria are influenced, and what is seen is then automatically reconstructed from economic premises. A corresponding (in)sensitivity goes for all social dynamics. Politics: will we gain votes, power? Science: does it generate new knowledge? News media: is it new information?

Empirically, during the latter half of the twentieth century, a critical mass of unintended side-effects of the blind reflexivity of society's functional filters strained society's environment, such as deforestation and oppression of human rights. The perspective of protest organized in social movements and caught onto mass media's selection criteria of sensation and conflict. Society's functional differentiation was gradually questioned. Decades of numerous legitimacy conflicts seemed to activate a general reprogramming of functional systems into reflection, which increased society's sensitivity to its environment. In the economic system, formerly extra-economic matters are gaining resonance within the meaning boundaries of business expressed, for example, in the concept of the triple bottom line of people, planet, profit.

The immediate problem on this structural dimension is the problem of too little resonance. Society's resonance is compulsively subject to the functional dynamics. Economy cannot see the relevance of considering people and planet until it increases profits. News media cannot see the problems of climate change if they do not meet with criteria such as new information, conflict, highest, greatest, worst, violation of norms, near, person, sensation. As for science, research into pollution or stress is subject to academic criteria of truth and of publication. As for politics, the resonance will follow the urge to gain power and to regulate. However, although this structurally determined resonance is a problem, it also solves problems – for without this structural resonance, there is no forceful resonance:

This reduction is the condition for noticing and processing environmental changes within the system as such. Coding is the condition that permits environmental events to appear as information in the system, i.e., to be interpreted in reference

> to something, and it causes this in a way that allows consequences to follow
> within the system. (Luhmann, 1989, p. 116)

Paradoxically, as also Luhmann warns, the threat may rather be too much resonance. The insensitivity and selective resonance in relation to the non-social environment of the functionally differentiated society imply an extremely high sensitivity and high learning capacity in the individual programmes of the different functional systems. When society finally sees the consideration of human beings and nature as relevant, it catches on according to the functional logics. The result is the risk of distortion and overreaction. Society's resonance to the strains on its environment tends to proceed unreflected, unproblematized, automatically when it has caught on to the functional logics. The market floods with CO_2-neutral products, and as the mass media burst with news on climate change when met with prospects of catastrophe and drowning polar bears promoted by celebrities from rock and politics, then other problems as well as most of the huge complexity involved in the issue tend to remain disregarded in the shadows. Climate change attracted most attention at the World Economic Forum 2007, and it pays for the business community to brand itself as climate conscious and to enter partnerships such as *Climate Savers* with the World Wide Fund for Nature (WWF) because this furthers competitiveness. As for politics, when a cause promises votes and electoral success, it automatically catches on even though considerations which please public opinion do not necessarily represent the most reasonable and efficient relief of the strains on society's environment. Furthermore, resonance is thrown around from one functional system to another, as I shall demonstrate in relation to theme three – the paradoxical interrelation between the independence and interdependence of functional systems. With a structural resonance and a tendency to black/white reductions of complex contexts, the risk prevails of distorting society's strains on its environment or of uncontrollable hyper-resonance to the effect that the strains are not relieved – and moreover, that society itself is strained by hyper-irritation. As Luhmann comments, then "such an oscillation of resonance [will] probably have destructive consequence within an evolutionarily highly improbable social system" (Luhmann, 1989, p. 120).

Organization: Decision-Maker versus Victim

On the second dimension, the focus is on the systemic principle of organization, and on the asymmetrical relation between decision-maker and those affected by a decision. With full functional differentiation, basic norms over the centuries have grown naturalized, anthropologized and integrated as tacit assumptions and *a priori* constructs in the self-description of modernity. During the late 1900s, protests against the rigid authorities that dominate society were increasingly activated and gradually provoked communication on communication and a second-order perspective which sees social filters as results of contingent choices. The general acknowledgement of contingency causes insecurity and uncertainty, and consequently increases worry and fear. However, as Luhmann (1993a) suggests as a criticism of Beck's *Risk Society* (1992), we cannot explain fear in the dangers we "really" face (the fact dimension) – but partly in the temporal dimension in regard to the principally unknown future, and partly in the social dimension in regard to who makes the decision which endangers others. Luhmann changes the distinction of risk as opposed to security applied in most observations on "the risk society" to risk as opposed to danger, and with this distinction the problem with which the topic of risk confronts society is seen differently: risk cannot be transformed into security, but is a question of attribution. From the dangerous position of potential victims the legitimacy of organizations' risky decisions is continuously questioned. Everything from global warming to AIDS and obesity is attributed to decisions. As Luhmann observes, "Refusing to assume risks or demanding their rejection has become dangerous behavior" (1993a, p. x).

The increasing acknowledgement of contingency has several implications for society's predominant decision-makers, organizations. *First*, the premises of decisions are no longer given but have to be generated along with the decision processes. The identity and legitimacy of an organization are continuously regenerated, and formerly tacit values are explicated. *Second*, when decisions are seen not as based in natural norms and common consensus but as products of contingent choice, they are made socially responsible for their consequences. Where a company was previously automatically seen as responsible by following society's well-established norms, today it must explicitly assume responsibility for the consequences of its decisions in the broader perspective – mantra: social responsibility. It must be able to account for its decision processes – cues: accountability, transparency. The demand for sustainability makes the company responsible for the future. *Third*, the whole social order is based on structures of expectations. In the normative society of yesterday, control and socialization guaranteed stability. Confidence prevailed and alternatives were unconsidered. With the recognition of contingency, norms and values have grown unstable (cf. also Jalava, 2003). In unfamiliar, unpredictable and uncertain situations we need trust, which makes it possible to interact on uncertain premises, without firm knowledge, knowing that it is possible to predict future events only with a certain amount of probability. Therefore, relations between organization and environment are no longer mediated by passive confidence, but by active trust. Moreover, organizations have to be constantly prepared for random "trust checks" by the mass media. *Fourth*, when universality is replaced by diversity and univocality by ambiguity, then it grows increasingly evident that what different observers consider as being the same thing generates different information for each of these positions. *Fifth*, when the environment is no longer given, but is acknowledged as contingent, then it has to be continuously reconstructed by the organization. A new environmental sensitivity is brought into focus, for instance in the form of stakeholder models which grow increasingly dynamic and fluid. However, as well as solutions to the problems involved in the increasing acknowledgement of the contingency of decision premises, new problems can be identified according to the social dynamics and societal structures.

As for corporate responsibility, who determines the degree and character? In engaging with stakeholders defined exactly as those influenced by the decision of a company (or those influencing the company, thus placing the company in the victim's position), fear, worry, feelings and a tendency to prejudice will prevail instead of reason (understood as insight into the complexity of the context) and will tend to paralyse decision-making and impede innovation. Moreover, company (decision-maker) and environment (potential victim) will consistently adopt different perspectives as to the risk involved in decision-making. In continuation of this, neither information nor transparency will solve the inherent conflict. It is more likely that, the greater the transparency, the more disagreement there is (Luhmann, 1993a; Holmström, 2005a).

In the case of *sustainability*, then, as Willke and Willke emphasize,

> Since it is impossible, with the presently available instruments and models, to predict and realise a specific future state of affairs, sustainability in its encompassing meaning is an empty concept, prone to be misused as a placebo moral formula to demonstrate good intentions and ethical highfalutin. (2008, p. 34)

First and foremost, the tendency to an oversimplification of the positions of decision-maker versus victim may pose severe problems to society, since the victim tends to be automatically seen as morally right. However, who is the victim and when? As Fuchs (2007) notes, with a hint to the moralizing discourse on nuclear power or genetic modification,

> Auch die Entscheidung gegen Kernkraftwerke oder gegen die Gentechnologie sei riskant und werfe für irgendjemanden (im Grenzfall für uns alle) entschiedene Gefahren aus.[5]

A moralizing discourse tends to catch on to mass media and to public opinion, and to create a general climate of hyper-irritation, fear and worry which generates distrust and hampers social interaction.

Independence versus Interdependence: Polygenous Sensitivity

The third interrelated frame for explaining the evolutionary changes of the interrelation between organization and environment is the increasing conflict between the independence and interdependence of functional systems as functional

---

5   "Even decisions against nuclear power plants or against genome technology may prove risky and may pose severe dangers to some (in borderline cases to us all)."

differentiation stabilizes. The higher the independence of functional systems, the greater their interdependence is. The level of knowledge, competency and specialization in today's full differentiation requires cooperation across multiple and diverse positions. On the one hand, the development of new medicine involves science, which depends on the educational system for qualified scientists and the health system for clinical tests, which depends on economics, which depends on law for intellectual property rights, which depends on the political system, and so forth. On the other hand, tight shutters are needed between, for instance, the rationales of economics and of science for the individual dynamics to function adequately. Verdicts of illegitimacy lurk in case of suspicion of economically biased scientific research results. So, on the one hand, the different spheres are increasingly interdependent with each other in a complex, polycontextual interplay. On the other hand, they are dependent on each other to function independently in their own way, with their individual function, knowledge, competencies and dynamics intact. Consequently, full differentiation on the one hand increases the mutual negligence of functional systems. However, on the other hand it increases the sensitivity and motivation to develop self-restrictions and coordinating mechanisms in recognition of the interdependence. The increasing interdependence does *not* imply reduced independence. Rather, the opposite is the case:

> Such dependencies are often interpreted as constraints on the autonomy if not as symptoms as the reversal of differentiations. Actually the contrary is the case. Functional differentiation promotes interdependence and an integration of the entire system because every function system has to assume that other functions have to be fulfilled elsewhere. (Luhmann, 1989, p. 42)

Empirically, since the late 1980s and the 1990s we have observed how the sensitivity provoked by this structural conflict also provokes sensitivity to society's irritating perspectives – such as protest, morale and fear (Luhmann, 1989, 1993a, 1996a, 1998) – as activated by the two structural conflicts analysed above, i.e. between society and environment, and between decision-maker and victim. When irritations are provoked in one functional system, then formerly irrelevant protests and turbulence grow relevant to other functional systems due to the growing interdependence of the functional systems. Gradually, decades of numerous legitimacy conflicts seem to activate a general reprogramming of functional systems into reflection. Although the structural problems originate from the functional dimension, they emerge in organizations. Consequently, reflection on this dimension implies that organizations intensify their sensitivity to diverse perspectives, and the primary functional rationale of an organization is no longer the undisputed trump in the decision-making processes. In the case of business companies, the economic rationale conventionally determining business operations is increasingly being filtered through other rationales such as science, education, family, care, politics, health and mass media. Furthermore, the monocontextual reconstruction of the environment as markets of consumption, employment and investment explodes in polycontextual ambiguity.

Some scholars criticize this polygenous sensitivity as endangering society's functional differentiation. For example, Beckert comments:

> In funktional differenzierten Gesellschaften trennen sich Wertsphären (Weber) voneinander. Gerade in diesem Organisationsprinzip liegt die enorme Leistungsfähigkeit moderner Gesellschaften begründet. Das Konzept der sozialen Verantwortung von Unternehmen unterminiert aber genau dieses Prinzip, indem von Unternehmen erwartet wird, nicht allein Kriterien wirtschaftlicher Effizienz in ihren Entscheidungen anzulegen, sondern auch nach nichtökonomischen Gesichtspunkten zu handeln. (2006, p. 9)[6]

Based on my analyses of the evolution of the interrelation between society and organization since the 1960s, as already indicated, I see the context in a different light. I suggest that we understand the learning processes towards reflection, which implies a polycontextual sensitivity, as a means of strengthening the societal skeleton by making it flexible and reinforcing boundaries at the same time, thus facilitating communicative processes. The mutual considerations by the functional systems are a way of strengthening the functional boundaries. New legitimating notions such as CSR, ethical programmes and triple bottom line reporting have strengthened functional differentiation – after a brief period of wavering, as for instance demonstrated by a moralizing discourse culminating within the Danish business community in 1997, following a series of legitimacy crises. The discourse fed from a distinction between profit and ethics, as exemplified by the following comment on a survey on the Danish business community: "The survey indicates a landslide in businesses' approach to ethical values. Formerly, the common perception was that the companies questioned should concentrate on doing business – i.e. earn as much money as possible" (Mandag Morgen, 1997). However, this challenge to economy's boundaries was quickly replaced by a reprogramming of the economic rationale and a strengthening of economy's boundaries. The Dow Jones Sustainability Index in 2000 was one among many empirical evidences. It concluded that "sustainable companies – defined as companies which in their strategies integrate economic aspects with environmental, ethical and social – give a larger yield on their shares than conventionally driven companies". Economy's former distinction between economic success and environmental, ethical and social considerations has been transformed into new distinctions which determine the legitimating ideals regulating the relations between the economic system and its

---

6 "In functionally differentiated societies value spheres differentiate (Weber). The enormous capability of modern societies lies exactly within this principle of organization. The concept of corporate social responsibility, however, undermines exactly this principle, because it is expected that companies not only adopt criteria of economic efficiency in their decisions, but also act from non-economic perspectives."

environment. Correspondingly, Krohn (1999) shows how the irritating perspectives of ethics and morals are absorbed and pacified by the functional systems.

This does not mean that the increase in mutual functional sensitivity does not present any problems in the social perspective since the risk of weakening the structures of expectations lurks. To an organization, to reflect decisions in several functional rationales multiplies, complicates and slows down decision processes. Moreover, it might grow uncertain for the environment as to what to expect from the organization: are we dealing with a humanitarian organization, a political party or a business company? Uncertainty may reduce the general level of trust in society.

Furthermore, the growing interdependence between functional systems activates a process where the resonance on problems of other structural dimensions – the strains of society's environment and the fear of decision-making – is thrown around between the independent functional system, finding a distorted, disproportional and uncoordinated hyper-resonance.

> It is [...] highly probable that the turbulences of one function system are transferred to others even if, and because, each proceeds according to its own specific code. For example, the economy is at the mercy of scientific discoveries and technological innovations as soon as these find economic use. The same is true *mutatis mutandis* for the relation of politics and law, for science and medicine and for numerous other cases. There is no superordinate authority that would provide for measure and proportionality here. Through resonance small changes in one system can trigger great changes in another. (Luhmann, 1989, p. 117)

Law versus Legitimacy: Polycontextreferential Self-Constraint

The fourth interrelated feature is that with full differentiation new political forms emerge which constitute new challenges to organizational legitimization. The political system is under increasing pressure from the structural problems dealt with above, in coordinating the resonance resulting from environmental strains, in being the major decision-maker of society and consequently the main source of risk, and in balancing the functional systems' independence and interdependence. Analyses show how the intervening law of the welfare state gradually grows overburdened and inadequate for flexibly containing the accelerating speed and complexity of social processes. Part of this picture is national legislation's impotence in the wake of globalization. Based on Luhmann's theories, these emerging forms of regulation are conceptualized as *context regulation* (Willke, 1994), *supervision state* (Willke, 1997; Andersen, 2004), *polycontexturality* (Sand, 2004) and *polycontextualism* (Holmström, 2007, 2008).[7]

---

7   Contexturality and contextuality are to some extent opposites. A contexture refers to an area which has self-referentially stabilized itself – in which case each functional

In polycontextualism, conventional law and authorities are substituted by increasing communicative complexity. For an organization to navigate legitimately it must be reflectively sensitive to several rationales and take an active part in society. Key features of polycontextualism are that, *first*, the political system relieves the pressure on own risky decision-making and increasingly sends on the responsibility, in particular to the economic system, by means of political initiatives aimed at internalizing the societal horizon within the business community. Corporations should take co-responsibility for society, should impose a sensitive self-control in areas where legal regulation does not set sufficient frames, and should do so in "multi-stakeholder dialogues" (EU Commission, 2001). Further, organizations become involved in policy networks and partnerships with other private organizations, public institutions and a multitude of NGOs to solve societal issues by producing tools for organizations' reflective self-restriction – ranging from child labour to global warming. *Second*, political initiatives not only endeavour to intervene from *outside* by conventional law – but increasingly influence organizations' *internal* reflections on their own role and responsibility by *reflexive law* (Teubner, 2005; Buhmann, 2007), acknowledging that "any system can steer itself only, with the modification that other systems can regulate it not against, but exactly through its self-regulation. Politics can only create conditions that influence the programme of another system and in this way the self-steering" (Luhmann, 1997b, p. 53).

In this context we may understand, for example, corporate governance guidelines, political incentives to environmental and social considerations and reporting, and encouragement of voluntary compliance with ethical standards. *Third*, political regulation relies on the regulating force of polycontextual interplays between the public perspective, news media, various NGOs and an increasing number of stakeholders. Correspondingly, sanctions take new, polycontextual forms such as mass mediated legitimacy crises and failing support from stakeholders. *Fourth*, when politics and responsibility are decentralized, the traditional legitimating reference of the political system, public opinion, increasingly grows relevant to organizations outside the political system. We see a pronounced increase in public relations structures.

However, on this dimension too, there may be drawbacks – or at least grey zones which deserve analyses from an understanding of the structures and dynamics of contemporary society. Political initiatives and legitimating notions such as CSR force companies into pseudo-political decisions and a societal responsibility without the possibility of securing adequate democratic legitimacy within the structures of contemporary society. Some scholars (e.g. Henderson, 2001; Michael, 2003) see CSR as a battle over the right to decide on societal goals and their financing. Where companies decide on societal policies instead

---

system is a contexture. Consequently, the functionally differentiated society represents a polycontexturality. Contextuality means discourses, networks, etc. Polycontextualism then is a network of polycontextures.

of democratically elected and monitored politicians doing so, then CSR implies a democratic deficit.

Moreover, CSR is seen as self-regulation with reference to partnerships, policy networks or "multi-stakeholder dialogues". However, given the premise that any organization can see the environment only from its own worldview, then stakeholders will be reconstructed from the company's criteria of relevance: will this lead to economic distortion of society's meaning formation? And as for partnerships and policy networks, how to avoid private politization? Accordingly, Offe and Preuß (2005, p. 9) identify "corporate governance" as "government without opposition".

Part of the politization of business companies is sensitivity to public opinion. How to avoid an over-investment of resources with "PR-sensitive" sectors which know how to promote their cause in mass media and public communication processes? The greater the complexity, the greater the compulsion is to make a selection – and public opinion reduces the immense and accelerating complexity involved in public communication processes with simplified, black-and-white causal attributions (Luhmann, 1995b). Steering a company by reference to public opinion may mean steering by over-simplified, populist criteria.

Globalization: Activation of Previously Passive Legitimacy Conflicts

The fifth structural dimension relates to the conflicts between legitimating notions and legitimization processes in different forms of society as globalization increases the interdependence and sensitivity between societal and cultural forms that were previously separated.

The analyses presented above are empirically founded in northwestern Europe, and since a principal conclusion is that organizational legitimacy and forms of legitimization are closely interrelated to a given society's specific coordination processes, then it follows that the premises of organizational legitimization differ in various regions of the world – although we also see traits of global policy-making and global opinion. Ideals of reflection and polycontextual coordination of the polycontexturality constituted by functional differentiation as analysed above work only in a specific type of society, characterized by the ideas of modernity and the structures of full functional differentiation, by a well-educated and active population, by freedom of expression and of free mass media not strained either by economics, politics, religion or other functional rationales (Luhmann, 1998). Based on Luhmann's societal categories, we basically differ between two types of conflicts: (1) between two fundamentally diverging societal forms, with function and stratification respectively as their primary differentiation; and (2) between contemporary variations of the functionally differentiated society.

Although expanding strongly during the centuries throughout large parts of the world, functional differentiation continues to face societies with *stratification* instead of function as their primary structure of society. In these kinds of societies, hierarchical relationships are basic and group belonging is the predominant way of giving meaning to individual identities (Luhmann, 1997a, pp. 678–706). There are variations of the balance between stratificatory and functional differentiation. However, to illustrate my point, namely that different types of societal constitution breed fundamentally different legitimating corporate settings, I intensify the differences by applying analytical archetypes of full functional differentiation and stratification. Based on Luhmann's analyses of the differences between a functionally differentiated society and a stratified society, decisive differences of organizational legitimacy and legitimizing practice can be identified. *First*, a functionally differentiated society values individual performances and expressions of personal diversity, whereas in a stratified society individual identity and social identity overlap, and consequently dissolve the boundary between a private and a public sphere. *Second*, in functional differentiation, modernist ideas of a public sphere with equal access to a diversity of individual expressions prevail. In stratification, the public sphere is regulated from above (or from a centre) with the function of maintaining a common collectivist identity. *Third*, the dynamics of a functionally differentiated society rests with a pluralist coding of societal values. Social responsibility and legitimacy are debated from differing positions, without an ultimate reason or privileged position. The coordination of society takes place in continuous legitimating and legitimizing processes in polycontextual, pluralist interplays without any centre or top. In a stratified society, societal coordination is hierarchical, most often with religion as the fundamentally legitimating reference of society. Notions of legitimacy are dictated rather than debated. *Fourth*, in functional differentiation, intermixture of functional rationales is illegitimate, such as for instance: (1) of politics and mass media – it is illegitimate if the political system dictates the boundaries of expression to mass media; (2) of religion and politics – it is illegitimate if any religion dictates the government and law of a nation; and (3) of economy and politics or law – bribery of politicians or public servants is illegitimate. In contrast, the stratified society implies no distinct boundaries between religion, politics, economy, mass media, family, etc. Even economics, politics, law and market mechanisms are subject to religion and stratificd group affiliation. *Fifth*, the modernist values of functional differentiation breed a culture of contingency as opposed to necessity and inevitability. Social norms and institutions tend to be acknowledged as contingent, i.e. as choices which could have been taken differently, and consequently as potential subjects to intentional change through reflection and discussion. In contrast, in a primarily stratified society social relations are based on perceptions of necessity, orthodoxy and belief in authorities; norms are assumed as inevitable and necessary to maintain society, as unquestionably accepted self-evidences, "and if someone harbours doubts, that person can scarcely be included in communication. Anyone who attempted to do so would be reproached with 'error'" (Luhmann, 1995a, p. 468). Freedom of expression without boundaries of necessity is illegitimate. Accordingly, the ultimate conflict is localized between the late modern society and societies dominated by stratification, where functional differentiation plays a secondary role, as experienced by Scandinavian dairy cooperative Arla Foods in 2006. Because of a Danish newspaper's cartoons of Muslim prophet Mohammed, publicized as "a test of freedom of expression" (Rose, 2005), first, the company was boycotted in Arab countries dominated by stratified structures. Later, after having tried to legitimize itself in Arab countries by publicly expressing respect of local values, Arla Foods was threatened with boycott back home in Scandinavia for betraying modernist values (Holmström et al., 2010).

In contrast, societies characterized by functional differentiation share the same basic values of individual choice, the attribution of responsibility within the framework of political democracy, free economic markets, modernist education and positive rights (Baraldi, 2006). Nevertheless, in variations of the functionally differentiated society corporate legitimacy – although apparently very similar with semantics and practices of CSR and business ethics – differs more than meets the immediate eye. First, we see different stages of functional differentiation, and second, we see different forms of political regulation. In particular, we can compare the degree of *monocentred versus decentred regulation, exterior other-regulation versus self-regulation, internal versus external complexity* with decisive implications for the legitimating notions mediating the interrelations between organization and society. Inherent conflicts surface for instance in differing notions of the stakeholder concept in the liberal economy of the USA and the negotiated economy of Denmark with a tradition for involving a plurality of perspectives in the policy-making processes (Campbell et al., 2006). In particular, the post-communist countries of Eastern Europe show different transitional stages from a politically monocentred dominance towards a society constituted by independent functional spheres. Economy is gradually developing on autonomous premises with private propriety rights and without political planning (Lawniczak, 2001, 2005). News media are gradually freeing themselves from their function as mediators of political propaganda. Correspondingly, companies are slowly learning to take on independent responsibility and to install measures of self-restriction after having been strictly politically controlled. However, transitive societies have not yet stabilized the specific societal constitution, which is a precondition of the notions of organizational legitimacy analysed above as reflection.

Therefore, when adding the dimension of globalization, the complexity increases decisively, since globalization is a process creating interdependence and consequently sensitivity among societies and cultures that were previously separated. The intensified relations activate previously passive conflicts between different societal forms, values and cultures. Although we see attempts of global ideals, they will be interpreted differently. We cannot identify common global ideals, but have to relate legitimating notions to the societal constitution. I shall suggest, however, that within the fully functional differentiated society we will see the principle of reflection evolving as the idea also at the meta-level, meaning that an organization with an identity basically rooted in a specific culture and in specific ideals of legitimacy is aware of this as a result of a contingent societal and cultural context – and at the same time is able to take into consideration different cultural and societal contexts within which the organization operates. However, not only will some legitimacy conflicts be unavoidable when a company addresses fundamentally different cultural and societal horizons; also, any company will have to apply blind spots in its observation of the world, based on the company's specific cultural and societal roots.

Why it Might Prove Unethical to Think with the Heart

Above, I have unfolded the social complexity involved in the legitimating notions evolved during the later decades on five structural dimensions. They all originate from the specific societal stage of full functional differentiation, and each in their way contributes to evolving new legitimating notions as to the interrelation between society and organization. *First*, society's strains on its environment – human beings, nature – increasingly activate questions as to the fundamental constitution of modern society as functionally differentiated. This questioning leads to, *second*, the increasing acknowledgement of contingency as the fundamental premise of decision-making, and consequently to demands of responsibility, transparency and sustainability. *Third*, the increasing interdependence and thus sensitivity between the highly specialized social filters of full functional differentiation intensifies the effects of the two first dimensions. *Fourth*, resonance is further boosted by the political system's endeavours towards polycontextual regulation in order to solve the problems of society's strains on its environment, the increasing sense of risk prevailing in society and the polycontexturality of the increasingly differentiated society. *Fifth*, with globalization, problems are multiplied as they are thrown around between different forms of society with their different values and different legitimating notions as to the role of economics and the interrelation between business and society.

On all five structural dimensions the social mechanism of reflection was provoked and embedded in the evolution of legitimating notions during the latter half of the twentieth century, as a reaction to the reflexivity of full functional differentiation, although on five different dimensions. In response to the blind side-effects of reflexivity expressed as society's strains on its environment, reflection implies an attempt for society to re-enter the difference between society and environment within society – expressed for instance in the triple bottom line of people, planet, profit. As for the inherent conflict between decision-maker and victim, reflection uncovers the contingent nature of social processes and opens up to acknowledging the responsibility involved in decision-taking. As for the increasing functional interdependence activated by increasing functional independence, reflection implies a respect for functional socio-diversity. As for polycontextual political regulation, the reflective perspective seems a precondition for organizations to navigate in a polycontextually coordinated (world) society. As for globalization, the principle of meta-reflection implies an understanding of the contingency of one's own societal and cultural context – and consequently considerations of different cultural and societal contexts.

Therefore, the new legitimating ideals empirically expressed as ethics, corporate social responsibility, triple bottom line, etc., and theoretically reconstructed as reflection, are provoked by a range of very different structural problems which – and this is a main conclusion – should be confronted with the utmost analytical stringency. We have to distinguish between the different problems if we wish to understand and confront the problems. As for practice, thinking with the heart, using gut feelings or good intentions in general will not suffice to prevent decisions from being made based on under-complexity or distorted complexity, or simply from trying to solve new problems with old ideas.

In the immediate analysis, reflection may seem a panacea. However, a prominent quality of Luhmann's theories is the unrelenting and unsentimental sensitivity to new problems resulting from solutions to previous problems. The backcloth of a reflective society is the acknowledgement of contingency and a hyper-irritated state of society which apparently cannot be suspended by more knowledge, or more information. Where organizations are forced, on the one hand, to make decisions, these decisions can, on the other hand, refer to no ultimate reason. These traits lead to public attention being continuously alerted, the position of fear being stimulated over and over, and prejudices and worries about the future prevailing. Consensus is not possible, partly because society is differentiated in irreconcilable perspectives, and partly because, since future consequences cannot be known in advance, there can be no unambiguously right solutions. Reflection copes with contingency, however it also increases the perception of flux, and may lead to hyper-irritation, feelings of powerlessness and indifference, paralysis of decision processes or distorted resonance, such as for instance extensive resources spent on social reporting and media alertness.

Moreover, reflection is a risky and resource-demanding form of communication. Risky, because it may raise doubt within an organization about its own boundaries and *raison d'être*. Resource-demanding because reflection doubles the communicative processes and makes decision processes far more ambiguous than reflexivity: "One becomes involved in drawing never ending distinctions between distinctions, which always transport the other side along with everything that is thought and said" (Luhmann, 1993a, p. 229). Empirically, we have observed how, as reflective processes diffuse, they are relieved into *best practice* routines which are adaptable to basic existing structures in the form of, for instance, certification, verification, sustainability accounts and business guidelines for social responsibility. Society canalizes its polycontextual self-regulation from unstable, hyper-irritable conditions into more secure patterns of expectation. It returns second-order observations to the level of first-order observations, and "it is by no means the old naïvety of direct common belief in the world but of finding a solution to inextricable entanglements in communication" (Luhmann, 1993a, p. 229). However, after this adjustment of modernity we may expect a gradual return to reflexivity, although with new perceptions of legitimacy stabilized

– upon which new evolutions can take their start. By gradually structuring new expectations, centuries of legitimacy crises seem to have helped the established society – including the business community – adjust and preserve itself rather than threaten it. New legitimating notions such as CSR, ethical programmes and triple bottom line reporting have apparently strengthened functional differentiation. This does not mean that learning processes and evolution necessarily lead to something better – but that society manages more complexity. On all five structural dimensions analysed, new legitimating notions and practices to some extent solve society's structural problems; however, although they are often presented as simple and self-evident solutions, they are embedded in complex contexts and often provoke new problems.

In conclusion, I shall suggest that the largest risk facing responsible business behaviour is a reduction of complex social dynamics to good intentions. They tend to overshadow and dwarf the social complexity within which the problems are embedded. Instead, responsible practice requires insight into the complexity of social structures and self-referential dynamics of social processes, and responsible science requires serious attempts to identify the complexity by avoiding resort to ideology, politics or morals in its own optics on social complexity.

References

Andersen, N. Å. (2004), Supervisionsstaten og den politiske virksomhed. [The Supervision State and the Political Organisation], in C. Frankel (ed.), *Virksomhedens Politisering* [*The Politisation of the Company*]. Copenhagen: Samfundslitteratur.

Baecker, D. (2003), Organisation som begreb: Niklas Luhmann om beslutningens grænser. [Organisation as Concept: Niklas Luhmann on the Boundaries of Decision], in H. Højlund and M. Knudsen (eds), *Organiseret kommunikation – systemteoretiske analyser* [*Organised Communication – Systems Theoretical Analyses*]. Copenhagen: Samfundslitteratur, pp. 17–34.

Baecker, D. (2006), "Niklas Luhmann". *Systemagazin*, http://www.systemagazin.de/beitraege/luhmann/baecker_luhmann.php (accessed 5 January 2006).

Baraldi, C. (2006), New Forms of Intercultural Communication in a Globalized World. *The International Communication Gazette*, 68(1), 53–69.

Beck, U. (1992), *Risk Society: Towards a New Modernity*. London: Sage.

Beckert, J. (2006), Sind Unternehmen sozial verantwortlich? Conference on *Unternehmensethik*. Zentrum für interdisziplinäre Forschung der Universität Bielefeld. Unpublished manuscript.

Buhmann, K. (2007), Emerging EU Regulation on CSR: Legitimacy Challenges and Reflexivity, in *Organisation and Society: Legitimacy in a Changing World*. Roskilde University/Lund University; www.euprera-loke-2007.ruc.dk.

Campbell, J. L. et al. (2006), *National Identity and the Varieties of Capitalism: the Danish Experience*. Quebec: McGill–Queen's University Press.

EU Commission (2001), *European Governance – a White Paper*. Brussels.

Fuchs, P. (2007), Ethik und Gesellschaft – eine Vorlesung; http://www.fen.ch/texte/gast_fuchs_ethik.pdf (accessed 5 March 2007). Unpublished manuscript.

Habermas, J. and N. Luhmann (1971), *Theorie der Gesellschaft oder Sozialtechnologie*. Frankfurt am Main: Suhrkamp.

Henderson, D. (2001), *Misguided Virtue, False Notions of Corporate Social Responsibility*. London: The Institute of Economic Affairs.

Holmström, S. (1997), An Intersubjective and a Social Systemic Public Relations Paradigm. *Journal of Communications Management*, 2(1), 24–39.

Holmström, S. (1998), *An Intersubjective and a Social Systemic Public Relations Paradigm*. Roskilde: Roskilde University Publishers; www.susanne-holmstrom.dk/SH1996UK.pdf.

Holmström, S. (2002), Public Relations Reconstructed as Part of Society's Evolutionary Learning Processes, in *The Status of Public Relations Knowledge*, D. Vercic et al. (eds). Ljubljana: Pristop Communications, pp. 76–91.

Holmström, S. (2003), *Grænser for ansvar [Limits of Responsibility]*. PhD thesis 41/2003, Roskilde University.

Holmström, S. (2004), The reflective paradigm, in *Public Relations in Europe*, B. v. Ruler and D. Vercic (eds). Berlin: de Gruyter, pp. 121–134.

Holmström, S. (2005a), Fear, Risk, and Reflection. *Contatti (Udine University: Forum)*, 1(1), 21–45.

Holmström, S. (2005b), Reframing Public Relations: the Evolution of a Reflective Paradigm for Organizational Legitimization. *Public Relations Review*, 31(4), 497–504.

Holmström, S. (2007), Co-evolution of Society and Organization: Reflexivity, Contingency and Reflection. *Alicerces, revista de devilgacao científica do instituto politecnico de Lisboa*, 1(1), 489–504.

Holmström, S. (2008), Reflection: Legitimising Late Modernity, in *Public Relations Research: European and International Perspectives and Innovations*, A. Zerfass et al. (eds). Wiesbaden: Westdeutscher, pp. 235–250.

Holmström, S., Falkheimer, J. and Gade Nielsen, A. (2010), Legitimacy and Strategic Communication in Globalization: The Cartoon Crisis and Other Legitimacy Conflicts. *International Journal of Strategic Communication*, 4, 1–18.

Jalava, J. (2003), From Norms to Trust – The Luhmannian Connection between Trust and System. *European Journal of Social Theory*, 6(2), 173–190.

Knodt, E. M. (1995), Foreword, in N. Luhmann (ed.), *Social Systems*. Stanford, CA: Stanford University Press, pp. ix–xxxvi.

Krohn, W. (1999), Funktionen der Moralkommunikation. *Soziale Systeme*, 5(2), 313–338.

Lawniczak, R. (2001), Transition Public Relations – an Instrument for Systemic Transformation in Central and Eastern Europe, in R. Lawniczak (ed.), *Public Relations Contribution to Transition in Central and Eastern Europe – Research and Practice*. Poznan: Poznan University of Economics, pp. 7–18.

Lawniczak, R. (ed.) (2005), *Introducing Market Economy Institutions and Instruments: The Role of Public Relations in Transition Economies*. Poznan: Piar.pl.

Luhmann, N. (1989), *Ecological Communication*. Chicago, IL: University of Chicago Press.

Luhmann, N. (1990), *Die Wissenschaft der Gesellschaft* [*The Science of Society*]. Frankfurt am Main: Suhrkamp.

Luhmann, N. (1993a), *Risk: a Sociological Theory*. Berlin: de Gruyter.

Luhmann, N. (1993b), *Legitimation durch Verfahren* [*Legitimation via Procedure*]. Frankfurt am Main: Suhrkamp.

Luhmann, N. (1995a), *Social Systems*. Stanford, CA: Stanford University Press.

Luhmann, N. (1995b), Brent Spar oder Können Unternehmen von der Öffentlichkeit lernen? [Brent Spar or Can Companies Learn from the Public?] Frankfurt: *Frankfurter Allgemeine Zeitung*, p. 27.

Luhmann, N. (1996a), *Protest: Systemtheorie und soziale Bewegungen* [*Protest: Systems Theory and Social Movements*]. Frankfurt am Main: Suhrkamp.

Luhmann, N. (1996b), *Die Realität der Massenmedien* [*The Reality of the Mass Media*]. Opladen: Westdeutscher Verlag.

Luhmann, N. (1997a), *Die Gesellschaft der Gesellschaft* [*Society's Society*]. Frankfurt am Main: Suhrkamp.

Luhmann, N. (1997b), Limits of Steering. *Theory, Culture and Society*, 14(1), 41–57.

Luhmann, N. (1998), *Observations on Modernity*, W. Whobrey (trans.). Stanford, CA: Stanford University Press.

Luhmann, N. (1999), *Die Wirtschaft der Gesellschaft* [*Society's Business*]. Frankfurt am Main: Suhrkamp.

Luhmann, N. (2000a), *Organisation und Entscheidung* [*Organisation and Decision*]. Opladen: Westdeutscher Verlag.

Luhmann, N. (2000b), *Die Politik der Gesellschaft* [*Society's Politics*]. Frankfurt am Main: Suhrkamp.

Luhmann, N. (2002a), *Art as a Social System*. Stanford, CA: Stanford University Press.

Luhmann, N. (2002b), *Die Religion der Gesellschaft* [*Society's Religion*]. Frankfurt am Main: Suhrkamp.

Luhmann, N. (2002c), *Das Erziehungssystem der Gesellschaft* [*Society's Education System*]. Frankfurt am Main: Suhrkamp.

Luhmann, N. (2003), Beslutningens paradoks [The Paradox of Decision], in *Organiseret kommunikation – systemteoretiske analyser* [*Organised Communication – Systems Theoretical Analyses*], H. Højlund and M. Knudsen (eds). Copenhagen: Samfundslitteratur, pp. 35–61.

Luhmann, N. (2008), Wirtschaftsethik – als Ethik? [Business Ethics – as Ethics?], in *Die Moral der Gesellschaft* [*Society's Moral*], D. Horster (ed.). Frankfurt am Main: Suhrkamp, pp. 196–208.

Mandag Morgen (1997), Den etiske virksomhed [The Ethical Corporation]. *Ugebrevet Mandag Morgen,* 24–30.

Michael, B. (2003), Corporate Social Responsibility in International Development: an Overview and Critique. *Corporate Social Responsibility and Environmental Management,* 10, 115–128.

Offe, C. and Preuß, U. (2005), The Problem of Legitimacy in the European Polity: is Democratization the Answer? Berlin. Unpublished manuscript.

Parsons, T. (1951). *Towards a General Theory of Action.* Cambridge, MA: Harvard University Press.

Pruzan, P. (1998), Hvad er etik i erhvervslivet [What is Ethic in Business], in *Etik i dansk erhvervsliv – fremtidens lederkrav [Ethics in Danish Business Life – Future Demands on the Leader]*, K. Boelsgaard (ed.). Denmark: Jyllands-Postens Erhvervsbøger.

Rose, F. (2005), Freedom of Expression: the Face of Mohammed. *Jyllands-Posten,* Århus, 30 September, p. 3.

Sand, I.-J. (2004), Polycontexturality as an Alternative to Constitutionalism, in *Transnational Governance and Constitutionalism*, C. Joerges et al. (eds). Oxford: Hart, pp. 44–66.

Teubner, G. (2005), Substantive and Reflexive Elements in Modern Law, in *The Law and Society Canon*, C. Seron (ed.). Aldershot: Ashgate, pp. 75–122.

Willke, H. (1994), Staat und Gesellschaft [State and Society], in *Die Verwaltung des politischen Systems [The Administration of the Political System]*, K. Dammann et al. (eds). Opladen: Westdeutscher Verlag, pp. 13–26.

Willke, H. (1997), *Supervision des Staates [The Supervision of the State]*. Frankfurt am Main: Suhrkamp.

Willke, H. and Willke, G. (2008), Corporate Moral Legitimacy and the Legitimacy of Morals. *Journal of Business Ethics,* 81, 27–38.

Chapter 11

Hide and Seek in the Dark – On the Inherent Ambiguity of CSR

Ole Thyssen

When civilizations clash, it is all about values, but the battlefield is not only civilizations, but also organizations. In the last 30 years, values have invaded business life and created new agendas, as not only economic, but also ethical, human, social, environmental and a host of other values fight for a place in the sun.

Values in Organizations

Working with values might be difficult. Working without values is impossible. According to Talcott Parsons (1951, p. 12), a value is "a standard for selection among alternatives". This definition may be specified: a value is a binary distinction with an in-built asymmetry, so that one side is preferred. So decision-making presupposes values. Only because *much* is better than *less* when it comes to values such as money, power, efficiency or reputation, can decisions be made.

Without values, decision-making degenerates and becomes arbitrary. If you do not know where to go, and do not care about the transport, one road is as good as another. In Kurosawa's movie, *The Bodyguard*, the Samurai Sanjuro throws a stick in the air and follows its direction after it falls. Even in this case of an arbitrary choice, values enter the stage from behind. Sanjuro presupposes that it is better to find a way than not to find it, so making even an arbitrary decision is automatically the expression of a value. Sanjuro needs to go *somewhere*. Even more radically, *not* doing anything may be observed as a choice of passivity. Consequently, there are no value-free zones.

Offering a simple distinction, a value accomplishes three tasks – simplification, a yardstick for success or failure, and motivation, but it only does so if accepted as a premise for decisions. This may not be the case. The existence of a value does not automatically mean that it is activated. It may be considered

1. normatively binding;
2. empirically relevant as a means to obtain other values; or
3. irrelevant or even harmful.

Whether a value is considered a goal in itself or just a means to achieve other goals is, as we shall see, a crucial question when it comes to corporate social responsibility (CSR) activities.

If values are inherent in any decision, talking about "value based management" seems superfluous, as management is only possible based on values. So the term needs specification. "Values" in organizations are normally soft values as opposed to hard values such as money, power and law. They have to do with welfare, environment, social benefits and human rights.

Somewhat arbitrarily the term "value" refers to the soft side of the distinction between soft and hard values. The reason is, of course, that only soft values need a normative backing. They are presented as an *ought*, a moral demand universally binding. Hard values, on the contrary, are in no need of support. It is not necessary to insist that organizations ought to make a profit, because economic gain is considered self-motivating. On the other hand, it is not self-evident that organizations fulfil soft values, even if they are considered beneficial for individuals or for society as a whole. Soft values are introduced in order to civilize organizations by curbing their greed, so that the distinction between soft and hard values has the same structure as the classical philosophical distinction between reason and passion, or moral and desire.

The rigid distinction between soft and hard values is softened when organizations consider soft values a useful resource. Soft values may be means to hard values as ends. By using soft values as tools for observing and premises for deciding, organizations make themselves sensitive to phenomena which are invisible in the light of money or power. Violating human rights may not be an economic problem. On the contrary, money can be made by accepting harsh working conditions, but in the long run such violations may damage the image and consequently harm the earnings. Not because of a feeling of moral obligation – an organization has no feelings! – but as a matter of sheer prudence, it may decide not to violate human rights and accept observation of its activities in this light.

Taking responsibility for a soft value is to accept being accountable, giving stakeholders *a licence to critique*. It is to claim that organizational activities are transparent and that responsibility is no lip service or a trick to fool the public.

By accepting soft values organizations change their self-description. As no organization is visible in detail, due to its complexity and the coexistence of too many simultaneous processes, organizations must produce models, images and texts to describe themselves. So values have to do with the past, the present and the future of organizations. They are rooted in their tradition and may be seen as *mémoires* of what at a certain time seemed important; they bind the present and they are visions for the future.

Focusing on the social responsibilities of organizations, the distinction between soft and hard values will be specified as a distinction between political and economic values. These two kinds of values pull in different directions, but there are interesting causal interconnections, because organizations are evaluated according to both political and economic performance. Even if economic and political values create their own worlds, they are coupled to each other. These couplings are not tight and do not allow simple measuring, but political values may create meaning and motivation, which are also economic resources. It makes more sense to die for lofty ideals than for a well-ordered budget.

Values and Value Conflicts

Introducing political values means a simplification because they offer an advantage of speed in cases where decision-making on a purely economic basis is complicated or impossible. Whether or not it is profitable to use a cheap labour force in low-wage countries such as India or China, considering the possible damage to the image and the cost of damage control, is not easy to decide. Using human rights as a criterion, the decision is easy. More values mean more sensitivity and an increased battery of selection tools.

On the other hand, the introduction of a plurality of values means a complication if values are conflicting, so that second-order values or super-values must be introduced to decide which values carry the greatest weight. As even super-values are values, third-order values must be introduced if it is questioned whether a super-value really is able to outweigh a "normal" value.

In theory, organizations run into the so-called "trilemma" of a vicious circle, a never ending regress or an arbitrary choice. In practice, such complications are avoided by creating frames with an in-built value orientation, thus making the problem of finding super-values superfluous. It is normally not questioned that a private organization must make a profit to exist. Tradition normalizes contingency by preventing "silly" questions being asked, thus hiding the fact that a choice has even been made. This also goes for public organizations, which have values inscribed in their names. A school must be interested in education and a hospital in health, and if a judge states that he does not care about the distinction between legal and illegal, he will be considered cheerful or mad.

Introducing political values re-opens the problem of choosing between values. If a private organization commits itself to human rights and at the same time is forced by competition to operate in a low-wage country, the question arises whether it is possible uncompromisingly to shoulder such obligations without being forced *out of business*. This raises the awkward question of whether it is ethically correct to withdraw and, consequently, to ruin the lives of poor employees in the name of ethical values.

Conflicts between different kinds of values are without objective solutions. As a value is a standard for selection, it takes second-order standards to solve value conflicts, but at the end of the line no imperative values can be found. Even if it is possible to identify some basic values in Western societies, they do not have the accuracy necessary to solve value conflicts in a neutral manner.

Even if a single value might look self-evident, observed in isolation, unsolvable conflicts arise when a plurality of values are introduced, each with a claim of being fulfilled. Money is the basic value for private organizations, but money can be made in many ways, and money is only a basic value in the economic field, not in the religious or cultural field.

That value conflicts have no objective solution does not mean that solutions cannot be found. An organization may solve value problems as it pleases, only it has to take full responsibility. Absence of objective solutions means the presence of responsibility, because an objective decision is anonymous, whereas a non-objective decision is ascribed to the decision-maker. The solution of a value conflict makes the organization visible and becomes part of its identity.

Economical and political values can be related in various ways. They may be (a) equally ranked or (b) hierarchically ordered. They may each (c) define a minimum threshold or (d) provide a vision for the future.

Equal Ranking

If economical and political values carry equal weight, problems arise when economic and political regards pull in different directions. Which value must be sacrificed? Equality creates an undetermined space where compromises must be made, but with freedom to choose *which* compromise. More values do not necessarily mean less freedom but, on the contrary, more freedom to choose according to what seems important in a specific context.

Hierarchical Ordering

If one value always carries greater weight than another, the "lower" value is in practice suspended. If profit is always of more importance than human rights, the organization will only make an appeal to human rights if it does not cost anything or if it is considered a means to economic gain. In this case, political values are just for show.

Hierarchy does not mean that the lower values are just illusions, only that no *direct* effort is made to fulfil them. They may, as we have seen, be used strategically if an organization can only get a *licence to operate* by fulfilling human rights. Considerations are only *indirect*.

However, can it be measured how political values affect the economic results of an organization? The answer to this question seems to be "no". Values are not small and hard objects. They include personal attitudes, they mean different things to different people, and talking about values it is hard to distinguish between fact and illusion. When it comes to values, David Hume's model of the causal relation, two billiard balls colliding, is simply not adequate. Neither causes nor effects exist in this simple form. They have to be constructed and isolated, giving ample space for "guesstimates", because an infinite past has to be connected with an equally infinite future through the small keyhole of the present. Some effects are unambiguous and lack alternatives, but others are ill-defined, contingent and depending on the preferences and aspirations of the observer, so that, in the words of Niklas Luhmann, the observer causes the causal relation (Luhmann, 2000, p. 452f). Whether a description of the causal connection between economical results and political values is accepted or not is an empirical question involving rhetoric more than logic. According to Aristotle, rhetoric is used in situations that are scientifically inaccessible.

As organizations are not persons, it is difficult to decide whether an organization assumes direct or indirect responsibility for political values. No scrutiny of managerial feelings will disclose the quality of the value. Managers take on a professional role in their decision-making and do not express personal feelings. The gap between feeling and decision may be wide. Therefore, the quality of organizational values cannot, in the spirit of protestantism, be decided by testing the goodwill of the decision-maker, but must, in the spirit of catholicism, be measured by the good deeds and their consistency over time.

Minimum Thresholds

Nothing prevents the fact that different values mark minimum thresholds, which an organization commits itself to remain above. Political values are accepted and may lower profits, but not too much. Conversely, economically promising projects might be rejected if they violate human rights too crudely. If both minimum thresholds are imperative, the organization only has to avoid moving into the red area in both places. How it balances the different kinds of values in the allowed area is, again, a purely empirical question.

Values as Visions

A value may present a rigid distinction between acceptable and not acceptable, but it may also be observed in the temporal dimension as a vision to be obtained in the future, even if it is not possible to fulfil it for the present. In this way, an organization may both accept and violate a value.

This, of course, is a complicated manoeuvre, and to avoid accusation of double talk and even lying, the organization must demonstrate an active interest in furthering the value. In the words of Niklas Luhmann, it must act in order to minimize the difference between reality and norm (Luhmann, 1992, p. 208). Just as an organization may accept less money now in order to gain more money later, it can accept violations of political values here and now, while at the same time working to minimize the difference between *status quo* and vision.

This approach is much used by Western organizations in low-wage countries. Even if it has its own risks, it is hard to deny that it is suicidal for an organization to demand perfection as a condition for operating in India or China.

Trying to reach perfection is not only impossible, but also foolish. Perfection allows no improvement. By keeping the distance between *status quo* and vision open, an organization keeps its values ready for different and unpredictable tasks. Political visions are not meant to be completed.

Normalization of Hypocrisy

If an organization has to fulfil both economic and political values, it is not unusual for it to exaggerate its commitment to both kinds. It mingles its present with a hoped-for future, *status quo* with utopia. In short, it plays the hypocrite and accepts, following Machiavelli, that managers must be great pretenders.

Hypocrisy is quite different from lying, but what is the difference? In short, lying is saying something which you know is not true. Hypocrisy, in a managerial context, is understating what you know is true in order to create a better future – better in the light of some value. Therefore hypocrisy is treated with more indulgence that lying. It may even be considered a managerial duty to be a hypocrite, but again there is a precaution: the manager must show that she is active in promoting the value. Otherwise the tolerance vanishes and she is accused of simply lying.

Managers are not theorists who must describe the reality as it is. They are practitioners, who must create a reality not yet existing. To do this, they must motivate employees, customers and the public. Like marksmen they do this by aiming in front of the goal in order to hit the goal. They present the present as if a desired future is already in existence. They do not tell the whole truth if it might hurt the motivation of employees or customers. This conjuring trick, if not double talk, is accepted as long as the organization makes a serious effort to fulfil the goal. Soft values represent long-range ends rather than actual achievements, but the borderline between present and future is deliberately kept blurred.

According to the Nils Brunsson, hypocrisy implies a decoupling of words, decisions and actions (Brunsson, 2003, p. 27). What is said is in conflict with what is decided, what is decided is in conflict with what is done, and what is done is neither said nor decided officially. If political values are considered both mandatory *and* impossible, they may form part of the self-description of an organization, not in order to be fulfilled, but in order to legitimate that they are *not* fulfilled. The mechanism is simple: because an organization claims that it will fulfil them, it is tolerated that it does not do it fully for the time being. The presence of words compensates for the absence of actions, and the fulfilment of the commitment is transferred into an open future. Trust is exploited as a joker in an equivocal game.

Hypocrisy protects actions by creating opaque situations, where words and actions are not easy to compare. It thrives on distance in space and time, so that words are uttered in one department, actions are done in another, or problems in the present are compensated for by visions of the future. As the public normally has no access to organizational activities or to what happens in distant Chinese villages, an organization gets a breathing space to construct an imaginary – and highly motivating – reality to cover the less spectacular realities. Brunsson enumerates a whole series of techniques to keep words, decisions and actions apart – or to avoid negative consequences if the trick is seen through. He mentions (a) silence or "drop a distinction", (b) political support by a dominating group, making the organization immune to critique, (c) decoupling of economic and political discourses by using different rhetoric to different groups, and finally (d) focus on consensus and repression of conflict (Brunsson, 2003, p. 10).

Hypocrisy is not an option, but a must, because management talk is a *positive genre*. A manager may criticize his organization internally, but externally he must present it as spotless and competent. In the stories he tells about his organization only solved or manageable problems are mentioned. Investors are only willing to risk their capital if prospects are bright.

It is no wonder that the stronghold of capitalism, the USA, has produced not only the greatest multinational organizations, but also Hollywood, which has the same unfailing optimism. In Hollywood stories have a happy ending and hope is always kept alive – a fact which Hollywood movies may use self-referentially when they compare American belief in success with a European sense of tragedy. Public talk of managers exudes optimism, because pessimism is self-fulfilling and, therefore, must be avoided.

Another American cultural product, rock music, also presents a business pattern. Hard rock and sentimental tunes alternate in the same manner as organizations alternate between insinuating PR-talk and harsh economic analysis.

CSR – Inevitably a Grey Area

A distinctive mark of CSR is that it must be voluntary. If responsibility is demanded by the law, it ceases to be *corporate* responsibility and is not part of the specific identity of an organization. Consequently organizations are free to choose how they define their social responsibilities. This is done by selecting areas with high public visibility, strategic interest and affordable costs. Vulnerable areas may be chosen to demonstrate goodwill and prevent criticism. As organizations are their own end, they consider political values as means to their own growth and prosperity. Basically, they do not care about society or the environment *except* as resources.

A further consequence is that the public do not trust the values statements or ethical codes of organizations. Commitments are not supposed to be absolute and everlasting, only strategic and temporary. It came as no big surprise when BP, British Petroleum, in October 2007 gave up its green image of going "Beyond Petroleum" and investing in renewable resources of energy. Instead it changed direction and went "Back to Petroleum", because its profits were considered too low and a promising business area was seen in the so-called "oil sands" – according to Greenpeace, the dirtiest way to extract oil from the ground.

Because of the diversity of CSR strategies and the desire to use them as tools for creating a unique identity, it is hard to compare the achievements of different organizations. Even if standards have been constructed, such as ISI 1300, standardization weakens the focus on CSR, because a standard is the same for all, nothing special for me.

So diversity seems to be an inherent feature of CSR strategies. Combined with their volatility, the whole area of CSR seems to be ill-defined and ever-changing. It might be argued that CSR is a new phenomenon which calls for patience and support rather than the barren pleasure of radical critique. One does not reject a new born baby just because it is unable to walk and talk. However, this defence overlooks that it is hard to imagine what kinds of improvements are possible. Regulation and standardization are possible, but not wanted, because they are looking backward, not forward and do not strengthen the image of an organization.

Therefore, the conclusion must be that, using CSR strategies, organizations try to combine economic and political values by playing hide and seek in the dark. They tell the public that good business has a double meaning, both economic and political, but the public is in doubt and with good reasons. Normally the public has no access to the activities of organizations, at home or abroad. This gives organizations ample space for constructing illusions, but every time an organization is exposed in prime time for using political values as a smoke screen to cover shady activities, or changes its CSR profile in order to adapt to fluctuations of the market, the general confidence in CSR is weakened.

So CSR is no panacea against the evils of capitalism. On the contrary, it is yet another organizational tool for adapting to the demands of the market place. Whether or not a CSR strategy can be trusted is a purely empirical matter which cannot be decided in general. This does not mean that CSR should be abandoned, but the pressure must come from the outside, from the political community and from the public or, to be more precise, from the mass media. Only by putting constant pressure on organizations and by criticizing them for using political values to obscure facts can there be an interesting future for CSR. The colour of CSR is grey, not red.

References

Brunsson, N. (2003), *The Organization of Hypocrisy. Talk, Decisions and Actions in Organizations*. Oslo: Liber.

Luhmann, N. (1992), *Beobachtungen der Moderne*. Opladen: Westdeutscher Verlag.

Luhmann, N. (2000), *Organisation und Entscheidung*. Opladen: Westdeutscher Verlag.

Parsons, T. (1951), *The Social System*. New York: The Free Press.

Chapter 12

"Ethics of Sensitivity" – Towards a New Work Ethic: New Age in Business Life

Kirsten Marie Bovbjerg

The relation between employees and their workplace has changed in recent decades – leaders show an increasing awareness of the importance of employees' competencies aside from strictly professional qualifications. A variety of techniques rooted in New Age philosophy have been applied in private and public organizations, either in order to identify the right employee for the right position through various kinds of testing, or as part of personal development and team-building efforts (Bovbjerg, 1995; Bovbjerg; 2001; Bovbjerg, 2007a, b; Salamon and Goldschmith, 2002; Auspers and Houtmann, 2006). Many of these techniques have their origin in modern religious thoughts and New Age practices such as Zen buddhism, Landmark, neuro-linguistic programming (NLP), transcendental meditation, fire-walking and meditation techniques.

The term "ethics of sensitivity" is developed in research I have completed on courses in personal development in working life. These courses are to a large extent inspired by New Age psychotherapeutic techniques. Key words in the ethics of sensitivity are: personal growth, self-management and searching for an authentic inner core. A range of techniques support this new ethic: therapeutic courses at work, coaching, team building, appraisals and stress-coping. Employees see their personal development as an individual project in which they experience the optimization of their opportunities for self-expression, and also of their human attributes, by the unveiling of their hidden resources. The cultivation of the individual's inner emotional life is a practice whereby modern management and New Age theories give way to the establishment of the ethics of sensitivity. Bizspirit, an American company selling spiritual courses to companies, have this to say on their website:

> Shamans have more in common with business leaders than anyone might expect. Within the indigenous traditions is a vast and deep knowledge waiting to be tapped by the businessperson who is ready to undertake the next step in developing personal power. (http://www.bizspirit.com/bsj/current/fea1.html; 'The Five Values of Shamans. How to Apply Them to Personal Power in Business', by José Luis Stevens, 11 May 2006)

Max Weber

The work of Max Weber provides an excellent starting point for the study of religious practice in modern business life. In his famous work on the rise of the protestant ethic in the early phase of modern capitalism, Weber points out that the new protestant ethic and the protestant idea of salvation had a significant impact on the development of a new economic behaviour and a new attitude towards work (Weber, 1958). Taking the religious approach, I want to introduce the concept "ethics of sensitivity" as an analytical frame for understanding a new work ethic based on a quest for employees' sensitivity, work on the self, and on the prospects for self-realization as a way to flexibility and productivity. Inspired by Weber's work on the protestant ethic, the concept "ethics of sensitivity" is intended to express a particular attitude to work which, I will suggest, is developed methodically through the various programmes for personal development during working life. The cultivation of the individual's inner emotional life is a practice whereby modern management and New Age theories give way to the establishment of the ethics of sensitivity. Could New Age philosophy be of crucial importance for the modern work ethic, in the same way as Weber considers the protestant ethic to be central to the development of early capitalism in Western society?

Gauchet and the Construction of the Unconscious

The premises for personal development are the notion of a mental "self" that can be explored, and the idea of personal transformation by transpersonal techniques such as therapy or mental training. I have tried, in my research, to determine how and why the development of the "inner life" of employees is relevant to their work. As a significant theorist of the role of the "inner life" and the "unconscious" in contemporary culture, the French philosopher Marcel Gauchet provides an explanatory framework for the emphasis on developing the personalities of employees (Gauchet, 1997). According to Gauchet, we cannot hope to understand the origins of either psychology or New Age theories unless we understand the fact that the modern interpretation and explanation of the human is oriented towards the unconscious. The individual's inner life becomes the intangible focus of religious practices, and the subconscious becomes a constituent part of the modern individual's understanding of the Self.

The primary concern in modern religiosity is the individual's potential, based on the notion that the individual has hidden subconscious resources waiting to be accessed through the development of the Self. For the modern individual there is an inner core, which is not immediately visible to the individual, and of which the individual is not immediately conscious, but which is considered to be of importance for the individualization of the subject (Gauchet, 1999). Within this analytical approach, I suggest that an understanding of personal development courses in business life and in organizations, as framed in modern religiosity and often described as "New Age", is important.

Psycho-Religious Practice

New Age can be used as a common denominator for "alternative" explanations of phenomena in very different fields: health, philosophy, management, personal development and others. It is an eclectic movement in the sense that adherents take inspiration from many different religious and psychotherapeutic approaches to assemble their own brand of faith. It consists of religious and therapeutic techniques, which the French sociologists Françoise Champion and Danièle Hervieu-Léger name "psycho-religious practice", and is centred on the conscious and unconscious self.

In the New Age movement, there is no conversion to a coherent faith as in a large number of traditional religious groups; instead the believer shops around in a loose network of attitudes and interests. The idea of authenticity frames the spiritual experience within the individual's narrative of his own being, and knowledge of the self is attained through personal emotional experiences (Champion and Hervieu-Léger, 1990). Through a certain practice, the psycho-religious practitioner expects to achieve self-perfection in a never-ending transformation of the self. The participant is thought to explore unconscious parts of his personal life and to liberate himself from external domination through therapeutic or meditative methods. Emotional problems are, in psycho-religious practice, associated with inauthenticity, and a failure to live in accordance with one's "true self" – in other words, one does not realize one's potential or one's inner convictions and opportunities. Therapeutic techniques are applied in psycho-religious practices, but it is emphasized in these practices that the human being has a fundamental "spiritual" or "divine" substance. A certain habit of sensitivity evolves through transpersonal methods in this psycho-religious practice (Champion, 1990).

Transpersonal Psychology and Personal Growth

Organizations changed dramatically in the 1960s. Since then the aim has been to create an environment within the organization that attempts to consider the autonomous individual in the employee. The employee should adapt herself to the aims of the company, which in turn is constructed in terms of being innovative, flexible and competitive. Modern management must, in Nikolas Rose's words, "work on the ego of the worker itself" (Rose, 1986, p. 112). In this way modern management has set a new agenda for employees. Maslow is a central figure in the modern management theory known as "Human Resource Management", which is based on the notion of personal growth and self-actualization through work. Maslow worked out a theory of the self-actualizing human being in the form of a transpersonal psychology in which the individual is encouraged to exceed his personal bounds. This theory comprises an understanding of the self, an ethic and a lifestyle that encourages authenticity, and consciousness of the body, self-realization and continuous personal improvement. In the late 1950s, Maslow developed a theory of motivation, depicted graphically as a pyramid of needs divided into five levels. According to Maslow the most significant human need is that of self-actualization, which is construed as the driving force in the growth of every individual and in the development of our personality (Savard and Deikman, 1986; Bärmark, 1985). Ethically "good" characteristics are associated with self-actualizing individuals – they have accomplished "personal mastery". Like humanistic psychology, personal development in business is concerned with the human capacity to "grow", and the opportunity to access untapped resources in the individual. References to buddhism, Gestalt therapy, intuition and meditation, among others, frequently crop up in different branches of management literature, and this is also the case in Maslow's work. He often serves as an important reference for New Age groups – especially within the groups known as the Human Potential Movement. There is an interesting connection between prominent management theories, humanistic psychology and New Age milieus such as the Esalen Institute in California (Hammer, 1997; Champion, 1990).

Personal Development in Working Life

We cannot ignore the economic aspect when approaching the rationale for personal development in business life. When the company pays for their staff to be trained they expect an outcome, whether it is the latest version of Microsoft Windows, or personal development of the employee. Rhetorically there is a discourse about personal development, commitment and meaning in work that ignores the economic aspect. From an international conference on business and consciousness quoted on the Bizspirit website it is put in this way:

> When business is done from a place of fullness, we don't so much work as play – to connect, to create, to manifest our potential, to actualize. You go to work to share your creativity, and you are full – and incidentally, you get a pay check. (http://www.bizspirit.com/bsj/current fea4.html, 'Bringing the Soul Into the Workplace'. A Report on the International Conference on Business and Consciousness, by Naomi Rose, 11 May 2006)

In the idea of personal development the economic aspect is recognized, but the application of spiritual methods in business life is often presented as a humane and committed attitude towards employees. Transcendental meditation (TM) has the slogan: "When heart and bottom line aren't opposites" (From the flyer, "Success without stress", about the use of TM in companies). The vision is that the economic goals should be achievable without putting the employee under pressure.

In this sense, personal development is presented as taking care of the employee in all aspects, both the emotional side of the employee and her success in the company. In my research, I have not examined whether participants in courses on personal development achieved the personal competences and personal growth they expected, rather I have explored the attendees' expectations and their notions of personal development.

Managers

In Denmark, managers talk publicly about their spiritual interests and how they use spirituality in their professional life. It is well known that managers from big companies in Denmark seek inspiration from the Silva method, Sai Baba and shamanism amongst other sources (Nielsen, 2006; Salamon and Goldschmith, 2002; Bovbjerg, 2001). Leaders see the purpose of leadership from a new angle. As John Seely, Director of Xerox, puts it "The job of leadership today is not just to make money; it's to make meaning" (Nielsen, 2006, p. 1). Apart from meaning, the leader also sees spirituality as a way to increase productivity. Spirituality in business life is, just like other management strategies, seen as a tool for managers to initiate organizational change and to improve performance at all levels – a strategy to improve the bottom line! From the manager's point of view, the company's need for new qualifications is related to the employee's personality. To become flexible and ready for change, employees have to work with their personality. Developing the employees' personal competences is not just to please them and improve staff relations and cooperation within the company, but also to improve vitally important client relations. As middle manager Karl Christiansen put it:

> I don't pay them [the employees] to like their job. I pay them to do a job. But the work we do is based on human relations, so I have to give them some flexibility and insight into how these things are. This is what they get their salary for. (Karl Christiansen, my translation)[1]

As he sees it, the company's needs for new competencies are related to the personalities of the employees. Becoming flexible and ready for change means that the employees have to work with their personalities. Personal development is used to give staff members new competencies and to change the organizational structure. Organizational change should solve a range of problems according to my informants, including reduction in number of staff and reduction of absence due to illness, and they also expected that the psychological work environment will be

---

1   Karl Christiansen stresses the importance of keeping a distance between work and employees' personal lives as an ethical demand, but at the same time he was responsible for introducing first gestalt therapy and later neuro-linguistic programming into the organization.

improved. The rationale described by my informants was that they believed that each and every human being possesses capacities and resources that we fail to use in daily life.

Employees

Employees often ask for personal development courses in the company. Some employees believe that personal development is a way to get in touch with their "authentic" self: they expect to find the right hidden resources to use at work, and they expect that this personal development and liberation of hidden resources will make them attractive employees. Some employees develop an interest in psychology through work, while others develop an interest in alternative thinking.[2] The majority of my informants consider personal development to be a way to change their lives. One of my informants considers insights about her unconscious self and liberation to be the key reasons to seek out personal development:

> If you are told by others what you are, and people do that all the time, you have limitations imposed on you, limitations that can be overcome. Again, I think you can learn, if you really want to. What I mean is, you can overcome your own conviction that – if I'm not very good at something, then I can at least learn it if I want to and if I can. (Hanne Mikkelsen, my translation)

Informant Hanne Mikkelsen believes her NLP training[3] is a way to get in touch with her "authentic" self, where she expects to find the right hidden resources to use at work. She expects that this personal development and the liberation of her hidden resources will make her an attractive employee. Only a few critical voices have appeared in my empirical material. In general, the employees meet the demands for flexibility and personal development with enthusiasm – even though some ambiguities also seem to be present. That was at least the case in the 1990s. Now there is a new kind of technique on the market – courses in stress-coping, very often using personal development as a way to cope with stress.

---

2   This shows how the psycho-religious practice as described by Hervieu-Léger is relevant for understanding courses in personal development in working life (Hervieu-Léger, 1990).

3   NLP is neuro-linguistic programming. It is one example of a personal development course that is firmly rooted in the field of New Age theory as well as modern management. It was in vogue in the 1990s and seems to be so still. Along with business counselling and other alternative methods such as fire-walking, meditation and Landmark, NLP competes in a market where services such as leadership training and courses in personal development are offered to companies and organizations (Bovbjerg, 2007a). As a "transpersonal" method, NLP conceives of training and therapeutic practice as the road to personal change. By adopting a perspective of change as the main goal, personal development is understood as a way to obtain personal and professional success (Bovbjerg, 2001, 2007a).

Consultants

For consultants, personal development is not just about raising employees' awareness. It is just as much about encouraging a particular kind of conduct and ensuring that employees think of themselves in relation to their company in specific ways. It seems that the relevant adjustments must occur in the mind of the employee himself, who in turn will align his own interests with those of the company. In the business community, personal development courses are aimed at nurturing a particular attitude towards work. The ideal modern working relationship is a compact between the company and the employee, where both parties share a common interest. The organizational theorist Peter Senge put it this way:

> The essence of this compact is the organization's commitment to support the full development of each employee, and the person's reciprocal commitment to the organisation. (Senge, 1990, p. 311)

The ideal employee no longer sees his work from a perspective of duty, but as work done *con amore* – as a way to self-realization. The well-developed employee is self-managing: he derives his devotion to his job from an inner necessity. Courses in personal development are part of the effort to communicate the correct *work ethic*, what I call the *ethics of sensitivity*. A consultant describes his role like this:

> You [as a consultant] have some clear attitudes, a clear understanding of people that you communicate and that you are a good example of, right? You have the ability to take the initiative, and you are more or less self-motivated, right? This means that suddenly there's no need [for the firm] to spend a lot of energy on me [as an employee] because I more or less run things myself. (Peter Soerensen, my translation)

At the time of the interview, Peter Soerensen was employed in a large consultancy firm where he took care of courses for both public and private organizations. He was very much into spiritual training. He notes in passing that development is a personal matter, but at the same time he says that professional development is synonymous with personal development. If the employees follow the right path of personal development, then their impulses towards work will come from within themselves – they will be self-motivated. The goal with the courses that Peter Soerensen and others design is to create an environment in which change becomes a permanent state of affairs, and employees are always ready to meet external changes. Peter Soerensen believes that this state of affairs will create inspiring and innovative workplaces that will foster joy, enthusiasm and creativity. Consultants and managers are supposed to demonstrate that personal change and progress is possible. Managers have to "walk the walk" as well as talk the talk.

A good work ethic is all about attitude adjustment, about a change in the way employees approach their workplace and their colleagues. The work must be driven by passion rather than duty. The American anthropologist Emily Martin suggests that employees in modern companies must establish a positive attitude toward change, and must take an active stance with regard to it (Martin, 1997). Martin describes this belief in change as a myth that has been imprinted in the organization that surrounds our social relations, and in which we comport ourselves on the basis of the opportunities that are given to each of us for development and self-realization. Modern employees should constantly be brought up to date, not just professionally, but also in a personal sense. Just as the company has to keep up with current trends in order to be competitive, the employee cannot just let herself go with the flow in the company. The individual sees herself as a mini-corporation, one that is primarily oriented towards its own interests in the global flow of capital. This is why people feel a need to invest in their own resources and "hidden potentials" to be successful, just as if they themselves were a firm, according to Martin.

The Inner Potentials

Personal development is a widespread idea in schools and other organizations, in sport, in childcare, at work, etc. It would be difficult to argue that personal development could be problematic, or not desirable in all situations, or not for everybody. It is often associated with the idea of lifelong learning. From a UNESCO Report, the former EU chairman Jacques Delors says about the aim for Life Long Learning:

> A broad encompassing view of learning should aim to enable each individual to discover, unearth and enrich his or her creative potential, to reveal the treasure within each of us. This means going beyond an instrumental view of education (…) to one that emphasizes the development of the complete person, in short learning to be. (In Hermann, 2003, p. 7)

"The treasure within" is the hidden potential. To be in the international competition we have to discover the hidden resources in European citizens and reveal the treasure within. In this way there is an essential correspondence between New Age thinking, modern management and neoliberal policy, which appears especially in the shared importance of the optimizing of people's capacities. The unconscious becomes an essential element in ideas surrounding human assets and liabilities. This is why Marcel Gauchet's account of the modern understanding of consciousness as bifurcated by the contemporary idea of the person/self is a central theme in our understanding of the modern culture of work, where personal development has taken a central place in the management strategies of firms.

From the Protestant Ethic to the Ethics of Sensitivity

Employees are encouraged to adopt a new attitude to their work, in which work is viewed as an opportunity to develop one's human potential and progress towards self-actualization. Personal development courses serve not just as paths to knowledge of the self and to self-realization, but also as objects of individual investment. They are considered to be a merging of professional and personal interests through change and improvement of the self. This change and improvement is considered to be for the benefit of the company, making it a reasonable investment to provide personal development for the employees.

New Age philosophy plays a natural part in this development because many of its methods make sense to the employees of modern companies. Employees see their personal development as an individual project in which they experience the optimization of their opportunities for self-expression and of their human attributes by the unveiling of their hidden resources. Personal development supports a work ethic that leaves little room for employees to make a distinction between their personal and professional lives. The person as a whole – conscious as well as unconscious – becomes of interest for organizations under the ethic of sensitivity. This challenges the employee's personal integrity in the sense that it is very difficult to negotiate working conditions in a culture where work is considered to be a way to self-realization. This seems also to be the case when the employee feels under pressure and stressed. Many courses are introduced as a way of improving working conditions and alleviating the problems of modern working life, such as stress and burnout.

According to this new work ethic, modern human beings must work in order to find their "authentic core", which is precisely the way to liberate the good human being and attain self-discipline, both at work and in private life. It is, by definition, an interminable process, which imbues lifelong learning and eternal change with meaning, but at the same time puts modern employees under increasing pressure at work. Ideal employees are seen as being in a permanent state of reflection, learning and experiencing, seeing themselves as being in a state of growth, and adopting an ongoing programme of work upon "the Self". In his work on the protestant ethic and the spirit of capitalism, Max Weber (1958) argues that a particular work ethic evolved from the protestant ethic in the sixteenth century. The ethics of sensibility constitute a new way of thinking about work that has emerged from post-protestant New Age spirituality. Work is no longer to the glory of God, as it used to be in the protestant era: contemporary work is to the glory of the Self.

References

Auspers, S. and Houtman, D. (2006), Beyond the Spiritual Supermarket. The Social and Public Significance of New Age Spirituality. *Journal of Contemporary Religion*, 21, 201–222.

Bärmark, J. (1985), Självforverkligandets psykologi. Ett centralt tema I Maslows tänkande. Sverige: Natur och Kultur.

Bovbjerg, K. M. (1995), Personality Analyses. *Ethnologia Scandinavica*, 5, 50–66.

Bovbjerg, K. M. (2001), *Følsomhedens etik. Tilpasning af personligheden i New Age og moderne management*. Højbjerg: Hovedland.

Bovbjerg, K. M. (2007a), Personal Development under Market Conditions. NLP and the emergence of an ethics of sensitivity based on the notion of untapped personal potentials. Working paper, Department of Educational Anthropology, School of Education, University of Aarhus.

Bovbjerg, K. M. (2007b), De menneskelige potentialer i en "stresstid", in *Medarbejder eller modarbejder – religion i moderne arbejdsliv*, J. Haviv (ed.). Aarhus: KLIM.

Champion, F. (1990), La Nébuleuse Mystique-Ésotérique, in *De l'émotion en religion*, F. Champion and D. Hervieu-Léger (eds). Paris: Centurion.

Champion, F. and Hervieu-Léger, D. (1990), *De l'émotion en religion*. Paris: Centurion.

Gauchet, M. (1997), *The Disenchantement of the World. A Political History of Religion*. New French Thought. Princeton, NJ: Princeton University Press.

Gauchet, M. (1999), Essai de psychologie contemporaine. Un nouvel âge de la personalité. *Le Débat*, March–April, 164–181.

Hammer, O. (1997), På jagt efter helheden. New Age. En ny folketro? Århus: Fremad.

Hermann, S. (2003), Fra styring til ledelse – om kompetencebegrebets udvikling. I *Uddannelse* 01/2003, Undervisningsministerie.

Martin, E. (1997), Managing Americans. Policy and Changes in the Meanings of Work and the Self, in *Anthropology of Policy. Critical Perspectives on Governance and Power*, C. Shore and S. Wright (eds). London: Routledge.

Nielsen, T. (2006), *Religiøs mening i arbejdslivet*. Maj: Kritisk Debat.

Rose, N. (1986), Governing the Soul. The Shaping of the Private Self. London: Routledge.

Salamon, K. and Goldschmith, L. (2002), Beåndet ledelse – en antropologisk analyse af managementkonsulenters nyåndelige diskurs og netværker, PhD series 11, 2002, Forlaget Samfundslitteratur.

Savard, D. and Deikman, A. (1986), Psychologie transpersonnel, in *Gnoses d'hier et d'aujourdhui*. Les Cahiers de recherches en sciences de la religion, Volume 7, R. Lemieux and R. Reginal (eds). Québec: Université Laval.

Senge, P. (1990), The Fifth Discipline. The Art and Practice of the Learning Organization. London: Century Business.

Weber, M. (1958), *The Protestant Ethic and the Spirit of Capitalism*. New York: Charles Schriber.

Chapter 13

Public–Private Development of CSR on the International Stage: Reflexivity and Legitimacy

Karin Buhmann

Introduction

In recent years, various initiatives to promote substantive corporate self-regulation have been launched at intergovernmental level. The UN Global Compact, initiated by then UN Secretary General Kofi Annan, is based on a multi-stakeholder process engaging intergovernmental organizations and business to define the 10 normative principles and other key features of the Compact, in cooperation with civil society. In Europe, the Multi-Stakeholder Forum (MSF) on corporate social responsibility (CSR), comprising business and civil society and headed by the EU Commission, was launched in 2002 to promote corporate self-regulation and public–private regulation of CSR pertaining to European companies. The results of the two initiatives differ: the Global Compact resulted in agreement on nine (now 10) principles on human rights, labour rights, environmental protection and corruption to which presently around 5000 companies have committed themselves. The principles are based on international declarations or conventions. The EU MSF resulted in a general reference to international human rights law as part of the normative framework for CSR in Europe but not in specific principles. In addition, business participants played the ball of responsibility back into the hand of governments, telling them to act themselves if they wanted public policy goals implemented rather than counting on companies.

The creation of CSR norms easily suffers from a democratic legitimacy deficit. Corporations have no democratic mandate but nevertheless engage in processes of creating behavioural norms that impact on society, including politics, but may also reflect societal concerns. CSR sometimes shifts tasks from the public to the private sector to deal with public policy interests (Reich, 2007; Haufler, 2001). This creates a need to consider if and how corporations may be embedded in democratic processes of defining rules (see also Scherer and Palazzo, 2007, p. 1098).

This chapter understands the legitimacy of CSR norms created through public–private rule-making processes as a perception among business and other stakeholders that the procedure was acceptable in terms of being representative, if not inclusive of all interests, and with the output – the resulting norms – being adopted by companies and respected by stakeholders.

With acute implications for CSR action at the practical level, legitimacy deficits risk making norms and resulting action vulnerable to outside criticism or dissatisfaction among various stakeholders. Civil society organizations arguing for CSR may prefer to attack rather than compliment companies for their CSR action if guiding norms are perceived to have been created in a closed forum, excluding significant societal actors. Media, politicians, investors and other stakeholders may react in related fashions.

Global society is witnessing a mushrooming of new forms and fora for creating norms whose effect may be likened to soft or even traditional hard law, many of which are related to corporate action and corporate accountability. Some of these engage actors at administrative levels of public institutions at national or international level who work with corporate and other non-state actors to develop norms on non-state actors' behaviour to accommodate societal concerns and needs. Many of these bodies, too, have no formal democratic mandate as law-makers (see further Kingsbury et al., 2005; Krisch and Kingsbury, 2006; Buhmann, 2009). There is a need to understand more about how corporations and other non-state actors contribute to norm creation in such fora and the legitimacy role of procedural aspects of public–private schemes for norm creation. With growing use of public–private regulation in a number of thematic fields and at a number of governance levels to address CSR relevant issues ranging from sustainable forestry to veterinary health and business responsibilities for human rights, there is a need to understand what makes such schemes successful in the sense of the process as well as the output being perceived as legitimate in the above sense. Without such perception, the likelihood that the norms will be applied by companies and valued by other stakeholders decreases. Legitimacy is therefore crucial for the actual success of public–private processes for creation of CSR norms.

Drawing on the UN Global Compact and the EU MSF as cases of public–private schemes for creating CSR norms, this chapter considers how those schemes have given business access to influence the creation and implementation of CSR norms. The two cases studies have been selected as both are intergovernmental efforts to develop CSR norms in a process that includes business and other actors, and because both are based on efforts to draw on international human rights law as a source for the resulting CSR norms. As such, the Global Compact and the MSF share important common features that lend themselves to comparison. The chapter argues that both initiatives contain features of reflexive law-making, drawing on the theory of German legal theorist Gunther Teubner. It argues that the Global Compact was more successful and the MSF less successful in creating CSR norms and defining international human rights law as a source, and argues that the difference in results was at least partly due to the procedural set-up of the MSF, which did not sufficiently handle power disparities between actors. It argues that the theory on deliberative discourse developed by Jürgen Habermas may complement the reflexive law theory through a procedural focus on discourse and participation that may contribute to handling power disparities and cater for a higher degree of perceived legitimacy. As indicated by Scherer and Palazzo (2007), parts of Habermas's work on deliberative discourse hold potential for management and other social sciences related to CSR as they suggest that legitimacy is constructed through joint communicative action. Because of space limitations, the discussion of both reflexive law and deliberative discourse is brief and skirts a number of complexities in both theories and their application. The former draws mainly on early writings on the subjects, found for the purpose of this chapter to be the most appropriate for the generalized discussion here. The discourse ethics theory of Jürgen Habermas, particularly as developed in *Faktizität und Geltung* (1992, translated into English as *Between Facts and Norms* 1996)[1] will provide the theoretical basis for a discussion of legitimacy aspects.

The overall aim of the chapter is to contribute to understanding the potential for establishing public–private norm-creating processes at the international level and to suggest new areas of research to further illuminate the field. Its point of departure in public sector regulation and regulatory modalities sets it apart from many other studies of CSR, many of which approach CSR from the perspectives of management and private regulation. Moreover, this chapter approaches the subject matter with a theoretical background in legal science. This too sets it apart from many others on CSR, and also means a different method and a different approach to data than in most other social sciences. The presentations and discussions on the development of the MSF as well as the Global Compact are both based on information provided on the websites of the two schemes.[2] These websites contain speeches, reports and statements which serve as empirical data. By necessity, this approach excludes the use of research articles prepared by other authors as direct sources on the evolution of the two initiatives. Such articles, however, may be included in other research and publications and, indeed, have been included in work by this author published elsewhere. Owing to space limitations, the presentations are generalized and based on more detailed presentations made elsewhere (Buhmann, 2008, 2009, submitted). The legal science approach also means that both the theory of reflexive law and that on discursive legitimacy are approached as law-making theories, with particular focus on consultative rule-making. In addition, the approach is informed by the particular focus on the integration of international human rights law into the output of the public–private regulatory process. This too differs from the application of the reflexive law and discursive legitimacy theories to CSR matters by authors with different academic points of departure (e.g. Hess, 1999, 2008; Scherer and Palazzo, 2007; Willke and Willke, 2007; Rasche and Esser, 2006), serving to contribute to the growing interdisciplinary character of CSR research based around shared themes and theories.

---

1   References in here are to the English translation (Habermas, 1996).

2   For the UN Global Compact see www.globalcompact.org, and for the EU MSF see http://forum.europa.eu.int/irc/empl/csr_eu_multi_stakeholder_forum/.

The UN Global Compact and the EU MSF

The UN Global Compact

The UN Global Compact initiative was announced by then UN Secretary General Kofi Annan in January 1999 at the World Economic Forum and launched for operation in 2000. Companies that participate in the Global Compact commit to 10 principles on human rights, labour rights, environmental protection and anti-corruption. A UN General Assembly resolution provides the Global Compact with its formal legal and organizational basis within the UN system. Funding is provided through voluntary contributions from governments. An initiative planned and launched through the UN under the UN Secretariat, the Global Compact is an intergovernmentally and state backed scheme for making companies self-regulate.

The Compact principles build on international law. The two human rights principles (principles 1 and 2) are based on the Universal Declaration on Human Rights. The labour standards (principles 3–6) are based on the ILO Declaration of Fundamental Principles and Rights at Work. Among the environmental principles (principles 7–9), principle 7 on the precautionary approach is based on the Rio Declaration. Principle 10 is based on the UN Convention against Corruption.

The Compact was developed during 1999 and the first half of 2000 in a consultative network process comprising the UN Secretary General and representatives for his office, the International Labour Organization (ILO), the United Nations Environment Programme (UNEP), the Office of the High Commissioner for Human Rights (OHCHR), the International Chamber of Commerce, business organizations and company representatives. During the process, focus shifted from business organizations to CEOs of transnational corporations (TNCs) that were considered leaders in CSR. They were expected to provide impetus for implementation. The international labour movement was reluctant initially but relatively late in the process decided to become involved. NGOs were involved even later, a few months before the official launch. Selected NGOs were invited on criteria of having a global reach and particular competences in a Global Compact issue area (Kell and Levin, 2004). The Global Compact website, which is the key instrument of information and guidance on the Compact and for facilitating the adoption, dissemination and implementation of the principles was constructed "with the help of" corporations, business associations, partner agencies and NGOs (Kell and Ruggie, 1999).

NGOs were not unanimously supportive of the approach of the Global Compact and have been particularly critical of the Compact's initial lack of integrity measures. Nevertheless, the initiative succeeded in having major NGOs cooperate in setting up the website and producing comments for it, and in many others joining later as stakeholders. As of late 2008, the website lists 46 global and 511 local NGOs.

According to its website, the Global Compact is purely voluntary. It is presented as an instrument to promote institutional learning and implementation of best practice based on the 10 principles, and the values that these reflect. Despite the explicit links between the principles and the informing instruments of international law, the Global Compact has been promoted as an initiative to realize a vision of a sustainable and inclusive global economy, rather than as an initiative to promote human rights, labour rights and/or environmental protection and anti-corruption.

The Compact promotes corporate self-regulation on the 10 principles through three main avenues: a learning-forum and learning networks, policy dialogue and public–private partnership projects (Ruggie, 2002). At its website and elsewhere, the initiative is described as a network and forum of dialogue, with an organizational structure and method of operation promoting the external consultation process and internal reflection among participating businesses (Leisinger, 2004; Ruggie, 2002; Kell and Levin, 2004).

The Compact currently (March 2009) has more than 5000 active participants. The number has been growing steadily since the initiative was launched in 2000.

The EU Multi-Stakeholder Forum

The MSF was established in 2002 by the EU Commission with the aim of promoting innovation, transparency and convergence of CSR practices and instruments, to develop problem understanding, discuss values and relevant action, and make recommendations. The background to the MSF was a Resolution of the European Parliament calling for codes of conduct for European TNCs, a subsequent Commission Green Paper and a Commission Communication on CSR (Buhmann, 2008). The Commission asked the MSF to address the relationship between CSR and competitiveness, effectiveness and credibility of codes of conducts based on internationally agreed principle, proposed that the MSF develop guidelines and criteria for measurement, reporting and assurance of CSR, and suggested that such schemes and labelling schemes be based on ILO core conventions and the OECD Guidelines for Multinational Enterprises (Commission of the European Communities, 2002).

The MSF was chaired by the Commission. Its 18 member organizations represented labour organizations, business organizations (industry, employers and commerce) and NGOs engaged in human rights, consumers' interests, fair trade and sustainable development. Observer status was held by 11 entities including the European Parliament, the EU Council, OECD, ILO and UNEP. The working method combined plenary ("High Level") meetings and thematic round tables. The end product was a report ("Final Report"). Among a number of topics related to CSR, two were particularly contentious: the possible role of international law on human and labour rights as a normative source, and whether CSR was to be mandatory and subject to regulation or continue to be voluntary. NGOs generally argued in favour of mandatory regulation and for international law to inform CSR. With some exceptions, business organizations maintained that CSR should be voluntary without any strong influence from international law. They also argued that public policy objectives should be implemented through government initiatives, not through business action.

The MSF did not lead to a concrete framework on CSR. The first and brief part of the Final Report reaffirms international and European agreed principles, standards and conventions of relevance to CSR. As the main reference for CSR the report notes the ILO Tripartite Declaration, the OECD Guidelines and the UN Global Compact (MSF, 2004, p. 6). These deal directly with issues of social responsibilities of business, but are all non-binding and, at the most, serve as guidance for corporations. The Universal Declaration of Human Rights, the European Convention on Human Rights, the 1998 ILO Declaration on fundamental principles and rights at work and some other instruments are noted with the comment that they contain values that can inspire companies when developing CSR (MSF, 2004, p. 6). The bulk of the report which contains its main recommendations and suggestions for future initiatives focuses on awareness-raising and improving knowledge of CSR, capacity building and competences to help mainstream CSR. It does not mention a common normative framework. Instead, it provides that authorities should ensure that a legal framework and appropriate economic and social conditions are in place to allow companies to benefit from CSR in the market place, both in the EU and globally. The implications of this are twofold: if governments do not ensure the legal framework for human rights and other CSR issues, business does not need to go further; and when companies do undertake CSR, this should translate into economic benefits for companies, supported by formal law and public policy.

The UN Global Compact and EU MSF Compared: Results of the Norm-Creating Processes

Reflexive law is a regulatory strategy rather than law *per se*. It builds on an assumption that effectiveness of regulation is strengthened when regulatory norms are developed with the participation of those who are to be subjected to the norms. The process is promoted through a procedural framework set up by governments. In the case of the Global Compact and the MSF, the procedural framework is established by the UN Secretariat and the EU Commission respectively.

The theory of reflexive law was developed in the 1980s as an alternative to traditional top-down, black-letter law as well as the other alternative, complete de-regulation. In the 1990s and 2000s it has been discussed and applied in the context of CSR to specific regulatory initiatives, particularly but not exclusively at national level (see e.g. Arthurs, 2008; Hess, 1999, 2008; Deakin and Hobbs, 2007; Lobel, 2005; Deakin, 2005; Scheuerman, 2001; Orts, 1995; Wilthagen, 1994; Rogowski 1994, 1998, 2001). For the discussion in here which aims at identifying reflexive regulatory features of the MSF and the Global Compact, early writings in which the theory was introduced have been found the most appropriate. The background to the development of reflexive law as a regulatory theory was an observation that regulatory strategies of welfare states were ineffective for addressing societal concerns, such as environmental problems, unemployment and social inequalities, which required the cooperation of non-state actors for their solution (Teubner, 1983, 1986, 1993). Teubner found that substantively rational regulation, designed for top-down intervention with generally quite specific goals, was unable to cope with many of the complexities of the welfare state, including societal needs, which required the active cooperation and engagement of the private sector for their solution. Reflexive law is procedural in the sense that it influences decision-making and communication processes. Reflexive law does not mean that substantive, top-down regulation is abandoned, but complements the latter as a regulatory strategy and offers an alternative. Reflexive law leaves organizations such as companies the freedom and choice to determine their own norms of behaviour discursively. Authorities intervene only by establishing procedures that guide self-reflection. Reflexive law allows public institutions to initiate self-regulation among other societal actors by offering a learning process that enables the latter to reflect and integrate societal needs and demands. The theory assumes to some extent that institutional procedural mechanisms should be designed to neutralize power disparities in order to limit the abuse of power by stronger participants in the process (see Teubner, 1986, pp. 316–317), but does not specify how power disparities should be procedurally handled.

Reflexive law offers an interesting theoretical perspective for understanding public–private regulation on CSR, because it is process and communication oriented. The terminology of reflexive law refers to learning and exchange between social sub-systems of their expectations and demands of each other as well as best practice, and other modalities to support reflection within and between social sub-systems.

Gunther Teubner developed his theory on reflexive law in partial reaction to the clashing theories which German social scientists Niklas Luhmann and Jürgen Habermas had formulated in the 1970s and early 1980s. Both also wished to address the inefficiencies of welfare-state, state-based regulatory systems. Reflexive law is particularly related to Luhmann's systems theory but also incorporates elements related to ideas formulated already then by Habermas on communication and the significance of creation of norms through a discourse with a balanced representation of interests. For the appreciation of the discussion in the remainder of this chapter, it should be noted that Habermas's deliberative democracy theory as developed in the work *Faktizität und Geltung* had not yet been formulated when the theory of reflexive law was introduced.

Assessed along these lines, the Global Compact and the MSF both contain features that suggest a reflexive law approach to creation of CSR norms, although not necessarily a "pure" approach. Both aim at corporate self-regulation but also have co-regulatory features. In both cases, the reflexive law character appears to be incidental rather than intended (for a similar finding on the European Environmental Management System, EMAS, see Orts, 1995, p. 1287).

The development of the Compact suggests a reflexive law approach which allowed companies a procedure to work directly with the UN Secretariat to develop the normative framework. The insistence on the Compact's website and in other sources that the initiative was developed as a consultative network process and that it is "not a regulatory instrument" but "a learning platform" suggests that it is considered significant for the Compact to strongly indicate that it is not an ordinary top-down (inter)governmental regulatory instrument, and that its norms are produced in collaboration with businesses who are the key non-state actors subjected to the norms. The Compact is a continuously evolving instrument, as evidenced by the addition in 2004 of the tenth principle, the development of the Communication-on-Progress reporting system and the delisting of non-reporting companies. This indicates that the Global Compact is a dynamic instrument which itself internalizes external concerns and addresses these through its multi-stakeholder structure. Its original as well as ongoing development and operation after adoption are based on a procedural framework established under the UN Secretariat and now the Global Compact Office. The Compact's objectives are clear: to induce business behaviour in accordance with the 10 principles and the informing instruments of international law, based on self-regulation. The network structure engages companies procedurally to share best practice and mutually learn how to integrate the normative goals of the 10 principles into daily business practice. In terms of working method after adoption, the Compact provides a normative framework to guide the behaviour of corporations and provide a shared global understanding of human rights, labour standards, environmental protection and anti-corruption. Participants are invited to embrace the global values contained in the principles and the international standards that inform them, by incorporating them into their mission statements and turning them into concrete corporate action. The network and partnership methods that bring UN bodies and companies together also assist companies in learning about societal expectations and concerns. The intention is to assist them in internalizing such concerns, to make them self-regulate, and through the 10 principles to provide normative guidance for corporate self-regulation.

The Compact is not a legal instrument in the ordinary sense. However, it is a regulatory instrument drawing heavily on instruments of international (mainly soft) law as sources of normative substance, and on the method of reflexive law to make companies internalize this normative substance through self-regulation. With nine principles based on international law and formulated in the course of around one year, the addition of the tenth principle to reflect anti-corruption concerns of many participants, around 5000 participants from around the globe after around 10 years of operation and significant NGO backing 10 years on, the Global Compact norms (the now 10 principles) and the process of establishing them show strong signs of being perceived as legitimate by stakeholders. This is despite the fact that the principles were developed with business as the main non-state actor together with the UN Secretariat, and the fact that many NGOs did not want to participate at the outset as they preferred hard regulation or found the initiative lacking in accountability measures.

The EU Commission's approach to establishing CSR norms for European companies involved a larger range of affected societal actors from the outset than did the Global Compact. The Commission has consistently suggested that corporate CSR self-regulation take certain substantive issues and normative sources into account, especially on human and labour rights, but has also indicated that CSR was not to be made in the form of legally binding mandated requirements. Through the MSF the Commission established a procedural modality for stakeholders to meet and learn about concerns of other societal actors and to take part in a shared regulatory process. Non-state actors were given the main stake in defining the substantive output. Commission documents indicate that the process was based on the recognition that public and wider societal interests and expectations require companies to take responsibility for their actions in society as well as the role they may play in promoting welfare policy objectives. This approach to regulation has the key characteristics of reflexive law. However, the outcome (Final Report) of the MSF seemed to neither meet the Commission's objective that the MSF would establish a framework for CSR nor establish the role that international law, especially human rights conventions, were to play for such a framework.

The differences in the results of the Global Compact and EU MSF as processes of creating norms suggest a crucial difference in the procedural approach. The speeches, statements and reports made during the MSF[3] indicate that the failure of the EU MSF to create a normative framework and to reference international law widely as sources of CSR norms may be due to power disparities within the MSF, with business having much greater political as well as discursive power than NGOs. The internal fight for power in the Commission among proponents of business interests versus proponents of social affairs may have added to the end result. NGOs did not find the general result satisfactory and were also dissatisfied with the later decision of the Commission to establish, as a new initiative and in response to the MSF Final Report, a "CSR Alliance" for companies without NGO representatives. Nor did NGOs support the decision to reconvene the MSF as a way of making up for lack of NGO participation in the CSR Alliance (Buhmann, 2008). The EU experience suggests that part of the failure was due to insufficient balancing of power disparities between businesses, especially those opposed to international human rights instruments as a clear source for CSR norms in the EU, and NGOs as proponents for the adverse stance.

We now turn to the deliberative approach which assumes that the legitimacy of the creation of norms rests on the discursive quality of the process, to see what this may contribute to our understanding of how to construct public–private norm-creating processes that lead to CSR norms with relatively wide acceptance.

---

3 Speeches, statements and reports are available at: http://forum.europa.eu.int/irc/empl/csr_eu_multi_stakeholder_forum/.

Deliberative Discourse in the Context of Creation of CSR Norms through Multi-Stakeholder Processes at International Level

The deliberative democracy theory developed by Habermas in the 1990s builds on and further develops his previous discourse ethics theory. The early works of Habermas as a discourse theorist focus on the conditions of ideal discourse, and ideal discourse as an avenue towards deciding on the justification and reasonableness of social claims and interests. With a somewhat different approach from the 1990s, Habermas's theory on deliberative democracy is directed at the conditions for production of law as valid norms subject to administration and enforcement in a constitutional–democratic legal order (Habermas, 1996). Such a legal order typically refers to a nation-state and does not correspond to the current conditions for production of international law, nor of norm-creation processes that take place within public–private schemes at international/intergovernmental level. Habermas's understanding of law mainly relates to binding, enforceable norms. CSR normativity is of a softer kind and, being "voluntary", generally neither legally binding, nor enforceable. Despite these differences between the immediate subject matter of Habermas's ideas and CSR normativity, his ideas on deliberative democracy do contain points useful for legitimacy of CSR norm creation. Through its focus on discourse as a form of communication to provide norms with legitimacy and conditions for establishing equal opportunities for public participation in law-making, Habermas's theory is relevant in the context of providing input to a process of producing behavioural norms, such as CSR norms.

To Habermas, norms are only valid if they are met with the approval of those potentially affected and on condition that these participate in rational discourses. Participants in a discourse strive towards forming a common will by each attempting to convince other participants through arguments. Habermas posits that law gains legitimacy through institutionalized procedures and communicative presuppositions. Through various forms of participation as well as general elections, public opinions feed into the legislature and legitimizing regulatory agencies. Positive law administered or enforced by the state derives its legitimacy through a broad discourse of citizens and their representatives, including the civil society. Public discourse mobilizes reasons and arguments drawing on citizens' interests and values and allows those subjected to legal norms to influence their substance. Discursive processes allow citizens to agree on normative positions for common coexistence. Like Teubner, Habermas is aware that some actors may be stronger than others. He stresses that, for the production of law to be legitimate, participants should have equal rights not just in formal but in actual terms. Such equality requires procedural regulation of the processes that draw on discourse to provide normative input. Discourse is both a condition for legitimate production of (positive) law and itself contingent on law, understood as rights guaranteeing the procedural equality of participants in the normative production process. Bargaining is an alternative when a common will cannot be formed through discourse. Bargaining aims at identifying compromises. Bargaining based on discursively grounded procedure to balance conflicting interests may lead to results that are legitimate (Habermas, 1996).

Political will-formation may be offset by moral, ethical or pragmatic reasons. Moral questions relate to our common life in the equal interest of all, including the protection of the environment, social policy, the distribution of social wealth or life opportunities. If they conform to the conditions for legitimacy, norms offset by such reasons are valid (Habermas, 1996, pp. 155–156).

Because of the different composition and roles of actors and institutions and state-centrist structure, deliberative discourse-based democracy as a foundation for the legitimacy of procedurally created norms cannot be transplanted directly to the international level (Habermas, 2004). However, in some of his more recent texts, Habermas deals with the challenges of producing norms legitimately at the level beyond nation-states. He transfers the application to this level with adaptations due to the institutional structure but does not come up with concrete proposals for how to deal with the number and variety of relevant actors at international and transnational levels. NGOs and other organizations may serve to establish links to deliberative processes at lower levels of decision-making. The absence of a political coordinative system at transnational market level and of effective powers of the UN to enforce human rights, ensures that environmental and social sustainability are key problems for global will-formation (Habermas, 2005b). A common practice for formation of opinions and will must also be established at post-national, global, international, supranational or transnational level. Deliberative discursive procedures may provide for legitimacy at these levels too. In terms of its formal (state-centrist) organization or procedures, the UN does not, in Habermas's view, live up to this. However, other avenues may be possible, e.g. through involving non-governmental forms of organization in international negotiations, as well as through other arrangements and procedures that promote compromises and negotiated results among independent decision-making actors. A shift of emphasis must take place from the embodiment of sovereign will through persons and electoral acts and specific organizations, towards procedural requirements to processes of communication and decision-making. Moreover, actors with the powers to act with regard to rule- and decision-making at the global level (under current formal conditions, typically states supported by intergovernmental agencies) should employ institutionalized procedures for international level will-formation with regard to bringing a satisfactory level of social standards and alleviating extreme social differentiation. They should consider themselves part of a community in which members take each other's interests as well as common interests into consideration (Habermas, 2005a, b).

As Scherer and Palazzo (2007, p. 1109) argue, the idea of the corporation as the "bad guy" representing economic interests and NGOs as the "good guys" representing moral interests is oversimplified and does not recognize that discourse quality derives from the analysis of arguments, not from actors. This suggests that the procedural aspect of discourse which leads to the production of norms through reflexive regulatory processes should not just be procedurally structured so as to even out formal or easily observable power disparities and to learn about social expectations. Just as importantly, they should provide for appropriate conditions for an exchange of arguments and a quality of discourse conducive to consensus or at least bargaining, leading to common acceptance of resulting norms. The EU MSF provided the formal procedure for social actors to meet, make speeches and exchange reports. The framework and discussion, however, were quickly politicized into non-state participants guarding already established positions and the Commission trying to engage business in implementing new political objectives. The framework does not seem to have been appropriate for exchange of arguments at a deeper level to provide for consensus. The UN Global Compact, on the other hand, appears to have set conditions for an exchange of arguments between individuals from within the UN Secretariat (and now the Global Compact Office) and business to engage in what appears to have been a more successful way of reaching consensus on nine (now 10) principles. In this context, it seems to be less significant that NGOs were not strongly represented in the process of establishing the normative foundation of the Global Compact and helping shape the principles. The limited degree of NGO participation, however, did result in severe criticism of the Compact from some NGOs. This has been somewhat met by the institution of integrity measures, including progress reporting and de-listing. This finding supports the arguments made by Scherer and Palazzo (2007, p. 1114) that legitimate CSR norms development should be made through procedures that remain open for dissent and promote the expression of marginalized interests and values. It also corresponds to the theoretical point that reflexive regulatory processes should handle power disparities but adds a perspective, that of weaker groups being allowed a real say and not just formal presence. NGO opposition to the EU MSF outcome and to the Global Compact for lack of accountability underscores this point of the significance of the deliberative approach.

In one sense, the Global Compact establishment and success seem to somewhat contradict the assumption that Habermasian discourse-based deliberative norm creation is the key to legitimacy. Rather, it underscores the significance of the reflexive law approach for (inter)governmental organizations to establish procedures and learning platforms for corporations to understand and internalize societal concerns and expectations. What we do not know, however, is whether the Global Compact would have been an even more successful instrument with even higher legitimacy if NGOs and labour organizations had been engaged more and at an earlier stage. There is no reason to doubt that the reservations against the Compact which were expressed by NGOs and parts of the labour movement, especially prior to the establishment of the still limited integrity measures, have reduced the attraction of the Compact to certain companies or companies within certain national settings.

In addition, the Global Compact arguably draws a great deal of its perceived legitimacy from the deliberative processes that led to the declarations and conventions which inform the 10 principles. Management- and policy-oriented literature suggests that the Global Compact draws its moral authority and global convening power from the UN Secretary General, and its moral and political legitimacy from the UN (McIntosh et al., 2004). For the purposes of this chapter, the legitimacy provided by internationally agreed standards as normative sources of the Global Compact principles may have been as significant (see also Waddock, 2002 on "hypernorms"). The process of the Compact's establishment was not exactly balanced with regard to representation of societal actors: business was invited to have a much stronger and earlier role than NGOs. Labour joined the process late, of its own will. Nevertheless, the result is a strong normative basis which appears to have significant global legitimacy. This indicates that legitimacy derives both from the Global Compact's particular way of engaging business and other stakeholders in defining norms as an ongoing process that adapts to outside concerns and criticism, and from basing those norms in international standards of global applicability which have been agreed to under the UN and ILO. Although the state-centrist structure of international law-making may be lacking in legitimacy in several ways in today's globalized and post-Westphalian world, the international human rights, labour and environmental norms do enjoy a high degree of global legitimacy, being developed by states members of the UN and ILO to address global concerns of peace and welfare.

Conclusion and Perspectives

The contextual framework provided by Habermas enables us to assess legitimacy and particularly legitimacy deficits in terms of process and output. This adds to the analysis of multi-stakeholder CSR norm creation through reflexive regulatory processes by throwing light on why some processes and arguments fail and why others succeed, both in terms of increasing the power of the process and/or the output and in terms of the legitimacy of the output. Although the MSF was successful in a number of ways to bring forward CSR awareness-raising in Europe, its process and output were not successful in terms of bringing international human rights law strongly forth and creating a strongly formulated normative framework for CSR. The Global Compact is much more successful in this respect. The combination of the theories of Teubner on reflexive law and Habermas on deliberative discourse-based norm creation provides guidance on the design of multi-stakeholder processes to promote CSR norm creation that may be broadly acceptable and not just reflect the power and position of the stronger/strongest participant.

In a context of reflexive law-making, Habermasian discourse theory adds additional perspectives that Habermas had not yet developed when Teubner formulated his ideas on reflexive law in the 1980s. As demonstrated in the discussion above, in a context of CSR norm creation through multi-stakeholder public–private schemes engaging TNCs and other business actors, reflexive law and deliberative democracy have much in common, with Habermasian deliberative discourse providing important suggestions for the legitimacy of the reflexive regulatory process and its outcome. In particular, Habermas's theory of deliberative democracy contributes to the provision of instructions on how to deal with the challenge that the procedure should mitigate power imbalances. In addition, the theory provides instructive ideas for promoting legitimacy through public participation in norm creation at the international level. For practical reasons, direct involvement of all citizens globally in such decision-making is not possible. Institutional non-state actors may serve as proxies, representing a representative range of business and civil society views. The crucial point to establish true legitimacy will be to provide for a wide and balanced representation of such views and ensure that they are indeed representative.

To understand more about how to achieve this while working through a necessarily limited number of actors, much more research needs to be done on the successes, challenges, failures and legitimacy of the many forms of public–private and/or multi-stakeholder norm creation that have seen the light in various national, international, supranational and transnational contexts in later years. Such work could take inspiration in one of the points made by the Special Representative of the UN Secretary General (SRSG) on Human Rights and Business in a report to the UN Human Rights Council, in which he referred to "innovations in soft law mechanisms that involve corporations directly in regulatory rulemaking and implementation [which] suggests increased state and corporate acknowledgment of evolving social expectations and a recognition of the need to exercise shared responsibility" (SRSG, 2007, para. 62).

Further study of developing legitimate CSR norms through public–private regulation would benefit from interdisciplinary approaches. Such research could include interviews and focus group studies of participants in the MSF and the Global Compact, and for the Global Compact also collection of admission, subscription and compliance data. The combination of organizational, sociological or communication analysis of such data with legal scholarship on regulatory strategies and legal theory as modalities for institutionalization of behavioural norms could provide valuable insight into the subject matter of legitimate CSR norm creation which has been sketched in this chapter.

References

Arthurs, H. (2008), Corporate Self-Regulation: Political Economy, State Regulation and Reflexive Labour Law, in *Regulating Labour in the Wake of Globalisation*, B. Bercusson and C. Estlund (eds). Oxford: Hart, pp. 19–35.

Buhmann, K. (2008), Retliggørelse af CSR gennem politisering: Refleksiv regulering af CSR i EU og begrebsudfyldning ved international menneskeret. *Politik*, 11(4), 27–37.

Buhmann, K. (2009), Regulating Corporate Social and Human Rights Responsibilities at the UN Plane: Institutionalising New Forms of Law and Law-making Approaches? *Nordic Journal of International Law*, 78(1), 1–52.

Commission of the European Communities (2002), *Corporate Social Responsibility: A Business Contribution to Sustainable Development.* EU Document COM(2002)347.

Deakin, S. (2005), Social Rights in a Globalised Economy, in *Labour Rights as Human Rights*, P. Alston (ed.), New York: Oxford University Press, pp. 25–60.

Deakin, S. and Hobbs, R. (2007), False Dawn for CSR? Shifts in Regulatory Policy and the Response of the Corporate and Financial Sectors in Britain. *Corporate Governance*, 15, 68–76.

Habermas, J. (1996), *Between Facts and Norms: Contributions to a Discourse Theory of Law and Democracy*, W. Rehg (trans.). Cambridge: Polity Press/ Blackwell.

Habermas, J. (2004), Folkeretten i overgangen til den postnationale konstellation. *Distinktion*, 8, 9–17.

Habermas, J. (2005a), Legitimering på grundlag af menneskerettigheder, in H. Andersen (ed.), *Jürgen Habermas: Demokrati og retsstat – en tekstsamling*. Copenhagen: Hans Reitzels Forlag, pp. 187–203 [translated from German original, 1998].

Habermas, J. (2005b), Den postnationale konstellation og demokratiets fremtid, in H. Andersen (ed.), *Jürgen Habermas: Demokrati og retsstat – en tekstsamling*. Copenhagen: Hans Reitzels Forlag, pp. 220–273 [translated from German original, 1998].

Haufler, V. (2001), *A Public Role for the Private Sector: Industry Self-regulation in a Global Economy*. Washington, DC: Carnegie.

Hess, D. (1999), Social Reporting: a Reflexive Law Approach to Corporate Social Responsiveness. *Journal of Corporation Law*, 25(1): 41–84.

Hess, D. (2008), The Three Pillars of Corporate Social Reporting as New Governance Regulation: Disclosure, Dialogue and Development. *Business Ethics Quarterly*, 18(4): 447–482.

Kell, G. and Levin, D. (2004), The Global Compact Network: An Historic Experiment in Learning and Action, in *Learning to Talk: Corporate Citizenship and the Development of the UN Global Compact*, M. McIntosh, S. Waddock and G. Kell (eds), Sheffield: Greenleaf Publishing, pp. 43–65.

Kell, G. and Ruggie, J.G. (1999), *Global Markets and Social Legitimacy: The Case of the "Global Compact"*. Paper presented at an international conference: Governing the Public Domain beyond the Era of the Washington Consensus? York University, Toronto, 4–6 November 1999; www.globalcompact.org/ NewsAndEvents/articles_and_papers/global_markets_social_legitimacy_ york_university.html (accessed 15 August 2008).

Kingsbury, B., Krisch, N. and Steward, R.B. (2005), The Emergence of Global Administrative Law. *Law and Contemporary Problems*, 68(3), 15–61.

Krisch, N. and Kingsbury, B. (2006), Introduction: Global Governance and Global Administrative Law in the International Legal Order. *European Journal of International Law*, 17(1), 1–13.

Leisinger, K.M. (2004), Business and Human Rights, in *Learning to Talk: Corporate Citizenship and the Development of the UN Global Compact*, M. McIntosh, S. Waddock and G. Kell (eds), Greenleaf Publishing: Sheffield, pp. 72–100.

Lobel, O. (2005), The Renew Deal: The Fall of Regulation and the Rise of Governance in Contemporary Legal Thought. *Minnesota Law Review*, 89, 262–390.

McIntosh, M., Waddock, S. and Kell, G. (eds) (2004), *Learning to Talk: Corporate Citizenship and the Development of the UN Global Compact*. Greenleaf Publishing: Sheffield.

MSF (2004), European Multistakeholder Forum on CSR. *Final Results and Recommendations*, 29 June 2004; http://forum.europa.eu.int/irc/empl/csr_eu_ multi_stakeholder_forum/info/data/en/CSR%20Forum%20final%20report. pdf (accessed 17 August 2008).

Orts, E.W. (1995), Reflexive Environmental Law. *Northwestern Law Review*, 89, 1229–1340.

Rasche, A. and Esser, D.E. (2006), From Stakeholder Management to Stakeholder Accountability: Applying Habermasian Discourse Ethics to Accountability Research. *Journal of Business Ethics*, 65, 251–267.

Reich, R.B. (2007), *Supercapitalism: the Transformation of Business, Democracy and Everyday Life*. New York: Knopf.

Rogowski, R. (1994), Industrial Relations, Labour Conflict Resolution and Reflexive Labour Law, in *Reflexive Labour Law: Studies in Industrial Relations and Employment Regulation*, R. Rogowski and T. Wilthagen (eds), Deventer: Kluwer Law and Taxation Publishers, pp. 53–93.

Rogowski, R. (1998), Autopoietic Industrial Relations and and Reflexive Labour Law, in *Advancing Theory in Labour Law and Industrial Relations in a Global Context*, T. Wilthagen (ed.), Amsterdam: North-Holland Press.

Rogowski, R. (2001), The Concept of Reflexive Labour Law: its Theoretical Background and Possible Applications, in *Law's New Boundaries. The Consequences of Legal Autopoiesis*, J. Priban and D. Nelken (eds), Aldershot: Ashgate/Dartmouth.

Ruggie, J.G. (2002), The Theory and Practice of Learning Networks: Corporate Social Responsibility and the Global Compacts. *Journal of Corporate Citizenship*, 5, 27–36.

Scherer, A.G. and Palazzo, G. (2007), Toward a Political Conception of Corporate Responsibility: Business and Society seen from a Habermasian Perspective. *Academy of Management Review*, 32(4), 1096–1120.

Scheuerman, W.E. (2001), Reflexive Law and the Challenges of Globalization. *Journal of Political Philosophy*, 9, 81–102.

SRSG (2007), *Report of the Special Representative of the Secretary-General (SRSG) on the issue of human rights and transnational corporations and other business enterprises*. UN Document A/HRC/4/035, 9 February.

Teubner, G. (1983), Substantive and Reflective Elements in Modern Law. *Law and Society Review*, 17, 239–285.

Teubner, G. (1986), After Legal Instrumentalism?, in *Dilemmas of Law in the Welfare State*, G. Teubner (ed.), Berlin: Walter de Gruyter, pp. 111–127.

Teubner, G. (1993), *Law as an Autopoietic System*. Oxford: Blackwell.

Waddock, S. (2002), *Creating the Tipping Point towards Corporate Responsibility*. University of Notre Dame, 21–23 April 2002; http://www.unglobalcompact. org/NewsandEvents/articles_and_papers/university_of_notre_dame_on_ global_economy.html (accessed 15 November 2008).

Willke, H. and Willke, G. (2007), Corporate Moral Legitimacy and the Legitimacy of Morals: A Critique of Palazzo/Scherer's Communicative Framework. *Journal of Business Ethics*, DOI: 10.1007/s10551-007-9478-1.

Wilthagen, T. (1994), Reflexive Rationality in the Regulation of Occupational Safety and Health, in *Reflexive Labour Law: Studies in Industrial Relations and Employment Regulation*, R. Rogowski and T. Wilthagen (eds), Deventer and Boston: Kluwer Law and Taxation Publishers, pp. 345–376.

Chapter 14

Business and Poverty – Bridges and Divides

Michael Blowfield

Introduction

Can business be a genuine agent in tackling poverty? Is it asking too much to expect business to go beyond its conventional economic roles to become a more active, conscious and accountable participant in the process of international development? What are the consequences both for business and wider society if the private sector becomes a development agent? Is it something to be welcomed for the additional resources and comparative strengths it gives access to, or is it something to be wary of because of how it might influence the development process?

In this chapter, I reflect on two issues: how business interacts with poverty, and how that relationship is affected by the approach to management called corporate responsibility. Some will say that the very idea that companies should be mindful of their responsibilities to society is dangerous. It is argued that companies exist to create value for shareholders, subject to legal constraints (Friedman, 1962). By so doing, they contribute to the public good: creating jobs, supplying goods and services, and helping to fund necessary social institutions. Yes, companies have a social responsibility, but it is not something that needs special consideration because profit maximization is a sufficient proxy for the various other contributions private enterprise can make.

However, a more interesting question in this era of globalization when things like disparities in wealth, the links between economic growth and climate change, and the ease with which good and bad news stories are transmitted around the world all have a demonstrable effect on how companies manage their relationship with society is not whether business has an impact on poverty, but whether or not it can and should be accountable for causing, preventing and alleviating poverty. For instance, the Friedmanite business might create jobs, but business as development agent takes responsibility for the number of jobs it creates, their location and their quality. The former might make products available in poor countries, but the latter makes products suited to the needs of and accessible to poor segments of the population.

The idea that senior managers in particular should recognize the "development agent" function of companies is not new. Khurana (2007) says that the emergence of management theory as something to be taught in public universities was because of concerns that the relationship between business and society was being poorly and damagingly handled, and that managers needed to be educated to be arbitrators between the competing claims of different constituencies – what would now be called stakeholders. He goes on to say that this idea of management for "higher aims" has been lost as managers have become "hired hands" serving the interests of investors.

In the last few years, there has been a marked increase in interest in business concentrating more on higher aims, not least in the developing country context. What emerges from the theory and concrete corporate examples is that there are three main ways that companies go beyond a narrowly prescribed economic role, and factor poverty into business decisions. These are: (a) when business is a cause of poverty; (b) when it is poverty's victim; and (c) when it identifies poverty as a commercial opportunity.

Business as a Cause of Poverty

In the free market system, an inefficient company has the potential to cause poverty if it fails to generate wealth, create jobs and provide goods and services. Advocates of free markets often make the case that business cannot cause poverty if it acts rationally because the market is the most effective way of determining price and allocating resources. However, it is the way seemingly efficient companies can cause or exacerbate poverty that is of interest here. For some, such as those in the Fairtrade movement, power asymmetries between different market actors mean that there are wide disparities in how the proceeds of trade are distributed, and that poor producers in particular (e.g. marginal smallholder farmers) can find themselves selling their produce for even less than the cost of production (Raynolds et al., 2004). Similarly, the power some brand-owners hold as gatekeepers to lucrative consumer markets means that manufacturers have limited bargaining power regarding price or specification, making labour one of the few areas where management can influence profitability. Hence, low wages, long hours and other abusive labour practices are the norm in places where low-skilled labour is plentiful, the opportunity cost of relocation is low and law enforcement is lenient (Graham and Woods, 2006). As one buying agent in Hong Kong said of Chinese manufacturers, "Suppliers still have places where they can cut fat, but the easiest fat to cut is workers' wages" (Chan and Siu, 2007, p. 8)

In the long run, developing economy labour markets may obey the scientific laws claimed of liberal economics, and if so wages will rise with the overall upgrading of a country's economy. However, in the short term, wages at less than the cost of survival and reproduction put enormous burdens not only on individual workers, but also on their families and social networks. For example, in a sample of factories producing for Wal-Mart, the hourly wage was less than the legal minimum, and overtime hours exceeded the legal maximum (Chan and Siu, 2007). Only by working excessive overtime (e.g. 12 hour days with only 1.5 days off in a month) could workers achieve earnings approximating a living wage.

Sudden injections of wealth, and unequal distribution, can have long-term consequences. For example, the promotion of cocoa production in parts of Sulawesi, Indonesia, in the 1990s together with weak enforcement of traditional land rights, allowed certain migrant ethnic groups to prosper using land alienated from the indigenous population (Blowfield, 2004). A more detailed analysis than is possible here would reveal how global trade impacts women differently than men, affects some ethnic groups more than others, and variously serves to empower and disempower people depending on their specific situations.

There are other areas where business relates to poverty, if not as the direct cause, then at least as the apparent beneficiary. The poverty that is behind child labour, forced labour and labour trafficking is something that has benefited business in some circumstances, even if few CEOs today would endorse the sentiment of Lord Cadbury in 1909 that slavery is essential to his company's competitiveness (Blowfield and Murray, 2008). Yet, in an indirect way, business is held responsible for these types of poverty, just as it sometimes is for bad or weak governance, not just because it is seen as a beneficiary of the global economic system within which such poverty exists, but because it is associated with the changing patterns of governance that are characteristic of that system.

It is tackling accusations that business is a cause of poverty that has led to a large number of initiatives whereby companies seek to protect their reputations, notably by adopting new regulatory systems promising some form of social accountability (e.g. the Ethical Trading Initiative, the Fair Labor Association). There are examples where new models of private enterprise have been developed to address the conditions of the poor, perhaps most famously in the Fairtrade movement, which seeks to ensure a fair return for producers and their communities. There are cases where business is attempting to ameliorate the negative effects of global competition, as happened when companies such as Nike, Carrefour, KarstadtQuelle and Levi Strauss joined with local manufacturers, unions and NGOs in the Multi-fibre Alliance to mitigate the consequences of ending the Multi-fibre Agreement that had been essential to supporting the garment and textile industry in many poor countries (Blowfield and Murray, 2008).

Business as Poverty's Victim

One only needs to look at the facets of poverty set out in the UN's Millennium Development Goals to see how business can be a victim of poverty. The goals are indicators of human development, and failure to achieve them is indicative of the insufficiencies that can hamper business in developing economies. For example, the facts that half the world lives on less than US$2 a day, and 1.1 billion people live in "extreme poverty" – less than US$1 a day – show how much greater the market for goods and services could be if only people had more income. The number of children who do not finish primary school is a warning of how difficult it can be for companies to fill even relatively low-skilled positions. Women are less likely to get an education, more likely to work at home, and less likely to obtain full-time salaried positions, and gender inequality and disempowerment can harm companies that need educated and independent workers and consumers.

Goals 4, 5 and 6 of the Millennium Development Goals (MDGs) concern health (child mortality, maternal health and major diseases such as HIV/AIDS, respectively), and high morbidity, failing health care systems, malnutrition and disabling or terminal diseases can all harm business. Companies such as L'Oreal and SABMiller in South Africa have invested in programmes to prevent AIDS and provide anti-retroviral drugs because of the attrition the disease was causing amongst experienced personnel.

Weak public governance and the failure of government as development agents are underlying themes of the MDGs. They are equally factors in business being a victim of poverty, and implicit in the goals is the idea that the private sector can compensate for weak government institutions. Moreover, if business does nothing to address rising inequality, this could result in all manner of uncertainties that risk-averse companies might rather not face, such as mass migration, conflict over natural resources and political unrest. Moreover, it should not be forgotten that an earlier era of economic globalization in the 1900s came to a halt because of a political backlash against globalization's distributional effects (O'Rourke and Williamson, 1999).

Awareness of these types of issue help explain the many examples of companies addressing issues that could affect their long-term prospects (e.g. Anglo-American education programmes in South Africa; Cisco Systems' network of academies worldwide; the numerous corporate AIDS programmes). The Forest Stewardship Council was established in response to the failure of conventional approaches to regulating forest management, particularly in parts of the developing world where tropical forests are typically located. Another example is Cadbury's multi-million pound Cocoa Partnership "to secure the economic, social and environmental sustainability of around a million cocoa farmers and their communities in Ghana, India, Indonesia and the Caribbean", spurred by the fact that the poverty associated with cocoa-growing over the past few decades posed a threat to Cadbury's core business.

Business as Solution

Following a period when business was often portrayed in the media and through campaigns as exploitative of poverty, or to a lesser degree its victim, increasing attention is being paid to the idea of business as a solution. This is not simply a restatement of the centrality of business to the capitalist economy as the source of employment, goods and services, and wealth. Rather, it is the belief that business can consciously invest in ways that are simultaneously commercially viable and beneficial to the poor. Hammond, Hart and Prahalad in their influential work on the "fortune at the bottom of the pyramid" emphasize that there are genuine commercial, market-based opportunities to be had by targeting the poor (Prahalad and Hart, 2002; Prahalad, 2005; Hart, 2005; Hammond et al., 2007). They argue that, whereas the richest 0.8 billion people represent a largely saturated and over-served market, and despite there being significant opportunities to serve the 1.5 billion emerging middle class, the greatest unexplored opportunity is the market of 4 billion people who individually or as households have low incomes, but as a group account for a significant percentage of national income and expenditure. For example, in Asia those at the bottom of the economic pyramid make up over 83 per cent of the population, and account for nearly 42 per cent of national income; in Africa, they make up 95 per cent of the population, and account for over 70 per cent of income (Hammond et al., 2007). All told, it is estimated that the poorest 4 billion people represent a market worth $5 trillion (ibid.).

These figures are controversial, and there is a lively ongoing debate about what is meant by the bottom of the pyramid (see for instance Karnani, 2007). Nonetheless, the insight that the poor control considerable wealth is important because it suggests that what is considered the untapped purchasing power at the bottom of the pyramid provides an opportunity for companies to profit by selling to these unserved or underserved markets.

This might imply that the poor represent a rational, if overlooked, business opportunity. However, bottom of the pyramid advocates say that, by meeting the needs of the poor, businesses can increase their productivity and incomes, and be an engine of empowerment, not least by allowing the poor to enter into the formal economy. In other words, by selling to the poor, companies can help eradicate poverty, and Prahalad (2005) particularly emphasizes the role multinationals can play in this by allowing the poor to benefit from both the quality of their products and the efficiencies of their systems. The poor can also benefit as producers, and organizations such as the Shell Foundation (e.g. through their collaboration with the retailer Marks & Spencer to promote flower growing groups on the Agulhas Plain, South Africa), and other large British companies involved in Business Action for Africa focus on the promotion of entrepreneurship.

Profit can be a contentious topic when considering the poor as an opportunity. There are successful examples of targeting the poor, such as Aravind in India, HealthStore Foundation in Kenya, and the Grameen Bank in Bangladesh, which have been run on a not-for-profit basis, or involve some form of subsidy or alternative funding. Moreover, being profitable can require unconventional business models, not only in terms of understanding the market, or designing products, but equally in the collaborations that are required. There are various examples of companies collaborating with NGOs to identify needs, and deliver products: these include Telenor and Grameen's collaboration to create Grameen Phone, ICICI Prudential's collaboration with women's groups in India on insurance products and Accion International's collaboration with ABN Amro on microfinance. Brugmann and Prahalad (2007) view these collaborations as part of a trend towards "co-creation", where business and NGOs create hybrid business models suited to the very different conditions for commercial and social success when dealing with poverty.

Conclusion

In summary, when we examine the role of business as a development agent today, what we are witnessing is part of a constantly shifting debate about business's contribution to society that plays out differently according to place, time and culture, but is ultimately about how the norms and values of capitalism, as embodied in the modern enterprise, can be accommodated, harnessed and utilized for society's good. Some would claim that companies fulfil their unique function by providing goods and services that people need at a profit to investors, and that to ascribe the role of development agent to firms is to distract managers from their primary duties. The framework of business's interactions with poverty used in this chapter shows that, even if a company focuses on its financial mission, there can be good reasons to consciously manage its relationship with society. However, companies are under no formal compulsion to do this, and some critics of business get frustrated that companies are not being told to do more. The reality, however, is that business's engagement in tackling poverty is not a radical shift, even if in recent years some companies are rethinking their relationships in developing countries. What the framework in this chapter sets out is that there are different ways in which business interacts with poverty, and that each of these both demand and create particular opportunities. Understanding the business–poverty relationship may not be the reason why companies engage in tackling poverty, but it is an important step in working out what actions to take and what outcomes to aim for.

References

Blowfield, M. E. (2004), Implementation Deficits of Ethical Trade Systems: Lessons from the Indonesian Cocoa and Timber Industries. *Journal of Corporate Citizenship*, 13, 77–90.

Blowfield, M. E. and Murray, A. (2008), *Corporate Responsibility: A Critical Introduction*. Oxford: Oxford University Press.

Brugmann, J. and Prahalad, C. K. (2007), Cocreating Business's New Social Compact. *Harvard Business Review*, 2007, 80–90.

Chan, A. and Siu, K. (2007), Wal-Mart's CSR and Labor Standards in China. *International Network on Business, Development and Society Workshop*, 12–14 September 2007.

Friedman, M. (1962), *Capitalism and Freedom*. Chicago, IL: University of Chicago Press.

Graham, D. and Woods, N. (2006), Making Corporate Self-regulation Effective in Developing Countries. *World Development*, 34(5), 868–883.

Hammond, A. L., Kramer, W. J., Katz, R. S., Tran, J. T. and Walker, C. (2007), *The Next Four Billion: Market Size and Business Strategy at the Base of the Pyramid*. International Finance Corporation/World Resources Institute: Washington, DC.

Hart, S. L. (2005), *Capitalism at the Crossroads: The Unlimited Business Opportunities in Solving the World's Most Difficult Problems*. Upper Saddle River, NJ: Wharton School.

Karnani, A. (2007), The Mirage of Marketing to the Bottom of the Pyramid. *California Management Review*, 49(4), 90.

Khurana, R. (2007), *From Higher Aims to Hired Hands: The Social Transformation of American Business Schools and the Unfulfilled Promise of Management as a Profession*. Princeton, NJ: Princeton University Press.

O'Rourke, K. H. and Williamson, J. G. (1999), *Globalization and History: the Evolution of a Nineteenth-Century Atlantic Economy*. Cambridge, MA: MIT Press.

Prahalad, C. K. (2005), *The Fortune at the Bottom of the Pyramid*. Upper Saddle River, NJ: Wharton School.

Prahalad, C. K. and Hart, S. L. (2002), The Fortune at the Bottom of the Pyramid. *Strategy + Business*, 26, 2–14.

Raynolds, L. T., Murray, D. and Leigh Taylor, P. (2004), Fair Trade: Building Producer Capacity via Global Networks. *Journal of International Development*, 16, 1109–1121.

Chapter 15

The Ethical Moment: Ethics and Economy in Public Administration

Ove K. Pedersen

Introduction

It has become common over the last 25 years to formulate general ethical standards for management of public administration, not only in developing countries, but in most Western democratic societies too. Standards of ethical conduct currently exist for public managers in USA,[1] the UK,[2] New Zealand,[3] Canada,[4] Australia[5] and a number of other countries.[6] They apply to members of the civil service on the basis of professional merits (meritocracy)[7] as well as to public officials on the basis of their political appointment (politocracy).[8]

The increasing use of ethical standards is a consequence of public administration being subjected to economic values concerning efficiency and productivity, and of administrative bodies being organized and managed to achieve several alternative

---

1   See American Society for Public Administration Code of Ethics, http://www. aspanet.org/ethics/coe.html.

2   See Public Administration – Seventh Report, http://www.parliament.the-stationery-office.co.uk/pa/cm200102/cmselect/cmpubadm/263/26302.htm.

3   See New Zealand Public Service Code of Conduct (2002), http://www.ssc.govt. nz/display/document.asp?docid=3423.

4   See Auditor General of Canada, Values and Ethics in the Federal Public Sector (2000), http://www.oag.-bvg.gc.ca/dominio/reports.nsf/html/0012ce.html; Office of Public Service Values and Ethics, Canada, Values and Ethics Code for the Public Service (2003), http://www.tbs-sct.gc.ca/pubs_pol/hrpubs/TB_851/vec-cve_e.asp; and finally Privy Council Office, Guidance for Deputy Ministers (2003), http://www.pco-bcs.gc.ca/default. asp?page=publication&language=E&doc=gdm-gsm/gdm-gsm_doc_e.htm.

5   See Western Australia Public Sector, Sustainability Code of Practice for Government Agencies (January 2004), http://www.sustainability.dpc.wa.gov.au/docs/submissions/Draft CodeofPractice.pdf.

6   See review of ethical codex, EthicsWeb.ca, http://www.ethicsweb.ca/resources/ government; or OECD, http://www.oecd.org/document/4/0,2340,en_2649_34135_2672772 _1_1_1_1,00.htmlT.

7   See e.g. Cabinet Office (1999), *Modernising Government*, White Paper, London, http://www.archive.official-documents.co.uk/document/cm43/4310/4310.htm.

8   See e.g. House Ethics Manual, Committee on Standards of Official Conduct, 110th Congress, 2nd Session, 2008 edn, Washington.

values and competing policy goals. The introduction of New Public Management (NPM) in public administration has led to economic values being introduced to the management of public organizations, and to public organizations being reorganized and new forms of policy regulation being implemented. Consequently, it is not only in the private sector that ethical codes are being implemented, but in public sectors as well. The role of ethical standards in regulating conduct in both public and private sectors is a characteristic of the period from the 1980s onwards.[9] In this chapter I will deal with only the development in public administration and only one specific aspect of this development – *the ethical moment*. The ethical moment happens on the one hand in situations where a civil servant is compelled to choose between competing values and policy goals and to do so with no clear and specific status for her bureaucratic discretion. On the other hand it happens in situations where – for the same reason – a manager is required to give ethical reasons for his decisions rather than referring to an already established set of legal rules on which his decisions can be judged. In the following I will argue that public managers are compelled to make decisions to an increasing extent in situations of "the legal void". In addition, I will use the introduction of NPM to explain why situations of ethical moments have become an important topic of contemporary public administration.[10] Much of this discussion focuses on the Nordic countries (Denmark and Norway), but it will also include examples from the USA and other Anglo-Saxon countries.

The chapter will be organized as follows. First, I argue for the use of a so-called "first person perspective" on the question of ethical standards of conduct. It is in this context that the concept of the ethical moment is introduced. Second, I read a number of general standards of ethical conduct to identify what can currently be identified as "public values". Based on this reading three areas (or categories)

---

9   A distinction can be made between different types of codex, e.g. for private companies and for public organizations. But the most important distinction is that between three types of codices for public sectors. The first is the codex on "Good Governance" which the UN, the World Bank, the OECD and other international organizations have developed as a guideline for developing countries' receipt of aid and financial assistance. See e.g. OECD (2001), *Public Sector Leadership for the 21st Century*, Paris: OECD, p. 34, see http://www.oecd.org/document/4/0,2340,en_2649_34135_2672772_1_1_1_1,00.htmlT. The second is the codex for international partnerships involving e.g. the EU. See the White Paper on European Governance, http://europa.eu.int/eur-lex/en/com/cnc2001_0428en01. pdf. The third is the codex for highly developed capitalist and democratic national states' administrations. See the introduction in State Services Commission (2001), Working Paper no. 13. A Cross-Jurisdictional Scan of Practices in Senior Public Services: Implications for New Zealand. Crown Copyright, www.ssc.govt.nz.

10   Bureaucratic discretion is certainly not only affiliated with the introduction of NPM; see for a longer time perspective, G. C. Bryner (1987), *Bureaucratic Discretion. Law and Policy in Federal Regulatory Agencies*, New York: Pergamon Press; and J. D. Huber and C. R. Shipan (2002), *Deliberate Discretion? The Institutional Foundations of Bureaucratic Autonomy*, Cambridge: Cambridge University Press.

of public values are identified: decisions-making ethics, organization ethics and communication ethics. Third, every area of public values is situated in relation to current stages of developments in the organization of public administration, enabling me to discover how NPM has initiated new dilemmas and conflicts and compelled civil servants to make decisions in situations void of legal instructions. Finally, this confrontation of values and trends is explored to create a tentative catalogue of moral doctrines. The purpose is to establish a summary of which ethical standards are needed in order to deal with the challenges created by NPM for the legitimate exercise of authority. Accordingly, the chapter is descriptive, as well as prescriptive.

Background

Even though it has been claimed for years that the separation of politics from administration is more formal than real and that officials have long had the independence to exercise discretion, the debate on how to separate political power and bureaucratic discretion has become intensified since the 1980s. In attempts to (re)order the relation between politics and bureaucracy, the Anglo-Saxon countries in particular (USA, UK, New Zealand and Australia) were pioneers in the development of ethical standards of conduct.[11] They were also the first to introduce NPM.[12] In addition, these countries have long traditions for using common law in regulating ties between politics and administration. Against this background, the appearance of general standards in the northwest European countries (Denmark and Norway in particular) is especially interesting. It is in Denmark and Norway that we find the longest and most formalized tradition of subordination of public administration to political control. In both countries the separation of politics and administration was introduced at the beginning of the 1800s, and has since been used as a basis for the formal dependency of public administration on political leadership and for not accepting public managers to

---

11   The present codex in the UK: *The Senior Civil Service Competence Framework – Leadership for Results*, is available at http://www.cabinet-office.gov.uk/civilservice/scs/documents/pdf/competenceframework.pdf. The American equivalent is the US Office of Personnel Management (1998), *Guide to Senior Executive Service Qualifications*, Washington, DC: US Office of Personnel Management, and is available at http://www.opm.gov/ses/ecq.asp. The codex in New Zealand is: State Service Commission (2001), *New Zealand Public Service – Chief Executives' Competencies*, Crown Copyright and is available at http://www.ssc.govt.nz/upload/downloadable_files/CECompetencies.pdf.

12   See presentation and review of these ideals in C. Politt and G. Bouchaert (2000), *Public Management Reform – a Comparative Analysis*, Oxford: Oxford University Press. See also T. Christensen and S. Lægreid (2002), *Reformer og Lederskap. Omstilling i den utøvende makt*, Oslo: Universitetsforlaget, pp. 38–59; and in C. Greve (2002), New Public Management – en kort oversigt over begrebets anvendelse og udvikling, *Nordisk Administrativt Tidsskrift*, 83, 74–90.

be selected based on their political affiliation (politocracy). The fact that general standards are now implemented in countries with traditions for both common and positive law is a sign that the appearance of standards is based on changes which cut across constitutional traditions. These changes appear to possess the following features:

- Public organizations have become subject to economic values concerning efficiency and productivity.
- They are organized and managed to achieve economic goals and results.
- They have achieved a certain bureaucratic autonomy (or "disestablishment") to prioritize their initiatives within economic frameworks, and through discretion to decide which specific services and benefits citizens are entitled to receive.
- Finally, they have become subject to professional management, either by boards of directors comprising experts or users, or by public managers empowered with independent responsibility.

In short, the NPM has led to the introduction of new values for public administration, and to the implementation of new forms of organization. The traditional values of the legal exercise of authority are supplemented by new economic values of efficiency and productivity; and the ties between public organizations and political leadership have been loosened and public organizations have been delegated a degree of autonomy to prioritize their resources and to decide which services and benefits citizens are entitled to. On the same basis, a substantial scope for management has been opened and placed with managers of public organizations and administrative bodies, including schools and hospitals, universities and nursing homes. This is how the conditions for *ethical moments* are created, i.e. situations where a person in a position of public authority is compelled to choose between competing considerations and to do so in situations of a legal void. Firstly, public administration is conducted in a situation of mutually competing legal, economic and professional values compelling officials to prioritize between alternative (in cases even opposite) values. Secondly, management of public discretion happens in the framework of competing organizational models including both hierarchy (subject to politically decided rules and directives) and decentralization (independent relative to politically decided rules and directives) inducing officials to prioritize between and to embed themselves in alternative (in cases even opposite) orders of authority. Thirdly and finally, public administration is governed by elected politicians, managed by professional managers and by politically appointed experts (and users) in many cases without a clear (and formalized) distribution of governmental power forcing officials to prioritize between alternative (in cases even opposite) lines of loyalty. As a result, a new situation is established for public administration and for street-level bureaucrats and professionals (doctors, nurses, school teachers, etc.). They are compelled to deliberate in situations with little (or no) guidance in their enabling status concerning how they should shape their regulatory agenda, set priorities and allocate scarce resources. Instead civil servants and professionals are required to make decisions which necessitate that they decide between competing values and goals within the framework of alternative models for the distribution of governmental power by choosing between alternative lines of loyalty. It is in these situations of legal void that they are required to give ethical reasons for their decisions rather than referring to their legal status.

The increasing use of bureaucratic autonomy is the basis for several theories. Among the most important is the principal-agent (PA) theory. In this theory it is assumed that the servant has (or has achieved) some form of autonomy relative to the politician and that the servant will use this autonomy to increase his own preferences. It is also assumed that the principal (the politician) and the agent (the servant) have their own interests and that each is framed by their own set of incentives. It is finally assumed that, when the administrative agent does not necessarily look after the principal's interests, the principal is interested in using incentives or other mechanisms of control to ensure that this is done.[13] In the USA, the UK and New Zealand, but also in Denmark and Norway, the PA theory has been applied in reforms to change the relationship between political leadership and administrative management as well as professionals.[14] Fixed-term employment and contractual controls have been introduced, individual salary arrangements have been created, and other incentive systems have been established with the object of ensuring the loyalty of management and professionals. In addition, general ethical standards for public administration have been formulated and implemented with the same object in mind.[15]

There is still discussion in public administration research of whether the NPM reforms have increased bureaucratic discretion by amplifying the independency of public organizations and administrative bodies. Even so, a general agreement is emerging that the management of public organizations has gained more independence, and that public managers have gained a significant influence on how the public administration is organized, which tasks it undertakes and how to set priorities and allocate resources. There is also discussion within political theory of whether public managers (especially top managers) have become more closely involved in political processes and in the political decision-making, or vice versa, whether politicians (or appointed users and organized interests) have become more involved in administrative processes. However, although the discussion is

---

13   For a review of the principal-agent theory and political control of the bureaucracy: see J. D. Huber and C. R. Shipan (2002), *Deliberate Discretion? The Institutional Foundations of Bureaucratic Autonomy*, Cambridge: Cambridge University Press.

14   C. Politt and G. Bouchaert (2000), *Public Management Reform – a Comparative Analysis*, Oxford: Oxford University Press.

15   See for example Code for Public Managers in Denmark, http://www. publicgovernance.dk/?siteid=635&menu_start=635; and Ethical Guidelines for Public Service in Norway, http://www.regjeringen.no/upload/kilde/mod/bro/2005/0001/ddd/ pdfv/281750-etiske_retningslinjer_engelsk_revidert.pdf.

still going on, there is an emerging unanimity in both fields that the governmental power of politicians has been changed, while public managers and administrative agencies have gained influence, but also that the politicians still possess political responsibility in formal terms, while the legal responsibilities of the official still are more limited than those of the politician.[16] Even so, there is agreement with the fact that the independence of public officials and the changes in the power relations between politics and administration have led to the introduction of new and more comprehensive ways for political institutions to control and steer the administration. Not only have administrative law and judiciary control been strengthened but also changes in administrative practice and formal agreements and contracts have been used with the same purpose, in many cases inspired by PA theory.

The Ethical Moment

Why have codes of conduct for public management become an important topic even if the actions of public employees are to an increasing extent being prescribed by law, administrative practice, agreements, contracts, customs and other formal and informal but binding standards?[17] The question can only be answered in a positive way if it is possible to argue convincingly for two points: (1) that public sector managers are subject to especially strict requirements with which civil servants in general are not required to comply; and (2) that public managers increasingly make decisions on a purely ethical basis. In the following, I will describe the public values which can be derived from the existing codes of conduct, and will on this basis argue why stricter requirements must now be set for public management. The pivotal point is the concept of the ethical moment, and I start by establishing the conditions which must be present for the ethical moment to arise. This leads us to "the first person perspective", i.e. towards the authority who finds herself in ethical situations where a choice which she cannot avoid has to be made.

The first condition is that there are certain values which it is taken for granted that all persons who exercise public authority must comply with. I call this first condition "the presence of public values". This condition includes that public managers must be able to demonstrate that every action they take can be said to have a common purpose.[18] The second condition is that public managers find themselves in situations where they have to make decisions with little (or no) guidance concerning how to set priorities, allocate scarce resources and distribute the costs and benefits involved in the budgets they are managing. I call this second

16   G. Peters and J. Pierre (eds) (2001), *Politicians, Bureaucrats and Administrative Reform*, London: Routledge.

17   L. Lundquist (1988), *Byråkratisk etik*, Lund: Studentlitteratur.

18   D. E. Thompson (1987), *Political Ethics and Public Office*, Cambridge, MA: Harvard University Press, p. 117.

condition "the presence of autonomy",[19] which presumes that, the more autonomy the executive enjoys, the stricter the requirement that both politicians and citizens are entitled to insight into and justification for the decisions made. I call the third condition "the presence of ethical choice". This assumes that, because managers can find little (or no) guidance in their status, they are compelled to give ethical reasons for their decisions in situations including an element of dilemma or conflict of values or goals. An *ethical conflict* thus arises when there are incompatabilities in a situation of choice between two considerations, and it is entirely obvious which consideration the decision-maker should favour from an ethical point of view.[20] An *ethical dilemma*, on the other hand, arises in situations where a choice has to be made in situations of two opposing interests, and it is not clear which of these interests the person making the decision should promote from an ethical point of view.[21] It is my claim that all three conditions must be present for the ethical moment to arise. The ethical moment therefore involves a person who finds herself in a situation where, void of legal instructions, she can only give ethical reasons for decisions she is compelled to make in situations of dilemma or conflict.

In the following I describe the public values which can be found in the existing codes of conduct in the USA, the UK, New Zealand, Australia, Denmark and Norway. I place these in relation to brief descriptions of actual trends in the last 30 years' implementation of NPM. Much of this discussion will be based on examples from Denmark and Norway and less so from Anglo-Saxon countries. Finally, I explore this confrontation to launch a catalogue of moral doctrines for management in contemporary public administration. I do this for several reasons, the first of which is because none of the existing codes identify ethical moments as reasons for why ethical codes are necessary in the first place. Some codes give no reasons at all, others point to the legal void, but none address the ethical nature of bureaucratic discretion in situations of legal void. The second is because none of the codes covers all of the challenges that are generally recognized as a consequence of the introduction of NPM ideals and thus identify the magnitude of the challenges in a systematic way. Some codes emphasize the professional qualities which must be present for good management, i.e. Codes of Competences (USA, UK, Canada, New Zealand, Denmark, and Norway). Others formulate moral doctrines for good management, i.e. *Codes of Conduct* (USA, UK, Canada, Australia, New Zealand); still others create employment policies with the purpose of ensuring good management by rules of mandatory training, evaluations and payment, i.e. *Civil Service Acts* (UK, USA, New Zealand).

---

19   L. Lundquist (1988), *Byråkratisk etik*, ibid., pp. 143–149.
20   Ibid., p. 168.
21   Ibid., p. 168; and M. L. Rhodes (1986), *Ethical Dilemmas in Social Work Practice*, Boston, MA: Routledge & Kegan Paul.

Public Values

Before identifying public values originating in codes of conduct, two points are worth emphasizing.

1. All values stated (explicitly or present by logical implication) are quite general. They are introduced as if they apply to all democratic forms of government at all times; and to all civil servants at all levels, even if – in the last case – they address only public managers (and not civil servants or professionals in general). In no cases do codes of conduct argue for the specific context in which they are introduced, neither with reference to the particular mode of government in which they are implanted, nor with reference to contemporary developments or trends or in this mode. All codes are – more or less – introduced without reference to context or history.
2. All values stated accept that existing laws, rules, administrative practice or other formal or informal but binding rules are "not enough" to assure appropriate action by civil servants or public managers. They take for granted – explicitly or implicitly – that public officials have gained some scope for independence, or that bureaucratic discretion sometimes happens in a legal void. All codes address persons constituted in a position delegated by public authority and take for granted that persons – qua their positions – have enough independence that their positions as agents (and not principals) must be checked by means other than existing laws and rules. All codes argue at the first person level, and address persons in public positions rather than public organizations or bodies.

In the political history of the Western democratic society, it has been widely accepted – and even taken for granted – that public managers and other public agents do not have the autonomy necessary to make decisions in a legal void or to be positioned in ethical moments without guidance in formal instructions. On the contrary, managers, like other public agents, have been regarded as servants of the law (subject to the principle of legal authority) and obeying a legally established impersonal order.[22] In addition, it has been widely accepted that it is in the authority of the elected representatives of the people (i.e. the politicians assembled in political institutions) to establish the body of law and by doing so

---

22 "That the person who obeys authority does so, (...) only in his capacity as a 'member' of the organization and what he obeys is only 'the law'", M. Weber (1978), On Legal Authority. With a Bureaucratic Administrative Staff, in *Economy and Society*, Berkeley, CA: University of California Press, p. 217.

to express what is to be understood as "the general will of the people" or "the common good", and it is not in the authority of the public agents to do so.²³

It is against this background that the ethical standards applied to public administrations set out to identify a set of general (or universal) public values as a framework for introducing ethical standards rather than letting "the body of law" or the established impersonal order of "the law" perform this role. It is also against this background that public values are derived from the premises that public authorities are implanted in democratic government (and not in "the law"); and also that democratic government unites public agents to follow standards different from those applied to private companies or to citizens in general. It is even against this background that the codes of conduct list two different roles of ethics in democratic government, and do so in the line of theories of political ethics.²⁴ The first is that democratic politics can be said to embed ethical decisions. The second is that a political ethic can be said to embed democratic government. In the first case the argument is this: many of the decisions which concern the basic conditions of life – life and death, imprisonment and others – must, in the final analysis, be decided by complying with some form of democratic procedure. It is thus by democratic legislation that it is decided whether or not, when and when not, an abortion may be carried out, or for how long and in what way criminals should be punished – and also in the final instance, it must be decided what is understood to be the proper democratic procedure to comply with. In the second case the argument is this: it is widely accepted that contemporary democratic government is based on the fundamental rights and freedoms of the individual; it is also widely accepted that bureaucratic discretion must be compatible with due regard for human dignity and human rights, even if the rights, the freedoms and the understandings can only be argued for in ethical terms and as such must be based on moral (or universal) principles. It follows from these arguments that there is a logical relationship between political ethics and democratic government, and that ethical decisions shall be made following democratic procedures, just as democratic politics must be justifiable by moral principles.

Thus, the basic public value to be identified in codes of conduct is that ethical decisions are embedded in democratic procedures, just as democratic government

---

23   The concept of common good or "the will of the people" is one of the most contested within democratic theory. For different readings, see I. Shapiro (2003), *The State of Democratic Theory*, Princeton, NJ: Princeton University Press; see also J. Schumpeter (2003), Capitalism, Socialism, and Democracy, in R. A. Dahl, I. Shapiro and J. E. Cheibub (eds), *The Democracy Sourcebook*, Cambridge, MA: The MIT Press, pp. 5–11. It is not my ambition to be involved in this discussion. Instead I take for granted that mainstream democratic theories from Aristotle to contemporary understandings of deliberative democracy base their theory of democracy on the normative conception that democratic methods (or institutions) should be geared to discover or manufacture some notion of the common good.

24   D. E. Thompson (1987), *Political Ethics and Public Office*, Cambridge, MA: Harvard University Press, p. 3.

is embedded in moral principles. The two are intertwined; together they constitute what can be called a logic of democratic government based on which the existing codes of conduct derive a number of more specific public values, two of which must be emphasized. The first is the public value of transparency and responsibility. It is taken for granted that the public administration as such exists to implement (or administer) common purposes, which is why society (or its citizens) has a special claim to be able to judge how officials act, and also has a special claim to be able to hold the people in question responsible for the actions they perform. Because the public administration exists to implement a common good and is required to act *for us* and *on our behalf*, public managers (as well as civil servants) have rights, but also obligations, which the general public does not possess. This applies especially to public managers, because they have a managerial responsibility. The second is the public value of promoting general values and representing a public interest. While it is taken for granted that public managers are expected to work for us, it is also expected that they will promote general values and represent a public interest. Among the general values they are expected to uphold is working within the frameworks of democratic governance, and implementing the interests of the public as such and not only their personal interests or the interests of their proper public organization. This too applies especially to public managers because they have a managerial responsibility.

Indeed, all codes of conduct are concerned with both sets of public values. They also point to three types of functions public managers are compelled to administer and in which they are supposed to have a certain autonomy to act. From this it follows that the object of all standards is two-fold, but also that the object has to be managed by three different functions. The object is two-fold in the sense that the purpose of codes is to formulate criteria for how citizens and politicians can assess executive actions (criteria for the assessment of actions) on the one hand, and on the other hand to equip managers with criteria for how actions can be appropriately exercised (standards for appropriate action). Codes of conduct equip citizens with criteria for assessing actions, and public managers with criteria for how to make appropriate decisions. Further, this is supposed to happen through the administration of three types of functions. All three are derived from codes of conduct and the types of functions public managers are supposed to act upon in their position as managers. Decision-making is the first and deals with how public managers can make appropriate decisions. Organization is the second and is related to how public managers can organize and manage their organization in appropriate ways. Communication is the third function and is oriented towards how managers can communicate and construct the knowledge to be communicated in appropriate ways.

I will now compare the two sets of public values with trends in public administration. Each of the trends is either explicitly described in codes or can be induced from these. The same goes for the three functions. Based on the comparison of trends with values I move from describing codes of conduct to prescribing 12 moral principles for how contemporary public administration can handle challenges created by the implementation of New Public Management. I do this by comparing (1) public values, with (2) moments where public executives find themselves in ethical moments, after which (3) four moral principles are formulated for each of the three functions. The result is 12 moral principles arranged within three areas of ethics:

Decision-making ethic	Organization ethic	Communication ethic
Principles of loyalty and distance	Principles of responsibility and ethical reflection	Principles of impartiality and analytical independence
Principles of political authority and anticipation	Principles of collective purpose and responsiveness	Principles of independence and dialogue
Principles of the common good and pluralism	Principles of employee care and caring management	Principles of generality and individuality
Principles of subjugation of own interests and professional leadership	Principles of proportionality and certainty	Principles of precedence of freedoms and free choice

Moral Doctrines for Ethical Moments: Decision-Making Ethics

The decision-making ethic comprises the doctrine of the appropriate way of making decisions. I concentrate exclusively on the decisions which involve ethical moments.

Public Values

Public managers are subject to the law, and expected to comply with constitutional norms and formal rules. In Western countries it is widely accepted that, in principle, every public servant is a neutral and objective administrator who is employed on her merits and whose job is to implement the legislation and the decisions adopted by political institutions following accepted democratic procedures. It is this value which creates the justification for the government's position relative to the officials, and the general role of the official in relation to the subordinate, and finally for the courts' authority to judge a law or a decision to be legally valid or invalid.

Ethical moments   As managers in the public sector become professionalized and develop their own form of professionalism, they come to possess a special set of skills relative to both the political leaders and the expert know-how of the various employees. On this basis, the manager's professionalization creates a "distance" from both sides in terms of information, knowledge and attitude. Conditions for asymmetrical information relative to the political leader are created. The executive possesses information which the political leader does not have. He also has a particular attitude towards competent and good management which the politician does not necessarily share. This applies especially to top managers who, all else being equal, may be assumed to have reached the top because they have built up a special knowledge during their career, have gained special experience, and have demonstrated a special attitude to management which on all points distinguishes them from other potential candidates. The building up of managerial skills creates, in other words, an asymmetrical relationship between political leaders and public managers, and gives the manager a measure of autonomy. For the same reason, the need to establish a relationship of loyalty between the two is sharpened. At the same time, the manager should be responsible under democratic doctrines to the law, the democratic form of governance and the principles of the rule of law. Together, this strengthens the need to base the relationship of loyalty on moral principles. In democratic theory, including bureaucratic ethics, there has long been discussion of how public executives can show loyalty to those who have been elected, while at the same time also being loyal to the law, the rule of law, and the spirit which should characterize a democratic administration. The first ethical standard derives from this question.

Ethical standard Top executives should show loyalty to their political leaders and use their managerial skills on behalf of the latter, and position their organization so that it accommodates the government's priorities. This implies a *principle of loyalty*, i.e. that the manager uses his special skills to promote and safeguard the president's or the government's or the minister's political interests. However, loyalty to the law also involves a second principle, namely the *principle of distance*, which assumes that, in showing loyalty, the manager upholds his or her duty to serve the common good and puts this duty before the duty to serve the elected politicians, and is therefore obliged in cases of a clear breach of the law, breach of agreements or setting aside of general considerations (including corruption, personal impropriety, etc.) to draw attention to this and possibly to pass the information on to other superior authority.

Public Values

Democratic theory holds the ideal that the organization of the public sector is determined by parliament by legislation and by the government by decisions. It is the government's (or the president's) prerogative to organize the government's administration and the minister's responsibility to lead it. It is taken for granted that the officials will work within organizational frameworks over which they themselves have no influence, and that they will work under a division of authority which they themselves have no authority to change. It is this doctrine which justifies the political leadership's prerogative to determine the government's organization and to arrange the government's or the municipality's management. It is also this ideal which will ensure that officialdom works within frameworks which serve a collective purpose.

Ethical moments   As public organizations have been made independent in various ways from the parliamentary chain of control, they have gained a measure of independency relative to the political institutions. This also applies to the political leadership. Further independence is gained when public managers are given managerial authority and extend its scope. Both forms of independence mean that the executive gains a responsibility – which is also imposed on him – for structuring the organization's powers and duties, and for its general performance, including achieving required goals and results. Other examples of how independence is gained could be given. For example, politicians let themselves be represented by officials in supranational and transnational contexts, or on boards of directors, councils, tribunals, centres and other organs locally or regionally, including in networks which lack the character of an organ, but in which political negotiations nevertheless take place or political agreements nevertheless are entered into. Political leadership is increasingly being exercised via "go-betweens". This function is left to public managers in particular, and they are consequently assuming a measure of independency in political decision-making processes. Public executives are basically appointed to undertake the duties prescribed by law, but gradually, as they gain increased independence, it has become a problem for democratic theory to justify why and how officials may legitimately take part in and make political decisions. This question is directed especially to top managers who have better chances, all else being equal, of becoming part of these processes than do other public employees. If we thus assume that public managers can make independent and political decisions, how can they do so by following principles which guarantee the politicians' right to lead and the principle of political loyalty? The second ethical standard arises from this question.

Ethical standard   Public managers should seek a political mandate for everything they do. This implies a *principle of political authority*, i.e. that executives enter into agreements with their political head on how they may use their special insights, and under what terms they may make independent decisions or influence decisions. This also implies a *principle of anticipation*, i.e. that executives not only possess adequate knowledge of which decisions the political leader wants made, and how the latter wants to be represented in various contexts, but also, via the procuring of information and knowledge, attempt to predict the problems and challenges which the political leader can be expected to have to handle.

Public Values

The public sector plays a special societal role. Its existence is based on the common good and its interests. There is no doubt that all members of society have a shared interest in the existence of organizations which guarantee the individual citizen's life, safety and welfare. Seen in this light, the public sector's societal role is based on making public goods available for members of society, including a legal system and guarantees of the individual's safety and welfare. It is this public interest which creates justifications for the constitutional state's principles of legality, equality before the law and transparency in its application, including the need for supervision by the courts.

Ethical moments The public sector has come to embed several types of special interests in step with the establishment of different forms of organization subject to essentially different forms of rationality (policy, administration, service and production). These could be sectorial interests where the interests of the municipalities and those of the central or federal state do not necessarily coincide. They could be organizational interests where the interests of a hospital and those of the health system as a whole do not necessarily coincide. They could be professional interests where the interests of the doctors and the hospital administrator do not necessarily coincide. And they could be many other competing interests. The basic point is this: that those who are appointed managers (and are employed as public professionals) are meant to represent the public interest. However, if we assume that, like politicians, public managers like public professionals can legally allow themselves to be influenced by, and show consideration for special interests, how can they do so by following principles which guarantee the common good? The third ethical standard arises from this question.

Ethical standard Managers should safeguard the interests of the common good when they allow themselves to be influenced by, and to show consideration for, special interests. This involves a *principle of the common good*, i.e. special interests must not be given advantages unless they can be justified as a public interest or as being a public good. A *principle of pluralism* is also involved, i.e. before consideration is shown for special interests, other special interests should also be heard so that a balanced weighing of interests can act as the basis for action on behalf of a public interest.

Public Values

The public sector employee is appointed on his or her professional merit and not because of any party-political affiliation, or on grounds of gender, race, religion, sexual preference or other characteristic. In this sense the appointment is based on the interests of the common good in ensuring that the public sector is staffed by persons who are equipped with the best possible and most appropriate skills. It is this public interest which creates the justification for the so-called meritocracy and for the bureaucratic tradition that employment in the public sector is not based on subjective (or ideological) considerations. It is also this tradition which creates the justification for the presence of rule-of-law principles underlying valid administration, and that employment, salary and advancement and other benefits are awarded to the individual employee on the basis of objective merit.

Ethical moments   As public managers are entrusted with increasing managerial responsibility and gain independent skills, not merely in relation to political leadership but also in relation to employees, the possibility of paternalistic relations is created. "Paternalism" here means situations where a superior influences others to do something against their will, but nevertheless in their own interest.[25] This could be accepting unreasonable working conditions or providing financial or sexual favours in return for a benefit – an appointment or promotion. Similarly, as managers are designated on the basis of professional merit and not in accordance with standards in a particular system of advancement, their options for advancement come to depend on the evaluations of peers and other employees. The conditions for a paternalistic relationship also exist here, where "paternalism" is to be understood as the situation where a leader prefers to remain blind to an employee's incompetence, slovenliness, corruption or neglect of ordinary conduct in order to achieve a benefit himself – to keep his position, avoid criticism or similar. And finally, as merit comes to be associated with salary, appointments and promotions, personal interests are coupled to the manner and degree to which the manager's organization meets goals for objectives and results or otherwise achieves status and reputation in the community. Here again, the possibility of paternalistic relations arises, where "paternalism" is to be understood as the situation where a superior induces his employees to produce inaccurate or wrong information on the organization's performance so that the superior himself or his employees can gain a benefit – additional resources, a better reputation, higher status. Officials are employed and given opportunities of advancement because they possess objective skills. It is therefore also a problem for democratic theory to justify why executives may look after their own personal (career) interests when they are simultaneously required to look after society's and/or the interests of political elected leaders. This problem of course applies especially to managers. If we assume that they can legally base the exercise of their managerial functions on their own interests, how can they do so by following principles which guarantee the common good? And if we assume that managers, like all others, are dependent on the evaluation of their peers and other employees and on collective performances, how can they perform their managerial duties without paternalism? The fourth and final ethical standard in the decision-making chain arises out of this question.

Ethical standard   Managers should safeguard the interests of society ahead of their own interests and always show loyalty to their own organization and its employees ahead of loyalty to their own careers and conditions of employment. This involves a *principle of subordination of own interests*, i.e. that her own interests may not be an important reason for the decisions made by the manager,

---

25   Ibid., p. 148ff.

including decisions on organizational changes, arrangement of the work processes, allocation of tasks, and appointment and remuneration of employees. In principle, public managers should also be free of suspicion that paternalistic rather than professional considerations are the basis for their decisions. This involves a *principle of professional management*, i.e. that management may not be based on paternalistic relations.

Moral Doctrines for Ethical Moments: Organization Ethics

Organization ethics are the doctrine of the appropriate way to organize public authority. This section focuses only on the organizational questions which involve ethical moments.

Public Values

The law is the basis for all public authority, and only public authority may award rights and impose duties. In principle, all civil servants are required to allow the law or other binding rule to decide by whom the decision must be made, under what circumstances and on which legal grounds and with what legal consequences this is to happen. Ideally, the legal framework does not grant any freedom to the public authority or official to make decisions in a legal void.

Ethical moments   The delegation of broad, policy-making powers to administrative bodies has empowered managers to issue regulations and to set priorities and allocate resources based on bureaucratic discretion, including by balancing different interests. At the same time, the delegation requires managers to make decisions in situations where several of these various interests rest on mutually competing or even mutually exclusive values or policy goals. These situations of competing values can be the regard for the freedom of the individual and equality before the law as against considerations of public security, or health, or the environment, or of society's economic growth. There can also be considerations regarding professional and ethically defensible treatment of patients or embryos as against the interest of the efficiency and productivity of public organizations or of technological development. Today many decisions are made by servants and professionals in situations where they are delegated autonomy to make decisions through discretion, and where the decision will inevitably involve a conflict or a dilemma. To the extent that street-level bureaucrats or professionals are systematically required to make decisions in ethical moments, problems arise which are particularly troublesome for public managers. Managers are responsible for the total performance of their organization, which is why they cannot avoid responsibility for the discretion of bureaucrats or professionals on their behalf, even if the discretion is made by "many hands", i.e. by several employees being part of a complex division of labour. The problem with "many hands"[26] has long occupied theories of bureaucratic ethics, but is accentuated by developments in the number of interests needing to be included in discretion, and as ever bigger and more complex operating units are established. If therefore we assume that it is legal to poise individual with public interests and to weigh several public interests against each other, how can public managers then ensure that somebody (or themselves) can be held responsible for decisions made by many hands? The fifth ethical standard arises out of this question.

Ethical standard Public managers are responsible for ensuring that citizens whose lives, welfare or property are affected by bureaucratic discretion can claim responsibility for the decisions made. This involves a *principle of responsibility*, i.e., that the manager is responsible for establishing a set of standards which specify where responsibility for every decision is to be placed, even for decisions made by "many hands". This also involves a *principle of ethical reflection*, i.e. that such a standard of conduct should include a set of procedures for how discretion made by many hands is to be made through deliberation. The theory of bureaucratic ethics includes a model for the "maximum responsible deliberation",[27] which requires *inter alia* the person (or persons) making the decision to be aware of all the interests and values involved in the decisions. In most cases it is impossible to live up to the maximum model. It is therefore up to the manager to ensure that standards of conduct are prepared which define the procedure for reflecting on how to rank and prioritize interests and values, making officials aware of how reasons can be known for prioritizing between values and how values are supposed to be prioritized – e.g. life before law, law before impartiality, impartiality before efficiency, and efficiency before expediency.

Public Values

The ultimate object of the public sector is to represent the common good. We need a public sector because, cutting across all our individual needs and interests, there are objectives which we cannot realize ourselves, and because in some cases tasks are best performed collectively. This is the criterion underlying the fact that it is up to political institutions like the Parliament to delegate powers to administrative bodies, or in the power of heads of governments to decide how to organize their government and its bureaucracy. Governments are appointed (or elected) to safeguard the interests of society as a whole and to do so through a public administration organized with that purpose.

---

26 Ibid., pp. 40–66; L. Lundquist (1988), *Byråkratisk etik*, ibid., p. 152ff.

27 H. Ofstad (1982), *Ansvar og handling. Inledning till moralfilosofiska problem*, Stockholm: Prisma, p. 23f. and (1987), p. 45ff.

Ethical moments   While public managers are required to amend and to adapt their organization to political purposes, managerial authority has been extended to included the authority to reform and change public organizations according to policy goals and results. In line with NPM ideas, reform programmes have delegated broad reform-making powers to public managers. So if we assume that public managers are empowered to reform their organization, how can it be ensured that this is done as a response to political or societal requirements or as a reaction to the needs and interests of a significant group of citizens and users? The sixth ethical standard arises out of this question.

Ethical standard   Public managers are required to reform their organization with the aim of improving the capability of the organization to fulfil policy goals or to meet the needs and interests of citizens. This involves a *principle of public interest* under which every change in the organization's structure and division of labour can be argued to enhance the capability of the organization to fulfil such goals. This also involves a *principle of responsivity*, i.e. the fact that the organization is structured so that it can be warned about, learn about or be informed about policy goals or the needs and demands of groups and segments of the population as well as of individuals.

Public Values

The ideal that the public sector looks after public interests and the needs of its citizens signifies that the sector should be staffed with competent and efficient employees. This ideal underlies the justification for employing the most suitable people, that salary follows merit and efficiency, that managers are appointed on merit, and that the employees' skills should always correspond to the duties required by the organization.

Ethical moments   The introduction of new forms of payment and the consequent competition between public employees imply that the official's loyalty to the organization depends on salary and promotion options. At the same time, the fact that public organizations are entering into ever more complex relations with other public and private organizations implies that public managers as well as public professionals are exposed to all sorts of attempts to exert influence or enter into situations where their loyalty to the organization is challenged. If we therefore assume that the manager has his or her own interests and that these do not necessarily coincide with those of the organization, and that the official's loyalty is always being tested, how can it be ensured that the officials who best match the organization's duties are always appointed, that they are equipped with the requisite skills, and that they are generally efficient, including always showing the necessary loyalty to the organization? The seventh ethical standard follows from this.

Ethical standard Public managers should ensure that their employees possess skills which correspond to their duties, and that they are otherwise efficient. This involves a *principle of staff care* which assumes that the executive should ensure that the organization is always staffed with skilled employees and that these are given opportunities to arrange and to develop their tasks so that they are able to execute their duties competently and efficiently and with quality. This also involves a *principle of caring management,* i.e. the executive should take the initiative to create perceptions of the organization's objectives and base these on values which ensure the staff's respect for the organization's objectives and their loyalty to its management. However, also the individual employee must gain respect for the executive as a person who shows loyalty and care for the employees as individuals with their own needs and special interests.

Public Values

Like other executives, public managers are equipped with independent managerial responsibility. This is formalized by law and in collective agreements and individual contracts, and it is also part of administrative practice and custom. The law is, however, usually quite broad in its instructions, which challenge the manager to create his or her concrete managerial space or scope. However, because this space is not (absolutely) delimited in advance, and because many people have an interest in how the managerial scope is delimited and which resources the manager is authorized to use, conflict must always be expected over the managerial space and the concrete use which the executive makes of it.

Ethical moments The battle for the managerial space is currently heating up. This is especially the case with respect to the public executive's managerial space, which is related not only to the fact that managerial responsibility for executives has been under constant expansion, but also to the fact that top managers in particular have been required to assume ever greater responsibilities. The same battle is taking place between the individual manager and the political leader, between the top executive and staff organizations, and between the executive and employees, but also between the manager and external competitors – e.g. other executives, public organizations and interest organizations. At the same time, the public organizations are becoming more complex, implying that the manager must delegate tasks to many levels and create bodies for cooperation in the organization and across several organizations. If we therefore assume that public managers carry a legally imposed managerial responsibility, how does a manager in question ensure that he can meet this responsibility and also provide competent and good management? The eighth ethical question, the last in the organization ethics, arises from this question.

Ethical standard Managers should secure their managerial latitude, but also take account of other moral doctrines for appropriate management. This involves a *principle of proportionality*, i.e. that managers should secure the managerial space required to be able to meet the obligations which have been formally and informally imposed on them, but such that there are always objective justifications for how they execute their obligations. This also involves a *principle of certainty*, i.e. that delegation of managerial powers to internal bodies may never be so vague as to cause doubt, and it may never be so permanent that it cannot be revoked. Even if, in the nature of the case, managers must delegate duties to many employees and must cooperate with many interested parties (including employees and staff organizations), he must always ensure that he possesses the necessary conditions for being able to provide competent management, even if this happens to be against the interests of a majority of employees.

Moral Doctrines for Ethical Moments: Communication Ethics

Communication ethics are concerned with the appropriate way of communicating.

Public Values

Public organizations are increasingly required to prepare reports, including prognoses and evidence-based knowledge. Public administration has increasingly become data-oriented. This is expressed in the use of scientific analyses or other forms of systematic gathering of knowledge. It is also expressed in the fact that analyses, evaluations and other forms of knowledge (including scientific knowledge) must be assessed for their administrative or political utility. The generation and use of such knowledge has various purposes. One is to devise policy goals to be included in legislation, or to point to policy problems on which to base policy proposals and public interventions. Another is to evaluate scientific research for policy or administrative use, or to evaluate social or organizational experiments for the purpose of identifying best practice. In democratic theory it is assumed that knowledge in general is generated and used with the object of manufacturing (or realizing) the common good, but also with the purpose of creating an informative and insightful platform for decisions to be made by political institutions and their leaders.

Ethical moments   Knowledge has become an important resource for political leaders and public management. The generation and use of knowledge has also become politicized. Like the business sector, politicians have an interest in how knowledge is accumulated, analysed, assessed, concluded and passed on. With the increased politicization, there are important political conflicts involved in the formulation of the public interest. For the same reason, knowledge cannot be deemed to be true or objective, relevant or applicable just because it is presented as if it is neutral or trustworthy. Competition for knowledge and the competition among those who generate knowledge are now of such a character that knowledge has become a tool for the safeguarding of special interests, and the formulation of the public interest is politicized. If we therefore assume that public organizations can legally generate and use knowledge, the ninth ethical standard then arises.

Ethical standard Public managers must ensure that knowledge is generated and used professionally. This involves a *principle of professionalism*, i.e. that the manager must create the conditions for ensuring that the knowledge on which political and administrative decisions are based has been generated and is used in such a manner that it is trustworthy, relevant and valid. This also involves a *principle of analytical independence*, i.e. that the manager ensures that the experts who are required to prepare the knowledge are guaranteed against interference in their obligation to gather data and analyse the information on the basis of professionally recognized theories and methods, including that their analytical assumptions and conclusions can be subject to critical reflection by both the general public and other experts.[28]

Public Values

Public organizations are increasingly using knowledge to influence public debate and the news cycle. This occurs when organizations issue press statements, or publish reports and blueprints, or when they conduct public campaigns or initiate processes in which social problems are identified and brought to the attention of the public, i.e. when authorities seek to influence the public debate or to create public attitudes and influence the awareness of the news media of the public debate. This also occurs indirectly when public authorities use the media in order to take part in the public debate, including influencing or controlling the political debate, i.e. the debate which includes or is conducted between political parties or elected members of parliaments or local councils. There is a democratic ideal which assumes that the public and the political debates must be free from the influence of public administration and able to house the expression of a plurality of attitudes and interests not influenced by the interests of public administration or administrative agencies.

Ethical moments The public and political moulding of opinions now occurs mainly by and in the media. The media agenda has become an important political institution. At the same time, political institutions (President and Congress, Parliament and Government, Municipal Councils and Mayors) are obliged to guarantee that the rivalry for public opinion remains open for deliberation, i.e. accessible to the bulk of the population and its collective organizations without interference from the public administration, but also that political institutions have

---

28 See J. D. Rendtorff (2003), *Videnskabsetik*, Copenhagen: Samfundslitteratur, about respect for freedom of research, pp. 42–45, Publication ethics, pp. 60–63, and Science fraud, pp. 63–66.

become obliged to be responsive to the needs of parties, organizations, institutions and individuals in their competition to influence the public opinion. This also applies to public managers to the extent to which they have achieved the independence to make decisions in situations where they have to balance oppositional views, evaluations and analysis. The tenth ethical standard derives from this.

Ethical standard   Public managers must ensure that it is possible to make decisions which are adequately independent of the media's agenda and news cycle so that decisions can be based on neutral and relevant knowledge and made without reference to the here-and-now turmoil of the news agenda. This involves the *principle of independence*, i.e. that the manager should ensure that her organization makes decisions based on appropriate and trustworthy expertise, independently of the media's agenda and volatile public attitudes. This also involves the *principle of dialogue*, i.e. that the organization is responsive to the needs of parties, interests and organizations in the public moulding of opinion, including that the public organization can enter into dialogue with citizens and users based on neutral and applicable information, and be available to the media and other interests for trustworthy and applicable information.

Public Values

Delivering services and distributing benefits to citizens is in the main a public duty. It is also done on terms which are predictable, universal or based on objective criteria for distribution. The modern welfare state is built on principles of social solidarity, equality and respect for the freedom or the dignity of the individual. A public ethos has developed in which it is assumed that the welfare state facilitates the needs and interests of its citizens (with the object of ensuring the welfare and safety of its citizens, but also maintaining and developing among its citizens a sense of national identity and a feeling of solidarity). This ethos rests on virtues, including a set of public values, which assume that it is the responsibility of the state to care for the welfare of its citizens and the social cohesion of its population, so that the individual can develop into a socially competent person.

Ethical moments   In recent years, the public sector has been required to perform additional, new and more complex tasks. At the same time, the terms for doing so are changing. For example, changes are occurring in the population's age distribution, in the cultural diversity of the populace, and in the religious creeds of the inhabitants, in general making it possible for individuals as well as groups to choose between alternative lifestyles and political and ideological attitudes, including between notions of gender, life and nature. Consequently, public values are under pressure; the same can be said about the public ethos. The public administration as well as the political institutions must perform tasks on behalf of numerous religions, multiple lifestyles, various ideologies and alternative understandings of gender and identity, and do so even in a situation where the administration is being integrated into transnational institutions and international organizations as well as being obligated to implement rules and norms decided by transnational and supranational entities (the EU for example). The standard operating procedures of action which have hitherto applied to direct contact and relations with the citizens are changing accordingly and the public administration is now involved in the same development as private business, becoming part of multinational companies, employing foreign labour, entering into transnational value chains and trading on global markets. At the same time, the public sector remains bound to the nation-state, to maintain and foster a sense of national identity and to service the national public interest. If we therefore assume that the public sector has gradually been required to perform tasks which involve clashes between numerous different values (national, religious, cultural, financial and gender-related), the eleventh ethical standard arises.

Ethical standard   Public managers must ensure that the values which underpin direct contacts between their organization and its customers are based on universal principles and that decisions can be justified on a rational basis. This involves a *principle of generality*, i.e. that values on which contacts, services and benefits are based are universal, or that, if they can be applied in one instance, they should also be able to be applied in others which in all relevant respects are identical. This also involves a *principle of individuality*, i.e. that the individual citizen is treated without prejudice and with respect for his or her sex, religion and lifestyle, and that companies are treated without regard to who they are owned by, by whom they are managed and which employees they appoint.

Public Values

Public authorities have a monopoly on the exercise of power. At the same time, they are required to look after the public interest, including by protecting the individual against the arbitrary exercise of power. Like political freedoms, human rights are at the base of democratic institutions, and it is the state (the public administration) itself – and its safeguarding of the public interest – which poses the most significant danger to the rights and freedoms of individuals (or collectives of individuals). For the same reason, the boundary between public authority and private freedoms is important; it is also important that the boundary for the execution of public authority is unambiguous, predictable and possible to monitor.

Ethical moments   It is increasingly the case that borders between legal and informal standards have become fluid. A distinction is made between "hard law" and "soft law", precisely to emphasize how a new set of non-binding but informal instructions is used by public authorities or semi-public bodies to implement public or semi-public authority. It is also the case that public administration, by contract or agreement with individual citizens, imposes a particular form of life on the latter, and that the administration, by campaigns and persuasion, requests companies to assume a social responsibility (CSR) with the object of extending state control to self-control. It is also the case that public authorities use marketing techniques when they advertise their own services in competition with other providers. Consequently, there has been a significant increase in the reservoir of tools for the exercise of public authority and many of the informal standards and new tools are being prepared and used without the involvement of Parliament or other legislating authority, and the monitoring of their compliance is either being left to private parties to do themselves or outsourced to private organizations. Such standards generally lack any binding effect, but are nevertheless associated with consequences for those who do not obey them. For the same reason, the boundary between authority and autonomy has become fluid, and the "administrative boundary" between public authority and privacy has become ambiguous, unpredictable and uncontrollable. The twelfth and final standard thereby arises.

Ethical standard   The public manager must ensure that his organization exercises new and soft forms of power with respect for, and taking account of, the personal, economic and political freedoms, rights and autonomies. This involves a *principle of primacy of freedoms*, i.e. that soft forms of power should only be used if citizens and companies voluntarily agree to be "exposed", and that their exercise must happen in ways that are transparent and open to public scrutiny. This also involves a *principle of free choice*, i.e. that, like private services on contract to public organizations, public organizations only provide customers with objective, relevant and honest information on services, their price and quality, so that customers are able to make an uninfluenced rational choice.

Summary

Twelve moral principles have been formulated within three categories of ethics, all of them derived by confronting public values with organizational and other developments in public administration. I assert that the introduction of NPM has made ethical moments an important part of the everyday work of public managers by compelling them to choose between competing values and policy goals and to do so with no clear and specific status for their bureaucratic discretion. I also assert that ethical standards of conduct have been introduced as a remedy for public managers in situations where they are compelled to give ethical reasons for their decisions rather than referring to an already established set of legal rules on which their decisions can be judged. This is particularly evident from the fact that NPM emphasizes economic interests (efficiency and productivity) in confrontation with a legally established impersonal order, and that the introduction of economic values has created conditions for ethical moments, i.e. situations where officials are required to choose among opposing values and goals in a legal void. For the same reason, public administration is currently a matter for discussions on ethics and economy, as are private companies. Considerations of corporate social responsibility or business ethics do not apply only to private companies. They increasingly also apply – on the basis of the special public values – to public administration.

Chapter 16

On Witnessing Global Ethics:
A Case of International Health Research
Involving Human Subjects

Janet L. Borgerson

Approaches to global ethics may require not an abstracted or universal judging subject to settle opportunities and potentials for understanding and action, but a multiplicity of attentions and voices – not all driven by narcissistic, powerful or profit-desiring interests. This chapter evokes the figure of the witness to articulate, manifest and even manage global ethics. Consider, for example, a film-maker who undertakes a process of witnessing, capturing a particular perspective and moreover illuminating or lighting up a landscape, a scenario and previously unrecognized others. Jacques Derrida has argued that a "witness" attempts to make present a singular and irreplaceable experience, not as proof, but as testimony (Derrida, 2000). From another perspective, Mohammad, the prophet, embodied the "Perfect Witness", one who could be trusted to present humankind to God without personal or self-imposing bias. The case in point here pertains to practices in the global industries of international health research involving human subjects and pharmaceutical drug development (Borgerson, 2005; Santoro and Gorrie, 2005). My witnessing position was that of a fellowship student at a globally powerful and pedagogically influential academic institution.

The context of international health research involving human subjects, and this should appear obvious, is the global human community. One might expect then that related ethical discourse would raise fundamental questions of how human beings *qua* human should be treated by other human beings, particularly in situations of unequal power – for example, relating to control, choice or opportunity. Of course, within the field's theoretical and practical discussions attempts *are* made to pinpoint relevant contexts and models of unacceptable treatment of human beings (see Harkness et al., 2001; Beecher, 1966); and reflections upon troubling research histories do serve as ballast for forming newer codes of conduct – apparently devised to avoid egregious repetitions of "inhumane" treatment.

Yet, the geography, both planetary and human, in international health research is so vast, and the boundaries of countries and the boundaries of acceptability so porous and moveable, that the concern for human beings, apparently so fundamental and the ground of basic concerns, may lose centrality (Garrett, 2000). Reasons, pragmatic, even heroic, are offered for this loss. Excuses are made, but the loss should shock; and the loss, this emptiness at the centre of discussions on international health research involving human subjects, should invite critical engagement in an attempt to call attention back to these all too human lapses that guide us into the future.

I am going to trace a narrative inspired by a programme in the ethics of international health research involving human subjects. I focus, in particular, upon the pedagogic rhetoric, then move to issues around a standard of care. I draw upon philosophers John Rawls, Claudia Card and Allen Buchanan to discuss concerns regarding the "least advantaged members of society" and "global basic structure" in the context of global inequality. What becomes clear is that inequalities in this so-called global basic structure leave the least advantaged members of any potential global society at considerable risk of continued exploitation.

Witnessing at "the Borderlands of Ethics"

Harvard Professor of Social Ethics and Clinical Medicine, Richard C. Cabot, asked in his 1926 book, *Adventures on the Borderlands of Ethics*, "What is the use of a code of ethics?" (Cabot, 1926, p. 79). How is it to be enforced? What of matters that are referred to in the codes but do not fall under legal prohibitions? Cabot suggests that a code of ethics allows a registering of ethical advance in periodic revisions and a brake "on our natural tendencies to slip back". Whereas persons involved in revisions of ethical guidelines for international health research involving human subjects appear to believe that such documents have some power to affect research practices, Cabot implies that the insight gained from writing and rewriting codes tells us more about the authors and less about what should, or will, be done. Have current revisions of international guidelines for biomedical research involving human subjects registered an "ethical advance", an opportunity to deter our natural tendency to "slip back"? I hope to maintain Cabot's insight: in the process of writing codes and guidelines, the authors are as much subjects of inquiry as the guidelines themselves.

Seventy-some years after Cabot's questions, I was awarded a fellowship to attend a programme on the Ethics of International Health Research Involving Human Subjects at Cabot's well-endowed institution. Researchers, policy-makers, academics and assistants to ministers of health attended – as students – from all over the world, in many cases as a result of the entrepreneurial generosity of fellowship funding such as I had received. Many of those present probably would go on to decide national policy and write influential curricula for similar courses in their own countries. Indeed, we were provided with hefty course packs to take with us. (Interestingly, a similar power of Harvard University to "export the American model" has been noted in Steve Fuller's discussion of James Bryant Conant – US Ambassador to West Germany who had been Harvard President – and scientist Thomas Kuhn's "manufacturing" of student course materials, including "the influential Harvard Case Histories in Experimental Science (1950)"; Fuller, 2003, pp. 204–205.)

In the present scenario, focus had fallen upon the World Medical Association's recent version of the Declaration of Helsinki (World Medical Association, 1964, revised 1996) and revisions of The International Ethical Guidelines for Biomedical Research Involving Human Subjects developed by the Council for the International Organization of Medical Sciences (CIOMS) together with the World Health Organization. The revision process, in conjunction with attention to cases of controversial conduct by HIV–AZT researchers using placebo control groups, had alerted philosophers and the public alike to the existence of these documents, and raised awareness of the potential global effects of the proposed changes.

Lectures from the corral of experts were led off by a lawyer who exposed many of us to an alternative story regarding the writing of the Nuremberg Code (1947), the document of guidelines for ethical human subject research that emerged from the Nuremberg trials of German doctors, research scientists and others accused of atrocities during the Nazi era. The Nuremberg Code, the foundation upon which more recent national and international ethical guidelines for research involving human subjects have been built, was written, the lawyer informed us, the night before the crucial trial date, and designed specifically to convict the particular men on trial for their particular crimes.[1] The language was universal, the speaker suggested, but the purpose of the document was singular. Why should international health researchers be held by the influence of this document's content?

A primary researcher responsible for AZT–HIV mother-to-child transmission trials in South Africa spoke. The doctor was under attack for using a placebo control group rather than providing the best proven effective treatment for his control group, as was done during trials in the USA. Marcia Angell, executive editor of *The New England Journal of Medicine*, had refused to publish this investigator's research results after condemning placebo use when "effective treatment exists". The doctor argued against "a standard of care" that would dictate a particular best effective treatment in all cases and, moreover, limited the range of trial outcomes. In short, a standard of care proposes a baseline that researchers – regardless of where, with whom and under what conditions they are working – must uphold and apply in relation to their research subjects. Moreover, the doctor queried, why should health researchers be bound to provide care to a control group beyond what would have been available to the population otherwise?

Another esteemed research physician's lecture concurred that a universal standard or level of care was true imperialism, requiring under-resourced clinics and researchers to adhere to Western standards that not only are unreachable, but limit "below standard" practices that could nevertheless save lives. Several further presenters argued that individual informed consent requirements in many cases

---

1   This argument draws upon a discrediting narrative that marks the Nuremberg Code as an illegitimate document biased by testimony-falsifying USA-based physicians. See R. Levine (1999), p. 240.

disregard cultural and contextual norms, including norms of consensus, or at least, hierarchy. "Can a chief", we were asked in one case-study exercise, "consent for a village?"

Thus, the first day's key points created doubt regarding the foundational status of the Nuremburg documents, favourably considered the notion that often something, no matter how much or what quality or for how long, is better than nothing, and in general cast to the winds traditional points of reference for international biomedical research involving human subjects. And was "something of value" offered in place?

Against the Western Imperialism of Personhood, Human Rights and Individual Consent

First among the programme's required readings was a paper by Yale Professor and physician Robert Levine. Levine's paper criticized existing international ethical guidelines for biases that he believed arose from Western "cultural imperialism" (Levine, 1999, p. 254). Levine played a strong – though in later discussions, largely invisible – role in the guideline revision process. (He is thanked extensively, however, in the Introduction of the 2002 CIOMS Guidelines – in which points sympathetic with his arguments are felt, articulated and often countered.) Arguing that international ethical guidelines should be considered global, but not universal – in that "universal" signifies true for all human societies in all historical periods, whereas "global" eschews permanence and accepts change – Levine echoed Cabot's assumption: codes of ethics require periodic revisions. However, whereas Cabot's concern for revisions was to register "ethical advances" or resistance to tendencies to "slip back", Levine's concerns for "advances" appeared more pragmatic.

From Levine's perspective, certain research must be done and various guidelines, as written, contained "conceptual errors" and other blockades to research. Concepts such as "personhood" and individual consent represented the substance of two such blockades. "Personhood", argued Levine for example, is a Western concept. In transporting ethical guideline-evoked "personhood" across cultural lines, well-meaning but naïve Westerners engaged in cultural imperialist domination. Levine also attacked imposed "imperialist" universal notions of autonomy and individual rights. In his view, revised versions of ethical guidelines for international health research involving human subjects must adopt a more "pluralist" approach.

In criticizing Western imperialism, the lack of attention to context and particularity, and invocations of a false "universalism", Levine's arguments often eerily echoed post-colonial or feminist theory. Yet, Levine's apparent lack of concern for the *impact* of his version of pluralism on subjugated populations manifested his failure to understand why imperialism and universalism had concerned these other disciplines in the first place. Indeed, any new vulnerabilities to which his "pluralist" approaches might subject populations were apparently not Dr Levine's focus. Thus, proponents of potentially exploitative revisions of international ethical guidelines for biomedical research involving human subjects were mobilizing notions of context and particularity against concerns for oppression and subjugation.[2] That is, what might be considered a form of cultural relativism, not usually a value associated with the scientific community, conveniently supported differing standards of care and consent.

For example, if current cultural practice in a community does not reflect norms of individual consent, the procedure generally required of researchers for gaining informed consent in Western contexts might be abandoned as intrusive or disrespectful.[3] Of course, attempts to excuse, defer, or even forbid, individual informed consent procedures raise fears of potential human subject abuse. Nevertheless, personal narratives passionately told by programme participants with "experience in the field" were presented as *reasons* for abandoning individual consent: one heard of the difficulty of following basic procedural requirements such as gaining access to individuals for information sessions, finding local translators to explain forms or the medical implications of trials, or the task of bringing along enough forms.

Another species of reason, apparently emerging from concerns to avoid Western imperialism, focused around potential subjects' inability to understand difficult and technologically advanced medical information, including descriptions of possible side-effects. Potential research subjects might be found to be not only embedded in communal or hierarchical procedures of decision-making, or be unable to read, write or understand technical language; but, Levine suggests, such subjects also might appear to lack the basic intellectual sophistication required to "decide for themselves". Such descriptions of field experience were prevalent among certain programme participants. Yet, pragmatic though certain desires for change may be, one cannot avoid parallels to other anti-democratic movements of the past that lobbied, for example in the USA, against voting rights for blacks, women and the non-property-owning public – said to be unintelligent, incapable of individual comprehension or in other ways lacking in basic qualifications of the mature, adult citizen. Although not the path pursued here, it would be worth reflecting further upon the histories of similar arguments and their guiding interests *cui bono*.

Is individual consent and deciding for oneself an imperialist demand? Is it truly the case that, in engaging with research procedures, diverse, globally dispersed communities find themselves forced to become "democratic" in necessary

---

2   This is a concern, for example, regarding women's positions in traditional societies. See Jones, "Culture and Reproductive Health: Challenges for Feminist Philanthropy", in Donchin and Purdy (1999), p. 234.

3   Whereas this particular debate has other aspects, it is interesting to note that similar appeals to a kind of cultural relativism have been made in arenas in which arguments for maintaining certain cultural traditions – while others fade – tend to disadvantage women. See U. Narayan (1998), Essence of Culture and a Sense of History: A Feminist Critique of Cultural Essentialism, *Hypatia*, 13(2), 86–106.

conjunction with a Western model of autonomous decision-making and individual rights that notions of "individual consent" may entail? Whereas compelling Foucauldian questions do emerge at such moments, the present discussion defers work in that direction.

One notices, then, that in many of what might be considered the most vulnerable geographic locations, researchers and spokesmen such as Levine have suggested that "informed consent" and a universal "standard of care" not only slow down and complicate their work, but that guideline processes and procedures may make some research impossible. Of course, one may respond, So what? If maintaining cautionary practices designated to protect human research subjects halts certain research procedures, might this not mean something more than that the guidelines are over-burdensome? We might ask instead: must, or should, such research be done?

Certainly, to ask such questions may mark ignorance, arrogance and academic distance from crisis situations. There are populations at terrible risk and dying, the frequently stated example being the impact of AIDS in some African countries. The needs are urgent.[4] Research on new drug therapies offers possible relief, treatments and cures. New drug therapies also offer the forefront of treatment, sometimes occasioning so-called "compassionate use". Nevertheless – although the assumption would make the ethical decisions easier – it is *not* the case that all research goals and drug treatment trials are universally good-willed, beneficent, compassionate or based upon a vision of cooperation for a satisfactory life. Such an acknowledgement, perhaps unpalatable, occasions consideration of to what extent research goals and drug trials must be related to the long-term health development in the test-group population. Should profit-making bodies, with no altruistic motives, be allowed to pursue growth, and researchers be allowed to pursue scientific knowledge and enhanced reputations for scientific contribution, in a context of testing scenarios that may, but may not, provide certain populations with access to hope, health or other resources?

There are four issues I would like to consider further: the notion of a standard of care; how some human beings become "perfect subjects" for research; concerns around the so-called "least advantaged members of society"; and conflicts regarding a "global basic structure".

Standard of Care: Some Considerations

One of the most basic conflicts between those who favour following a local standard of care (SOC) – which may be recourse to no resources or care at all – and those who do not favour a local SOC centres on the kind of care, both during

---

4   Of course, many research efforts have to do with medical and non-medical treatments for long-standing diseases such as malaria and tuberculosis, as well as parasite infestations, such as schistosomiasis.

the trials and after, that will be made available to those upon whom drug trials and non-standard treatments are imposed. Emerging concerns from the anti-local SOC perspective imply that, if a local SOC is employed instead of the best proven effective therapeutic method, particularly in the control group, researchers and others with interests in international health care research, including pharmaceutical companies sponsoring such research, will view this as a justification to (1) save money during trials through removal of requirements for expensive or time-consuming care regimes, particularly in regard to the control group, and (2) implicitly agree to ultimately long-standing, substandard care for populations in which something appears to be better than nothing.

The authors of a September 2000 letter to Dr Delon Human, head of the World Medical Association, stated that failure to maintain the requirement that research subjects shall have access to "the best proven prophylactic, diagnostic and therapeutic method" during the trial will result in "a de facto institutionalization of two-tiered research".[5] Apparently, a fine line separates new treatments representing an unacceptable substandard care and those treatments for diseases for which curative treatment does exist, but for which researchers believe a process currently conceived of as substandard may prove more effective locally than the imported standard treatment.

Dr Adetokunbo Lucas, one of the university programme speakers, has argued that some treatment protocols that are designed in wealthier developed countries may not meet the needs of developing communities (Lucas, 2000). He asks, for example, if the standard of care for tuberculosis in developed nations is traditional institutional care in sanatoria, how might a study on an alternative supervised ambulatory care – which would be defined as substandard – be carried out (Lucas, 2000, p. 3)?[6] Arguments for implementing standards of care that fall below the best, proven effective therapeutic method may represent attempts to find workable methods of care at local levels. Currently "below standard" treatment does not necessarily mean worse treatment – in the tuberculosis case the non-institutionalized patients fared better (Lucas, 2000, p. 3). Further, should a trial lead to a "better than nothing" solution, such a solution need not be considered the final word in the health care development of that community. This is what Lucas calls "Ethical Progressive Improvement".[7]

Lucas argues that an approach such as his can escape degeneration "into a system of double standards in which people in developing countries receive less

---

5   Letter from Peter Lurie, M.D., and Sidney Wolfe, M.D., Public Citizen's Health Research Group, www.citizen.org/hrg/Publications/1538.htm.

6   See, e.g., the *Letter From Brasilia*, a document authored during a forum on the Helsinki revisions held in Brazil, which suggests that using new methods of treatment should be allowed "in treating people with progressive, incapacitating or potentially fatal diseases for which treatment does not exist or is not curative" (National Forum, 2000).

7   Lucas describes "ethical progressive improvement" in a July 2000 letter to Professor Sir Kenneth Calman of the Nuffield Council on Bioethics (p. 4).

protection from ethical guidelines" by assuring a "context of direct responsibility for providing care" (Lucas, 2000, p. 3). Such a context of care speaks to the necessity of promoting the research capacities in developing nations and among these nations' citizens. Of course, Lucas's recommendations do not begin to confront situations in which (1) and (2) above appear to be operating, creating mean exploitation in the context of severe inequality.

It is interesting to note that, in the revised 2002 CIOMS Guideline 11, the phrase "established effective intervention" replaces a notion of "best" in use of a comparator. Nevertheless, the AZT–HIV researcher's reasoning for using a placebo comparator is considered in detail in the 2002 Guidelines and dismissed, although this is still potentially hazy territory and much is left up to particular ethical review boards. This includes distinguishing between cases in which "established effective" can replace "best effective". However, in the 2002 Nuffield Report, and in the follow-up discussion paper, a strong tendency emerges against a universal standard of care, promoting instead local standards, including "best intervention available for that disease as part of the national public health system" (Nuffield Council on Bioethics, 2002, pp. 94–97, 2005). Whereas this development may please some researchers, given the global variability of what is available through national public health systems, it is clear that the notion of providing human subjects with only "that which would have been available to them otherwise" has gained legitimacy and would mean that in some locations clinical trials can provide the control group with nothing.

The Burden of International Inequality

The assumption that health is a virtue united with a concomitant "blaming the sick," argues Helen B. Holmes, has serious consequences in the context of bioethics' failure to critically examine the assumptions upon which it rests (Holmes, 1999, 55). Similar critical failures lead to a focus upon "treatment" procedures, rather than on prevention. Blaming the sick contributes to a vision, or a representation, of those who live in impoverished, unhealthy conditions. For example, in positing generations of children who might be saved by the sacrifices of human subjects undergoing current research procedures, individuals become reasonable sacrifices, shouldering situationally appropriate burdens, in a utilitarian attempt to gain the greatest good for the greatest number.

Further, the impoverished and ill often are described as perfect research subjects. "Everybody is worried that we will use Africa, develop a vaccine there, say thanks and then take it back to Europe and America", said Dr Peter Piot, the executive director of the United Nations AIDS Programme.[8] "I don't believe that will happen. But we are in a terrible position. The process is perilous. It is unfair. And it is filled with inequalities – because the world is filled with inequalities."

---

8   Piot is quoted in a *New York Times* article by Michael Specter, 1 October 1998.

Americans diagnosed with HIV immediately start drug treatment, and hence are useless in testing vaccines, Piot says. "Since people in Uganda cannot hope to afford drug treatment, which can cost more than $15,000 a year, they are the perfect subjects for such a vaccine test."

Thus, an inability to pay for treatment qualifies one for research subject status. Moreover, inability to pay is treated as a reason to deny a certain form of care. In the US context this reason may sound familiar, but many countries do not treat individual inability to pay as a reason to withhold care.[9] Given the dangers around blaming the sick and treating ill and impoverished people as ideal research subjects, a familiar question is often raised: why do drug and treatment testing on these vulnerable populations and in these vulnerable areas? Researchers reply that, if a drug, vaccine, or other form of treatment is to be used in an area at all, it must be tested on local populations. Of course, in order for this to be a relevant argument to promote research in vulnerable groups, there must be an assumption that the local population can reasonably expect access to the drug, vaccine or other treatment once developed. In the best scenario, a vulnerable group is involved in the testing of treatments that will be available to, used in and benefit their own population. Most international health research does not involve such tidy cases, however, and researchers desire the cooperation of populations before evidence exists for future availability or levels of benefit.

The Least Advantaged Members of Society

In an early attempt to articulate the possibilities for cooperation between the least advantaged members of society and those "more fortunate in their social position", John Rawls wrote:

> It may be expedient but it is not just that some should have less in order that others may prosper. But there is no injustice in the greater benefits earned by a few provided that the situations of persons not so fortunate is thereby improved. The intuitive idea is that since everyone's well-being depends upon a scheme of cooperation without which no one could have a satisfactory life, the division of advantages should be such as to draw forth the willing cooperation of everyone taking part in it, including those less well situated. Yet this can be expected only if reasonable terms are proposed. (Rawls, 1971, p. 15)

We assume here that "willing cooperation" means something like an uncoerced participation based upon an understanding of advantages – understood, perhaps,

---

9   Of course, there may be other reasons, perhaps considered more egalitarian, that may result in a similar lack of care. That is, the focus falls upon distribution of available resources, rather than on inability to pay. Questions around how and why certain resources are "available" are, of course, another issue.

because of transparency of conditions, expectations, and so on. How seriously the term "everyone" should be taken is also relevant when speaking of the distinctions between individual consent and acting in concert with a group.

Cooperation might be accomplished, wrote Rawls, if his two principles were used as the basis for an agreement. That is, a just agreement could be made based upon equality in assignments of rights and duties, and a check on social and economic inequalities such that inequalities are just "only if they result in compensating benefits for everyone" (p. 15). Inequalities that are "arbitrary from a moral point of view", contends Rawls, should not figure into the kinds of agreements that can be made, nor the terms of the agreements.

This important point indicates that many factors that affect the positions of human lives should not influence persons' abilities to enter into important negotiations that influence lifetime opportunities and options. Unfortunately, such inequalities are probably those inequalities that are most relevant and debilitating in the scenario under consideration. That is, morally arbitrary inequalities result from the very conditions most likely to arise in the situations of the least advantaged members of society and under which Rawls's sense of agreement may be impossible. We cannot solve this difficult pragmatic point here, but again, tracking such inequalities certainly will serve a crucial role in any project that hopes to implement a Rawlsian solution to situations of inequality and injustice.

In reference to "natural distribution" of "talents" and the "contingencies of social circumstances", Rawls writes:

> The natural distribution is neither just or unjust; nor is it unjust that persons are born into society at some particular position. These are simply natural facts. What is just and unjust is the way institutions deal with these facts. Aristocratic and caste societies are unjust because they make these contingencies the scriptive basis for belonging to more or less enclosed and privileged social classes. The basic structure of these societies incorporates the arbitrariness found in nature. But there is no necessity for men to resign themselves to these contingencies. The social system is not an unchangeable order beyond human control but a pattern of human action. (Rawls, 1971, p. 102)

Rawls includes in his unnecessary, or contingent, human scenarios the unjust "basic structure of ... societies [that] incorporate the arbitrariness found in nature".

Whereas little time in the ethics of international health research programme was given to the compromising context of unjust societies, related arguments often do mirror Rawls's articulation of the conditions of just cooperation. Generally, Rawls captures an intuitive sense of many in the realm of bioethics and international health research involving human subjects: that is, no one could have a satisfactory life without the various forms of cooperation that make possible health research. We find ourselves in, perhaps, a "community of fate" (Birnbaum, 2008, p. 16).

However, are we really in the Rawlsian situation of "cooperation without which no one could have a satisfactory life"? Proposing just proportions of benefit and burden to participating parties may require calculations, both qualitative and quantitative – for example, the once popular Disability Adjusted Life Years – of questionable validity and value. Moreover, burdens exist in global industries of health research and drug development that may not be balanced by appropriate benefits. Yet, as long as there is some sense in which the vulnerable populations do benefit, researchers may argue that something is better than nothing. For example, short term, researchers entering a community might point to the availability of vitamin supplements or the construction of a building that will house the temporary clinic. Long-term benefits might include the possibility of valuable knowledge emerging from research that could aid treatment of disease and ill health in the local population.

Apparently, placing Rawls's articulations in conjunction with these considerations could mean designating almost any procedure or state of affairs that benefits these populations a "just" undertaking – and regardless of the magnitude of parallel benefit expected for the sponsoring countries or agencies, in terms of health care improvements, knowledge acquisition or corporate profits. If inequalities "arbitrary from a moral point of view", some the result of contingencies of social circumstance, are *not* to figure into "the kinds of agreements that can be made" between the more fortunate and the least advantaged members of society, then the inability of vulnerable populations and countries in situations of desperation to have an influential seat at the negotiating table poses a monumental difficulty in working out terms of agreements (e.g. Loriaux, 2008). I turn now to related concerns around the unnatural lottery and global basic structure.

The Unnatural Lottery and Global Basic Structure

Rawls's inadequate articulations around the "natural lottery" have been noted especially by those concerned with the well-being of subordinated populations, including Claudia Card's (1996) attention to the "unnatural lottery" and Allen Buchanan's (2000) focus upon unjust global structures.[10] Card writes:

> It is not enough to confront the inequities of the "natural lottery" from which we may inherit various physical and psychological assets and liabilities. It is important also to reflect on the unnatural lottery created by networks of unjust institutions and histories that bequeath to us further inequities in our starting positions and that violate principles that would have addressed, if not redressed, inequities of nature. (Card, 1996, p. 20)

In other words, where one is born may be a "natural fact", but how the nation or race into which one is born has been treated historically and how various effects

---

10   See W. McBride (1980), *Social Theory at a Crossroads* (Pittsburgh, PA: Duquesne University Press).

emerging from these historical variables will place a newborn are not natural facts. Contingent – though not necessarily accidental – historical circumstances, shaped and held in place by systems of power and status, may be ascribed to the just and unjust functioning of "institutions". Furthermore, such institutions may be as intimately related to an individual as her family relations, her skin colour and her gender.

Allen Buchanan's criticism of Rawls's "law of the peoples" echoes this awareness of underlying structural injustice that affects one's starting point, one's day-to-day relationships with others and one's character in morally important ways. Buchanan is particularly concerned with Rawls's inability to address issues of international justice outside a "vanished Westphalian world", and further marks the more general "marginal" status of these concerns (see e.g. Collste, 2005; Hurrell, 2001; Risse, 2005; Tasioulas, 2003). Rejecting Rawls's conjecture that, with little regard for resources, "reasonably and rationally organized and governed" societies could become "well-ordered", Buchanan argues that "a well-governed society might be seriously disadvantaged by the global basic structure" (Buchanan et al., 2000, p. 705). A global basic structure, argues Buchanan, is "a set of economic and political institutions that has profound and enduring effects on the distribution of burdens and benefits among peoples and individuals around the world" (p. 705). Surely then, he writes, such a structure is an important subject of justice.

A society may be unable to provide food or health care for its citizens, or to "determine how wealth is distributed within its borders", failing in what Buchanan calls "economic self-sufficiency" and "distributional autonomy". That is, the way in which goods are distributed, a fundamental aspect of Rawls's "basic structure", creates crucial justice-oriented concerns not simply within autonomous states, but among such states. As much international health research involving human subjects by definition requires agreements, cooperation and exchange among nations embedded in a global basic structure, inequalities between, and within, states must be honestly and directly attended.

In addressing the lacunae in Rawls's work, Buchanan raises another point relevant to ethical guidelines for international health research involving human subjects. The populations of states, writes Buchanan, "are collections of different groups, often with different and conflicting views concerning justice and the good" (p. 721). Indeed, in seeking access to populations within the borders of countries around the globe, researchers and bioethicists may not rest easy after gaining the opinion or permission, for example, of a country's public health representative, or alternatively the head of a country's dominant social group or institution. In both cases, the status or social position of the individual "representative" calls into question his ability to speak for others.

We might ask, recalling the rhetoric of the university programme on international biomedical research involving human subjects, whether avoiding Western imperialist domination implies respecting a centralized authorization as consent for all? Respect for local cultural norms – and not merely claims about feasibility and ease of gaining such consent – it has been argued, would require putting aside individual informed consent in favour of various forms of consensus or decisions made within an appropriate hierarchy. How, Buchanan might ask, are we to know which group the decision-maker speaks for, what biases the decision-maker might harbour, and which vision of good and justice, in the midst of conflicting visions, this representative represents? Reflecting upon scenarios unveiled in an unnatural lottery, including confronting the institutionalized injustice of the global basic structure, let us turn our concern to the human being present in the "subject" of international health research.

Ethical Ontology and the Human Research Subject

Feminist bioethics calls for an awareness of oppression – especially of historically vulnerable groups (Tong, 1997; Wolf, 1996). How have various principles and forms of reasoning been used to justify exploitative treatment and subordination? How have designated categories of race, class and sex functioned to grant or deny access to certain important resources? Who should be able to decide on behalf of whom when someone – often women or black people in general, or a non-English-speaker in the USA – is considered not "intelligent or curious" enough to understand relevant risks and benefits? (Levine, 1999, p. 241). This section looks briefly at the ethical nature of dilemmas that lead to abstract, rather than human, relations.

Particular forms of social relations subscribe to and reinforce hierarchical orderings of dualities that, throughout history, and within philosophy as well, have favoured the male, the white and the rational (Plumwood, 1993).[11] In such a context, those associated with the privileged elements stand in the position to claim knowledge of all that is important to know about those associated with the subordinated elements. That is, the dualistic relation engages with the potential for epistemic closure (Gordon, 1997, p. 81). A worldview informed by epistemic closure essentializes being and tends toward creation of a recognizable "authentic" identity while knowing next to nothing "about the typical Other beyond her or his typicality" (p. 81). Epistemic closure leads us to believe that we know the other's being completely – who they are and what their purpose is – denying the other status as human being and erasing any possibility for human relationships (see Borgerson, 2001; Borgerson and Schroeder, 2008). Moral recognition or standing is often denied to those whose human status is contested, particularly in racist and sexist settings of unequal power (Gordon, 1995). Characterizations of typical ways of being and representations of subordinate groups – particularly representations

---

11 For a discussion of race, racism, and meaning, see D. T. Goldberg (1993) *Racist Culture: Philosophy and the Politics of Meaning* (Oxford: Blackwell).

circulating within media culture, but including biomedical and bioethical research literature – rarely contradict, and typically reproduce, versions of subordination.[12]

Recent philosophical theorists have written on the relation between identity, identity representation and ontological status.[13] Some forms of representation that are exoticized, stereotypical, sexist or racist damage the reputation of members of the represented group and manipulate their being for consumption by others. Harm of this type disrupts the represented group's ability to exist as fully human. Philosophers concerned with ethical norms and behaviour have traditionally proceeded as though problematic situations of moral recognition can be handled through constructive definitions of personhood, the formal requirements of universality or universalizability, and substantive demands for impartial or equal consideration (Walker, 1997, p. 179).

Margaret Urban Walker argues that these three prescriptions lack sufficient conceptual strength to handle representations that often manipulate and damage the identity of subordinate groups. Moreover, because of the kind of problems these prescriptions were meant to handle, not only do they fail to provide sufficiently complex considerations to deal with problems of representations, but damaging representations often fail to qualify as moral problems. Walker writes that the assumption that people are a kind is propagated and created by representational practices. Representational practices are among those practices that "construct socially salient identities for people" (Walker, 1997, p. 178). She argues that, if practices of representation "affect some people's morally significant perceptions of and interactions with other people, and if they can contribute to those perceptions or interactions going seriously wrong, they bear on fundamental questions for ethics" (p. 179). By "going seriously wrong" Walker implies that a person influenced by such images may treat members of the represented group, including herself, as less than human, and undeserving of moral recognition. Walker explicates "moral understandings" – forms of interpersonal relation based upon "practices of responsibility" – that she believes can provide ethical guidance in this difficult terrain. Such a project provides an important step toward comprehending, resisting and moving beyond hierarchical ontological positioning that has ethical import, particularly important in abstracted relationships that turn human beings into research subjects.

---

12   This concern points to the necessity for an ethics that takes representation seriously, emerging from the ethical significance of ontological divisions and hierarchies and the reality of epistemic closure (Borgerson and Schroeder, 2008).

13   See S. Bartky (1991), *Femininity and Domination* (New York: Routledge); J. Butler (1999) *Subjects of Desire* (New York: Columbia University Press); and I. M. Young (1990), *Throwing Like A Girl and Other Essays in Feminist Philosophy and Social Theory* (Bloomington, IN: Indiana University Press).

Openings and Conclusions

As part of the university programme on the ethics of international health research involving human subjects, and since that time, Lucas has argued that "Ethical Progressive Improvement" can escape degeneration "into a system of double standards in which people in developing countries receive less protection from ethical guidelines" by assuring a "context of direct responsibility for providing care" (Lucas, 2000, p. 3). Such a context of care speaks to the necessity of promoting the research capacities in developing nations and among these nations' citizens. Indeed, a crucial point in international health research involving human subjects is the ease with which human beings become research subjects and are represented as research subjects, particularly as these subjects tend to exist outside Lucas's "context of care". Abstract and medicalized relations within research situations challenge human abilities to maintain an understanding of research subjects' full human status.

Moreover, concerns such as Card's – emerging from her notion of the "unnatural lottery" – and Buchanan's insistence on the international relevance of a moral theory of global distributive justice must be included in the discourse addressing ethical guidelines for international health research involving human subjects, including attempts to teach about conditions of vital and ongoing research. Further, international health research involving human subjects by definition requires agreements, cooperation and exchange among nations embedded in a global basic structure; thus, inequalities between, and within, states must be honestly and directly attended to.

Excluding these issues – as the pedagogical rhetoric of the university programme arguably did – denies core ethical territory. Understandings of subordinated groups at risk of exploitation must be formed through practices of responsibility, possibly as conceived by Lucas's "context of direct responsibility for providing care", and including an awareness of the potential damage caused by epistemic closure in the research context. Cabot suggested that revision of ethical codes and guidelines should mark an advance. Without continuing attempts to recognize humanity and human relations in places, and in populations, in which we previously saw abstract research subjects, those who debate, teach and revise the ethics of international health research involving human subjects may indeed be "slipping back". Moreover, a notion of *witnessing* that evokes the giving of testimony, not simply the proving of one thing or another, opens possibilities for understanding scenarios that otherwise remain obscured.

Earlier versions of this chapter were presented at the "Morality in the 21st Century" Conference in Delaware, Maryland, 2001, and at the "Feminist Approaches to Bioethics" Conference, London, 2000. An earlier published version appeared in the *Journal of Philosophical Research*, 2005.

References

Beecher, H. K. (1966), Ethics and Clinical Research, *The New England Journal of Medicine*, 274(24), 1354–1360.

Birnbaum, K. (2008), Meeting the Unprecedented Challenges of the 21st Century, *Swedish Institute of International Affairs Papers* 3, 1–17.

Borgerson, J. (2001), Feminist Ethical Ontology, or Why Contest the 'Bare Givenness of Intersubjectivity'? *Feminist Theory*, 2(2), 173–187.

Borgerson, J. (2005), Addressing the Global Basic Structure in the Ethics of International Biomedical Research Involving Human Subjects. *Journal of Philosophical Research*, special supplement, 235–249.

Borgerson, J. and Schroeder, J. (2008), Building an Ethics of Visual Representation: Contesting Epistemic Closure, in *Cutting Edge Issues in Business Ethics*, M. Painter-Morland and P. Werhane (eds). Berlin: Springer, pp. 89–110.

Buchanan, A., Brock, D., Daniels, N. and Wikler, D. (2000), *From Chance to Choice: Genetics and Justice*. Cambridge, UK: Cambridge University Press.

Cabot, R. (1926), *Adventures on the Borderlands of Ethics*. New York: Harper and Brothers.

Card, C. (1996), *The Unnatural Lottery: Character and Moral Luck*. Philadelphia, PA: Temple University Press.

Collste, G. (2005), Globalisation and Global Justice. *Studia Theologica – Nordic Journal of Theology*, 59(1), 55–72.

Council for International Organizations of Medical Sciences (CIOMS), in collaboration with the World Health Organization (WHO) (1993; 2002), *International Ethical Guidelines for Biomedical Research Involving Human Subjects*.

Derrida, J. (2000), 'A Self-Unsealing Poetic Text': Poetics and Politics of Witnessing, in *The Revenge of the Aesthetic*, M. Clark (ed.), R. Bowlby (trans.). Berkeley, CA: University of California Press.

Donchin, A. and Purdy, L. (eds) (1999), *Embodying Bioethics: Recent Feminist Advances*. Lanham, MD: Rowman & Littlefield.

Fuller, S. (2003), *Kuhn vs Popper*. Cambridge: Icon.

Garrett, L. (2000), *Betrayal of Trust: The Collapse of Global Public Health*. New York: Hyperion.

Gordon, L. (1995), *Bad Faith and Antiblack Racism*. Atlantic Highlands, NJ: Humanities Press.

Gordon, L. (1997), *Her Majesty's Other Children: Sketches of Racism from a Neocolonial Age*. Lanham, MD: Rowman & Littlefield.

Harkness, J., Lederer, S. and Wickler, D. (2001), Laying Ethical Foundations for Clinical Research. *Bulletin of the World Health Organization: The International Journal of Public Health*, 79(4), 365–366.

Holmes, H. (1999), Closing the Gaps: An Imperative for Feminist Bioethics, in *Embodying Bioethics: Recent Feminist Advances*, A. Donchin and L. Purdy (eds). Lanham, MD: Rowman & Littlefield.

Hurrell, A. (2001), Global Inequality and International Institutions. *Metaphilosophy*, 32(1–2), 34–57.

Levine, R. (1999), International Codes and Guidelines for Research Ethics: A Critical Appraisal, Paper included in programme on Ethics of International Health Research Involving Human Subjects, School of Public Health, Harvard University, Cambridge, MA.

Loriaux, S. (2008), Global Inequality of Opportunity: A Proposal, *Journal of International Relations and Development*, 11, 1–28.

Lucas, A. (2000), Ethics of Clinical Research in Developing Countries, Paper delivered to programme on Ethics of International Health Research Involving Human Subjects, Harvard University, Cambridge, MA.

National Forum on the Declaration of Helsinki: Brazilian Perspective (2000), *Letter From Brasilia*.

Nuffield Council on Bioethics (2002), *The Ethics of Research Related to Healthcare in Developing Countries*. London: Nuffield Council on Bioethics.

Nuffield Council on Bioethics (2005), *The Ethics of Research Related to Healthcare in Developing Countries: A Follow-Up Discussion Paper*. London: Nuffield Council on Bioethics.

Plumwood, V. (1993), *Feminism and the Mastery of Nature*. New York: Routledge.

Rawls, J. (1971), *A Theory of Justice*. Cambridge, MA: Harvard University Press.

Risse, M. (2005), How Does the Global Order Harm the Poor? *Philosophy and Public Affairs*, 33(4), 349–376.

Santoro, M. and Gorrie, T. (2005), *Ethics and the Pharmaceutical Industry*. Cambridge: Cambridge University Press.

Specter, M. (1998), *New York Times*, 1 October.

Tasioulas, J. (2003), Global Justice Without End? *Metaphilosophy*, 36(1–2), 3–29.

Tong, R. (1997), *Feminist Approaches to Bioethics: Theoretical Reflections and Practical Applications*. Boulder, CO: Westview Press.

Walker, M. (1997), *Moral Understandings: Feminist Studies in Ethics*. New York: Routledge.

Wolf, S. (1996), *Feminism and Bioethics: Beyond Reproduction*. New York: Oxford University Press.

World Medical Association. (1964; amended 1975, 1983, 1989, 1996), *Declaration of Helsinki: Recommendations Guiding Physicians in Biomedical Research Involving Human Subjects*.

Chapter 17

The Cosmopolitan Story

Peter Kemp

The Crisis of International Law

The current crisis of the world economy follows nearly eight years of crisis of the international law. The political reaction, in particular by the Bush administration (2001–2009), to the terrorist attack on 11 September 2001 shook for many people their conviction that international law was respected, at least to some degree, by the major powers in the world. The idea that all nations must respect a certain world order, including the right to basic goods for all people, was developed from Francisco Vitoria (1483–1546), Francisco Suarez (1548–1617), Hugo Grotius (1583–1645) and Samuel Pufendorf (1632–1694) up to the international agreement on the Charter of The United Nations in 1945 and the Geneva conventions from 1949 adopted by all major powers (Laghmani, 2003; Truyol Y Serra, 1987; Sudre et al., 2005). However this idea came into deep crisis after 11 September. People became demoralized.

Not only was a military intervention made against Iraq without the required permission from the Security Council of the United Nations, but prisoners from the wars in Afghanistan and Iraq were also treated inhumanely in prison camps at Guantánamo and elsewhere. These prisoners have not been given the right to a fair trial according to the Geneva conventions and later supplements.

The Crisis of World Economy

Then came the economic crisis in autumn 2008 that also was a consequence of the politics of the Bush administration. In both cases it was the belief in the free market economy that motivated the politics. However, whereas this market should be free internally, i.e. without political intervention, it should be defended externally by political force, including military interventions.

We know today that the attack on Iraq was not made in order to stop terrorism, but the fear of terrorist actions and the lies that promoted this fear (for instance the lie that it had been proved that Saddam Hussein possessed weapons of mass destruction) were used as a pretext for a military intervention to ensure US economic domination in the Near East and thereby the power of the USA over the world economy. Moreover, this intervention was made with a brutality and inhumanity that the aggressor found permitted by an end that justifies every means.

This end was the wonderful free market that Francis Fukuyama advocated in his book on *The End of History and the Last Man* in 1992 (Fukuyama, 1992). The idea was that the economic systems will always solve their own problems by an inner mechanism, the invisible hand of Adam Smith.

However, this idea of the end of history came itself to an end when the great majority of economists and politicians in October 2008 were obliged to recognize that it had created the biggest crisis in the world economy since 1929. It became clear that, without political control and in particular control by the state, the economy will not be able to serve the people in the future. Even Fukuyama declared that the state should now intervene in the world economy (Fukuyama, 2008).

It also became clear that a global crisis cannot be overcome without interconnection of national and regional measures. Both the crises of international law and the crisis of the world economy are global and demand a new world order and a new sense of global justice.

The Crisis of the State

The two crises are both crises of the state itself, as it has been conceived since Jean Bodin (1529–1596), who defined sovereignty as "the absolute and perpetual power of a State" (Bodin, 1999). This sovereignty, which means command over a territory and over the people belonging to that territory, is today increasingly challenged by many new players who, in addition to the states and across all state borders, have appeared. The strongest of them are the economic and financial players.

There have always been non-state actors like religious movements and institutions, revolutionary movements, etc., but at the end of the nineteenth century and throughout the twentieth century, transnational players such as international employers' and workers' organizations, multinational corporations and global banks have emerged. Also international courts have been created, not only to solve fights between states, but to also protect individuals and groups against transnational crimes, in particular the so-called crimes against humanity, and to insure individuals and groups against violations committed by states against their own citizens and refugees on their territories.

Among the non-state actors are also non-governmental organizations who challenge states and state institutions in relation to the environment, food, clothes and the treatment of prisoners, such as Greenpeace, Red Cross, Amnesty International and Médecins Sans Frontières.

A Particular Non-State Actor: The UN Climate Panel

Moreover, transnational networks of scientists play an increasing role in critiques of states, for instance in the domain of climate, such as the Intergovernmental

Panel on Climate Change (IPCC) set up in 1988 by the World Meteorological Organization and by the United Nations Environment Programme (see http:// www.ipcc.ch/ipccreports/assessments-reports.htm). Although the members of the panel are designated by states, they act independently of the states to provide the decision-makers and others interested in climate change with an objective source of information about climate change based on hundreds of scientists all over the world who contribute to its work as authors, contributors and reviewers. Thus, its only role is to assess on a comprehensive, objective, open and transparent basis the latest scientific, technical and socio-economic literature produced worldwide relevant to the understanding of the risk of human-induced climate change. Thereby it has a transnational power and can determine political awareness in the domain of climate change, as was the case in 2007 with the publication of the four parts of the Fourth IPCC Assessment Report, *Climate Change 2007*.

The Right of the Human Individual

Finally, as a consequence of the World Declaration of Human Rights in 1948, ratified by all member states of the Untied Nations, the human individual has gradually obtained status as a non-state actor whose rights are not only the right given by its state, but also recognized as belonging to the individual as such.

This is the background for the creation, according to the European Convention on Human Rights from 1950, of the European Court of Human Rights, which allows a single individual in Europe to bring a lawsuit against his or her own state.

This recognition of the right of the individual as such is quite new in international law which, since Grotius and Pufendorf, was mainly law that regulated relations between states and did not allow an individual to be considered a legal subject. It is precisely the violation of this right of the individual to limit the role of the state on the international scene that is the real and deep reason for the crisis of international law, and it is the same conception of right that was brought into crisis by lack of control of the financial market, causing millions of individuals and families to lose their jobs and homes.

Summa summarum, political, economic and legal decisions today are not only determined by governments and parliaments, but for better or for worse also by the new players who, rather than being universally accepted by the states, are sometimes, and must sometimes be, in direct conflict with the states.

Towards a New World Order

In this situation we are now obliged to look for a new legal order that can take into account the new players in international politics and law. One must ask what the foundation should be for the new rules for a new international order if this order should be accepted by all people around the globe. This foundation must be a new idea that not only is built on the recognition of the common global problems that no individual state and no individual non-state actor can solve alone, but also must take into account the moral necessity of a common global responsibility (Kemp, 2010).

We must look at the world and our history in another way than with what Ulrich Beck has called a self-sufficient national look; we must fundamentally tell the story of humanity in a new way that opens our eyes to a new horizon of possibility and order. The cosmopolitan look must take over (Beck, 2002). In other words, we must tell the story of mankind as a cosmopolitan story.

The Fall of the Grand Narratives

This means the return of the grand narrative. In his book on *The Postmodern Condition: a Report on Knowledge*, published in French in 1979, the philosopher Jean François Lyotard analysed the change in legitimation of knowledge since the Enlightenment (Lyotard, 1979, 1984). This legitimation was expressed in what he calls "meta-narratives" or grand narratives. He understood grand narratives as total philosophies of history, which justify ethical and political prescriptions for society, and generally determine decision-making and ideas of truth. According to Lyotard, grand narratives formed the basis of the social bond, and the founding story of the Enlightenment was the narrative about the progressive liberation of humanity through science.

However, Lyotard claimed that the credibility of the grand narratives was now lost because of the way they were used in the twentieth century to legitimate totalitarianism, whether in the form of the Marxism adopted by Stalin in the Soviet Union or in the form of nationalism adopted by Hitler in Germany and by Mussolini in Italy.

Left over are small narratives that Lyotard describes as "language games" in the sense of Ludwig Wittgenstein, i.e. rules for understanding and behaviour. Instead of legitimating our action by grand narratives, we should therefore refer to a lot of smaller contexts in which we act. Because of this fragmentation of life into thousands of localized roles, we do not need grand narratives as social kit any more. We should judge ourselves in the context of our performance in limited roles as good teachers, poor drivers, and so on.

The Age of Post-Modernism

Lyotard claimed that the role of the grand narratives was not to open the world but to limit it. The Enlightenment story developed a vision of the world and history that only accepted knowledge that could serve the ethico-political goal that was the perpetual peace; later the hegelian story only accepted what conformed to the development of his view of world history reaching its summit in European culture; and the Marxist story only accepted what would fit the vision of capitalism and its end.

However, in the age of what Lyotard called "post-modernism", these grand narratives have lost their guiding force. Instead small stories express the heterogeneity of reality today. We now have a diversity of narratives and a noncommensurability of language plays corresponding to the loss of power of old institutions and in particular the national states. It is in this perspective that Lyotard considers the transfer of power from the classical political class to new actors.

The Limit of Post-Modernism

The analysis of Lyotard contributed in his time to the post-modern movement that rejected all kinds of grand narratives as false legitimation of knowledge and action, even when the narrative did not intend to justify knowledge. However, this movement was founded on the negative statement of the weakening of the political and social institutions established in connection to traditional institutions of the national state and the state itself in its classical form (claiming to have absolute sovereignty). It was right in its criticism of the ideology of the state in the nineteenth century. Nevertheless it was incapable of proposing a new political world order after the reign of modernism, because it did not understand the new world problems that were emerging before its eyes. Thus, it did not recognize the importance of the end of a world order completely structured politically by the armed neutrality between states of the Westphalian type (named after the peace treaty of Westphalia that cemented the concept of the state as totally sovereign in its domain). Consequently it did not recognize the emergent new world order, including a network of new political actors and confronted with a number of common global problems not only in economy, but also in the encounter between cultures and in the handling of environmental problems, especially climate problems that mean that humanity cannot survive without a common will to live together and create a common habitable world.

Cosmopolitanism in Recent Philosophy and Sociology

All these problems have no immediate solutions and therefore they need a vision of history that makes the cosmopolitan the central figure for a new means of coexistence, working towards solution of the problems. That has been recently recognized by an increasing number of philosophers and sociologists. Of the philosophers, the first was Jacques Derrida in France (Derrida, 1997), and then Jürgen Habermas, Otfried Höffe and Francis Cheneval in Germany and Switzerland (Habermas, 1999; Cheneval, 2002; Höffe, 2004), and Martha Nussbaum and

Kwane Anthony Appiah in the USA (Nussbaum, 1997; Appiah, 2006). Among the pioniers in sociology let us mention David Held in the UK and Ulrich Beck in Germany (Held, 1995; Beck, 2005).

According to these thinkers, history is not only about the past and the cosmopolitanism not only about the rehabilitation of the cosmopolitan ideas in the Stoics, in Montesquieu and Voltaire, in Christian Wolff, Kant and others, but it is also and particularly about the present and the future, trying to make history and establish a new world order guided by global responsibility. Thus, the grand narrative has returned, not as a bed of Procust for closure of knowledge and wisdom, but as a guide and horizon for the life of humanity in search of the good life on all levels that will permit us to develop new ideas to handle the big transnational problems of our time for the benefit of our own and future generations.

Defence of Diversity: Ordered Plurality

The return of the grand narrative in the form of the cosmopolitan story does not mean that diversity of knowledge and action once more are oppressed as they were by the totalitarian stories of Marxism, national-socialism and fascism. The true cosmopolitan takes care of the individual and defends the individual against all repression by the state or other political actors who behave like a state, which considers itself as the foundation of all social values and all human rights.

In that sense cosmopolitism is an individualism, it follows that the cosmopolitan world order does not abolish plurality; on the contrary the cosmopolitan order is what the French philosopher of law Mireille Delmas-Marty has called an "ordered plurality" (Delmas-Marty, 2006). Therefore the grand narrative about the cosmopolitan is not authoritarian, but brings different individuals, groups and peoples together in one world. On the other hand, it is not limited to Immanuel Kant's cosmopolitan law prescribing the "right to visit all regions of the world" (Kant, 1996, p. 121) that should be enough to ensure the perpetual peace needed for the development and preservation of world trade.

There are today other big problems than that of ensuring free commerce in the world. It is also a big problem how to control financial speculation on the global market and to protect everybody's right to work and to have a home. Moreover it is a major problem how to avoid war between people with roots in different cultures and different traditions of how to organize democracy in society. Finally it is a major problem how to mobilize every society in the world and in particular the societies who have contributed most to pollution and climate change.

The Grand Narrative of Hope and Courage

Thus, the only way to overcome peacefully the major crises of our time in economy, mutual cultural understanding and protection of nature is to think and act according to the cosmopolitan story. This grand narrative expresses a strong hope in our time and encourages peaceful action for the establishment of a cosmopolitan world order.

As Kant says in *The Metaphysics of Morals*:

> The attempt to realize this idea should not be made by revolution, by a leap, that is, by violent overthrow of an already existing defective constitution (for there would then be an intervening moment in which any rightful condition would be annihilated). But if it is attempted and carried out by gradual reform in accordance with firm principles, it can lead to continual approximation to the highest political good, perpetual peace. (Kant, 1996, p. 124)

References

Appiah, K. A. (2006), *Cosmopolitanism. Ethics in a World of Strangers*. New York: Norton.

Beck, U. (2002), *Macht und Gegenmacht im globalen Zeitalter. Neue weltpolitische Ökonomie, Edition Zweite Moderne*, Suhrkamp, Kapitel III, 13, S. 177ff.

Beck, U. (2005), *Power in the Global Age*. Cambridge: Polity Press.

Bodin, J. (1999), *Les six Livres de la Republique*, I, VIII, p. 122 (quoted in S. Goyard-Fabre, *Jean Bodin, ellipses*. Paris, 1999, p. 32).

Cheneval, F. (2002), *Philosophie im weltbürgerlicher Bedeutung*. Basel: Schwabe.

Delmas-Marty, M. (2006), *Les forces imaginantes du droit, Vol. II. Le pluralisme ordonné*. Paris: Éditions du Seuil.

Derrida, J. (1997), *Le droit à la philosophie du point de vue cosmopolitique* (1991). Editions UNESCO.

Fukuyama, F. (1992), *The End of History and the Last Man*. New York: Penguin Books.

Fukuyama, F. (2008), The Fall of America, Inc. *Newsweek*, 13 October.

Habermas, J. (1999), Kants Idee des ewigen Friedens – aus dem historischen Abstand von 200 Jahren (1995). *Kritische Justiz*, 28, 293–319, in *Die Einbeziehung des Anderen*, Suhrkamp, 192–236.

Held, D. (1995), *Democracy and Global Order: From the Modern State to Cosmopolitan Governance*. Stanford, CA: Stanford University Press.

Höffe, O. (2004), *Wirtschaftsbürger, Staatsbürger, Weltbürger. Politische Ethik im Zeitalter der Globalisierung*. München: C. H. Beck.

Kant, I. (1996), *The Metaphysics of Morals*, M. Gregor (trans.). Cambridge: Cambridge University Press.

Kemp, P. (2010), *The Cosmopolitan*. New York: Prometheus Books, forthcoming.

Laghmani, S. (2003), *Histoire du droit des gens du jus gentium imperial au jus publicum europaeum*. Paris: Editions A. Pedone.

Lyotard, J. -F. (1979), *La condition postmoderne*. Paris: Minuit.

Lyotard, J. -F. (1984), *The Postmodern Condition: A Report on Knowledge*. Manchester: Manchester University Press.

Nussbaum, M. (1997), *Cultivating Humanity: A Classical Defence of Reform in Liberal Education*. Cambridge, MA: Harvard University Press.

Sudre, F. et al. (2005), *Les grands arrêts de la Cour européenne des Droits de l'Homme*, 3rd edn. Paris: PUP.

Truyol Y Serra, A. (1987), *La conception de la paix chez Vitoria*. Paris: Vrin.

Chapter 18

Conclusion: Outline of an Epistemological Methodology for Integrating Ethics and Economics

Jacob Dahl Rendtorff

In this conclusion I will propose a concept of the epistemology of business ethics and of the task of ethical analysis in economics and business. The aim of these foundational reflections is to situate the concept of business ethics within research in management, economics and social sciences. The object of analysis of business ethics is first of all the concept of the firm and how ethical reflections can be applied to corporations. Ethics is about the values and values-driven management is about the ethical norms that should govern corporate decision-making. I consider the discussions of this book as a pluralistic approach to ethics in business and economics. The object of study is business organizations and firms. This includes both their internal relations and ethics in organizational behaviour on the one hand and on the other hand the interaction of the organization with different environments, people and other organizations. However, business ethics does not stop with the study of international external organizational behaviour. It also concerns the level of individual ethical choices and actions in organizations and it can be extended from micro-economics of organizational studies of firms and individuals to a shift of perspective focusing on the macro-level of the role of the corporation in the political economy of a given society or state. Moreover, it includes the study of ethics of business systems and market structures, which cannot be understood exclusively at the level of the study of individual corporations. We may also mention global efforts and formulations of rules in order to regulate the behaviour of international corporations in global markets.

In this context I would like to stress that we may define a broad basis for business ethics. Business ethics can be conceived as a critical reflection over prevailing technical and economic "conceptual schemes" (Werhane, 2002, p. 83). It focuses on the impure nature of economic rationality and it considers the support of human needs and self-actualization as the basic significance and importance of economics. Business ethics looks for a holistic conception of the relation between human beings and society as the basis of investigation in economics and ethics. It does not exclude the neoclassic vision of economics as based on efficiency and utility, but includes this perspective in a broad and interdisciplinary perspective on the social sciences. This view implies an institutional and historical perspective on ethical issues, norms and values. Business ethics is not a field of pure philosophy but a kind of social theory and applied philosophy that addresses normative issues of values and norms in economic systems. Business ethics should be conceived as an interdisciplinary field of study, which proposes a broad and open concept of economics. Business ethics is in my view conceived as a normative argument about good business values. However, the field of study does not only depend on philosophical methods of arguments of meaning and interpretations of relevant textual material. Although it is a field of theoretical clarification of arguments as the basis of concrete action, business ethics also relies heavily on the type of knowledge that is generated by the social sciences. Therefore, research in business ethics cannot be separated from social sciences because it is enriched by the knowledge and methodology of the social sciences. However, this implies reflection about the kind of research to be undertaken in this intersection between business ethics and social sciences.

In this analysis of the epistemology of business ethics I will begin with a discussion of the relation between business ethics and the epistemology of economic sciences. After this I will define the epistemological basis for business ethics as emerging in the intersection between descriptive positivist economics and deconstructive discourse analysis (1). A further basis for my methodology of business ethics is the perspective of "critical hermeneutics" (Habermas, 1971; Ricoeur, 1991) as well as an interdisciplinary approach to social science and institutional sociology in business (2). From this point of view I go on to discuss the concept of the firm in organization theory and I propose to define business ethics in close relation with institutional theory (3). In the broader perspective of ethics and society we can talk about "integrative business ethics" integrating business ethics, economics and social sciences in the study of business ethics in practice in organizations (4). Thus, the function of this critical paper is to propose business ethics not as something external and fundamentally different but rather as an integrated part of social sciences and economics as "moral sciences".

Impure Economic Reason and the Methodology of Business Ethics

The reason why we need business ethics is both the "pure" and "impure" nature of modern economic science. In order to be pure this science has tried to formulate its own foundations as an autonomous science based on the ideals of a predictive natural science searching for clear causal links among economic events. However, this has excluded the tradition of political economy. Also, in business studies, the theory of the firm was not integrated into a larger context of political economy. There was a tendency to ignore the impure aspects of economics. The reaction to this strong positivistic trend in economic sciences has been the use of social constructivist and discursive methods as the methodology of economics. This development has in both cases excluded the old view of economics not only as descriptive predictions, but also as a normative and moral science about the just and good community.

Analysing the methods of economics, business and organization studies we can say that the twentieth century in the 1950s and 1960s was dominated by an empiricist and positivist conception of business economics. From the 1970s this was replaced by increased recognition of the necessity of other conceptions of epistemology in economics and social sciences.[1] Moreover, there has been recognition of the need for a multidisciplinary approach in the social sciences, and also in economics and business studies.

The study of business ethics can indeed be conceived as an acceptance of the impurity of economic reason and the alternative methodologies in business studies and economics. In particular, the method of business ethics can be distinguished from the dominating concept of epistemology in economics. This theory may be called the modernist paradigm of economics as based on logical positivism. This paradigm of descriptive economics can be said to imply the view that economics and business studies should be based on empiricist and inductive criteria for proposing meaningful economic statements and predictions about economic behaviour. Representative of modernist economists is, for example, Paul A. Samuelson, who in his important textbook *Economics* from 1946 tried to reproduce some of the insights into the positivist conception of economic reason on a post-Keynesian basis (Hutchisons, 1938; Knudsen, 1991). Samuelson tried to reformulate economic theory in accordance with logical positivism and he accepted the foundations of economic anthropology in individual wealth maximization that replaced the neoclassical consumer theory of marginal utility (Samuelson, 1971).

Taking into account contemporary criticism of positivist methodology by, among others, Karl Popper, who argued for the fundamental theory-dependence

---

1   My presentation of Milton Friedman's view of positive economics may be criticized for representing an outdated and old viewpoint that is not representative of economics today. However, those critics forget that the neoclassic concept of rationality is still predominant in economic theories like the welfare economics of Samuelson, principal/ agency theory, property right economics, transaction cost theory and mainstream concepts of rational choice in strategy and management sciences. Looking closely at the fundamental economic concepts of mainstream economics of fact and value, preference maximization, efficiency, methodological individualism, empiricism, etc., we find all those concepts in the programme of Friedman described as positive economics. I therefore find it relevant to propose Friedman's conception of economics as representative of what we can refer to as the dominant paradigm of epistemology in mainstream economics. Even though theory of science with authors like Popper and Kuhn and Feuerabend has moved beyond mainstream economic theory, the concept of positive economics remains extremely influential within mainstream economics, even though economists are not very conscious of their positivistic epistemologies. With critical hermeneutics we propose another concept of economics that is closer to a concept of interpretive economics. In fact, we can say that business ethics represents a heterodox approach within economics that integrates economics with social sciences and philosophy (Knudsen, 1997).

of observation and that inductivism and verification should be replaced by falsification, Milton Friedman made one of the most influential formulations of the empiricist conception of economics (Friedman, 1955).

Friedman considers economics as a kind of natural science. What is particularly important in this moderate view of economic empiricist method is the distinction between the logic of discovery and the logic of justification. Friedman emphasizes the instrumental function of the use of the covering law model in economics. The issue is the capacity of economic theories to predict concrete economic human behaviour in the future. The science of economics should formulate economic statements as clearly as possible with regard to the capability of economic theory to predict economic behaviour, even though it is a paradox that it seems nearly logically impossible to predict universal laws of economics.

In "The Methodology of Positive Economics" (1955) Friedman proposes a more precise description of his theory of prediction (Friedman, 1955). He argues for the instrumental view of economic methodology in opposition to a realist interpretation of positivist economics. Friedman states "The ultimate goal of positive science is the development of a 'theory' or 'hypothesis' that yields valid and meaningful (i.e. not truistic) predictions about phenomena not yet observed" (Friedman, 1955, p. 21). Friedman defends a theory of underdetermination with regard to the relation between theory and empirical data. The problem of economics is that it never operates with pure experiments but always relies on real events in the empirical reality. This can, for example, be illustrated by the idea of profit maximization. We can only *a posteriori* and by an "as if" causality determine that there has been selection on the basis of profit maximization because those who survive in the market by definition are those who have survived according to the theory of profit maximization (Friedman, 1955, p. 31).

Donald McCloskey has given a very concise description of Milton Friedman's concept of economic modernism (McCloskey, 1986, p. 7). He argues that the following characteristics are predominant in mainstream views of economic sciences, including economic business and organization studies:

> 1) Prediction and control is the point of science. 2) Only the observable implications (or predictions) of a theory matter to its truth. 3) Observability entails objective, reproducible experiments; mere questionnaires, interrogating human subjects are useless, because human subjects might lie. 4) If and only if experimental implications of a theory prove false is the theory proved false. 5) Objectivity is to be treasured: subjective 'observation' (introspection) is not scientific knowledge, because the objective and the subjective cannot be linked. 6) Kelvin's dictum: 'When you cannot express it in numbers, your knowledge is of a meager and unsatisfactory kind'. 7) Introspection, metaphysical belief, aesthetics, and the like may well figure in the discovery or hypothesis, but cannot figure in its justification: justifications are timeless and the surrounding community of science irrelevant to their truth. 8) It is the business of methodology to demarcate scientific reasoning from non-scientific, positive from normative.

9) A scientific explanation of an event brings the event under a covering law. 10) Scientists – for instance – economic scientists – ought not to have anything to say as scientists about the ought of value, whether of morality or art. (McCloskey, 1986, p. 8)

We see that it is important for the modernist paradigm to work with a strict separation between empirical, *a posteriori*, synthetic knowledge on the one hand, and analytical, *a priori* statements on the other hand. This has also been called Hume's fork that excludes all knowledge, which is neither empirical nor analytic or mathematical.[2] According to McCloskey, Friedman represents this concept in his essay on positive economics, although he is also very pragmatic, giving economics an instrumental justification, which means that he is more interested in the uses of knowledge than in knowledge in itself.

Research in business ethics does not deny that such a view of economic knowledge as descriptive predictions of economic behaviour based on mathematical models can be of great instrumental use for business corporations. It is rather the denial of all other forms of possible knowledge that is problematic from the perspective of business ethics. What we need is not only descriptive predictions and formalization of general laws, but also interpretations of real behaviour and normative evaluation of economic actions. Moreover, it is not clear that economic positivism gives us sufficient basis for empirical claims about economic behaviour. Although it is a great ideal, the promise of objective knowledge seems too ambitious. It is impossible to keep a strict separation between economic theory and normative and ethical values statements. As it is proposed by Donald McCloskey in *The Rhetoric of Economics* (1986), even with strict methodological restrictions, economic modernism cannot avoid relying on specific rhetoric assumptions, which are presupposed without being seriously questioned. This means that a strict positivistic conception of economics functions as a kind of discourse or an instrument for strict exclusion of major knowledge of social sciences, which could have enlightened the economic research (Samuels, 1990).

Business ethics may be one of the issues that would be excluded as an object of study for economics from the point of view of positive economics. Business ethics is about normative values and how to create just institutions and it does not directly accept the presuppositions of economic anthropology, which are proposed by positivist economics. Therefore research in business ethics, in order to be relevant for economics, would welcome a broader view of economic methodology. We are on our way to such a broad view of economics when Donald McCloskey proposes rhetorical criticism and re-evaluation of economics as a *science of conversation* in the perspective of the criticism of the positivist methodology of

---

2   It could be argued that McCloskey already with this proposal sees the importance of business ethics for economics. In fact, that this is an important new direction for economics is confirmed by a later book by McCloskey (2006).

Paul Feuerabend, Richard Rorty and Wayne Boot.[3] Understanding economics as a science of conversation without objective foundations does not have to exclude the work of hard mathematical economics, but it opens up a field of study of the normative and political implications of economic behaviour, which was excluded from the modernist view of economics. As a science of conversation the business ethics of economics may be understood as hermeneutic analysis of business organizations, their values and their economic behaviour. McCloskey's rhetorical reconsideration of the modernist project of economics as a critical evaluation of the language of economics – and his proposal to consider economics as a kind of discourse which, like other sciences, is determined by the conversational norms of that science – opens up a debate between economics, ethics and politics which was not possible on the objectivist and positivist basis.

In the rhetorical perspective economic scientific models are never exact duplications of the world, but are rather like metaphors, constituting an invitation to conceive the world in a specific way. Scientific models are ideal redescriptions of the world, which like all other theories as metaphors function like literary pictures of the world. We might even say that the use of mathematical formalization in economics sometimes has a rhetorical function in order to promote certain arguments about the world. Classical concepts like "supply and demand", "Homo economicus", "the invisible hand", "social capital" and "human capital" are kinds of metaphors that are not objective concepts but elements of philosophical theories. Other examples are the use of terms like exit/entry, competition, equilibrium, lemons in capital markets and islands in labour markets (McCloskey, 1986; Samuels, 1990, p. 7). In many cases economists take concepts from the non-economic sphere in order to develop economic theories, for example Gary Becker, who defines "children as durable goods like refrigerators" (Becker, 1993). When using such concepts, economics cannot be objective, but it uses techniques of rhetorical and ethical persuasion in order to impose economic arguments.

What is essential in McCloskey's view of economics as rhetoric is that economics should be serious about its status as a moral and conversational science, where we can apply Jürgen Habermas's view of ideal speech situation and the "force of the better argument" in order to understand that a good science is a science that has developed conversational norms. Here it is the task of the economic rhetorician to mediate between the conversational norms of different schools of economics and of social sciences. To use the word rhetoric means that economics fundamentally

---

3   To perceive economics as a science of conversation does not lead to pure relativism and lack of rationality in economic sciences. Rather it means that there is no ultimate instrumental justification of economics and that there is no pure instrumental conception of economic rationality. It is based on another kind of communicative or conversational rationality – for example the communicative rationality which is proposed by the critical theory of Jürgen Habermas.

should be understood as a hermeneutic science.[4] To make scientific research is in this pragmatic and anti-foundationalist perspective to contribute to development of this kind of open scientific discussion. When McCloskey following Richard Rorty argues that the quest for certainty of positivist economics should be replaced by the search for wisdom, we are not far from considering economics as a whole as a moral science, which is not value-free, but a discipline, where economists basically function as good persuaders (Samuels, 1990).

To introduce normative and rhetorical arguments in economic sciences and business studies is not an invitation to be imprecise or to make these sciences irrational. Rather it is to do consciously what is already done in economic sciences. The function of rhetoric in conversation should rather be seen as part of an effort to make plausible arguments in economics and social sciences. We may say with McCloskey that the uses of conversational and rhetorical analysis in economics contribute to understanding of the foundations of business and improve awareness of implicit value-conceptions in economic analysis. I would interpret this urge for rhetorical analysis of basic economic concepts and postulates as a search for elaboration of the ethical foundations of business. The view of economics as rhetorical conversation moves business ethics from being an irrational and esoteric discipline into the role of critical evaluation of the normative consequences of economic action and their impact on society. Business ethics becomes an important measure for evaluating the values and norms of different economic paradigms of business studies and economic organization theory.

---

4   Lavoie discusses the relation between hermeneutics and economics as hermeneutics being in a narrow sense about interpretations of economic texts and in a broader sense about understanding the "text" of the economy (Lavoie, 1991, p. 2). Hermeneutics is an interpretive philosophy, which as a powerful theory in the second half of the twentieth century conceived the aim of science as understanding meaningful products. It is a question of communication and it is a communicative philosophy. With Hans Georg Gadamer hermeneutics is conceived as a dialogical process of communication. This ideal is a process of good communication with the fusion of horizons of different points of view. However, economics seems very far from hermeneutics having natural science as a model. We can say that hermeneutics in economics is about the meaning of economic phenomena. With regard to organizations and business, it is the science of the meaning of business organizations in society. It emerges as the study of both the meaning of business texts and the meaning of business practices as we observe them in the social and cultural reproductions of mankind. Critical hermeneutics proposes a critical evaluation of this meaning of economic phenomena in society. To talk about meaning and understanding in economics, business and organization theory does not exclude explanatory approaches and hermeneutics can make use of "explanation" to clarify issues of hermeneutic interpretation of meaning. In this sense economics is understood in terms of the interpretive philosophy of hermeneutics.

Institutional Sociology and Critical Hermeneutics in the Epistemology of Business Ethics

The rhetorical criticism of traditional economic epistemology implies that the study of business ethics and values-driven management in organizations cannot be restricted to the literature of economic sciences. In order to understand and describe the role of ethics and values in the firm, we need a pluralist social sciences perspective. My criticism of the rhetoric of economics should not be conceived as a total exclusion of empirical research of the social sciences. However, I would not consider positivist economics as the only acceptable kind of empirical research that can shed light on business ethics.

Already Karl Popper's theory of falsification was a critical reply to the use of naive empiricist methods in the social sciences (Popper, 1957). Moreover, with the emergence of Thomas Kuhn's theory of scientific paradigms it was argued that theories, because of their dependence on specific paradigms, can only be partially falsified (Kuhn, 1962). Thus, we need more sophisticated and theory-dependent research methodologies in order to deal with questions of norms, ethics and values in organizations.

Furthermore, the question is whether the perspective of business ethics can be compared at all with the approach of the social sciences. Like economists social scientists are often sceptical towards normative business ethics as a normative discipline evaluating business practice and proposing ideas for action. Social scientists working with values and ethics in business agree with philosophy about the importance of the object of research, but they tend to approach values and norms in business and economics in a very different manner (Treviño, 1999, p. 218). Rather than asking normative questions about the appropriate moral action, social scientists are doing descriptive research of the structure, origins and causes of ethical or unethical behaviour. In opposition to the normative approach, social sciences explain contextual and institutional factors that influence normative behaviour.

I agree with Treviño and Weaver when they argue that we need to find a symbiosis between social sciences and ethics when studying values, norms and unethical or ethical behaviour in organizations (Treviño and Weaver, 1994). Even though there are considerable misunderstandings and confusion among social scientists and business ethicists because of the differences between normative–critical and descriptive–hermeneutic–explanatory approaches to the focus of common areas of values and morality, it would be counterproductive to argue that the two approaches should be separated. Moreover, a symbiosis between the two perspectives might help towards common enlightenment about the nature of values in business life.

This is why our approach in this discussion conceives business ethics as a combination between philosophical ethics and selected methodology from the social sciences. Social sciences can help to give useful information about the origins of ethical deviance and moral conduct in business. By investigating origins of institutional practices and the development of moral action in organizations, social sciences can give important knowledge for normative reflections. Moreover, social science can make investigations about the effect of specific ethical programmes and policies in organizations, for example with regard to the problem of the impact of codes of conduct and policies of corporate social responsibility on the social and financial performance of the firm (Treviño, 1999, p. 228).

Now the issue is what kind of social sciences methodology would be appropriate for such a symbiosis between normative business ethics and descriptive studies of the values and norms of ethics in corporations. Given the rhetoric conception of economics as a kind of conversation and my criticism of the covering law model and positivist empiricism in economics and business studies, I would like to propose an interdisciplinary critical hermeneutics (Habermas, 1971; Ricoeur, 1991) and social constructivist institutionalism (Powell and DiMagigio, 1991) to the studies of ethics and values in business.

We find the justification of an interdisciplinary approach to the social sciences in the report of the Gulbenkian Commission on the future of Social Sciences, prepared by Immanuel Wallerstein (1995). This book rejects the positivist ideal of value free social sciences based on the covering law model from the natural sciences and argues for a plurality of methods in the social sciences. Recent social changes at a global level, globalization, the end of ideology and the emergence of new world order have made it necessary to rethink the foundations of social sciences (Wallerstein, 1995, p. 237). We need an interdisciplinary conception of the social sciences, including many different disciplines to the traditional sciences of sociology, political science, but also law and economics. In particular it is necessary to include the findings and methods of geography and history as well as epistemology in the debates about the social sciences.

Instead of holding on to a nineteenth century paradigm of social sciences as representations of the national state imperial paradigms, it is necessary to propose a more unified conception of economics, political science and sociology, considering the objects of these sciences in simultaneously geographical and historical perspectives. To see a close connection between past and future was very important to get a real historical perspective in the social sciences. Moreover, it put more focus on the social sciences by including forms of life, mentalities and cultures and not particularly focusing on the covering law generalizing homothetic social sciences. At the same time it is not possible to exclude elements of psychology and philosophy when analysing the objects and presuppositions of the social sciences. The objects of economics should therefore be considered in an interdisciplinary perspective integrating methods from human sciences and natural sciences.

The need for an interdisciplinary approach to economics and business is based on the fact that mainstream social sciences of economics, political sciences and sociology in the modernist project have considered science as based on universal laws and they have considered hermeneutic or ideographic elements as insignificant in these sciences. Indeed, the sharp repartitions of social sciences in concrete disciplines have proven not to be very productive for new knowledge. It is necessary to approach the objects of economics and business in an interdisciplinary perspective, integrating aspects from economics, sociology and political science.

This ideal of interdisciplinarity demands an inclusion of knowledge and methods from many different perspectives. In particular, it is argued that social sciences have to drop the ideal of being a neutral, value-free science. Instead they must appear as critical social sciences being aware of the limits and boundaries between different disciplines in order to improve knowledge of the social sciences. Research programmes in major universities may be considered as an indication of this concept of interdisciplinarity in the social sciences. This makes it possible for us to leave a focus on individual events and open up the concentration on the institutional processes based on historical explanations of change and actions in institutions. In this sense interpretations of institutional factors and environments are important for understanding economic markets. For the social scientist and organizational sociologist values and norms have to be analysed in a broad institutional perspective.

Institutional theory is a general definition for many different approaches to organizations (Nielsen, 2005). We can distinguish between economic, political and sociological institutional theory. With their different theoretical perspectives they propose important differences and tensions for conceiving values and ethics in organizations. The research programme of new institutionalism in sociology (Powell and DiMaggio, 1991) was proposed by sociologists like Walter W. Powell and Paul J. DiMaggio, and an anthropologist such as Mary Douglas can help to explain the broad social sciences' focus on institutions that can be considered as the methodological basis for research in social sciences, which can deliver important factual information to business ethics.

A general definition of the institutional approach is recognition of the importance of institutions and scepticism towards the view of social institutions as a result of individual rational choice. An interdisciplinary sociological approach to institutions and organizations regards them as something more than the sum of individual and atomistic agents. The focus of research moves from individuals to institutional arrangements, cultures, rules, values and assumptions. With this general agreement we can detect great varieties among the institutional approaches in economics, political science and sociology.

In economic institutionalism we can distinguish between old and new institutional economics (Rutherford, 1995). Old or "original" historical institutional economics goes back to nineteenth-century Germany and was inspired by the conceptions of culture and history as important for economic development as proposed by the German historical school in philosophy and human sciences (Hodgson, 1994). Later this conception of economics was defended by the Norwegian and American economist Thorsten Veblen, who argued that economic institutions are cultural and social creations and therefore ethics and values are conceived as important for social change within this old school of economic institutionalism (Nielsen, 2005). The economy is from the point of view of this institutional economics considered as a process of "learning, negotiation and coordination" (Mirowski, 1991). Economic rationality is closely dependent on culture and social relations. Economics must be studied from the point of view of history and anthropology, focusing on the values of community. Economics is defined by habits and customs and the capacities of individuals to adapt instinctively to their environments. There are no objective rules of economics, but it is a result of human social interaction in given historical and cultural institutions. The science of economics should be based on hermeneutical analysis of the signs and social relations of economics. Veblen can be said to have a hermeneutic and pragmatic approach in his economic theory, where he combines the interpretive study of symbols with economic analysis. Another old institutionalist is John R. Commons, who wrote *Institutional Economics* (1934). In this work economic phenomena are considered as interpretive and it is argued that economists should also work with the interpretations of meanings of economic institutions. Such holistic and interpretive analysis of institutions can be revitalized in modern economics with the help of hermeneutic philosophy and social theory.[5]

The institutional research programme in new institutional economics includes authors like Douglass North and the transaction cost economist Oliver Williamson. The economic institutionalist emphasizes the limits of the neoclassical concept of the possibilities of rational decision-making by economic agents. In order to deal with imperfect information, insecurities and cognitive limits, institutions arise as a reduction of transaction costs. Following Coase the firm is in Williamson's idea of transaction cost economics conceived as a governance structure providing the necessary protection for opportunism (self-interest seeking with guile; Powell and DiMaggio, 1991, p. 4). The institutional approach provides an extension of the behavioural basis of economics and a prioritization of process analysis instead of analysis of equilibrium conditions. This implies analysis of the impact of different institutional arrangements and not only a focus on individual economic actors (Williamson, 1989). For Douglass North the extension of economics implies that mentalities, cultures, institutions and deep values have direct impact on economic analysis and the conceptions of organizational behaviour (North, 1992).

Even though they are open to the importance of institutions and governance structures for economic action, economic institutionalists are reluctant to change their view of the economic actor as fundamentally rational, self-interested and goal-maximizing. This view of the basis for institutional action has, however, been

---

5 Institutionalist economics in this sense criticizes the cartesian presuppositions of neoclassical economics. With Veblen and Karl Polanyi economics is considered as a historical and cultural science where pragmatism and hermeneutics replace formalism and mathematics. Economic science is no longer considered to be objective, mathematical and mechanic with presuppositions of the possibilities of absolute knowledge. Moreover, an economic science is not reduced to prediction or an instrumental or technical manipulation of economic markets. Instead institutionalist economics uses pragmatism and hermeneutics to approach institutions with a plurality of inductive, deductive or abductive methods, where economics is combining different methods in order to reach interdisciplinarity in economics.

seriously challenged by the developments of institutionalism in political science and sociology. Moreover, this concept of economic anthropology is questioned by the concept of human beings as autonomous responsible actors who, although they are embedded in institutions, are morally committed in their choices of action.

Institutionalism in political science has not been looking primarily at transaction costs and efficiency, but it has also been focusing on how institutions and organizations create stability and shape decision-making in political institutions. This approach is indeed inspired by hermeneutic conceptions (Torfing, 2005). The aim has been to research into ways in which institutions can help to create stability and coherence even when individuals are following their own motives. Rules, norms and culture play a role in shaping these institutions. In the study of international relations the theory of regime-building in order to overcome the situation of conflict among states has been helpful as a basis for how to shape and stabilize international cooperation (Powell and DiMaggio, 1991, p. 7).

The new institutionalism in sociology represents a stronger reaction towards functionalism and rational choice theory in organizational analysis. In sociological theories of institutionalization, establishment of social relationships is based on a process of creation of common cognitions, values and customs, which constrain individual behaviour and create a common rationality that goes beyond individual rationality and created organizational forms in which individuals have to adapt to common understandings and narratives.

Even though they are critical towards social constructivism Walter W. Powell and Paul J. DiMaggio admit that the phenomenological theory of Berger and Luckman in *The Social Construction of Reality. A Treatise in the Sociology of Knowledge* (1966, p. 21) plays a role in the formulation of the new institutionalism in sociology. In my view, this approach to understanding organizations and institutions is particularly apt for analysing questions of values and ethics in organizations because of the phenomenological and hermeneutic approaches to the human reality and life world in organizations. Indeed, I would like to stress that convergence between institutional sociology and this kind of social constructivism as well as their roots in the phenomenology of the human daily life was proposed by Alfred Schütz, who was one of the great sources of inspiration for Berger and Luckman (1966). We may also identify the roots of social constructivism in the phenomenological tradition of Husserl and Heidegger. Heidegger's concept of the world lies behind the idea of social construction as a cognitive institutionalization of a set of beliefs and values. Institutionalization conditions the individual to social reality in different forms of roles and implicit understandings of reality, which shape individual identity and routines for action and interactions between different human beings in different social settings.

I would like to propose an interdisciplinary institutionalism in the social sciences, which is founded on the insights of hermeneutic phenomenology and sociology. We can, inspired by Jürgen Habermas, identify this approach to institutions as "critical hermeneutics" based on an interpretive approach to human actions in institutional contexts (Habermas, 1971, 1973; Ricoeur, 1991). Habermas helps to reconstruct social theory as a criticism of Friedman's positivism and the implied mathematization of economics. According to critical hermeneutics, economics should not be instrumental manipulation but a contribution to the understanding of the universal conditions of human existence (Wisman, 1991). Habermas distinguishes between labour and communicative interaction. Labour is based on scarcity and human reproduction based on needs and wants in relation to the material world (Habermas, 1973; Wisman, 1991, p. 114). Communicative action is the level of human interaction and symbolic self-interpretation and transformation where human beings interact with language, meaning and intentions. At the level of labour, actions are based on instrumental goal rationality, while the level of communicative action is governed by consensual norms.

From this point of view Friedman's economics seems to reduce economic science to a technical instrumental science with no relation to the level of communicative action. This is the result of the dominance of instrumental rationality in modern technocratic society. However, it is impossible to reduce economics to be a mere technical science determined by labour, because it is also concerned with political, ethical and social goals for society (Habermas, 1981, p. 171). Instead of conceiving economics in terms of manipulation, positivist economics has to acknowledge that economics is also a normative science based on the rationality of intersubjective communication. We can say that economics should be based on a critical hermeneutical methodology of mutual discussion and examination of arguments. Friedman's instrumentalism in "The Methodology of Positive Economics" leads to control and manipulation, and reduces economics to a science of predictions. With Habermas economics is based on discussion of ends, not only on manipulation. Habermas would criticize laissez-faire economics and instrumental descriptive economics by arguing that the aim of economics is political practice and normative argument about ends of economics. Prediction is not the aim of social science, but as Habermas suggests it is also evaluation of socio-economic goals in terms of communicative interaction (Wisman, 1991, p. 118).

In contrast to Habermas's concept of practice based on the ideal speech situation, neoclassical economics and positivist economic methodology is limited to the level of labour and circulation in an ahistorical manner. Habermas would argue that this kind of economics focuses on formal freedom in markets without taking into account the historical conditions of economic action. Profit and utility maximization are based on individualistic and instrumental concepts of economic action which stand in contrast to discursive will formation based on the best argument in intersubjective dialogue. The market place as conceived in neoclassic economics based on strategic goal maximization and opportunistic instrumentalism is founded on a narrow concept of human exchange and practice because it does not take into account the intersubjective dimensions of communicative rationality.

In accordance with our defence of a normative approach to business ethics and social sciences, Habermas can be used to insist that values are not beyond science and reason, but instead science is founded on values. Economics should not be restricted to end–means rationality, but goals of economics should be determined in the light of the practice of social interaction. Economics is a question of discussion of the public sphere of public opinion and of democratic society. In the public sphere people discuss the general social interests as citizens who deliberate about the future of society. In this context economics is viewed as part of the future of society (Wisman, 1991, p. 118). Habermas's approach to critical hermeneutics therefore implies a possible criticism of modern capitalist institutions. Economics is not separated from society and the issue of economics in society is a problem of the social legitimacy of economics. Money and power have been replacing communicative interaction. Habermas would argue that economics cannot replace politics as scientific economics, but rather that economics should be integrated in the other social sciences with communicative hermeneutic rationality as the reason of social sciences.

Critical hermeneutics regards institutions as fields of human interaction and spheres of meaning, which cannot be reduced to the minds of individual actors. In talking about critical hermeneutics with Habermas we may emphasize that, even though hermeneutics is considered to be very friendly to the object of interpretation, the hermeneutic project may still include a critical attitude towards implied conditions of power and structural domination (Habermas, 1973). Critical hermeneutics also agrees to criticize positivistic conceptions of relevant empirical data. The social order in institutions is conceived as a symbolic system requiring hermeneutic interpretation rather than objective description. Such hermeneutic social constructivism in institutional analysis does not only approach institutions directly in their concrete phenomenological and empirical reality, but also discourses, textual expressions that are considered as symbolic objectivations of the life world and horizon of meaning of institutions. With Paul Ricoeur we can argue that objectifications of human life in language, culture, institutions and other kinds of human expressions constitute productive distanciations of universes of meaning that it is possible to grasp in hermeneutic interpretation (Ricoeur, 1987).

In order to deal with these expressions of human reality we can use Paul Ricoeur's methodological conception of the hermeneutic circle of interpretation as a "triple mimesis" of prefiguration–configuration–refiguration (Ricoeur, 1983–1985). According to such a model, expressions of meaning relate to the prefigurative reality of human action in institutional contexts. This reality is put into configuration by textual discourse or symbolic interpretation of the prefigurative life world, which is conceived as a narrative configuration (emplotment). Configurations are metaphors of human action, cross-referential in the sense that they are both fictional and historical because they are imaginary reinterpretations of the life world (Ricoeur 1983–1985 (1), p. 101). Configurations are then reinterpreted at the refigurative level of interpretations of institutional behaviour and we should hopefully experience an increase of knowledge about the life world of institutions during this hermeneutic process of deciphering human action.

Critical hermeneutics agrees with social constructivism in institutional analysis about the idea that institutions are reflections of human actions and creations of meaning. This kind of analysis is in accordance with Durkheim, on understanding institutions as factual social realities. Institutional integration is both cognitive and moral in the sense that an individual internalizes social structures of meaning and truth during the integration in specific institutional settings. Institutions are defined by a common social world which is constructed, internalized and subjectified in the human individual who takes part in these institutions. Individuals are becoming social products of earlier institutionalizations and historical constructions. It is an important task for critical hermeneutics to describe the origins, genealogy and meanings of different institutions. In contrast to functionalism or structuralism in the social sciences, hermeneutics does not exclude the perspective of subjective motivations of individual actors as important for the framing of institutions. Personal responsibility and motives for action matter even though individuals are shaped by their institutional context and history.

Organizations and Business Ethics: The Concept of the Firm

With this interdisciplinary approach to business ethics, social sciences and economics we propose critical hermeneutics as an approach to understanding the integration of business ethics and values-driven management in organization theory. Business ethics can be conceived as a part of strategy theory in order to develop the corporation strategically and rationally, for example as a part of mainstream strategy theory of evaluation of the strengths and weaknesses of the corporation (SWOT analysis). In this sense business ethics challenges the dominating paradigm of organization theory after the Second World War, which was to a large extent inspired by pure economic approaches to organizations. According to such a strategic concept of organizations, it is possible to manage organizations from predetermined strictly economically defined aims. Therefore, we have to perceive business ethics as an integrated element of the formulation of the mission and vision of an organization. When we argue for an interdisciplinary and institutional approach to business ethics we can, from the point of view of different institutionalisms, talk about fundamental levels of institutional analysis as the basis for business ethics of the firm: (1) the firm as a symbolic structure; (2) the firm as an economic institution; and (3) the firm as an open social system. With the institutional approach we can, from an anthropological perspective, consider the firm in a broader perspective than is the case in neoclassical theory (Bonnafous-Boucher, 2005). This theory was inspired by the concepts of competition, profit maximization and full information which dominated neoclassical economic theory. The view of the economic agent is based on the idea of "Homo economicus", a rational profit maximizer who is able to act rationally and use the corporation as an instrument to maximize utility.

From the anthropological point of view the organization is not only a closed system of rational interaction among isolated individuals but the firm takes part in social reality with its different forms of religious, political and familial institutions. According to Mary Douglas, the firm is not exclusively determined by pure economic rationality, but combines elements of different forms of rationality. The firm is instead a social construction based on relations between human beings grounded on "naturalized conventions" based on common rules of coordination (Douglas, 1986; Bonnafous-Boucher, 2005, p. 7). Mary Douglas argues that organizations are never established beforehand, but are constructions of social interactions and that to conceptualize organizations is to understand how they think and construct a common social horizon and structure of interaction (Douglas, 1986). This anthropological conception of institutions is close to the idea of critical hermeneutics in the sense that it combines deductive and inductive approaches and accepts a close relation between researcher and the field of research. Moreover, it accepts the study of the organization as an independent level of research which is different from both micro- and macro-approaches to social relations.

From the interdisciplinary perspective on organizations, the anthropological concept of institutions confirms that the firm is an open concrete system of action where functions are formed by interactions between actors in the system. In this system there is no predetermined structure but the system is a result of concrete social and historical processes leading to specific constitutions of a specific organization as a basis for cultural and social identification. Accordingly, with Maria Bonnafous-Boucher we can argue that rational organization is dependent on cultural forms and organizations. This means that concepts of rationality in firms are founded on broader social ideas based on the cultural and social institutions of society (Bonnafous-Boucher, 2005, p. 16). To have an institutional approach to the study of organizations implies therefore that strategies of actors in firms are not only rational in the pure economic sense but founded on corporate culture, strategies of actors and stakeholders and also dependent on the values and norms of other social institutions in society. The firm is a social structure that is separated from society but at the same time dependent on the norms and structures of society.

With this approach to the relation between institution and organization we may welcome the criticism of neoclassic theory by new institutional economics based on the idea of a transactions costs concept of the firm. New institutional economics shares the point of view of rationality of neoclassic economics, but it also realizes the need to develop an economic theory at the meso-level of organizations between the micro-level of individual actors and the macro-level of large economic systems. Ronald Coase and his follower Oliver Williamson acknowledge the importance of conceiving the firm in an institutional and interdisciplinary perspective. We may say that the authors agree to consider the firm as a social system, which as a social construction is an open system of interaction. As a social construction the firm is an institution because it is a place where people meet and interact with each other. When Coase describes the firm as an institution we can say that he emphasizes that it is a place where people agree about contracts in social interactions. Maria Bonnafous-Boucher argues that Coase seems to be aware of some of the same insights as anthropological theory of institutions when he says that institutions are a place where people work together for a common goal and agree about simple economic affairs. We tend to forget that it is this social relation which is the foundation for formalized concepts of institutions and firms which are constructed in law and legal regulation (Bonnafous-Boucher, 2005, p. 109). In fact, social agreement based on values, norms, culture and ethics can be argued to have important significance for the framework of organizations (Boltanski and Thévenot, 1991; Bonnafous-Boucher, 2005).

The institutional theory of organizations of Williamson in his transaction cost economics helps to answer the question of Coase "Why firms exist" or with the words of Mary Douglas "How institutions think". Organizations help to reduce transaction cost and therefore they are economic tools for acting more efficiently in markets. Firms are instruments to reduce costs and make contracts more efficient. The advantage of the firm is that it can replace a plurality of individual contracts with one single contract with the firm. Moreover, it ensures security in work and other social relations. With this explanation transactions cost economics understands the importance of conceiving the firm as an institution. However, it does not really accept the importance of the social level of forming institutions. In order really to understand firms as institutions we have to include the broader historical and social concept of institutions as historical forms that include aspects of the social and cultural life of society. In fact, the anthropological concept of institutions argues that the concepts of new institutional economics of property rights and contracts are grounded in collective social structures.

We can find support for such a critical argument against the concept of rationality within the institutionalist conception of organization theory in sociology questioning some of the central principles of neoclassical economic thought (Powell and DiMaggio, 1991). This was already the aim of the research of organization theorist Herbert A. Simon, who integrated social psychology in his studies of administrative processes in organizations (Simon, 1965). In particular, the behaviouralistic paradigm of organization and management theory questions the purity of the neoclassical concept of economic rationality (Cyert and March, 1963). These approaches to organization theory both argue that the ideal of economic man as a rational self-interest maximizing actor does not correspond to the reality of corporate action or to the idea of the firm as a "loosely coupled system" (Knudsen, 1995, p. 114). Simon and March stated in 1958 that the concept of maximization of profits does not explain how individuals act in daily economic life. Economic actors are not rational in any ideal sense, but depend on many different personal interests, preferences and property rights (Knudsen, 1995, p. 118). The firm does not represent a rational hierarchical engine of production, but may be viewed as an open political system of interacting individuals in a complex environment (March and Simon, 1958, pp. 2–3).

This view of economic action does not necessarily introduce a normative theory of foundation of economics in ethics and politics, but it implies that economic systems cannot be viewed as closed systems of efficiency and rationality. Organizations are much more complex, because they are social systems with mutually dependent actors who act according to organizational goals and particular structures of reward and incentives. Moreover, individuals take part in organizations according to personal judgments of possible benefits and organizations only function if there are good reasons for individuals to work in the firm.

By considering organizations as "political coalitions", March and Cyert developed in 1962 a criticism of the neoclassical conception of economic markets and firms as "black boxes" determined by ideal economic rationality (Cyert and March, 1963; Knudsen 1995, p. 124). Emphasizing imperfect knowledge and open complexity in firms, organizations are in opposition to fully rational systems viewed as adaptive rational systems characterized by the "garbage can model", where ideal economic rationality is dependent on particular decisions and horizons of decision-making.

This view of organizational rationality has further been described by Herbert Simon by the concept of "procedural rationality", which considers factual decision-making as dependent on "bounded rationality", meaning that alternatives are limited, absolute knowledge is impossible and full knowledge about personal future preferences is impossible (Knudsen, 1995, p. 159). James March argues that the neoclassical "logic of consequences" must be replaced by the "logic of appropriateness" as a condition for economic action. Bounded rationality means that it is impossible to work with a strict separation between exogenous and indigenous aspects of economics. Internal economic rationality is influenced by external social values and conditions.

Accordingly we may say that the evolution of organization theory supports the idea of external ethical and political limitations of economic rationality. When Simon argues that the substance of neoclassical economic rationality is replaced by "procedural rationality" in organizations as "adaptive, political coalitions", we may say that this shows how ethics and other values than economic values cannot avoid influencing organizational decision-making. Thus, organizational theory and the institutionalist paradigm in economics help to give descriptive arguments for a close relation between ethics and economics (Powell and DiMaggio, 1991). In this sense economic stability and competitive equilibrium are dependent on institutions and institutional arrangements. These arrangements cannot exclude ethical values and political considerations, which become part of a bounded and procedural rationality in firms as political coalitions.

From this level of social interaction of organizations we can go on to mention the third level of institutional analysis of organizations. This is the level of symbolic interactions where we can also situate values and norms. At this cultural level, theory of cultures and symbolic interpretations joins the analysis of critical hermeneutics (Gertz, 1973). The firm is considered as a complex totality with many complicated processes and events. According to the anthropology of culture, the study of the firm is a process of interpretation of a cultural and historical field. We can say that analysis of ethics institutions is very compatible with this approach. While being an economic institution for coordination of interventions on economic markets, the firm is also a symbolic structure with values and norms that aims at satisfying the desires of individual members of organizations. At this level of collective action an organization is also a unit for coordination, but this is based on a process of institutionalization where certain norms of interaction are created in the social process (Bonnafous-Boucher, 2005, p. 121). Accordingly, we can say that an institution is more than a formal agreement or convention. From the point of view of the anthropological and institutional approach, organizations are "rationalized myths" of social relations that are shaped in interactions with their environments (Powell and DiMaggio, 1991; Pesqueux, 2002). We can say that economic relations in organizations are embedded in social relations in the sense that they depend on the symbolic and cultural forms of society. New institutional economics should move from a conception of a contract as a legal fiction to a realization of the dependence of juridical forms on other social relations. Moreover, the firm should not only be considered from the point of view of individual contracts, but also holistically from the perspective of organizational culture and influences from the environment and other institutions in society. Therefore, we combine the approach of new institutionalism in economics with the broader anthropological and sociological view of the firm in order to consider the values and norms of this embeddedness (*l'encastrement*) in social relations, cultural and political affairs of society. Accordingly, even though neoclassical economics regards the firm as independent from social relations, the cultural view of the firm inscribes economic actions in general relations of social exchange and reciprocity of society (Polanyi, 1957; Bonnafous-Boucher, 2005, p. 131).

We have to consider the firm as part of the market and based on the social relations of exchange in society. Corporations are social constructions that depend on the social relations of society and have to follow the institutional framework of societies in their economic development. I can agree with Mary Douglas, who argues that the formal legal property rights concept of the firm is too limited for understanding the role of corporations in society. Corporations are based on social processes and this is also the basis for development of corporations in search of legitimacy and formation of ethics and values. With their description of organizations as open systems, organizational theorists like Simon and March give room to conceive business ethics and values-driven management as fundamental aspects of organizational strategies and functions. With these approaches to management an organization combines systemic features with issues of practice and norms. Organizations are systems that are governed by symbolic generalization and ethics is part of this creation of meaning. In contrast to purely systemic actions, ethics is capable of conceiving the plurality of institutional dimensions of organizations. In this sense ethics represents a broader concept of rationality that challenges the one-dimensional economic rationality of personal preference maximization and profits within limited legal and economic frames of the organization.

Therefore, values-driven management and business ethics is a way to deal with issues of legitimacy in organizations. Following Habermas, we can once again emphasize that communicative rationality emerges as an important alternative to instrumental and economic rationality (Habermas, 1981). In organization theory the method of critical hermeneutics implies that interactive deliberation about ends should replace the scientific concept of strategy. The ideal of communicative reason and communicative interaction is a democratic ideal. It is based on the idea of the ideal speech situation and rational consensus. In this context it is important to argue that the concept of the ideal speech situation is oriented towards truth (Wisman, 1991). Communicative actions should instead be the basis for evaluating decision-making in organizations. In business organization ethics and values can be conceived as responses to the need for management based on deliberation and open communication. Values-driven management and business ethics in corporations represent a communicative way to deal with management in modern organizations by integrating deliberations about ethics in the heart of corporate strategy.

Business Ethics and Institutional Analysis:
Towards an Integrative Approach

In-so-far as we use critical hermeneutics to interpret institutional processes and organizations and how institutions shape individual action, we are also in accordance with the new institutionalism in sociology. In the perspective of this tradition problems of business ethics and values-driven management in organizations would be analysed as problems of how values and ethics shape institutions and how individuals are determined in their value choices and ethical choices by the institutional schemes of cognition, path-dependencies of selection of values, institutional isomorphism with regard to the powers of institutions in shaping discourses and legitimacy in interaction with the environment (Powell and DiMaggio, 1991, p. 63). These are important questions about how the movement of business ethics influences economic, social, legal and political institutions and how these institutions may respond to institutional agendas of values-driven management and corporate social responsibility. Institutional economics, sociology, political science and law will help to answer these questions by looking at concrete institutional processes within the fields of business ethics in different organizations, markets and countries. In this context it is important to stress that institutional analysis based on critical hermeneutics addresses micro, meso and macro levels of institutionalization by values and ethics in business.

Accepting this important task of descriptive hermeneutics and genealogical analysis of the role and function of business ethics and values-driven management in corporations, markets and political institutions, critical hermeneutics also goes beyond these questions by proposing normative evaluations of values and norms of business ethics. According to Habermas's theory of communicative action, we can argue that critical hermeneutics in business ethics and organization theory is oriented towards possible development of democratic institutions in modern society, because the issue of legitimacy is becoming increasingly predominant. We may say that neoclassical rationality of economics and organization in modernity is submitted to requests of legitimacy in order to avoid colonization by the instrumental reason of the human life world. Business ethics can be considered as a part of this effort to request increased communicative reason in organization theory and economic sciences. It represents a contribution to workplace democratization and communicative reason in the workplace. It contributes to the critical self-reflection of economics and it helps people to react critically to power and domination. In this sense hermeneutics is a critical science of emancipation arguing for the importance of democratic legitimacy of business corporations. The task of institutional analysis is in my view not only to understand institutions but also to change them in order to work for the normative ideal of what we, with Paul Ricoeur, have called "the good life with and for the other in just institutions" (Ricoeur, 1990, p. 202). We can compare this concept with Habermas's concept of political democracy. This means that the hermeneutic analysis of institutionalization of business ethics cannot exclude matters of justice and moral integrity of organizations and business institutions. Critical evaluation of the norms of ethical practice and justice in institutions is an important methodological concern of my analysis of institutionalization and organizational behaviour in economic institutions.

Thus, the aim of critical hermeneutics in institutional and organizational analysis is not only to understand values in institutions and organizations as instruments for economic efficiency, political constructs for stability in decision-making, sociological frames for creation of cognitive schemes for common understandings or international regimes for cooperation. In addition to these important functions of values in business institutions I would rather like to analyse institutionalization of business ethics in the perspective of normative ethics dealing with what Habermas conceives as the general interest of society and what the legal scholar Ronald Dworkin has focused on in regard to legal systems (Dworkin, 1986), namely the role of concepts like "integrity" "political morality", rights, fairness and justice with regard to particular institutional arrangement and market structures.

In order to show how the ethical perspective goes beyond the descriptive, genealogical and interpretative aspects of institutional theory, we will now discuss the definition of ethics. In business ethics institutional analysis is about the requirements for just institutions in economic life. I argue for integration between institutional analysis and normative ethical analysis in business ethics and values-driven management. The ethical perspective is about responsible behaviour in business. In contrast to the debates about agency in most institutionalisms focusing on the possibility of rational preference maximization of individuals, the concept of subject in the ethical approach to institutional analysis relies on the idea of human beings morally committed to an ethical vision of the good life. Paul Ricoeur argues that the starting point of ethics is a hermeneutics of the self (Who am I?) and the responsible ontological conscience of moral obligation (Ricoeur, 1990).

Institutional actors are likely to reflect in the dialectics of what Weber calls an "ethics of conviction" (of personal religious belief) on the one hand and an "ethics of responsibility" (for consequences of actions) on the other hand (Maesschalck, 1999, p. 7). This view of agency presupposes moral autonomy and capacity for moral action of individuals and this commitment is considered as the basis for normative values of economics and business corporations when acting on economic markets.

This institutional perspective is different from other kinds of institutionalisms because the object of institutional analysis and ethical deliberation in organizations is first and foremost what may be called the ethical field (*champ éthique*; Maesschalck, 1999, p. 27). The concept of "ethical field" originating in Bourdieu's sociology indicates that ethics in institutions and markets can be conceived as a social and institutional space with specific actors, practices, technologies and methods. In this social space ethics is part of a game between different economic actors and it is the field of systematic production of ethical decision-making with regard to organizational action. Marc Maesschalck argues that the ethical field may be conceived as the place where the social cohesion of the firm is tested (Maesschalck, 1999, p. 31). The ethical field is a second-order domain of reflection where different rationalities in the enterprise are confronted with one another. In the institutional perspective we may say that the ethical field is space in the corporation where we experience the emergence of intersection between economic concepts of allocation of resources, efficiency, growth, competition, risk and reward, incentives and free exchange, political concepts of power, procedures of decision-making, organizational stability and resistance to change, and sociological concepts of culture, legitimacy, norms, values and communication, and most importantly legal rules and regulations. This ethical space of reflection of action and decision-making is not situated in one place of the institution and its application as a possible discourse may be without borders, even though the scope of ethics is constantly limited by the other social fields and institutional rationalities (Maesschalck, 1999, p. 33).

When we deal with such an institutional field we can see the importance of considering socio-economics and business ethics as conversational and normative sciences. According to the work of Habermas, the battle over decision-making in the ethical field can be said to constitute a procedural process of argumentation in which actors in search for mutual recognition are searching for collective norms of cooperation (Habermas, 1986). Discourse ethics searches for universal justification and reasoned consent among the participants in the ethical process (Habermas, 1981). When we enter into a possible field of ethical reflection, we encounter an intersubjective dialogue about ethics and values. Particular and personal norms are tested according to a model of deliberation about the validity and justification of norms. Thus the ethics of communication provides us with demands of legitimacy of justification of values and norms.

Peter Ulrich and Thomas Maak have proposed a definition of business ethics as "integrative business ethics" (Ulrich and Maak, 1997), which can be said to propose mediation between economic and political rationality and ethical reasoning within the field of ethical reflection. The integrative approach to business ethics argues for critical reflection of economics and considers that we should discuss the foundations of economics as a truly value-creating science (Ulrich and Maak,

1997, p. 28). We can maintain that this task of covering human needs and wants has always been a moral project as part of the search of human beings for the good life and just institutions. Business ethics is about finding the right principles for human social life and our relationships with the natural environment. Therefore we should not separate economics, politics and law from ethics, but rather consider them as serving the common purpose of the good life of humanity.

I think this is very convincing in responding to the kind of normative ethics that is required within the symbiosis with institutional analysis. Integrative business ethics starts with Habermas's analysis of the division of system and life world in modernity. Instead of operating with a sharp divide between different kinds of rationalities, critical ethical reflection is about the foundations of business economics and overcoming the strict separations between economics and ethics. Business ethics should generate knowledge about values and norms in corporations and their social environments, but it should also discuss foundations and preconditions for business and economic systems. Peter Ulrich and Thomas Maak think that rational business practice would relate practical reason to instrumental and strategic rationality (Ulrich and Maak, 1997, p. 31). Ethical reflection in business should be concerned with foundational normative issues and then apply these insights to the institutional context of business organizations.

Thus, integrative business ethics argues against the opposition between an "applied ethics of business" and economics. If we only understand ethics as the task of formulating outer limitations of economics, we might be able to impose some restrictions on business, but business ethics will remain external to economic rationality and therefore we would probably enlarge the divide between ethics and business. However, it would not be a better solution to argue for an "economic theory of morals" in which ethics is reduced to morals and only taken into account in-so-far as it would contribute to economic efficiency. This endorsement of the morality of the market would make ethics dependent on economics and ignore the search for just institutions and rights beyond the free market (Ulrich and Maak, 1997, p. 32).

Instead the integrative approach considers the aim of business ethics to formulate a global concept of practical reason and rationality in business, which combines economic rationality with a concern for social and political legitimacy (Ulrich and Maak, 1997, p. 33). This concern for legitimacy situates value creation with economics and business within a larger horizon of the political and social aims of democratic society. Integrative business ethics here concerns the institutional limitations of markets based on political and legal regulations of business activities in national economies, but also in the global market with creation of international regimes. At the level of values-driven management in corporations, integrative business ethics concerns the obligations of corporations as members of a community, their responsibilities towards employees and consumers and concern for stable and just business systems.

With this theoretical analysis I have proposed the institutional and integrative perspectives on business ethics on the basis of the methodology of critical hermeneutics. This epistemology respects the idea of business ethics as a critical practical rationality integrating ethics and the social sciences disciplines. As a search for principles of legitimacy and professional ethics of business, this critical perspective combines insights about norms and values from economics, social and political theory, but elements from theories of legal regulation in complex societies will also be useful in order to analyse the search for institutional legitimacy at different levels of business ethics.

References

Becker, G. S. (1993), *Human Capital: A Theoretical and Empirical Analysis, with Special Reference to Education*. Chicago, IL: University of Chicago Press (first published 1964).

Berger, P. and Luckmann, T. (1966), *The Social Construction of Reality. A Treatise in the Sociology of Knowledge*. New York: Doubleday.

Boltanski, L. and Thévenot L. (1991), *De la Justification*. Paris: Gallimard.

Bonnafous-Boucher, M. (2005), *Anthropologie et Gestion, Collection Connaissance de la Gestion*. Paris: Economica.

Commons, J. R. (1934), *Institutional Economics*. London: Macmillan.

Cyert, R. B. and March, J. G. (1963), *A Behavioral Theory of the Firm*. Prentice-Hall International Series in Management and Behavioral Sciences in Business Series. Englewood Cliffs, NJ: Prentice-Hall.

Douglas, M. (1986), *How Institutions Think*. New York: Syracuse University Press.

Dworkin, R. (1986), *Law's Empire*. Cambridge, MA: Harvard University Press.

Friedman, M. (1955), The Methodology of Positive Economics, in *Philosophy and Economic Theory*, F. Hahn and M. Hollis (eds). Oxford Readings in Philosophy. Oxford: Oxford University Press.

Gertz, C. (1973), *The Interpretation of Cultures*. New York: Basic Books.

Habermas, J. (ed.) (1971), *Hermeneutik und Ideologiekritik*. Frankfurt am Main: Suhrkamp.

Habermas, J. (1973), *Zur Logik der Sozialwissenschaften*. Frankfurt am Main: Suhrkamp.

Habermas, J. (1981), *Theorie des kommunikativen Handelns. Band II. Zur Kritik der funktionalistischen Vernunft*. Frankfurt am Main: Suhrkamp.

Habermas, J. (1986), *Kommunikativen Handelns und Moralbewusstsein*. Frankfurt am Main: Suhrkamp.

Hodgson, G. M. (1994), The Return of Institutional Economics, in N. J. Smelser and R. Swedberg (eds), *The Handbook of Economic Sociology*. Princeton, NJ: Princeton University Press.

Hutchisons, T. W. (1938), *The Significance and Basic Postulates of Economic Theory: A Logical Positivist Conception of Economic Reason*. New York: Alfred A. Knopf.

Knudsen, C. (1991–1997), *Økonomisk Metodologi*, Bind 1–2. Copenhagen: Jurist og Økonomforbundets forlag.

Kuhn, T. S. (1962), *The Structure of Scientific Revolutions*. Chicago, IL: University of Chicago Press.

Lavoie, D. (ed.) (1991), *Economics and Hermeneutics*. London: Routledge.

Maesschalck, M. (1999), L'Éthique professionelle et son champ de compétence, in *Éthique des affaires et finalité de l'entreprise*, R. Cobbaut and M. Maesschalck (eds). DUC, Université catholique de Louvain.

March, J. G. and Simon, H. A. (1958), *Organizations*. New York: Wiley.

McCloskey, D. (2006), *The Bourgeois Virtues, Ethics for an Age of Commerce*. Chicago, IL: University of Chicago Press.

McCloskey, D. N. (1986), *The Rhetoric of Economics*. Brighton: Harvester University Press.

Mirowski, P. (1991), The Philosophical Basis of Institutional Economics, in *Economics and Hermeneutics*, D. Lavoie (ed.). London: Routledge, pp. 96–97.

Nielsen, K. (2005), *Institutionel teori. En tværfaglig introduktion*. Roskilde: Roskilde Universitetsforlag.

North, D. (1992), *Institutions, Institutional Change and Economic Performance*. New York: Cambridge University Press.

Pesqueux, Y. (2002), *Organisations. Modèles et représentations*. Paris: PUF.

Polanyi, K. (1957), *The Great Transformation. The Political and Economic Origins of Our Times*. Boston, MA: Beacon (first published 1944).

Popper, K. (1957), *The Poverty of Historicism*. London: Routledge & Kegan Paul/ Boston, MA: Beacon Press.

Powell, W. W. and DiMaggio, P. J. (1991), *The New Institutionalism in Organizational Analysis*. Chicago, IL: University of Chicago Press.

Ricoeur, P. (1983–1985), *Temps et recit I–III*. Paris: Le Seuil.

Ricoeur, P. (1991), *From Text to Action: Essays in Hermeneutics II* (1986), trans. K. Blamey and J. B. Thompson. Evanston, IL: Northwestern University Press.

Ricoeur, P. (1987), *Du texte à l'action. Essais d'herméneutique II*. Paris: Le Seuil.

Ricoeur, P. (1990), *Soi-même comme un Autre* (*One-Self as Another*). Paris: Le Seuil.

Rutherford, M. (1995), *Institutions in Economics. The Old and New Institutionalism*. Cambridge: Cambridge University Press.

Samuels, W. J. (ed.) (1990), *Economics as Discourse. An Analysis of the Language of Economics*. Dordrecht: Kluwer Academic.

Samuelson, P. A. (1971), *Foundations of Economic Analysis*. Cambridge, MA: Harvard University Press.

Simon, H. A. (1965), *Administrative Behavior. A Study of the Decision-Making Processes in Adminstration Organization*. New York: Free Press.

Torfing, J. (2005), Institutionelle teorier inden for politologi, in *Institutionel teori. En tværfaglig introduktion*, K. Nielsen (ed.). Copenhagen: Roskilde Universitetsforlag.

Treviño, L. K. (1999), Business Ethics and the Social Sciences, in *A Companion to Business Ethics*, R. E. Frederick (ed.). Oxford: Blackwell.

Treviño L. K. and Weaver, G. R. (1994), Business ETHICS/BUSINESS ethics: One field or two? *Business Ethics Quarterly*, 8(3), 447–476.

Ulrich, P. and Maak, T. (1997), Integrative Business Ethics – a Critical Approach. *CEMS Business Review*, 2, 27–36.

Wallerstein, I. (1995), *Unthinking Social Science*. London: Polity Press.

Werhane, P. H. (2002), The Very Idea of a Conceptual Scheme, in *Ethical Issues in Business. A Philosophical Approach*, 7th edn, T. Donaldson, P. H. Werhane and M. Cording (eds). Upper Saddle River, NJ: Pearson Education/Prentice Hall.

Williamson, O. E. (1989), *The Economic Institutions of Capitalism*. New York : The Free Press.

Wisman, J. D. (1991), The Scope and Goal of Economic Science. A Habermasian Perspective, in *Economics and Hermeneutics*, D. Lavoie (ed.). London: Routledge.

Index